INVESTING IN CANADA

THE PURSUIT AND REGULATION OF FOREIGN INVESTMENT

by

Russell Deigan, M.A., LL.B.

De Boo

© 1991 by Thomson Professional Publishing Canada
A division of Thomson Canada Limited
A Richard De Boo Publication

This publication is designed to provide accurate and authoritative information. It is sold with the understanding that the publisher is not engaged in rendering legal, accounting or other professional advice. If legal advice or other expert assistance is required, the services of a competent professional should be sought. The analysis contained herein represents the opinions of the author and should in no way be construed as being either official or unofficial policy of any governmental body.

Canadian Cataloguing in Publication Data

Deigan, Russell
    Investing in Canada

Includes bibliographical references and index.
ISBN 0-459-56764-0

1. Canada.   Investment Canada Act.   2. Canada.
Foreign Investment Review Agency.   3. Investments,
Foreign — Law and legislation — Canada.
4. Investments, Foreign — Government policy —
Canada.   I. Title.

KE1575.D45 1991   346.71'07   C91-095225-6
KF1575.D45 1991
      74769

Thomson Professional Publishing Canada
Corporate Plaza
2075 Kennedy Road
Scarborough, Ontario
M1T 3V4

Toronto		416-609-3800
Canada & U.S.		1-800-387-5164
Fax		416-298-5094

PREFACE

The purpose of this book is to explain how Canada encourages and regulates foreign investment. The first chapter presents a history of the Foreign Investment Review Agency and a brief overview of Canadian nationalism in the 1970s. The changes that have since occurred in the Canadian and global economies are then discussed. This leads to an explanation of why Canadian government officials decided to set up this country's "Investment Development Program". The factors influencing Ottawa and Washington to adopt different stances towards the promotion of foreign investment are mentioned as well.

The focus of the book then shifts to the *Investment Canada Act* and other laws affecting foreign investment. Topics examined include: the meaning of de facto control; the reasons why many foreign acquisitions of Canadian oil and gas properties are not reviewable; the circumstances when foreign investors can obtain the minister's approval to buy a business before the review process is completed; and the criteria government officials use to determine whether a foreign takeover benefits Canada. Insights into the role of the Competition Bureau in the foreign investment review process are also offered.

A major highlight of this book is the Free Trade Agreement and its impact on Americans wanting to invest in Canada. Particular attention is paid to the special rules in this Agreement governing Canada's cultural industries and oil and gas sector.

The last chapter portrays the intense competition among Canada and other nations for foreign capital and technology. This chapter also describes the strategies being used by Canada to attract more foreign investment.

The topics mentioned above should be of interest to several audiences:

- lawyers and accountants;

iii

- government officials (federal/provincial/municipal) engaged in economic development;
- foreign: business executives, lawyers and government officials;
- Canadian nationalists and continentalists;
- members of the general public interested in foreign investment or free trade issues;
- employees in certain foreign-owned plants and labour leaders; and
- students of law, economics and political science.

Through this book, these readers can benefit from my work experience at the Foreign Investment Review Agency, Investment Canada, the Competition Bureau (Mergers Branch), and as corporate counsel.

This book breaks *new* ground in several ways. For instance, the history and rationale for the branch business exemption—which has puzzled many lawyers—is recounted. The "Delaware merger anomaly", which always surprises lawyers when they learn about it, is also mentioned. Chapters 7 and 8 explain which foreign takeovers need government approval under the *Investment Canada Act*. Instead of wondering why the Canadian government did not examine the purchase of a high tech company, or a utility company, Canadian nationalists can now understand the legal reasoning. These days, the environment and pollution are at the forefront of many people's concerns. Chapter 13 examines—for the first time—the extent to which environmental considerations may be relevant in the government's review of a foreign takeover. Workers in foreign-owned plants, which are rationalizing operations and reducing staff, often contact their members of Parliament. Before doing so, these employees (and their union leaders) should read chapter 14, which clarifies what the Canadian government can and cannot do in such circumstances.

Chapter 16 describes the "creative ideas" lawyers and some accountants use when attempting to avoid legislation like the *Investment Canada Act*. Unlike the presentations in articles and seminars on the *Investment Canada Act*, the emphasis in this book is on the risks and dangers. This emphasis may cause professionals to seriously reflect before using such schemes. Incidentally, this is one topic I thought about not even discussing. However, the members of Canada's top law firms are well aware of all the possibilities. Similar creative techniques—such as different classes of shares—are used by those seeking to circumvent the *Income Tax Act* as well. I decided that the only effect of ignoring this topic would be to keep the general public, and some legislative drafters, in the dark about the ways in which certain corporate lawyers and accountants attempt to assist their clients.

Chapter 21, which discusses Canada's Investment Development Program, is also original. This is Canada's program to attract foreign investment (capital and technology), and encourage more Canadian companies to invest abroad. As this chapter points out, Canada should engage in self-promotion overseas. Otherwise, potential foreign investors may think only of the U.S. and overlook the more amiable nation to the north. However, Canada's Investment Development Program raises many issues. The most interesting ones are presented in this chapter.

One reason for encouraging selected foreign companies, such as those with advanced technology, to come to Canada, is that Canadians must have an internationally competitive economy if they are to achieve their social goals. If the economy is not competitive, even Canadians employed in industries apparently insulated from foreign competition will be adversely affected. For example, if jobs are lost in the import-competing sector (eg., consumer electronics, clothing), and if the exporting sector (eg., lumber and paper products) cannot create a sufficient number of new positions, the resulting army of unemployed workers will drive down wages in domestic industries, such as retailing and construction.

However, perhaps there should be a new perspective when Canada's Investment Development Program and other programs designed to make the Canadian economy more 'internationally competitive' are being planned. At present, the ultimate aim of these programs is to increase the rate of growth of Canadians' real incomes. One concern is that our standard of living, although improving in absolute terms, may otherwise slip relative to the rest of the world. Most other nations are pursuing their own similar goal, and naturally, such a goal is very appealing.

Nevertheless, because of the ecological consequences of economic growth and the social costs of high unemployment, many people in Canada should realign their aspirations. The rationale for achieving a more competitive economy should be to provide employment and an adequate, but not necessarily an increasing, material standard of living for all Canadians.

The inspiration to write this book came from the business and legal communities, and from my wish to share my knowledge as an observer of a changing scene.

In 1981, the operations of Canada's Foreign Investment Review Agency ("FIRA") were causing controversy in several world capitals. Three years later (December 1984), a newly elected Prime Minister, Brian Mulroney, declared that Canada was "open for business". In July

1985, FIRA was axed and Investment Canada was created. Thereafter, the Canadian government proceeded to lure more foreign investment through a series of measures that included advertising; overseas seminars and missions; a major conference; the negotiation of the Free Trade Agreement; and by sending investment counsellors abroad.

Publicity generated by this "investment promotion campaign" and the startling shift in government policy from Trudeau's rhetorical nationalism, prompted many phonecalls to Investment Canada. Lawyers had questions about the new statute. Businessmen wanted information on a compendium of topics related to establishing and operating a business. After I had assisted them, some of these callers suggested I write a book on investing in Canada. This book is the result of those suggestions.

Russell Deigan
Ottawa, Canada
November 4, 1991

FOREWORD

The publication of this book on Canada's legislation relating to foreign investment comes as a welcome and timely event. It is now almost twenty years since Canada first adopted a comprehensive law dealing with foreign direct investment. Since that beginning, the administrative approach and the legislative structure have evolved in response to a variety of factors, including the benefits of experience and both domestic and international debate. The replacement of the *Foreign Investment Review Act* with the *Investment Canada Act* in 1985 marked a major change in direction, with a new emphasis on the desirability of foreign investment. The adoption of the Canada-U.S. Free Trade Agreement furthered that development in respect of U.S.-sourced investment. At the same time, the retention of a scheme of significant legislative control for foreign investment confirmed to many that foreign investment continues to call for a level of governmental attention in this country. These developments have, of course, taken place in a context that is not static. Canada's position and prospects in the global economy have evolved over the past two decades and continue to evolve; sound public policy must be responsive to such changes. Indeed, we may hope that when, at some time in the future, these two decades in the history of Canada's approach to foreign investment are appraised, a consistent effort to address both national benefit and international confidence will be seen to be the identifying features of our public policy.

No one can doubt the importance of a careful and supple approach to these sensitive matters of national significance. Thoughtful analysis of the laws relating to foreign investment and the manner in which they operate is essential for the community of those concerned with such matters. I am pleased that this book makes its appearance at this juncture in the continuing evolution of Canada's approach to foreign investment. I hope it will further the effort of careful attention and critical scrutiny which the subject requires on the part of policy-makers and practitioners alike.

James M. Spence, Q.C.
Tory, Tory, DesLauriers & Binnington
Toronto, Canada
September 17, 1991

ACKNOWLEDGMENTS

I wish to express my sincere appreciation to the many government officials and lawyers in private practice who helped with this book. Without their expertise, time and support, it would have been very difficult for me to complete a project as ambitious as this one. For that reason, I am exceedingly grateful to:

W. Gordon Brown (Bennett, Jones, Verchere), Paul G. Findlay (Borden & Elliot), Catherine MacLean (Nelligan, Power), Paul McKenzie, The Hon. Donald S. Macdonald, Ursula Menke, George Woods, Marie-Paule Scott, Q.C., Yash Lamba, John Martin, Gilles Menard, David Doherty, Andre Charette, Larry Kiez, Heather Black, John Barker, Matt Van Neste, Alan Walker, Dave Swimmer, Richard Lepage, Brian McGivern, Bill Wood, Jim Downer, Richard Lovatt, Paul Fecser, Bruce Murat, Greg Kinlin, Romy Peters, Mike Sullivan, Helene Bernier, Alexandra Wood, Hedy Kirkby, Dimitri Pantazopoulos, Ash Ahmed, Louise Lanoy, Peter Humber, Cal Gundy, Margaret Sanderson, Jeff Bregg, D'Leap Hall, Gordon Dewhirst, Marilyn Eades, Ted Zahavich, Marilyn Arditti, Dennis Shanley, and Nicholas Veliotes (Association of American Publishers).

Special thanks are also due to a member of Canada's Free Trade Negotiating Team and other officials at Investment Canada, the Department of Justice, Office of the Superintendent of Financial Institutions, Consumer and Corporate Affairs Canada and Employment and Immigration Canada.

The development of this book was not uneventful. I began writing this book (a private project) in 1986, with the knowledge and approval of senior Investment Canada officials and a Department of Justice official. In July 1989, I started distributing draft chapters to officials in several government departments. The response was enthusiastic and helpful. In 1990, serious problems unexpectedly arose. Despite my many offers to make amendments, the few officials involved would not identify any passages that they wanted amended.

I wish to thank the Minister of Justice, the Hon. Kim Campbell, and a second Conservative M.P., for taking an interest in some difficulties that had arisen. Also, Walter Regan, Q.C., of the Department of Justice, for the same reason. He is an excellent representative of that department. In addition, I am indebted to Iris Craig, President of the Professional Institute of the Public Service, and staff, and Joe Pelisek (at the time Vice President of the Commerce Group), for trying to protect established rights of civil servants. Although the Supreme Court of Canada has ruled that public servants have full political rights, in practice, not all government managers believe that public servants should be allowed to write even articles of a professional nature. Most of all, however, I would like to thank a number of current and former Investment Canada employees for their steadfast support.

Partial funding to write this book was received from the Law Foundation of Ontario. I appreciate the faith of the Law Foundation's trustees that I would complete this project.

Lorraine Reynolds did the word processing. Despite having two full-time jobs, she still found the time, after work, to make revisions to the manuscript. Her performance was outstanding. I am also grateful to several employees at the publishers, including Victoria Parker, Jilean Bell, Sherry MacIsaac, Sonia Nigam, David Keeshan and Joel Saltsman, for the assistance they rendered in many different ways.

Any opinions expressed in this book are my own, and are not necessarily held by anyone who assisted with its preparation. If there are any errors or omissions, I assume sole responsibility for them.

Although the topic of foreign investment is by its nature, controversial, this book was intended to be non-partisan and non-political. It should be read and construed in that fashion.

CONTENTS

CHAPTER 4 THE EXISTENCE OF A CANADIAN BUSINESS 99

CHAPTER 5 ESTABLISHING A NEW CANADIAN BUSINESS 111

CHAPTER 9 OBTAINING AN OPINION 189

CHAPTER 10 FILING A NOTIFICATION 195

CHAPTER 11 EARLY IMPLEMENTATION: FILING AN APPLICATION FOR REVIEW 201

CHAPTER 14 AFTER THE DECISION

CHAPTER 15 REMEDIES AND PENALTIES

CHAPTER 16 THE RISKS IN ATTEMPTING TO AVOID REVIEW

CHAPTER 17 THE FREE TRADE AGREEMENT AND THE AMERICAN INVESTOR

CHAPTER 18 THE BANK ACT AND THE INVESTMENT CANADA ACT 345

CHAPTER 19 THE ACCESS TO INFORMATION ACT AND THE INVESTMENT CANADA ACT 355

CHAPTER 20 THE NATIONAL TRANSPORTATION ACT, 1987 AND THE INVESTMENT CANADA ACT

CHAPTER 21 CANADA AND THE INTERNATIONAL COMPETITION FOR FOREIGN INVESTMENT

TABLE OF CASES

CHAPTER 1

SUNSET ON FIRA: THE BACKGROUND TO INVESTMENT CANADA

Canada's law governing foreign investment, the *Investment Canada Act* ("*IC Act*"),[1] was proclaimed in force on June 30, 1985. It is a significant date in Canada's economic history, not so much for what the new Act accomplished, but because it dramatically highlighted the nation's changed attitude towards foreign investment and the ebbing of nationalist sentiments. Canada, in the words of its prime minister, was open for business again.[2]

Up to that time, and for the preceding 11 years, the gateway to investment in Canada had been guarded, at least symbolically, by the Foreign Investment Review Agency (created under the *Foreign Investment Review Act*). Better known by its acronym FIRA, the Foreign Investment Review Agency had come into being in April 1974, during a period of great public concern over the extent to which control of Canadian industry and natural resources had been acquired by non-Canadians.[3]

The roots of this concern had been growing during the 1960s and early 1970s. This was a period of relative prosperity during which thoughtful people in many parts of the world had begun to question the value system of industrial society. Stoked by stories about the newly independent nations in Asia and Africa, the issue of national sovereignty was receiving much attention.

---

[1] R.S.C. 1985, c. 28, (1st Suppl.), as am. S.C. 1988, c. 65. It might have been called the Canada Investment Act were it not for the existence of an American organization with the same initials that also monitors the activities of foreigners (the C.I.A.).

[2] Prime Minister Brian Mulroney, speaking before a meeting of the Economic Club of New York, December 10, 1984.

[3] The *FIR Act* came into force in two phases. On April 9, 1974, the takeover provisions went into effect; on October 15, 1975, the provisions dealing with the establishment of new businesses were proclaimed in force.

1

At the same time, political economists were beginning to investigate the behaviour and characteristics of the multinational firm, which was in the process of assuming an unprecedented importance within the world economy. These political economists were quick to note that the central characteristic of multinational firms—their ability to organize production across national boundaries—was posing an immediate challenge to the nation-state and raising questions about the long-term viability of nations.[4]

The idea that the most efficient allocation of resources can be achieved through the free flow of international capital was also under attack. That proposition was true in a "perfectly competitive world" (thousands of firms, no barriers to entry, no one able to affect market price). In such a (nonexistent) world, restrictions on the free flow of foreign investment would protect inefficient domestic firms and prevent capital from being used in the most productive fashion.

However, as Canadian-born economist Stephen Hymer pointed out, multinational firms operate in oligopolistic markets (few sellers, as in the automobile industry). In an oligopolistic market, it is impossible to prove that "competition allocates resources efficiently, and that there is a harmony between private profit maximization and the general interest".[5]

That meant—theoretically at least—that foreign investment could have a negative effect on a country's economy. It might impede the formation of domestic capital. Or, if the advantages that a multinational firm had over domestic companies were rooted in advertising or restrictive practices (e.g., the foreclosure of sources of supply), the net effect might be to curtail competition and raise prices with no gain in efficiency. Even if multinational firms always made positive contributions to (national and global) economic welfare, government intervention could increase or alter the distribution of those benefits in favour of host countries. In theory, this could be done without affecting other aspects of the firm's behavior (and was therefore a "costless" remedy).

Proponents of this theory argued that multinational firms earned high profits because they had a competitive advantage (e.g., unique technology, marketing skills) over domestic firms. In order to maximize these profits, multinational companies often bought their inputs from cheaper home country suppliers, or filled export orders from

---

[4]Gilles Paquet, *The Multinational Firm and The Nation State*, (Don Mills, Ontario: Collier-Macmillan Canada, 1972).

[5]Stephen Hymer, "The Efficiency (Contradictions) of Multinational Corporations", *American Economic Review*, LX, 2, May 1970, Papers and Proceedings of the 82nd Annual Meeting, 441 at p. 443.

branches in low-cost countries. By forcing a multinational company to buy locally, export part of its production, and sell equity to local citizens, a host country could supposedly capture some of these profits without affecting the company's decision to invest.

1. New Thoughts: The Impact on Canada

In Canada during the 1960s, these novel currents of thought were both reviving and spawning nationalist sentiments. At the same time, they were causing Canadians to ponder the extensive foreign control of Canadian industry. Oblivious to the silent sprouting of Canada's own multinational companies, many Canadians became increasingly alarmed at what they perceived to be a growing Americanization of Canada.

The issue was debated in the press and subjected to four government-sponsored studies.[6] Canadians read that foreign investment brought a package of assets to Canada that might include capital, technology, management skills, licences to use brand names, and increased access to world markets or sources of supply. This package increased the country's economic growth and prosperity.

But the picture had more than one side. Of foremost importance was that foreign investment was both an economic and political phenomenon. Through the foreign ownership link, the laws and policies of other nations—especially the U.S.—could be transmitted to Canada. That possibility led the authors of the Watkins Report to warn the nation that foreign direct investment represented a "potential shift outside the country of the locus of some types of decision-making".[7]

Canadians were also discussing the performance of foreign-owned firms and debating whether this performance was primarily determined by nationality of ownership or Canada's economic and social environment. The studies that were done sometimes came to conflicting conclusions or no conclusions at all.[8]

---

[6] The Gordon Commission (*Royal Commission on Canada's Economic Prospects*, Ottawa, 1958); the Watkins Report (*Foreign Ownership and the Structures of Canadian Industry*, Ottawa, 1968); Wahn Report (*Report to the House of the Special Committee Respecting Canada-U.S. Relations*, 1970); and the Gray Report (*Foreign Direct Investment in Canada*, Ottawa, 1972).

[7] *Foreign Ownership and the Structure of Canadian Industry. Report of the Task Force on the Structure of Canadian Industry*, M. Watkins, Chairman, (Ottawa: Queen's Printer, 1968) p.27.

[8] It is very difficult to determine the effect of foreign investment on people's living standards, their freedom of economic choice and the distribution of income. (The study of such issues is part of "welfare economics".) For a summary of the research that has been done, see A.E. Safarian, *Foreign Direct Investment: A Survey of Canadian Research*, (Montreal: The Institute for Research on Public Policy, 1985).

Nonetheless, many Canadians were aroused by allegations that foreign-owned firms in Canada discriminated against Canadians when filling senior management positions, thus hindering the development of Canadian entrepreneurial expertise; that they bought goods and services from traditional foreign suppliers even when similar goods and services were available in Canada; and that they prevented Canadian subsidiaries from exporting because of the existence of affiliates abroad. Canadians were also concerned about the reverse flow of interest, dividends and capital and what some economists called the "miniature replica effect" which occurred when foreign firms followed each other in establishing subsidiaries in Canada. These subsidiaries sometimes mirrored their foreign parents in every respect—except that they could not operate on an efficient scale.

Then there was the issue of transfer pricing. A multinational company, critics contended, might manipulate the prices of goods and services moving between itself and its subsidiaries to keep reported profits and taxes low or to keep competitors at bay.

But what probably agitated Canadians the most were suggestions that foreign multinational companies centralized almost all research and development activities at their head offices and during recessions, first cut back on employment at their subsidiaries. According to the exaggerated rhetoric of some nationalists at the time, Canadians were in danger of becoming mere hewers of wood and drawers of water in a branch plant economy.

2. The Purpose of FIRA

The *Foreign Investment Review Act* ("*FIR Act*") was designed to meet some of these concerns[9] by filtering investment from abroad. To receive government approval to establish a new business or acquire a Canadian business, foreign investors had to submit their proposals to a review process, during which they were obliged to show that the proposed transactions were likely to be of significant benefit to Canada. The purpose of this review was not to reduce foreign ownership in Canada. Instead, it was to push foreign firms to alter their

---

[9] What other measures did Ottawa take to control foreign investment? It passed key sector legislation to ensure that banks, other financial institutions and companies engaged in broadcasting (radio, television and cable T.V.) would remain under Canadian control; established the Canada Development Corporation (to attract Canadian savings into the development of Canadian-controlled businesses); changed the tax system to favour Canadian-controlled firms; and passed legislation to require that a majority of the directors of federally-incorporated companies be Canadians. Through Crown corporations, Ottawa also participated directly in rail and air transportation, nuclear energy and oil and gas exploration.

behaviour and thereby increase the package of benefits the country obtained through foreign investment.

Transactions of both major and minor socio-economic significance were caught by the *FIR Act*. That meant the government had to examine not only sizeable acquisitions but also new businesses and rescue operations and the takeover of small companies that lacked the technology, the funds, or the management and marketing expertise to expand.

This examination of small transactions was criticized by certain business people and politicians. However, it was justified by the government of the day as a way to protect sensitive industry sectors and infant companies in which public funds had been invested. The government was also concerned that if small transactions escaped the review net, a large international company might use a small investment as a foot in the door to expand without review.

The administrative mechanism created to receive and evaluate applications for approval was FIRA. The agency often received the credit or blame for decisions but in reality its role was to provide advice and recommendations to the minister and the Cabinet.[10] Ultimately, it was a committee of Cabinet, known as the Governor in Council, which issued the order that allowed or disallowed the proposed investment.[11]

FIRA and the *FIR Act* were never a great obstacle to foreign investment in Canada. To begin with, there were major loopholes in what the Act covered. Excluded from the Act's ambit was the expansion of existing foreign-controlled businesses. In addition, foreign investors who already had a business in Canada could establish a new but "related" business without review.[12]

This meant that FIRA had little impact upon the largest source of foreign investment—the reinvestment by foreign corporations of their Canadian earnings. Multinational companies which had set up operations in Canada before FIRA was created, like Ford and General Motors, and those admitted under the Act, could grow and expand without hindrance.[13] Moreover, by interpreting the concept of a "related" business (and certain other provisions of the Act) in a way that

---

[10] Some of this blame or credit was deserved. FIRA administrators did not make the final decisions but they influenced the outcome through the information and recommendations (the "case summaries") they sent to the minister, who in turn sent the summaries to the Governor in Council.

[11] See: R. Schultz, F. Swedlove, K. Swinton, *The Cabinet as a Regulatory Body: The Case of the Foreign Investment Review Act*. Working Paper No. 6, Regulation Reference Series, (Ottawa: Economic Council of Canada, 1980).

[12] Despite its importance, the concept of relatedness was undefined in the *FIR Act*.

[13] Except for a few companies whose expansion was limited by undertakings given at the time of the initial approval.

favoured investors, the administrators at FIRA deliberately narrowed the scope of the Act even further.[14]

In theory, even the smallest investor with only a few thousand dollars available to start a new business was challenged under the *FIR Act* to prove that the proposed business would be of significant benefit to Canada. In practice, if the small investor could show that any benefit existed, that was usually sufficient to meet the test. Although opponents of FIRA liked to dwell on the senselessness of reviewing the plans of a budding entrepreneur to establish a corner grocery store, to such an entrepreneur, FIRA was a cause of inconvenience but also a rubber stamp.

After the *FIR Act* became fully operational, the greatest number of cases turned down annually was in 1981 when 13.1% of decided cases were disallowed. In 1983, the figure was only 3.1%. And following the election of the Progressive Conservatives in 1984 until the repeal of the Act nine months later, there were no disallowances at all.[15]

If FIRA was a serious barrier to investment, its impact should have been most dramatic in 1981, when the number of disallowances and the profile of the agency itself were at their heights. In its Speech from the Throne of the previous year, the Trudeau government had promised to publicize foreign takeover bids in order to encourage counter-offers from Canadians. Trudeau also wanted to enlarge FIRA's mandate by instituting performance reviews of large foreign firms operating in Canada.[16] However in 1981, as Chart 1 indicates, the flow of foreign investment dollars into Canada was greater than before.

---

[14] Foreign companies already in Canada could establish a new "related" business without government approval. The word "related" could have been given a narrow or wide meaning. FIRA (and the minister) chose to give it a very wide meaning in the minister's "Guidelines Concerning Related Business". Why did FIRA administrators tend to interpret the Act in a way that narrowed its scope? Sometimes this was done to achieve policy goals, such as to reduce the number of real estate transactions that would otherwise have been subject to review. (See the "Guidelines Concerning Real Estate Businesses".) However, this tendency was also a natural response by government administrators to one-sided pressure from lawyers for foreign investors. (The interpretations of FIRA administrators formed a body of "unwritten FIRA law".)

[15] The percentages of cases disallowed and the corresponding years are as follows: 19.5% (1974); 15.3% (1975); 10.5% (1976); 4.3% (1977); 9.1% (1978); 6.7% (1979); 10.7% (1980); 13.1% (1981); 8.0% (1982); 3.1% (1983); 3.6% (January to September 1984); average: 7.4% (1974-84).

[16] *House of Commons Debates*, 1st Session, 32nd Parliament, Vol. 1, April 14, 1980, p.6. The Governor General in his speech from the throne stated: "The *Foreign Investment Review Act* will be amended to provide for performance reviews of how foreign firms are meeting the test of bringing substantial benefits to Canada." The government intended to examine the level of R & D done by Canadian subsidiaries of foreign firms, their sourcing practices and any export restriction imposed by the parent company, etc. Some

3. A Growing Hostility

These statistics, however, don't tell the complete story. They neither reflect applications that were withdrawn before a decision could be rendered nor investors who were deterred from applying either because they feared delays or that they could not meet the significant benefit test.[17]

Unfortunately, investors did, at times, experience unconscionable delays in the rendering of decisions. A few had to wait months.[18] Occasionally deals collapsed as a result. Such delays and the attendant costs sent out a message that Canada did not really welcome any foreign investment. However, simple administrative changes,[19] instituted after June 1982, considerably reduced those delays to the extent that criticism of FIRA as an administrative body had lessened by the end of 1984.

So, why a new Act? The problem was that misconceptions about the role and impact of FIRA had assumed monumental proportions.

---

newspaper writers speculated that the results of the examination would be published. Others believed that it would lead to discussions between the government and foreign firms on how the latter could improve their performance.

[17] Or for other reasons. Using a questionnaire survey, MacDowall investigated the deterrent effect of "foreign investment controls". He found that 11% of respondents claimed to have been deterred from investing in Canada by such controls. MacDowall did not define the phrase "foreign investment controls" in his survey. However, he intended that the phrase include various forms of controls. D. MacDowall, *A Fit Place for Investment?*, Study No. 81, (Ottawa: Conference Board of Canada, 1984).

[18] These delays were caused by dilatory investors (who filed incomplete applications and took weeks to provide the necessary information); the need for FIRA to consult with other government departments and the provinces and to assess third party representations; the negotiating process and the drafting of undertakings; plus competing demands on the time of ministers.

[19] These administrative changes included: monitoring the progress of applications; reducing the number of legally deficient applications by amending the application forms and regulations; being more liberal in interpreting what information constituted a complete application; and raising the ceilings for eligibility under the "quick" review process. Had these simple changes been introduced at an earlier stage in FIRA's life, U.S. hostility might never have reached the depths it did. (The demise of FIRA was caused not so much by the scope of the legislation as by the way it was administered. At one point, the average turnaround time from the receipt of an often incomplete application to a decision was 156 days. This angered foreign business people. In 1982, an irritated Prime Minister Trudeau said that he could not even eat dinner without hearing complaints about FIRA.)

In addition, FIRA had become a high profile target for critics of government regulation of investment.[20]

In the U.S., an increasingly hostile attitude had developed after the election of the Reagan government. This new attitude—a change from the previous grudging acceptance—had come about through a combination of factors.

In 1981, Canadian companies had made several takeover bids for American businesses (e.g., Bronfman-owned Seagram's bid for Conoco). These bids caused an uproar in Washington. Americans who were adversely affected by the takeovers got sympathy in the U.S. Congress by alleging that FIRA treated American companies unfairly when they tried to buy Canadian businesses.

A more profound reason for the changed attitude was the concern of U.S. officials over their country's economic performance (high unemployment, inflation). Once the dominant force in world commerce, the U.S. was facing stiff competition from Europe and the newly industrialized countries. During the previous decade (the 1970s), almost two million manufacturing jobs had been lost because of imports. Over the same period, the world market share held by U.S. manufactured goods had suffered a 23% decline.

The operations of U.S. multinationals overseas were one of many factors blamed for these economic changes. In the 1960s, U.S. companies had gone abroad to better serve foreign markets. This resulted in new opportunities for U.S.-based suppliers of parts and components. During the 1970s, however, Americans had become aware that U.S. companies overseas were buying many of their inputs locally, often at the insistence of foreign governments. U.S. companies that had established plants in low-wage countries were also exporting to the U.S. Commitments obtained by FIRA from U.S. companies were criticized by some Washington officials for worsening this situation. In a 1981 speech, the U.S. Secretary of Commerce stated that: "Canada's present policies may be injurious to United States' companies profitability, as well as to our balance of payments and trade".[21]

---

[20] Until 1980, FIRA was perceived by U.S. government officials as being relatively inoffensive. What changed U.S. attitudes? Stephen Clarkson, in *Canada and the Reagan Challenge*, (Ottawa: Canadian Institute for Economic Policy, 1982), sheds light on the political factors. The Trudeau government's promise to expand FIRA's mandate to include performance reviews of established multinational companies focused American attention on FIRA. The belief of U.S. officials in the benefits of free investment flows, their willingness to protect the interests of U.S. companies abroad, and U.S. economic problems are three other reasons. (In 1981, Robert D. Hormats, Assistant Secretary of State, said: "We have also pledged to help defend U.S. investors adversely affected by foreign laws and regulations." For citation, see *infra*, n. 31.)

[21] "Remarks by Secretary of Commerce Malcolm Baldrige for delivery before New York University International Business Conference, July 20, 1981, New York City", *Commerce News*, July 21, 1981, p. 1, at 4.

In U.S. eyes, FIRA was distorting trade by encouraging American subsidiaries that were being established in Canada to import less from the U.S., and export more. There were also complaints that, as a condition of approval, American companies were being forced to transfer more of their operations from the U.S. to Canada than would otherwise be the case; that Canadian law was being applied extraterritorially when a merger of two companies in the U.S., one of which had a Canadian business, led to a review by FIRA; and that U.S.-owned assets in Canada were being reduced in value because American subsidiaries couldn't be sold to the highest foreign bidder. Delays in the approval process and a belief that some proposed takeovers were disallowed in order to permit a Canadian to purchase the target company at a bargain caused further irritation among some American business people and their supporters in Congress.

And then, there was the hated National Energy Program ("N.E.P.") with its "back-in provisions"[22] in favour of the Canadian government, and higher incentive grants to Canadian-owned companies. These two initiatives had hit U.S. oil interests hard. The object of the N.E.P. was to increase Canadian ownership of the oil and gas industry from 30% in 1980 to 50% in 1990.[23] One way to achieve this goal was to increase the growth of Canadian-controlled companies. Under the N.E.P., a company which spent money to explore for oil and gas received a grant. Foreign-owned companies were eligible for these grants, but companies with a high level of Canadian ownership received a much larger grant. American officials called this "discrimination".

FIRA's role in the "Canadianization" of the oil and gas industry was also criticized. Although there was no direct effect on Canadian ownership levels when a merger of two U.S. companies led to the indirect acquisition[24] of Canadian oil and gas assets or when an American purchased a foreign-owned oil company in Canada, the Canadian

---

[22] The "back-in provision" was a term invented by industry spokespeople. It described the right conferred on the Canadian government by the N.E.P. to claim, retroactively, a 25% interest in oil found on Crown lands (chiefly in the far north and offshore). In industry eyes, this was retroactive confiscation. For further details on the N.E.P., see: Jean-Paul Lacasse, "Legal Issues Relating to the Canadian National Energy Program" (1983), 16 *Vanderbilt Journal of Transnational Law* 301.

[23] One objective was 50% Canadian ownership of oil and gas production in 1990, as measured by production revenues. Another objective was to have Canadians control a number of industry leaders in the oil and gas industry. By 1984, Canadian-controlled Petro-Canada, Dome Petroleum and PanCanadian Petroleum were ranked among the top ten oil and gas companies operating in Canada. *Financial Times*, "'Times' Exclusive Ranking", July 9, 1984, p.7.

[24] An indirect acquisition occurs when a foreign company with an existing Canadian subsidiary is purchased by, or merges with another foreign company. There is no direct effect on the Canadian subsidiary, but its ultimate controllers change. Under FIRA, this triggered a reviewable transaction.

government sometimes used FIRA to negotiate benefits consistent with the National Energy Program. To receive approval for an acquisition, a U.S. company might have to agree to sell the upstream assets[25] of the Canadian business to Canadians, increase Canadian ownership or sell shares in another of its resource-based subsidiaries.[26]

Unfortunately for FIRA, the result was that the agency became identified with the National Energy Program in the corridors of Washington.[27] There, FIRA was viewed as another instrument through which the Canadianization goals of the National Energy Program were being carried out. Some Americans also complained that FIRA was blocking investments in other sectors on the basis of undisclosed government policies.

To a degree, this U.S. reaction was understandable. On occasion, any review process is a zero-sum game.[28] To the extent that FIRA increased the benefits that foreign firms brought to Canada, the rewards that foreign countries hoped to derive from their direct investments abroad would sometimes be correspondingly reduced.

This in essence was the complaint of the Labour-Industry Coalition for International Trade ("LICIT")—an American labour-business lobby group, whose members included the United Steelworkers of America, the Boeing Corporation, the International Brotherhood of Electrical Workers and St. Joe Minerals Corporation. LICIT pointed out in its submissions to American politicians that performance requirements—such as commitments to export a fixed percentage of production, to source locally and to transfer technology—were being imposed by several western and Third World governments. These performance requirements, warned LICIT, could have undesirable consequences for the U.S.A. In particular, they could "lead to a direct

---

[25] Upstream assets are those used in exploration for, development and production of oil and gas. Refining and marketing of petroleum and petroleum products constitute the downstream side.

[26] For instance, after Occidental Petroleum acquired Canada-Cities Service in 1983, the assets of Canada-Cities Service and Canadian Occidental were combined into a new company, whose shares were later issued to the public. This diluted the parent company's ownership to a little less than 50%. See: Jack Hanna, "Big Change of Style at Canadian Occidental Petroleum", *Financial Times*, Oct. 31, 1983, p.6. Mobil Corp., on the other hand, got approval to buy the Canadian assets of General Crude Oil by agreeing to sell half of the proven gas reserves it had acquired to Canadians. Dunnery Best, "FIRA—Less Canada—First Bite", *Financial Post*, Sept. 25, 1982, p. 1.

[27] Hyman Solomon, "N.E.P. and FIRA at the Top of Reagan's Hit List", *Financial Post* (Special Report), July 3, 1982, p. s3.

[28] In a zero-sum game, a gain by one party is at the expense of the other. For a summary of the literature of game theory, see Katheryn Harrigan, *Strategies for Joint Ventures*, (Toronto: D.C. Heath and Company, 1985), p. 74.

transfer of investments, jobs and production to the country which imposes them and away from other countries".[29]

Particularly reprehensible to LICIT, as France, Mexico and Brazil embraced performance requirements, was that Canada was setting a bad example for the rest of the world. Canada was giving the impression that performance requirements were an acceptable practice. Pointing to FIRA's annual reports, which summarized the commitments that foreign investors had given, LICIT described the government of Canada as "probably the most assertive advocate of the benefits of performance requirements".[30] A top U.S. government official expressed the same concern: "Canadian investment policies, if unchallenged, are likely to encourage other countries to adopt similar measures".[31]

The U.S. therefore had some understandable misgivings about FIRA. What disconcerted many Canadians was that the U.S. had magnified the small "achievements" of FIRA out of all proportion and ignored the many legislative obstacles, both state and federal, that faced "alien" investors in the U.S.A.

Although the U.S. and other countries have a myriad of legislative hurdles[32] that investors must overcome before being allowed to proceed, their laws and regulations are administered not by one body but by a host of different government bodies—sometimes in a most discretionary fashion. It is frequently difficult for critics even to find out what the laws are, much less mount a sustained campaign of attack against them.[33]

---

[29] The Labour-Industry Coalition for International Trade ("LICIT"), *Performance Requirements: A Study of the Incidence and Impact of Trade-Related Performance Requirements and an Analysis of International Law*, p. viii. Published in March 1981 and distributed by LICIT from its headquarters in Washington, D.C. Reprinted in *U.S. Policy Toward International Investment: Hearings before the Subcommittee on International Economic Policy*, 97th Cong., 1st Sess. (1981), n. 29, at 49 (insertion to the statements of Alan Wolff).

[30] Ibid., p.8.

[31] Statement of Robert D. Hormats, Assistant Secretary of State, Bureau of Economic and Business Affairs, Department of State, before the Subcommittee on Oversight and Investigations of the Committee on Energy and Commerce, House of Representatives, Washington, D.C., July 9, 1981, p. 5.

[32] Some nations have review processes built into foreign exchange control systems.

[33] A foreign investor in the United States must cope with an enormous number of laws. Michael Seitzinger, "Foreign Investment in the U.S. Major Federal Restrictions" in *Foreign Direct Investment Effects on the United States*, Subcommittee on Economic Stabilization of the Committee on Banking, Finance, and Urban Affairs, House of Representatives, July 1989, p. 48.; Joseph Norton, *Regulation of Business Enterprise in the U.S.A.*, (New York: Oceana Publications Inc., 1985); New York State Bar Association Committee on

Canada, however, was different. Canada had centred the most important of its regulatory powers within a single agency with an acronym that was a bit frightening. Moreover, Canada had carefully spelled out through legislation and guidelines the procedure and criteria for obtaining governmental consent to an investment.

Not surprisingly, FIRA quickly became a lightning rod. By 1984, some domestic critics were portraying FIRA as being responsible for almost everything that was wrong with the Canadian economy:

> The two biggest economic problems in this country—why people don't have jobs—are FIRA and the N.E.P., which have been an absolute disaster. Basically both policies should be scrapped.[34]

The cycle was at this point complete. Born amid popular sentiments that overestimated the negative consequences of foreign investment, the impact of the agency, whose role was to curtail these consequences, was itself being misjudged.

The perception that FIRA was a barrier to foreign investment and that Canada did not want foreign investment was partly, if not substantially, incorrect. However, perceptions are one of the most important determinants of capital flows.

With Canada's economy just coming out of a recession, and unemployment at high levels, the new Conservative government wanted to solicit foreign investment, and to soothe Canada's largest trading partner, particularly when the Canada-U.S. free trade talks were on the horizon. Some way had to be found to alleviate foreigners' fears of FIRA.

International Trade and Transactions, *Federal and State Disclosure Requirements and Restrictions in Connection with U.S. Acquisitions By Foreign Purchaser*, (mimeo) pp. 1-108; American Bar Association, Division for Professional Education, *Foreign Direct Investment in the United States*, (Chicago: American Bar Association, 1988).

An amendment to the 1988 Omnibus Trade Act (the "Exon-Florio Amendment") now allows the President of the U.S. to block foreign takeovers of U.S. firms that threaten "national security". An inter-agency committee called the Committee on Foreign Investment in the U.S. ("C.F.I.U.S.") receives notices of acquisitions, undertakes investigations, and makes recommendations to the President. The maximum review period is 90 days. One interesting sideline: the C.F.I.U.S. is negotiating takeover terms. In one case (Heuls AG's takeover of Monsanto Electronic Materials), the foreign (German) firm gave a pledge to retain R&D in the U.S.

[34] Stu Eagles, Chairman of Marathon Realty as reported in the *Toronto Star*, June 19, 1982, p. A3. See also David Crane, "U.S. Trying to Scuttle Our Trade Safeguards", *Toronto Star*, June 23, 1982, p. A24.

4. The Conservative Government Changes the Law

How was this to be done? Through a public relations campaign? More administrative changes to the agency? Amendments to the Act to exclude smaller investments? It was decided that the easiest way to change perceptions was to abolish FIRA itself. But the new *Investment Canada Act* did more than just abolish FIRA. It propelled Canada from near one end of the screening spectrum towards the other.

Under FIRA, at least when Mr. Herb Gray was the responsible minister, the majority of investment proposals were given a rigorous examination, with undertakings being sought as a guarantee of performance. If a proposal involved a large investment, the negotiation of undertakings was often a lengthy process.

The preamble to the *Investment Canada Act* expresses a different outlook. It says, in a nutshell, that most investments are of benefit to Canada and should be encouraged. It thus implies that only when investments are of major economic significance should discussions and perhaps undertakings be necessary in order to obtain government approval.

As an accompaniment of this new philosophy, the Act changed the scope of the review process and imposed strict time limits to prevent delays. Irritants to foreigners, such as the review of indirect acquisitions of Canadian businesses when takeovers occurred in other countries, uncertainty over when the Act applied, and the lack of openness caused in part by the umbrella of Cabinet secrecy were (to some extent) addressed.[35]

To the surprise of many observers, the Act also gave the new Investment Canada agency a novel mandate:

(i) to review major foreign takeovers to ensure that such transactions benefited Canada;

(ii) to encourage Canadians and foreigners to invest in Canada;

(iii) to conduct research and provide policy advice on investment issues.

Trumpeting Canada's potential as a profitable place to invest, protecting the country's culture from foreign investors, and scrutinizing large takeovers—that was to be the new role. Investment Canada

---

[35] For further complaints about FIRA's screening process from a legal practitioner, see E. James Arnett, *"FIRA and the Rule of Law"* (1984), 62 *Can. Bar Rev.* 121, at 126. Also see R. Schulz, F. Swedlove and K. Swinton, *supra*, n. 11.

was to be, symbolically at least, Canada's economic guardian and, for a time, its leading salesman in Canada's effort to attract foreign investment.

Chart 1

GROSS & NET FLOWS OF
FOREIGN DIRECT INVESTMENT
1976 TO 1990

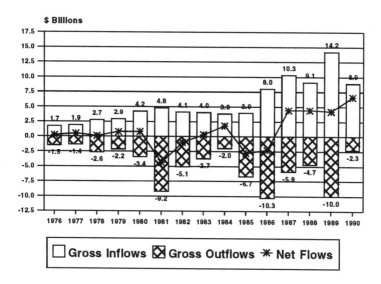

Source: Statistics Canada, Quarterly Estimates of the Canadian International Balance
of Payments, Cat.# 67-001.

Note: Gross inflows of FDI refer to debt and equity investments that a foreign firm makes in a subsidiary in Canada. For instance, if a foreign firm purchases a Canadian business, or loans money to a subsidiary in Canada, the result is a gross inflow of FDI. A gross outflow occurs when the loan is repaid, or a Canadian buys a business owned by non–Canadians in Canada. Gross outflows must not be confused with the payment of interest and dividends to foreigners (which are part of the current account of the Canadian balance of payments, not the capital account) nor with Canadian investment abroad. Net flow is, of course, the difference between gross inflows and outflows. Portfolio investment (trade in stocks and bonds) is not shown in these figures.

CHAPTER 2

INVESTMENT CANADA AND THE NEW WORLD ECONOMY

Investment Canada is a federal government agency which performs two distinct roles. The one that generates the most controversy is its review of takeovers by foreign investors. The other role—which may be of greater long-term significance—has been to participate in Canada's Investment Development Program by *promoting* foreign investment in Canada.

1. The Pursuit of Foreign Investment

This pursuit of foreign investment startled many Canadians when it began in 1985. After so many years of nationalist rhetoric (e.g., Trudeau: "If we abolish FIRA now . . . we would be selling the birthright of our children."),[1] the announcement that government officials would encourage *more* foreign investment sounded like a revolutionary change had occurred in federal government policy. Newspapers headlined the event: "Investment door opens"[2] and "Canada for sale, but who's buying?"[3]

---

[1] "P.M. Says Abolishing FIRA Means 'Selling Our Children's Birthright'", *Montreal Gazette*, Sept. 8, 1982, p. A1. Trudeau said in part: "If we abolish FIRA now, in the weak state of our industries and businesses, they [foreign investors] could come in and pick it up at a pittance."

[2] Giles Gherson, "Investment Door Opens: Big Push for More Foreign Money Here", *Financial Post*, August 24, 1985, p. 1. Former FIRA employees at Investment Canada discovered their duties had substantially changed. Ruth Hubbard, Investment Canada's executive vice president at the time said: "Part of our job is to help define the government's investment policy and that means trying to temper or restrain other moves toward nationalist policies elsewhere in the government." Op. cit., p. 2.

[3] Deborah McGregor, "Canada for Sale, but Who's Buying?", *Report on Business Magazine*, Mar. 1, 1985, p. 76. Her question was answered two years later when several

17

Reality was less dramatic. The scale and intensity of Canada's marketing effort was unprecedented. However, the direction of actual government policy had not shifted all that much. Indeed, with the exception of two periods when nationalists in the Liberal Party were on top, (1973–75 and 1980–81), the decision of the Conservatives to promote foreign investment did not really constitute a significant change in the Canadian government's orientation.

Many Liberal government ministers had never accepted the goals of the economic nationalists. When Jean Chretien was responsible for FIRA (1976–77), critics called the agency a welcome mat.[4] Jack Horner, FIRA's next minister, said the agency's role was to encourage foreign investment![5]

In 1980, the Liberal left wing was in the ascendency. Trudeau wanted to strengthen FIRA. (Trudeau proposed that FIRA examine the performance of foreign firms already in Canada, publicize takeover bids, and provide financial assistance to Canadians seeking to buy foreign-controlled firms.)[6] Industry Minister Herb Gray, who was responsible for FIRA, was comparatively tough on foreign investors. In his speeches, Gray also spoke of a new industrial strategy that the Liberal government was working on which would "address the very prominent foreign presence in our economy".[7]

---

large Canadian companies (e.g., Husky Oil, Carling O'Keefe) were purchased by foreign investors. Barry Critchley and Eric Reguly, "Canada for Sale: Foreign Buyers Rushing in After Historic Shift in Our Investment Nationalism", *Financial Post*, Mar. 16, 1987, p. 1.

[4] Ian Urquhart, "The Welcome Wagon", *Maclean's*, Nov. 1, 1976, p. 40n. Urguhart wrote: "In the Cabinet, ministers who opposed FIRA in the first place and only agreed to its formation under pressure from the NDP are seizing the opportunity to do the agency in." At the time, Jean Chrétien had said: "There are a lot of places in Canada where people don't give a damn who owns what."

[5] Paul Jackson, "FIRA Approach to Takeovers Changes Completely", *Calgary Herald*, July 28, 1978, p. B14.

[6] Pierre Trudeau's election campaign speech, Feb. 12, 1980; the Speech from the Throne, Apr. 14, 1980. On Feb. 12, Trudeau said: "Through government guarantees of bank loans, FIRA will help provide financial assistance to Canadian companies that want to compete for foreign takeovers or repatriate foreign ownership of assets."

[7] Stephen Clarkson, *Canada and the Reagan Challenge*, op. cit., p. 88. Reporting on a meeting at Meech Lake on June 14, 1981, *The Globe and Mail* mentioned that Cabinet ministers have discussed "the prospect of Canadianizing certain key sectors, as is now being attempted in energy". (At the time, the Liberal government, through its National Energy Program, was aiming for 50% Canadian ownership of the oil and gas industry by 1990.) R. Sheppard, "Industry Strategy, Inflation at Centre of Cabinet Think-in", *The Globe and Mail*, June 15, 1991, p. 1, at 2.

The result was a crisis in Canada-U.S. relations,[8] threats of counter-measures against Canadian investment and energy policies, congressional hearings on the role of FIRA and pressure by Washington for the elimination of all FIRA-imposed performance requirements.[9] Trudeau finally backed down. The Liberal government's budget document, issued November 12, 1981, referred to the proposed changes to the *Foreign Investment Review Act*, then stated: "For the time being, no legislative action is intended on these measures."[10]

By then, a recession accompanied by high interest rates had hit the Canadian economy. The flood waters of a new mood began rising fast. In the spring of 1982, a battle took place in Cabinet over whether to retain FIRA. By September 1982, nine out of ten provincial premiers had condemned FIRA.[11] The following month, Prime Minister Trudeau shuffled his Cabinet. Economic nationalist Herb Gray was ousted as FIRA's minister. A man well liked by the business community, former bottling company manager Ed Lumley, took over.[12] Thereafter, few investors—except in the oil and gas and cultural sectors—experienced difficulty in getting government approval. (The approval rate for the period from April to June 1983 was 99%.)[13]

---

[8] This crisis was ignited by several Canadian takeovers of American companies in the spring of 1981. For further details, read: Stephen Clarkson, *Canada and the Reagan Challenge*, op. cit.

[9] "U.S. Urges Canada to Ease Foreign Investment Rules", *Montreal Gazette*, Oct. 22, 1981, p. 80. Also: David Macdonald, deputy U.S. trade representative, Opening Statement before a joint hearing of the Subcommittee on International Economic Policy and Trade and the Subcommittee on Inter-American Affairs of the House Committee on Foreign Affairs, Oct. 21, 1981, p. 4.

[10] Budget Document entitled *Economic Development for Canada in the 1980s*, p. 13.

[11] *The Economist*, Sept. 18, 1982, at p.83. Michael Doyle, "10 Premiers Seek Summit on Economy", *Winnipeg Free Press*, Aug. 27, 1982, p.1. When Quebec Premier René Lévesque suggested to a group of American senators that an independent Quebec would be more receptive to American investment, the *Toronto Star* asked whether the price of Lévesque's dream would be the transformation of Quebec into another Louisiana where French culture is a "quaint shadow in an economy controlled elsewhere". "Courting U.S. Domination", *Toronto Star*, July 16, 1982, p. A12.

[12] John King, "U.S. Businessmen Like New FIRA Head", *The Globe and Mail*, Oct. 1, 1982, p. 10. At the same time as a new minister was being appointed, Bob Richardson took over as commissioner of FIRA. Three weeks later, Prime Minister Trudeau told a group of U.S. business people that he was not an economic nationalist and that economic nationalism was a policy pushed on the Liberals by the Ontario caucus. James Rusk, "FIRA to Be Revised, U.S. Executives Told", *The Globe and Mail*, Oct. 21, 1982, p.1.

[13] FIRA Commissioner Bob Richardson played a role. Like all deputy ministers he controlled the type of information and advice that his political boss received. The nature of Richardson's advice is confidential. However, in January 1984, *The Globe and Mail* reported that Richardson was considering getting in touch personally with investors

About the same time, the attitude of the general public began to change. In June 1984, a Gallup poll of 1,000 people found that 67% wanted the prime minister to encourage more foreign companies to invest in Canada.[14] Some government officials—and candidates at the Liberal leadership convention (June 1984)[15]—had not changed their minds. They still thought that the level of foreign ownership of Canadian industry was too high. Three months later, the election of the Conservatives largely swept the remnants of that thinking out the door.[16]

2. The Forces of Change

What had transformed public opinion and policy? It was more than the 1982 recession and "the outs" (the Progressive Conservatives) assuming power. According to Tory party officials in 1984, Conservatives believed that "rather than assuming that it (foreign investment) is bad until proven good", foreign investment should be "judged good until demonstrated not to be beneficial".[17] This stance caused the Conservatives, after their election, to lower the regulatory hurdles facing foreign investors. But such views do not explain why the Conservatives (in general, supporters of less government intervention) gave government officials an expanded role: to seek out foreign investment and partners for Canadian industry through a campaign of unusual intensity.

To understand the forces behind this transformation and Canada's pursuit of foreign investment, we must travel back in time to

---

whose applications for approval had been rejected and asking them to try again! Norman Webster, "FIRA Head Warms Tone in Pitch to Executives", *The Globe and Mail*, Jan. 31, 1984, p.1. "99% of Foreign Bids Get FIRA Approval", *Montreal Gazette*, Aug. 19, 1983, p. D5.

[14] "Majority Favours Investment from Abroad: Gallup", *Toronto Star*, June 14, 1984, p.A3. By contrast, a 1975 Gallup poll found that only 16% of Canadians wanted more foreign investment; 71% thought there was enough.

[15] *Toronto Star*, June 14, 1984, pp. B 4-5. Three of the seven Liberal leadership candidates wanted FIRA strengthened. Turner supported FIRA. Chretien was non-committal.

[16] Many former FIRA employees at Investment Canada left during the first couple of years. A document entitled *Investment Canada: Senior Management Data Feedback* (July 19, 1985, released under the *Access to Information Act*) provides some of the background: "Too many similar faces in certain roles may add to the difficulty of altering the public's perception of the agency".

[17] Christopher Waddell, "P.C.'s Investment Bombshell Defused", *Financial Post*, Aug. 4, 1984, p. 5.

the early 1960s. Key features to observe are the changes in the Canadian and global economies. The impact of these changes on the mood within Canada's business community should also be noted. (The new international economy is the main reason given by government officials for establishing Canada's Investment Development Program, discussed in Chapter 21 of this book.)[18]

(a) Canada and Asia: 1964–65

What was Canada like back then? In some ways, it was similar to the Canada of today. The establishment of the Carter Royal Commission on Taxation was generating talk of tax reform. Edmonton and several other Canadian cities were trying to attract Japanese investment.[19]

Another similarity was that Canadian nationalists and free traders were at loggerheads. Early in 1964, the nationalists were upset because an American company (Joseph Schlitz Brewing Co.) had bought John Labatt's Ltd. According to press reports of the time, that takeover stirred rumours that Canadian Finance Minister Walter Gordon might revive his proposed 30% tax on the sale of Canadian public companies to non-residents. (Gordon introduced this proposal in his June 1963 budget speech. Confronted by sharp criticism from the business community, the Liberal government withdrew it.)

Certain Canadian business people, on the other hand, wanted more American investment in Canada. They applauded when the chairperson of U.S. Steel, Roger Blough, in a 1964 speech to Toronto's Canadian Club called for a freer flow of capital and trade.

One significant difference between the mid-1960s and today was that, in 1964–65, inflation and unemployment were much lower. Unemployment hovered around 4.2%. ("That's too high," said economists. "It should be 2%.")

Another highlight of the mid-1960s was the agitation on Canadian university campuses. The Vietnamese War was one cause; the worldwide proliferation of American businesses was another.

---

[18] In their speeches, government officials frequently refer to the "new international economy" (such as the growing importance of Asian and European markets) to explain the need for more foreign investment (By way of example, see: Alan Nymark, Executive Vice-President, Investment Canada, "Globalization—-Lessons For Canadian Investment Policy And The Federation", Notes for an address, IRPP Conference on Canadian Federalism: Global Economic Challenges, Mont Gabriel, March 30, 1990).

[19] "Edmonton Is Confident Japanese Investment Coming Its Way", *Financial Post*, Apr. 11, 1964, p.65.

American companies had usually expanded horizontally, by establishing "miniature" branch plants in developed countries. This form of expansion (an alternative to exporting), characterized the American presence in Canada. In the 1950s, however, American companies began to expand vertically to Third World countries. Attracted by the low wages in Asia and Latin America, American companies set up affiliates in those regions to produce labour-intensive products, or to supply themselves with components. Other companies established assembly operations (to purchase the end products of American factories).

Some Canadian scholars thought these new businesses would benefit nations like Brazil, Taiwan and South Korea. However, a vocal minority described the growth of American multinational companies as "economic imperialism" and "the last stage of American capitalism". American investment overseas, these critics maintained, would only leave the Third World in a permanent state of dependency and poverty.

Idealistic Canadians formed CUSO (Canadian University Service Overseas) to alleviate this poverty. Under its banner, several hundred Canadians laboured and taught in Africa and Asia (Thailand, India, Singapore, Sarawak — now part of Malaysia).

CUSO volunteers never went to South Korea. However, Canadian teachers, nurses and missionaries were active there.[20] South Korea apparently needed their assistance. Despite massive American financial aid, that country was still struggling for economic self-sufficiency. By 1964, American officials were expressing optimism that, in another year or two, South Korea would be self-supporting. South Korea, these officials declared, has "a bright future as a reservoir of highly skilled but low priced labour that could turn out cheap manufactured goods for *developing* countries".[21]

(b) Canada and Asia: 1991

Much has changed since 1964–65. Unemployment in Canada is much higher (10.2% in September 1991), even in good times. Yet economists today just offer excuses. Meanwhile, technically sophisticated goods from Third World countries jam Canadian store shelves.

In a reversal of roles, Canadian politicians seeking foreign investment journey to the teeming cities in Asia. In Hong Kong, six Canadian provinces[22] and the commission for Canada chase after

---

[20] Canadian missionaries had been in Korea since the 1880s. Department of External Affairs, "Relations Between Canada and Korea", *External Affairs*, Feb. 1963, p. 80.

[21] Robert Trumbell, "U.S. and Seoul Officials See South Korea Moving Toward Self-Support", *New York Times*, Dec. 11, 1964, p. 2.

[22] Ontario, Saskatchewan, Alberta, British Columbia, Manitoba and Quebec.

millionaires. At the same time, multinational companies from Brazil, Hong Kong, South Korea, Singapore, India and Taiwan (which was receiving American foreign aid until 1965) ponder where to locate their overseas subsidiaries.

Some of these multinational companies have selected Canada as an investment location. Brazilian steelmaker Grupo Gerdau, for instance, recently purchased Canada's Courtice Steel (an ultra-modern mini-mill located in Cambridge, Ontario). Other Brazilian multinationals have invested in the U.K., Portugal, and Latin American countries.[23]

South Korean companies have found Canada to be an attractive location as well. The Shinho Group has invested $120 million in a Thunder Bay pulp mill. Hyundai Motors has a $325-million car assembly plant in Bromont, Quebec. Sammi Steel (traded on the Korean stock exchange) spent $200 million to modernize Atlas Stainless Steels (which it purchased from Rio Algom). A fourth Korean company, Hyundai Engineering and Construction Ltd. (based in Vancouver) provides Canadians with construction management services.[24] These multinationals will be joined soon by multinationals from Taiwan (which so far has invested principally in the U.S., the Philippines and Malaysia) and cash-rich Singapore companies (which are being encouraged by Investment Canada and provincial government officials to set up branch plants in Canada).[25]

As for Hong Kong manufacturing companies, they have invested in India, Indonesia, Pakistan, even some African countries. They have also invested in Canada and the U.S., but principally in real estate, not manufacturing. Hong Kong is home to 375,000 squatters. Yet some Hong Kong residents, like billionaire Li Ka-shing, have lots of funds to invest overseas (e.g., Husky Oil and the former site of Expo'86 in Vancouver). After interviewing him, two Canadian authors wrote:

> When Li retires . . . (his two sons) Victor and Robert . . . will end up owning almost one third of downtown Vancouver, some of the country's top hotels and a giant slice of the nation's energy sector, and according to their father perhaps even a grocery chain or two.[26]

---

[23] Christopher Wells, "Brazilian Multinationals" (1988), 23:4 *Columbia Journal of World Business* 13.

[24] By December 31, 1990, companies in the Republic of Korea had invested $298.5 million (US$) in Canada and $807 million (US$) in the United States. (Source: Bank of Korea.) Total project value (including borrowed money and government grants) of Korean investment in Canada and the U.S. is several times greater.

[25] See: Pang Fong, "Singapore Multinationals" (1985), 20:2 Summer *Columbia Journal of World Business* 35, for some background information.

[26] John DeMont and Tom Fennell, *Hong Kong Money*, (Toronto: Key Porter Books, 1989), p.45.

In 1965, a *Maclean's Magazine* reporter visiting Hong Kong noted that "millionaire mansions and squalid slums share the same mountainsides . . . ragged children besiege the bus at every stop".[27] That same year, four men who are now billionaires were making their fortunes. Stanley Ho was running a government-granted gambling casino monopoly in Macau. Li Ka-shing, Cheng Yu-tung and Lee Shau-kee were buying land wherever it was cheap.

Today Cheng Yu-tung and Lee Shau-Kee are buying commercial and residential projects across Canada. With Li Ka-shing (through Concord Pacific Developments Ltd), they have built a mini-city (office buildings and condominiums, sold in the Far East) on Vancouver's Expo'86 site. Total cost: Cdn. $2 billion. Meanwhile, billionaire Stanley Ho has bought hotels in Vancouver, a mansion in Toronto and an interest in Canada's garment industry.

Not everyone who worked in Hong Kong's sweatshops in 1965 has accumulated so much capital. More than 1.2 million Hong Kong residents still live in substandard housing. (For thousands of families, that means one room, no private toilet or kitchen.) Another 2.5 million live in public housing. Some have only cages—a bed surrounded by a wire mesh—in rotting Kowloon apartment buildings.[28]

There is also immense poverty among Indonesia's 170 million people. In 1965, Indonesia was receiving foreign aid. In 1988–89, Canada gave $48 million in financial assistance to that country. Other countries gave much more.[29] Nevertheless, Indonesia (like Hong Kong) has become another source of foreign capital (Indonesia has investments in Vietnam, the U.S. and elsewhere).

First Pacific International, for example, has affiliates in 21 nations. In 1988, it bought Hegemeyer Canada (an import/export firm). First Pacific is controlled by Indonesian billionaire Liem Sioe Liong. Liem, a friend of the Indonesian president, has prospered through government-granted monopolies.

Even multinational companies from the People's Republic of China are investing in Canada. In 1966, Red Guards were beating up suspected capitalists. China's economy was in disarray. Recently, Great Wall International Investment (Canada) Ltd. helped in the building of

---

[27] Fred Bodsworth, "The Land that Lives on Borrowed Time" *Maclean's Magazine*, Nov. 1, 1965, pp. 27, 35.

[28] Reuters, "I've Got the Best Cage Now", *The Gazette*, Dec. 4, 1988, p. B4.

[29] In 1988–89, other countries and lending agencies provided Indonesia with over $5 billion in soft loans and grants. Michael Vatikiofis, "Optimists Pour in More Money", *Far Eastern Economic Rev,* June 30, 1988, p. 59.

an International Trade Centre in Scarborough, Ontario, and condominiums in B.C.

Despite these astounding changes since the mid-1960s, some aspects of the Canadian and global economies remain the same. In 1965, Canada exported wheat and industrial raw materials (newsprint, asbestos, lead, nickel and wood pulp) to South Korea. That same year, South Korea sold textiles, clothing and rubber footwear to Canada.

Canada still exports mostly raw materials and unfinished goods to South Korea. (In the intervening years, however, Canada's agricultural, mining and forestry sectors have become highly automated). South Korea's exports to Canada, on the other hand, now consist mainly of highly technological, manufactured goods (cars, television sets, computers, microwave ovens and textiles).

What has happened?

3. Narrowing Comparative Advantage

There is no simple explanation. Some economists blame automation, which has eliminated many clerical jobs. In an automated factory, production can be sharply increased in boom times, with little change in the level of blue collar employment. Other economists point to Canada's monetary, tax and industrial policies, the rapid pace of technological change, the high cost of Canadian labour, foreign protectionism, and excessive or insufficient foreign investment.

Insufficient foreign investment? According to the continentalists, multinational companies facilitate the spread of existing technology. They make Canada more productive. It is trade barriers which have kept Canadian companies from being more competitive in world markets.

Nationalists have a different perspective. Canadian companies are inefficient because there are too many foreign-owned firms. Foreign ownership, these nationalists maintain, stultifies Canada's innovative capacity (R&D, market research).

One cause of the new trade and investment patterns has no direct connection with foreign investment: the relative levelling of factor endowments and costs (e.g., manpower skills, cost of capital, level of technological achievement) between countries. Technology, for instance, now diffuses easily around the world. Capital has been accumulated in numerous centres. Institutes of higher education are located all over the globe.

These forces of convergence have narrowed the distinctions between countries. Thirty years ago, the nations of Europe, North America and Japan had strikingly different industrial structures, income levels, and factor endowments. What is remarkable today are the similarities.

These same forces have affected the traditional basis for comparative advantages between nations. In the past, these advantages have been founded upon disparities in the allocation of capital, labour and resources. Over the last twenty years, as these distinctions have begun to blur, there have been corresponding shifts in trade flows and the location of industry. The experience of Canada illustrates this.

During the 1950s and 1960s, Canada was an attractive location to establish a business. It offered political stability, an educated labour force, an excellent transportation system and a storehouse of raw materials. Three decades later, Canada still offers the same enticements. But these enticements have declined in relative importance as other nations have reached a stage when they can trumpet some of the same advantages.

A number of Third World countries, for instance, have developed their own mining and resource-based industries. Educational campaigns have also been successful. This has created an army of skilled workers in the newly industrialized countries. As for the nations of southern and eastern Europe, with their favourable cost structures, they have become second rank industrial powers.

As these changes were occurring, the technology for producing cars, appliances, and other consumer durable goods was being standardized. Trade barriers were falling. World-wide communications were improving. Attracted by the possibilities, and the low wages in Third World countries, many owners of capital established factories there.

These factories have poured their products onto world markets. Particularly affected have been Canada's labour intensive industries such as textiles, leather and footwear. However, Canadian firms that produce consumer durables (like cars, appliances, and electrical goods) and intermediate manufactured products (such as chemicals, papers, and metals) have faced growing competition as well.

(a) The Product Cycle

To an extent, these transformations are an outgrowth of the product cycle. This cycle begins when a product is first manufactured in an advanced country like the U.S. or Germany, which has the research capabilities to conceive and develop it. Foreign demand is served through exports. Over time, the "bugs" in the product are ironed out and the manufacture of the product becomes standardized. It is then easy for the technology to be transferred to other developed countries or to the Third World through direct investment or licensing. Once production begins in a Third World country, its ample supply of cheap labour can give it an advantage over the nation which created the product in the first place.

Rising income levels in the Third World have shortened this cycle by making it profitable to manufacture products abroad at an earlier stage. Reductions in transportation costs and the greater familiarity of multinational companies with the requirements of Third World countries have added extra impetus to this phenomenon.

Today, in part because of this product cycle, countries such as Mexico, Singapore, Taiwan, Brazil and South Korea are selling television sets, military vehicles and computers in competition with Canadian industry. At the same time, new challenges are coming from southern and eastern Europe.

4. Response of the Mature Economies

In response to these changes in the world economy, western nations are seeking new ways to maintain their lead. Increasingly, they are turning to technology. This is not a new phenomenon. Technology has been the motor of international trade since World War II.

What is new is the importance it has assumed. Technology "is America's only comparative advantage", Hewlett-Packard's Chief Executive, John Young, has declared.[30] Twenty years ago, he would have pointed to the American worker.

One result of this realization is that industrialists are embracing a new strategy. They are concentrating on the production of new products, improvements in the quality of conventional products and are seeking to reduce costs through robotics. At the same time, their political leaders are preaching that entrepreneurship, more R&D and better managerial skills are needed to compete in the global marketplace.

Two other factors, pushing western nations along this road, have been demographic and trade-related. The labour forces in developed countries have been growing as the late baby boomers and a greater percentage of women have entered the job market. At the same time, automation has been reducing the level of employment in the manufacturing sector. Because these new entrants to the labour market are

---

[30] Quoted by Richard Kirkland, "The Economy of the 1990s. We're All in This Together", *Fortune*, Feb. 2, 1987, pp. 27, 29.

well-educated and politically visible, the attention of governments has been focused on the limited number of good jobs.

Trade liberalization, however, has threatened the existence of many well-paid jobs (while holding out the prospect of job creation). Trade liberalization (the lowering of tariff and non-tariff barriers) has allowed companies to compete across national boundaries almost as easily as they do across Canada's provincial boundaries. This phenomenon, known as the global market-place, has caused hardship for many companies (while offering opportunities to others). At the same time, trade liberalization has encouraged the global rationalization of production. A multinational company can transfer a profitable operation from one country to another country where costs are lower, and export to its former host. Finally, trade liberalization has unleashed a feeding frenzy of mergers and joint ventures with obvious consequences for employment.

In the last few years, West Germany's Continental AG has acquired General Tires of the U.S.; in the process becoming the world's fourth largest producer of tires. Philip Morris has become the world's largest consumer goods maker by buying Kraft. In the communications field, German giant Bertelsmann AG bought U.S. publisher, Doubleday and Co. There are hundreds of other examples.

Some of these transnational mergers have been motivated by the prospect of giant companies with global economies of scale, or by the need for mega-companies able to absorb the high costs of research and development. But often, raw market power on a global scale has been the silent magnet.

Whatever the motive, the phenomenon is self-generating. To ensure that their companies can effectively compete, many countries have set aside some of their anti-trust and xenophobic worries and opened their doors to foreign investment.

5. Sources and Destinations of Funds

Unfortunately, the task of locating potential foreign investors is not so simple these days compared with the 1960s. Back then, the United States was the leading source of foreign investment (accounting for 70% of total investment by O.E.C.D. countries). Today, although the U.S. has not exactly been displaced, there are a host of other sources of capital.

If reinvested earnings are excluded, the largest source country, on a flow basis, is now Japan. Another change is that Sweden and Italy have become significant foreign investors. Hong Kong has stepped on stage. Even some former recipients of foreign investment (South Korea, Taiwan, India, Brazil and Singapore) have become exporters of capital.

The traditional European sources of foreign investment (the Netherlands, Germany, France and the United Kingdom) have retained their stature, except for the U.K. That country has resurged in importance; today, the U.K. is among the top three providers of direct foreign investment in the world.[31]

What about Canada? In a rather dramatic reversal from the 1960s, Canada is both a major source and recipient of funds. In 1981, 1984 and 1985, Canada was actually a net exporter of direct investment. It is presently a net importer.

There has also been a change in the destination of funds. In the early 1960s, 65% of all investment flowing into "developed market economies" went to Canada, Australia, West Germany and Italy.[32] Currently, the U.S. is the major magnet for foreign investment, attracting over half of all inward investment. Other investment dollars that might have been enticed by Canada's potential of two decades ago are now flowing to Brazil, Mexico and the newly industrialized countries of Asia.

6. Ottawa's Response

Ottawa's response to these developments has diverged from that south of the border. In the U.S. at the national level, there is no agency that promotes foreign investment *per se*. One reason for this is "ideological":

> U.S. policy with regard to international investment is based on the premise that the total benefits from international investment are maximized if Governments seek to take no action either to accelerate or hinder investment flows into or out of their territories. We believe that intervention into investment by home or host national governments may distort the efficient allocation of economic resources. . . . Hence . . . the Government

---

[31] For recent figures, see O.E.C.D., *International Direct Investment and the New Economic Environment*, (Paris: O.E.C.D., 1989).

[32] O.E.C.D., *International Investment and Multinational Enterprise: Recent International Direct Investment Trends*. (Paris: O.E.C.D., 1987).

should neither promote nor discourage inward or outward investment flows or activities. . . .[33]

Instead, the U.S. federal government has generally restricted itself to a passive policy of providing a "good" climate for business. In the view of the Reagan and Bush administrations, any structural problems in the U.S. economy could be solved by *free market forces*,[34] provided the regulatory climate was relaxed and taxation levels reduced. (The 50 American states disagree. Most promote foreign investment by offering financial incentives. Some, e.g., Ohio, have anti-takeover statutes.)

Deregulation, tax reform and privatization were goals of the Canadian government too. In the area of "investment", however, Ottawa took a different course.

In 1985, the Canadian government adopted a new mercantilist policy, which focused on attracting foreign investment and organizing Canadian industry to meet foreign competition. Canadian companies were to be encouraged to enter into national and international partnerships and licensing agreements. In addition, there was to be a new emphasis on technology and the need for co-operation between industry, labour, universities and government. It was a significant step for a Conservative government philosophically committed to "less of a role for government" and the notion that the market should determine which industries emerge as leaders.

It was also a rather audacious step since it was based on apprehension about the future, rather than economic data derived from past performance. There was certainly a mountain of evidence that Canada was a relatively high-cost producer of manufactured goods.[35] However, some studies indicated that Canada's manufacturing sector was holding its own, with increased penetration of the Canadian market by

---

[33] Remarks by Hon. C. Fred Bergsten, Assistant Secretary of the Treasury for International Affairs, before the Second Annual Conference on International Trade and Investment Policy of the National Journal, Washington, D.C., May 11, 1979. His remarks were entitled: "The Need for International Co-operation in the International Investment Area". Bergsten also characterized U.S. policy towards international investment as including these two elements: "The government should avoid measures which give special incentives or disincentives to specific flows or activities". Also "the government should avoid intervention in the activities of individual companies regarding their international investment".

[34] However, the U.S. Department of Defence pumps billions into private sector projects involving critical "defence" technologies—like biotechnology, robotics, fibreoptics.

[35] Productivity in Canada (output per worker) is below that of the U.S. However, in several sectors (e.g., transportation), Canada's productivity growth rates have exceeded those in the U.S. See: Economic Council of Canada, Twenty-sixth Annual Review, 1989, *Legacies*, (Ottawa: Supply and Services Canada, 1989), pp. 10–16.

foreign companies being matched by Canadian export success abroad.[36] (Indeed, Canada's share of world trade had gone from 4.6% in 1965 to 5.1% in 1984.)[37]

Still, these studies were not of much comfort. Canada had remained competitive in part because of slowly growing labour compensation and the depreciation of the Canadian dollar. That depreciation (30% between 1976 and 1986 compared with the U.S. dollar) had given Canada a competitive advantage in terms of exchange rate adjusted unit labour costs.

However, currency rates are volatile. The Canadian dollar may quickly go up. In addition, disturbing shifts had taken place within the manufacturing sector, with some "winning" industries being significantly less labour-intensive than some of the "losing" industries. Canada's trade balance deficit (exports minus imports) in several high tech industries and low rate of R&D spending were other harbingers of future trouble.

(a) Political Cultures: Canada Versus the U.S.

One reason the federal Conservatives adopted their proactive strategy of seeking foreign investment was because they had the support of a political culture quite different from that in the U.S. In Canada, the state has historically played a significant role in the economy. This role began with the National Policy in 1879, which was designed to foster manufacturing through the erection of a high tariff wall. It continued through state ownership of businesses and a myriad of incentive programs.

Generally, Canadian politicians of all stripes have accepted this degree of state intervention. Many business people, particularly if they benefitted, have welcomed it. Thus, the noisy and ideologically-rooted

---

[36] Roy A. Matthews, *Structural Change and Industrial Policy: The Redeployment of Canadian Manufacturing, 1960–80*, (Ottawa: Supply and Service Canada, 1985), a study prepared for the Economic Council of Canada. Between 1982 and 1985, Canada's merchandise trade surplus averaged $17.8 billion per year. Between 1979 and 1988, the cumulative trade surplus was $122.8 billion.

[37] Andrew Sharpe, "Can Canada Compete? Part 2: Canada's Position in the World" *Canadian Business Review*, Spring 1986, p. 34. A different view on Canada's ability to compete was provided by Joseph D'Cruz and James Fleck, *Canada Can Compete*, (Montreal: Institute for Research on Public Policy, 1985). (By choosing different reference periods, it is easy to manipulate productivity and unit labour cost figures to support any point of view.)

Canada had also scored seventh out of 22 countries in a survey of competitiveness, "We're Getting Better at World Competition", *Financial Post*, Jan. 19, 1985, p. 2.

debate that has taken place in the U.S. over industry policy and how to respond to changed economic conditions, has been more muted in Canada.

Another reason for Ottawa's different response was that several economic problems confronting Canada had no counterpart in the U.S. Many of Canada's manufacturing industries had been established to serve a relatively small domestic market. This was partly a consequence of Canada's high tariff barriers erected earlier in this century, which persuaded foreign companies to set up "miniature replica" subsidiaries. Some of these subsidiaries were high-cost, low-volume producers but, sheltered by Canada's tariffs, they remained profitable.

The General Agreement on Tariffs and Trades threatened to change that. By 1985, tariffs were dropping among GATT signatories to a level where they would provide almost no protection at all.

Ottawa officials were concerned that, if Canadian companies didn't become more competitive so that they could protect their market share, there would be a flood of imports. A related worry was that foreign parent companies would decide to shut down their subsidiaries in Canada or relegate them to performing sales, distribution and service work.

(b) The Intellectual Underpinnings

While these factors were propelling Ottawa to choose an activist industrial strategy, writers like Reich and Thurow, and, ultimately, the example of Japan, were influencing its content. In fact, it was the success of Japan that originally caused policy-makers within the Ottawa bureaucracy to question mainline economic thought.

From the days of David Ricardo the majority of western economists have believed that the most competitive economy was a free market economy. According to these economists, a country with a comparative cost advantage in, say, textiles, should concentrate on manufacturing textiles and buy its food from countries which can grow food cheaply.

The post-war economic history of Japan, on the other hand, presented a different message. The message was that industrial policies that favour some industries over others can have a significant impact on the ability of nations to compete in the international market-place. Another part of the message was that comparative advantages between nations were not merely static or slowly evolving, but instead were partly dynamic. Some changes in comparative advantages could be engineered, and quickly too.

After World War II, unemployment was high in Japan. Had that nation's policy-makers been wedded to the traditional "static" theory of comparative advantage, they would have asked what factors of production were most abundant and then emphasized the development of industries that used those factors. Such thinking would have led Japan to concentrate on labour-intensive industries that required little capital.

Instead, Japan's Ministry of International Trade and Industry (M.I.T.I.) embarked on a different national strategy. At a time when capital was scarce, it chose to emphasize steel and chemicals. M.I.T.I. also set out to make Japan competitive in industries with great potential for cost decline through technological progress as well as industries with a high income elasticity of demand (that is, industries where demand for their products would rise very rapidly as people's income increased).

To protect these infant industries, Japan also adopted a strategy of restricting both imports and foreign direct investment. When a foreign investor's proposal was approved, it was for the purpose of obtaining not capital, but the best foreign technology.

The result was a demonstration that technology, plus organizational and marketing skills could be more important than natural resources in determining which nations became winners. Another lesson was that the State, regarded by some business people as a dead weight, could have a significant impact on economic success (if government officials were far-sighted enough).

Brazil, Taiwan and South Korea[38] demonstrated one more point. Low-wage countries, where industry can ignore the cost of pollution,[39] could become serious competitors to western industry if just one element was present: a university-educated elite with entrepreneurial ambitions.

Such an elite could acquire western technology through licensing or copying, then organize workers into efficient units. These workers

---

[38] How did Korea's Samsung (currently $40 billion in sales) do it? One-dollar-an-hour labour; long hours; immense dedication from its labour force; design copying; sending its engineers to meet the customers; seeking long-term growth in volume, not short-term profits. See: Ira Magaziner and Mark Patinkin, *The Silent War: Inside the Global Business Battles Shaping America's Future*, (New York: Random House, 1989), pp. 21–44.

[39] The deputy secretary general of Taiwan's opposition party states: ". . . part of the reason for (Taiwan's) successful export business is that we have a lot of polluting industries and they haven't had to pay the cost of pollution." Quoted in Alison Maitland, "Green Factor Enters Centre Stage in Run-up to Election", *Financial Times*, Survey: Taiwan, Oct. 10, 1989, sec. III, p. 6.

could then produce manufactured goods at prices below those in developed countries. If productivity was a problem, the money to purchase modern machinery could be borrowed from international banks.

Singapore, too small and poor to set up its own industrial structure, chose another strategy. It wooed foreign companies (after creating an infrastructure of roads and communications facilities). The newly arrived companies then funded a network of employee training centres which the government had established.

Developed countries like Canada could compete through automation. An automated factory can produce products cheaper than even a low-wage country. Xerox and RCA had regained the market for copiers and televisions sets by following this route. But to automate, a nation needs capital. And automation may put workers on the street, unless new businesses are created.

Another way for the developed nations to retain an advantage was to emphasize products that require skilled labour, such as bio-technologies, fibreoptics, precision machinery, and telecommunications equipment. However, to produce such products, companies would need the most up-to-date technology and, to achieve optimum plant size or recover R&D costs, access to global markets.

Many policy-makers in Ottawa thought they had the prescription. Canada should move towards an economy based upon trade in high technology products. Canadian companies should also reduce their costs of manufacturing existing products (to below that of overseas rivals) and establish a physical "presence" in overseas markets. A new trade development strategy (e.g., more trade shows and sellers' missions to bring together foreign buyers and Canadian manufacturers) would be required as well.

To achieve these goals, Canadian industry would need to invest in the latest technology and switch to "capital intensive, skill intensive" means of production. At the same time, new competitive advantages would have to be created through R&D and entrepreneurship.

But this would require more risk capital, not just on a one-time basis, but continuously since technology is forever advancing. And to sell the products, access to new markets in Europe, Asia, and the U.S., would have to be opened up through partnerships between Canadian and foreign companies.

Where was the capital to come from? The existing savings of Canadians? In 1972, the Gray Report (*Foreign Direct Investment in Canada*) had concluded that Canada's domestic savings were sufficient to meet the country's capital investment requirements at full employment (although Canada's financial institutions often refused to lend to small businesses). In 1972, however, Canada had a current account surplus (not a deficit, as in 1985). Moreover, although some of Canada's savings were being invested abroad in 1972, that amount had increased by 1985.

The adequacy of domestic savings must be measured against the amount of investment a country desires. If it is insufficient, people must consume less (spend less on private or public goods) and save more.[40]

An alternative is to rely on foreign capital. That was the decision the government took in 1985. Government officials decided to encourage a massive inflow of foreign capital into Canada. Hopefully, it would go into productive capacity (new plants and machinery).

What about technology? Canada, government officials noted, had spent only 1.24% of its GNP on R&D in 1984. Other O.E.C.D. countries were spending an average 2.2%. Nearly 98% of all technology was being developed outside of Canada.[41] One way to make Canadian companies more competitive, officials decided, was through the acquisition of more foreign technology.

Technology can be transferred through direct investment, licensing, and importing the final product. The central issues are the costs, the most efficient form of transfer and the rate of diffusion.

According to some economists, not much technology is diffused by international direct investment. The benefits are monopolized by the foreign firm itself. Other economists disagree. They argue that technology is disseminated as local manpower is trained and local subcontractors are hired. Even more technology is transferred through international ventures. (The amount depends upon which nation performs the research and the complex portion of the production process.)[42] By encouraging foreign investment, Canadian government officials concluded, state-of-the-art technology could be brought to Canada.

---

[40] The Japanese save as much as 18% of all personal income. This is one reason Japanese companies can raise capital at remarkably low cost, which gives them a true competitive advantage.

[41] Ministry of State for Science and Technology ("M.O.S.S.T."), *Science, Technology and Economic Development*, (Ottawa: Supply and Services Canada, 1985). M.O.S.S.T., *Innovation: The Canadian Strategy for Science and Technology*, (undated publication distributed in 1987).

[42] Robert Reich and Eric Mankin, "Joint Ventures with Japan Give Away Our Future" (1986), 2 *Harvard Bus. Rev.* 78–86.

The final need was for entrepreneurship. Could more Canadians become world business people? Canadian officials decided to look overseas. Canada, they concluded, should import a lot of entrepreneurs, especially from southeast Asia.

7. A New Program: "Investment Development"

Might this greater inflow of foreign capital and the restructuring of Canadian industry be achieved by itself through the price system? Government officials apparently did not think so. The price system, whose signals are those of the present moment, could not guarantee an adequate response.

Broad macroeconomic policies were not sufficient either. Instead, the government would have to become actively involved in business development at the micro (individual firm) level. A corollary was that Ottawa would have to devise a strategy aimed at engineering comparative advantages by assisting enterprises in promising economic sectors to become internationally competitive.

Salesmanship would be required as well. Canada was only one of many competitors for foreign capital and technology. In addition, investors in those nations which were new sources of capital, such as Japan, had only a foggy understanding of the Canadian economy.

In the minds of senior government officials, a new program was needed. Because it would seek to encourage foreign investment, it would have to be significantly different from the grab-bag of incentive programs that characterized much of Canada's industrial policy.

In June 1985, Ottawa set up such a program. Termed the "Investment Development Program", at the beginning it was just a shell. However, in the years that followed, the bureaucracy gave it some content.

More will be said about Canada's Investment Development Program in a later chapter, but first, let us see how the *Investment Canada Act* overhauled Canada's screening mechanism.

8. Reviewing Foreign Investments

Screening major takeovers by foreign investors is the second arm of Investment Canada. This is the function that brought FIRA so many headlines and eventually led to its demise.

The activities of Investment Canada have generated less criticism. In part, this is because its screen was made smaller and the mesh wider.

Size limits, for instance, were never a constraint on FIRA's authority. A foreign investor who wanted to buy a small store, or set up a new business, had to obtain government approval.[43]

With one exception (the cultural sector), Investment Canada does not even review the establishment of new businesses. As for takeovers, except for the cultural sector, government intervention is limited to "economically significant" transactions. What is "significant" is a question that could have been answered in several ways. However, the asset size of the Canadian business was the criterion that the government chose.

(a) Trimming the Review Net

Not all foreign investors, on the other hand, face the same size criterion. Depending upon the nationality of the investor, the review net either expands or shrinks. For Americans, who are governed by the Free Trade Agreement, this net is tiny. Only very large American investments are subject to Canadian government scrutiny, unless these investments are in one of five sensitive economic sectors.

For nationals of other countries, and Americans investing in a sensitive sector, investments which require review are:

(1) direct acquisitions of Canadian businesses with assets of $5 million or more;

(2) indirect acquisitions of Canadian businesses with assets of $50 million or more;

(3) indirect acquisitions of Canadian businesses with assets between $5 and $50 million, if the Canadian business constitutes more than 50% of the value of the total international transaction.

In addition, acquisitions below the $5-million threshold and the establishment of new businesses may be reviewed if they are culturally sensitive. This is the government's reserve review power.

There exists a particularly high threshold for indirect acquisitions. These occur when a non-Canadian buys a foreign-incorporated company which has a Canadian subsidiary. This high threshold reflects Ottawa's intention to intervene only when there is an indirect change of control of a major business in Canada. After 1991, because of the Free Trade Agreement, indirect acquisitions by Americans will not be reviewed at all.

---

[43] Foreigners who already had a business in Canada could establish a *related* business without approval.

During the FIRA decade, all indirect acquisitions were reviewed. Some foreign business people were very irritated by this. They complained to the highest levels in Washington that such interventions were "retroactive" and an extraterritorial extension of Canadian laws. The issue became a source of friction between Canada and the U.S., with potential political and economic consequences that might have offset the benefits of screening foreign investment. The drafters of the *IC Act*, wishing to maintain amicable relationships with Canada's trading partners, calibrated the degree of government intervention with this concern in mind.

When the Act was being formulated, certain business community representatives complained that the thresholds for review were too low. In reality, the thresholds are far higher than they appear. This is because the test is not the fair market value of the assets being purchased, but their balance sheet value, in other words, their *historical* costs.

If a transaction is not reviewable, a notification must still be filed by the foreign investor. However, this is a minor obligation imposed to gather statistics.[44]

(b) Paring the Scope

At the same time as the review net was being trimmed, the framers of the *Investment Canada Act* slashed the number of people (and organizations) who needed government approval for their investments. Unlike FIRA days, Canadians can now live abroad forever without being treated like foreign investors.[45] Some foreign-controlled companies can become "deemed" Canadians. Finally, FIRA's *de facto* control test, designed to ascertain who really was in control of a company, was replaced by a simpler ownership test that made "Canadian" status easier to achieve.[46]

---

[44] The inspiration for the Act's notification requirements came from U.S. anti-trust legislation, in particular, the Premerger Notification Rules issued by the F.T.C. under the Hart-Scott-Rodino Antitrust Improvement Act of 1976.

[45] During the FIRA era, Canadians who lived abroad for more than five years were treated like foreigners when making an investment in Canada.

[46] Canadians who favour an "ownership test" may be more interested in ensuring that the profits from multinational companies remain in Canada. Supporters of a *"de facto* control test" may place a greater emphasis on national sovereignty and company performance. For further discussion, see David Anderson, *Foreign Investment Control in the Canadian Mineral Sector: Lessons from the Australian Experience*, (Kingston: Queen's University, 1984), p. 103.

(c) Forms of Control

The significance of this latter change can best be appreciated by those readers who understand the mechanisms of control. There are two forms of control which legal commentators like to identify:

(1) legal control, which is founded on legally enforceable rights and obligations; and

(2) *de facto* control, which cannot be clearly defined in legal terms but manifests itself through minority control, personal influence and informal agreements.[47]

De facto control (also called "control in fact") is obviously the more unstable of the two forms.

Under the *FIR Act*, *de facto* control ("control in any manner that results in control in fact") determined whether a corporation, partnership, or joint venture was foreign-controlled. This encompassed control through share ownership, but also control through many other means, such as distribution agreements, family relationships, debt instruments, technical expertise and financial clout.

Because *de facto* control is often distinct from the division of equity ownership, shareholder, partnership, and joint venture agreements had to be examined with care. Although a Canadian had a majority interest, a unanimous shareholders' agreement sometimes transferred real control to a foreign investor.[48]

Frequently, it was also necessary to search for negative control through quorum rules and by-laws governing signing authority. In a widely-held company, if the role of the board was mainly advisory, control might be with the senior officers.

De facto control, through any means whatever, was therefore a formidable concept, one that had never been used in Canadian legislation before.[49] And some lawyers loathed it. It was not like the objective

---

[47] Adolf Berle and Gardiner Means, *The Modern Corporation and Private Property*, (New York: Harcourt, Brace, 1968); Murray Pickering, "Shareholders' Voting Rights and Company Control" *L.Q. Rev.*, 81:322 April 1965, p. 248.

[48] Why might *de facto* control of a joint venture differ from the division of equity? Because of lack of time and expertise, some joint venturers only want a voice in a few major decisions. In addition, the joint venturer which does the staffing (the hiring and rewarding of key personnel) has an important instrument of control. J. Michael Geringer and Patrick Woodcock, "Ownership and Control of Canadian Joint Ventures", *Business Quarterly*, 54:1 Summer 1989, p. 97.

[49] In 1987, Parliament put *de facto* control into subs. 256 (5.1) of the *Income Tax Act*. The meaning being given to this concept by Revenue Canada is discussed by Richard

tests ("counting shares") which they had studied in law school. Instead, it subjected the investments of their clients' corporations to review on a subjective basis, namely, whether foreigners actually directed the affairs of the company.

This test, these lawyers complained, gave FIRA bureaucrats too much discretion. They seldom mentioned their other concern. Many of these lawyers wanted to put Canadian faces on corporations while allowing their foreign clients to pull the strings. The FIRA *de facto* control test frustrated them!

What was the rationale for such a test? The Hon. Alistair Gillespie, who was the minister when the draft *Foreign Investment Review Act* was being debated, explained on November 20, 1973 to the House of Commons that:

> . . . this bill focuses on control, not ownership, because it is the actual power to make decisions, rather than the mere fact of share ownership, that affects the performance of subsidiaries in Canada.[50]

Unfortunately, the *de facto* control test had serious drawbacks. The principal one was the uncertainty about who was subject to the legislation. This, in turn, imposed a financial cost on some corporate executives wishing to avoid review because they had to hire legal counsel to argue with FIRA merely to learn if their corporation was foreign-controlled.

(d) Control Under the IC Act

The rules in the *Investment Canada Act* are quite different. They are based upon the ownership of voting shares in the case of a corporation, and equity ownership in the case of a partnership, trust, or joint venture.[51]

These rules, when applied to a corporation, recognize certain forms of legal control, such as proprietary control (or control through the ownership of a majority interest) and control through constitutional means. An example of the latter is loaded voting rights.

Bennett, "*De facto* Control Is an Extremely Broad Net", *The National*, July 6, 1990, p. 29 (*The National* is a C.B.A. publication).

[50] *Hansard*, November 20, 1973, p.7967.

[51] The *FIR Act* classified partnerships, trusts and joint ventures as "groups" of investors. They were subject to different rules from those that applied to corporations. Those who drafted the *IC Act* wanted to treat all forms of association in the same way. Consequently, the rules for determining who controls a partnership (trust or joint venture) treat the partners (etc.) as if they were the owners of shares in a corporation.

The *IC Act* also acknowledges that two forms of *de facto* control can exist. One of these forms is minority or working control. Working control occurs when a shareholder (or group) with less than 50% of the votes can impose his or her will. A minority shareholder who can attract sufficient proxies to control a majority of the votes has such power. So does a minority shareholder who has considerable influence over or affinity with company management. Management in such cases will vote the proxies it receives from other shareholders in the way the minority shareholder wishes. When these proxy votes are combined with the votes of the minority shareholder, the result is a majority of the votes and working control. Another way working control can arise is when attendance at shareholders' meetings (in person or by proxy) is very low. The minority shareholder will then be in a majority position.

Working control is frequently found in large publicly-traded companies. Its continued existence depends upon the apathy and indifference of the other shareholders.

The other form of *de facto* control that the Act recognizes is control through a community of interests. This often leads to majority control. Many smaller corporations are controlled by family groups on this basis.

However, several *de facto* control mechanisms are disregarded in the *IC Act*. So are certain types of legal control, such as irrevocable voting trusts and management contracts. Moreover, it is open to question whether, and to what extent, the legislation recognizes the concept of negative control, and shareholder agreements, which are a type of legal control.

One further restriction on the Act's scope is the model around which it is built. According to this model—the traditional one of corporate governance—the shareholders elect the board of directors. These directors then determine corporate policy and strategy. The company's officers play a subordinate role.

This model describes reality in small companies. In such companies, ownership and management are identical. However, the model fails when confronted by the practice in a few widely-held companies. In these companies, the president sets company policy. (The outside directors don't have the time or knowledge.) The president also selects the outside directors, then uses the proxy machinery to elect them. The result is that the president has *de facto* control of the company. (In between these two extremes are many possible combinations of centres of control.)

The rules in the *IC Act* are therefore less accurate in locating real control and more easy to evade than the *de facto* control test of FIRA.

But because factual evidence as to ownership is readily available, these rules have two attributes prized by the business community: greater clarity and certainty!

(e) Narrow Acquisition Rules

The 1985 legislation narrowed the scope of the review process in yet another way. By changing the acquisition of control rules, the number of times when a purchase by a foreigner would be considered in law to be an acquisition of control was reduced.

Widely-held companies can be controlled through very small interests. Consequently, the *Foreign Investment Review Act* had low trip-wires. A foreign investor who purchased 5% of a publicly-traded company (20% of a private company's shares) had to show that control had not been acquired.

Parliament raised the tripwires in the *IC Act* and removed the distinction between private and public corporations. Now, a foreign investor need not worry if he or she purchases less than one third of any company's shares. The Act simply does not apply. In many circumstances, there is no acquisition of control even though 50% of a company's shares have been purchased.

(f) The Process of Decision Making

In addition to paring the scope of the review mechanism, the *IC Act* changed the decision-making process. Under FIRA, the basic period during which the government had to make a decision was 60 days. However, unlimited extensions of time were legally possible if the government so wished.[52] And the government had that wish quite often.

The *Investment Canada Act*, on the other hand, keeps the bureaucracy moving. The Act provides for an initial time period of 45 days. Without the consent of the investor, the minister cannot avoid reaching a decision for more than 105 days. The government can no longer unilaterally reset the clock.

Secondly, under the *Investment Canada Act*, it is the minister who makes the final decision. Compare that with the FIRA era when a committee of Cabinet made the formal decision.

---

[52] The *FIR Act* gave government officials 60 days after an application was received, to determine if an investment was likely to be of significant benefit to Canada. By sending a letter stating that the minister was unable to complete the assessment, FIRA officials could extend the 60-day time period indefinitely.

Finally, the 1985 legislation remodelled the benefit test. During FIRA's reign, an investor had to prove that his or her proposal would likely be of "significant benefit" to Canada.

The *Investment Canada Act* uses a "net benefit" criterion. It sounds easier and suggests a weighing of the positive and negative aspects of a proposal. When the preamble to the *Investment Canada Act* and the net benefit test are read together, they imply that foreign investment is *presumed* to benefit Canada, unless the review process discloses the contrary.

By introducing strict time limits, thresholds for review, and an ownership test to ascertain control, government officials involved in formulating the legislation achieved their two goals. They rendered the administration of Canada's screening legislation more precise and they blocked the possibility of future "regulatory creep" back to a more interventionist state of affairs.[53]

Not even the Cabinet can change the thresholds for review. A return to the FIRA era can never happen without Parliament amending the *IC Act*.[54]

(g) Transparency

The business community applauded these changes when they were announced in 1985, but not all of their complaints were met. Because investors wanted confidentiality and the government some flexibility in applying the net benefit test, the review process was not made as predictable and transparent as some business people would have liked.

What is transparency? If investors could anticipate the outcome whenever they file an application, Canada's screening mechanism would be very transparent. But to achieve such clarity, the government would have had to provide reasons for its decisions, make public departmental policies, disclose the identity of intervenors, and publish

---

[53] Why didn't the Conservative government simply amend the *FIR Act*? The government could have raised the thresholds for review and instructed administrators to exercise their discretion in favour of foreign investors. One likely reason is that it would have been easier for a future government to return to a FIRA-type regime. Also, merely amending the existing legislation would have permitted greater "regulatory creep" (by cautious officials wanting to avoid risk by asserting jurisdiction). However, the principal reason the Conservative government wanted a new statute was to convey a message to the world that Canada welcomed foreign investment.

[54] However, the reserve review power may allow a future government to enlarge the scope of review without amending the legislation.

guidelines on the meaning of net benefit. The government never journeyed far down this road.

9. This Book

In the chapters that follow, the *IC Act* will be examined in detail. The various questions that an investor must address in order to determine if the Act applies, will be discussed.

Other legislation such as the *Bank Act* and the *National Transportation Act*, which intermesh with the *IC Act*, will be mentioned. Finally, Canada's Investment Development Program, which is designed to attract foreign investment to Canada, will be highlighted.

Foreign investors and their advisers have an obvious need for such a detailed explanation. So do executives whose firms are potential targets of hostile takeovers, and union leaders who want to intervene.[55]

Paradoxically, even Canadian investors in the United States should understand the *IC Act*. Several legal concepts in the Free Trade Agreement were lifted from this legislation. Nonetheless, the purpose of this analysis is not limited to assisting professionals.

Canadian nationalists and continentalists will be interested in knowing just what transactions are "caught". Private sector employees engaged in business development overseas, and economic development officials working for municipal and provincial governments may want to learn more about how Ottawa pursues foreign investors.

Lastly, the chapters that follow may provide students of government administration[56] with some insight into the difficulties faced by administrators who must give some meaning to legislation drafted in

---

[55] How may executives of a company subject to an attempted hostile takeover by a foreign investor use the *IC Act* as part of their defence strategy? If the foreign investor is seeking the minister's permission to purchase their company before the completion of the review process (see Chapter 11), the executives can submit counter-arguments. Also, they can stress the negative effects of the proposed takeover and urge the provincial governments to oppose it. If the company's ownership of a Canadian oil and gas subsidiary or cultural business will make it difficult for another potential foreign purchaser (a "white knight") to comply with Investment Canada's requirements, they might consider selling the subsidiary.

[56] Students may ask how Ottawa can screen foreign investment when Canada's Constitution makes no mention of it. The constitutional basis for a screening mechanism is Ottawa's authority over aliens and trade and commerce. See *A.G. v. Cain*, [1906] A.C. 542, at 546. Also: J. Nixon and J. Burns, "An Examination of the Legality of the Use of Foreign Investment Review Act to Control Intra and Extraterritorial Commercial Activities by Aliens" (1984), 23 *International Comparative L.Q.* 57.

generalities. Also, this material may highlight why— because administrators have the power to choose between several possible interpretations of legislation, and to control the flow of information to their political bosses—the thought processes of bureaucrats are as important as those of the judiciary in constructing the regulatory framework within which business people must operate.

CHAPTER 3

THE MEANING OF "NON-CANADIAN"

Because the *Investment Canada Act* only regulates non-Canadians, the first question that must be answered is whether the investor is a Canadian or a non-Canadian. Usually, the answer will be obvious. An individual's status should be clear and a series of rules govern the status ("status rules") of investment vehicles, such as corporations and joint ventures. However, the Act contains several surprises. Moreover, a few corporations whose owners have hidden themselves behind nominees may have a difficult time in trying to ascertain their status.

1. The Economic Implications

These "status rules" are discussed in detail in this chapter. Readers should ponder how the competing policy considerations were resolved. A "Canadian" could have been defined in more than one way. Under the *FIR Act*, for instance, there were more "potential foreign investors" than exist under the *IC Act*. By increasing the number of persons and companies which qualify as Canadians and by moving from a control-based system in the direction of an ownership-based system, those who drafted the *IC Act* were making "policy". These policy decisions involved:

(1) the flow of foreign funds into Canada,

(2) data collection,

(3) the need for government regulation of business,

(4) the acceptable level of influence by foreigners over a "Canadian" company.

2. The Individual Investor

(a) Canadian Citizens

If the investor is an individual and a Canadian citizen, the Act does not apply. The investor may have resided in a foreign country for the last twenty-five years and have severed all links with Canada, but if the investor is still a Canadian citizen, and wants to invest in this country, the *Investment Canada Act* can be ignored. (Until 1985, when FIRA was abolished, Canadians who had lived abroad for more than five years were classified as foreigners.)[1]

This absence of a residency requirement will please wealthy Canadians who have moved to the Bahamas (to escape Canadian taxes) or the United States. It will also benefit immigrants who have obtained Canadian citizenship and subsequently returned to their country of origin. Since the only stipulation is that the investor be a Canadian citizen, dual citizenship (which is permitted under the *Citizenship Act*) poses no problem.

(b) Landed Immigrants

If the investor is a landed immigrant (the wording in the Act is "a permanent resident within the meaning of the *Immigration Act, 1976*"), the Act *may* not apply to him or her. A landed immigrant ("permanent resident") is exempted from the notification/review provisions of the Act if he or she "has been ordinarily resident in Canada for not more than one year after the time at which he or she became eligible to apply for Canadian citizenship".[2]

This means that a landed immigrant who has never resided in Canada until obtaining permanent resident status will be treated as a Canadian under the *Investment Canada Act* for four years from the date of arrival. After that time, his or her "Canadian" status will be lost unless Canadian citizenship is obtained.

---

[1] The drafters of the *Foreign Investment Review Act* wanted Canadians who had moved to another country to be treated like foreigners. They argued that these Canadians had abandoned Canada. Conservative M.P. Don Blenkarn disagreed. He condemned the creation of "second-class citizens". House of Commons, *Minutes of the Standing Committee on Finance, Trade and Economic Affairs*, July 12, 1973, Issue No. 40, p. 36.

[2] See the definition of "Canadian" and "non-Canadian" in s. 3.

Why did the government choose this four-year time period? A landed immigrant can apply for citizenship after three years of residency. The additional year of grace is to provide for the processing of the documentation.[3]

Some landed immigrants have lived and worked in Canada for ten or more years without becoming Canadian citizens. They are not pleased to learn that they have the same status as a foreign investor. However, there is a certain rationale behind the provision. A landed immigrant who does not take out Canadian citizenship may not be deeply committed to Canada, and, therefore, should not enjoy all the benefits of Canadians.

What happens to the investments made by landed immigrants during their first four years in Canada if they never take out citizenship or if they return to their country of birth? Nothing. The *Investment Canada Act* is not retroactive. (The notification/review provisions apply only to those investments made *after* the landed immigrant has lost Canadian status.)

(i) The Charter and the IC Act

Is this treatment of landed immigrants discriminatory? That is an interesting question. Since two classes of landed immigrants are created, a potential "equality" issue does arise. The first class consists of landed immigrants who are not yet eligible to become citizens. They are regarded as "Canadians". The second class of landed immigrants, namely, those who decide not to become Canadian citizens within one year of being eligible, must abide by the provisions of Canada's screening legislation.

Subsection 15(1) of the *Canadian Charter of Rights and Freedoms*[4] declares:

> 15.1 (1) Every individual is equal before and under the law and has the right to the equal protection and equal benefit of the law without

---

[3] Absences from Canada (and prior residency) will change this cut-off date. A landed immigrant must have resided in Canada for a total of three years within the four years immediately preceding his or her application for citizenship. Within these four years, each day he or she resided in Canada after becoming a landed immigrant is counted as one day, and each day he or she resided in Canada before becoming a landed immigrant is counted as one half-day. Therefore, some immigrants may not become eligible to apply for citizenship until the end of their fourth year in Canada, with the result that they will not lose their Canadian status until the end of the fifth year. On the other hand, landed immigrants who resided in Canada before becoming permanent residents need not wait three years after being "landed" before applying for citizenship. See the *Citizenship Act*, R.S.C. 1985, c. C-29, s.5.

[4] *Constitution Act, 1982*, as enacted by Canada Act 1982 (U.K.), 1982, c. 11.

discrimination and, in particular, without discrimination based on race, national or ethnic origin, colour, religion, sex, age or mental or physical disability.

There is no mention in section 15 of distinctions based on citizenship or the length of residency. Nonetheless, if section 15 is interpreted broadly, any distinctions constituting discrimination might be caught.

The courts may one day rule that the treatment of landed immigrants in the *IC Act* violates section 15 of the *Charter*. If so, the courts will probably also rule that the objectives underlying this differential treatment are reasonable and uphold it under section 1 of the *Charter*. This section states:

> The *Canadian Charter of Rights and Freedoms* guarantees the rights and freedoms set out in it subject only to such reasonable limits prescribed by law as can be demonstrably justified in a free and democratic society.

(ii) The Meaning of "Ordinarily Resident"

Some foreigners obtain permanent residency status in Canada, then return home to operate family businesses. Do such immigrants remain Canadians? This question is of crucial importance to some families in the Far East. Why? These families want to safeguard their fortunes by investing in Canadian businesses, yet work in Asia where more money can be made.

Under the *Immigration Act*,[5] immigrants can leave Canada for considerable periods of time yet remain "permanent residents" of Canada. Section 24 sets out the law on this point:

> (1) A person ceases to be a permanent resident when
>
> (a) that person leaves or remains outside Canada with the *intention of abandoning* Canada as that person's place of permanent residence . . . [Emphasis added.]
>
> (2) Where a permanent resident is outside Canada for *more than one hundred and eighty-three days* in any one twelve month period, that person shall be *deemed* to have *abandoned* Canada as his place of permanent residence *unless* that person satisfies an immigration officer or adjudicator, as the case may be, that he *did not intend* to abandon Canada as his place of permanent residence. [Emphasis added.]

However, section 24 is not the complete answer to the concerns of wealthy families living in other countries. This is because it is possible

---

[5] R.S.C. 1985, c. I-2.

for an immigrant to retain his or her status as a "permanent resident", yet lose his or her status as a "Canadian" under the *IC Act*.

How could that happen? In the *IC Act*, a Canadian is defined as "a permanent resident within the meaning of the *Immigration Act* who has been ordinarily resident in Canada for not more than one year after the time at which he first became eligible to apply for Canadian citizenship". The issue, then, is whether a recently landed immigrant (i.e., a "permanent resident"), who lives in the U.S. or Hong Kong for several months, remains "ordinarily resident" in Canada.

Those who read statutes literally say the answer is no. An immigrant must be ordinarily resident in Canada during the entire four-year period after becoming a permanent resident if he or she wishes to be treated like a Canadian for investment purposes. (This is also Investment Canada's interpretation.)

Needless to say, not all solicitors with foreign clients share that view. Some solicitors believe that the law only requires a "permanent resident" to be "ordinarily resident" in Canada during the fourth year after becoming landed (that is, during that one-year period following eligibility to apply for citizenship).

This latter interpretation (if upheld by the courts) would allow a "permanent resident" to be a Canadian for investment purposes even if he or she lives in Hong Kong or Manila for most of the first three years after arrival in Canada. Of course, there is a risk. Canadian immigration officials might rule that the person is no longer a "permanent resident" because he or she has abandoned Canada. To avoid this possibility, solicitors tell their clients to get a returning residency permit. Subsection 25(2) of the *Immigration Act* explains the legal effect of these permits:

> Possession by a person of a valid *returning resident permit* issued to that person pursuant to the regulations is, in the *absence* of *evidence* to the *contrary*, *proof* that the person did *not leave* or remain outside Canada *with the intention* of abandoning Canada as his place of permanent residence. [Emphasis added.]

3. Governments and Their Agencies

The *IC Act* applies to foreign governments and their *agencies*. They are all "non-Canadians". Sometimes it is unclear whether a company is the agent of a foreign government. If the statute permitting the establishment of a corporation does not state that the corporation is to be a government agent, the common law must be examined.

The test used by Canadian courts in determining issues of agency is based upon the degree of control that a government can exercise over the company or, conversely, the degree of independence that the company has. The courts have reached some surprising decisions on this point.[6]

If, after examining the law, the directors of a corporation are still in doubt about whether it qualifies as an agent of a foreign government, they should read the status rules in the *IC Act*. Under these rules, it may be clear that the corporation is not Canadian-controlled.

4. Corporations

The rules for determining the status of corporations are found in section 26 of the *IC Act*. The legal adviser to a corporation must peruse these rules, as if he were climbing down a ladder until he finds a provision which indicates that his client is or is not Canadian-controlled.

These rules represent a significant change from the law as it existed under the *FIR Act*. Under that Act, the status of a corporation was determined by a control in fact test (also called a "*de facto*" control test).

That test had its origins in theories about decision making within organizations—theories that had been in the process of development since the turn of the century. In 1904, for instance, Thorstein Veblen (*The Theory of Business Enterprise*) noted that management became more and more separated from ownership as corporate size increased. Brandeis (*Other People's Money and How The Bankers Use It*) and Lenin (*Imperialism*) observed that the banks were controlling companies. In 1932, Berle and Means (*The Modern Corporation and Private Property*) described how shareholder control had been replaced by managerial control in the largest public companies. Berle and Means also developed a classification scheme grouping together various types of control. All of these writers implicitly recognized that "control" was really a bundle of rights which could be subdivided into lesser control rights and end up in the hands of different people.[7]

---

[6] Robert Flannigan, "Crown Agency Status" (1988), 67 *Can. Bar Rev.* 229.

[7] For an overview of some of the literature on control, see Edward Herman, *Corporate Control, Corporate Power*, (New York: Cambridge University Press, 1981), ch. 1. A.A. Sommers discusses some ways control can be exercised in "Who's in Control? - S.E.C.", *Business Lawyer*, April 1966, p. 559. Adolf Berle, "The Price of Power: Sale of Corporate Control" (1965), 50:4, *Cornell L.Q.* 628-40. Because there are so many types

The framers of the *FIR Act* liked the *de facto* control test, because they too recognized the distinction between ownership and control, and wanted to draft a statute which focused on the real locus of power. Although this locus could be among the shareholders, the drafters also realized that control could lie with one or more directors or senior officers.

That could happen because many boards ratify the decisions of senior management, and provide advice when asked for it, but do not normally make the decisions themselves. In other cases, pursuant to a management contract, or a licensing, distributorship, supply, or technology agreement, the levers of power might be exercised by someone outside the corporation, such as a supplier or franchisor. Sometimes a lender under a debenture would be dictating to management. Rarely, other factors such as interlocking directorships, domineering personality, an option to buy a controlling block of shares or the technical expertise of a company officer could be a consideration. This is because *de facto* control under the *FIR Act* could arise in any manner whatsoever.[8]

The *IC Act* did not completely abandon this *de facto* control concept, but in the interest of simplicity, the concept was circumscribed. Fixed rules were partly substituted. This enhanced certainty of application,[9] but with the loss of some accuracy in pinpointing who is moving the levers of power.

Under the *IC Act*, ownership levels determine which of the rules governing Canadian/non-Canadian status is to be applied. The concept of control in fact is found in only some of the rules and is restricted to the exercise of control in fact through the ownership of voting shares. Thus, the impact of franchise agreements, tied supply agreements and management contracts on the locus of decision making need not be considered. The possibility that the chairman and chief executive officer or senior management as a group, might be selecting the directors of large companies and through control of the proxy machinery, ensuring their election, is not a consideration either.

---

of "control" and the word appears frequently in statutes, it has been called "the albatross around the neck of many corporate transactions".

[8] Liberal government ministers (Pepin, Gillespie) spoke about *de facto* control through management contracts, licensing arrangements, debts, voting trusts, and long-term supply contracts. House of Commons, *Minutes of the Standing Committee on Finance, Trade and Economic Affairs*, June 7, 1972, Issue No. 17, p. 16; June 5, 1973, Issue No. 26, p. 3; July 10, 1973, Issue No. 39, p. 71. In addition, see: *The Foreign Investment Review Act*, (Toronto: The Law Society of Upper Canada, 1975), p. 8.

[9] *De facto* control depends upon the co-operation or passivity of other shareholders. Sometimes it is impossible for a shareholder with a minority interest to know whether he has *de facto* control until he tries to elect directors.

These changes have made it easier, in comparison with the prior legislation, to determine who controls a corporation. However, there are still many puzzling concepts. The three most perplexing are "voting shares", "voting group", and "control in fact through the ownership of voting shares". Each of these concepts is explained below. Then the status rules are examined.

(a) The Meaning of "Voting Shares"

When determining who controls a corporation, the central concept to focus on is a "voting share". This concept is defined in a two-pronged fashion. A "voting share" means a share in the capital of a corporation to which is attached:

- a voting right *ordinarily exercisable* at meetings of shareholders of the corporation

—and—

- to *which is ordinarily attached* a right to receive a share of the profits, or to share in the assets of the corporation on dissolution, or both."[10]

In other words, a voting share is a share that usually carries the right to vote and the right to participate in the growth of the company. It was given this two-pronged meaning in an attempt to prevent lawyers from circumventing the statute by separating equity rights from voting rights.[11]

However, there is also a deliberate vagueness to this definition. It is a vagueness that lawyers who like to design escape routes based upon technicalities had best be wary of.

A voting share will normally carry the right to vote and an equity interest, but exceptionally it may mean something different. When combined with the anti-avoidance provision in paragraph 39(1)(g) of the Act, the definition of a voting share gives the minister considerable flexibility in dealing with strange shares from which various rights have been stripped.

For instance, a foreign jurisdiction may permit the issuance of shares with voting rights only, and no equity rights. If the right to share in profits, or in the assets of the corporation on dissolution

---

[10] *IC Act*, s. 3.

[11] E. James Arnett, "From FIRA to Investment Canada" (1985), 24 *Alta. L. Rev.* 1, at 8. Mr. Arnett was Special Counsel to the Government of Canada in connection with the draft *Investment Canada Act*.

would *ordinarily* be attached to such shares, they could still qualify as voting shares for the purpose of the status and acquisition rules in the *IC Act*, despite the absence of equity rights.[12]

(b) Partial Vote Complications

After reading the definition of "voting share", investors ask: what is "a voting right ordinarily exercisable at meetings of shareholders"?

This phrase obviously encompasses voting rights exercised by the common shareholders. They elect the directors, appoint auditors, adopt the company by-laws and approve fundamental corporate changes. In this way they control the corporation.

But what about class votes of other shareholders? In many jurisdictions, shares that are nominally non-voting are given mandatory voting rights in certain circumstances. Under the *Canada Business Corporations Act*, for instance, non-voting shareholders have the right to vote on an amalgamation, the sale of substantially all the company's property, and other fundamental matters. Other non-voting shares, because of a "coat-tail provision", may acquire voting rights if there is a takeover bid. Should the voting rights of these shareholders be ignored on the grounds that they do not elect the directors and, therefore, do not *ordinarily* participate in control?

One view is that a share is not a "voting share" if any voting rights attached to it are exercisable for only limited purposes. This is the prevailing view.[13] It means that preferred shares that become voting in the event dividends are not paid do not affect a company's Canadian status until the day that right to vote arises.

However, a few solicitors disagree. These solicitors are alarmed that a foreign corporation could buy 30% of a Canadian company's voting shares and a huge number of convertible preferred shares without falling into Ottawa's review net. The foreign corporation could

---

[12] *Investment Canada Act: Briefing Document* (undated, released under the *Access to Information Act*), p. 12.

[13] The courts will probably define "voting share" in terms of a present ability to vote. If so, there can be no acquisition of control until conversion rights are exercised. Although not directly on point, see: *Arctic Geophysical Ltd. v. M.N.R.* (1967) C.T.C. 571; *Rous & Press Ltd. v. M.N.R.* (1953), 7 D.T.C. 326. On the subject of preferred shares that have a contingent right to vote, see *Lou's Service (Sault) Ltd. v. M.N.R.* (1967), 21 D.T.C. 5201 (Ex.Ct.). Under the *FIR Act*, preferred shares, which only became voting if a dividend was not paid, were not taken into account when determining who controls a company. House of Commons, *Minutes of the Standing Committee on Finance, Trade and Economic Affairs*, July 12, 1973, Issue No. 40, pp. 71–72.

then browbeat other shareholders by threatening to convert its preferred shares. In the view of these solicitors, a preferred share is a voting share if it becomes voting when fundamental matters (like an amalgamation) arise.

A more difficult issue occurs when preferred shareholders are given partial voting rights, such as the right to elect a certain percentage of the directors. Must such partial voting rights be taken into account? Should three preferred shares be equivalent to one common share? Such fine points of law become important to a foreign investor who owns a majority of a company's preferred shares.

Subsection 30(2), which provides a formula for dealing with shares which carry multiple and fractional votes, may help in fashioning an answer. However, even mathematicians may become confused if they try to incorporate the partial voting rights of preferred shareholders into the "share ownership percentages" found throughout the statute.

(c) Voting Group

The second concept that puzzles investors is a "voting group". This concept distinguishes those shareholders who tend to vote together from the remaining shareholders, who often constitute a much larger, but amorphous, group. For instance, Canadian or foreign shareholders who have a community of interests and own 35% of a company's shares may well exercise *de facto* control over that company. Conversely, a number of shareholders who have no association with each other can own 60% or more of a company's shares and exercise no real control. It was in recognition of this phenomenon that the concept of a voting group was placed in the Act:

> "voting group" means two or more persons who are *associated* with respect to the exercise of rights attached to voting interests in an entity by contract, business arrangement, personal relationship, common control in fact through the ownership of voting interests, or otherwise, in such a manner that they would ordinarily be *expected to act together* on a continuing basis with respect to the exercise of those rights. [Emphasis added.][14]

Solicitors who must work with this concept complain it is too fluid. In their minds, it places "undue" discretion in the hands of administrators and the courts.

There are two preconditions for the creation of a voting group. Obviously, the first one is the ownership of shares (or other voting

---

[14]*IC Act*, s. 3. The concept of a voting group is only used to determine Canadian/non-Canadian status. A voting group is not considered to carry on a business. That is one way the *IC Act* differs from the *FIR Act*.

interests) by those alleged to be group members. The other is the existence of a relationship between those alleged members leading to the expectation that they will ordinarily vote together. Such a relationship can arise in any fashion—through a contract, business arrangement, personal relationship or otherwise.

When trying to discover if these preconditions have been met, it may be useful to examine voting patterns at shareholders' meetings over a number of years. History can be a harbinger of the future. If members of a possible voting group have been at odds on important issues in the past, it is unlikely that they can be "expected to act together on a continuing basis" in the future.[15]

Shareholders who have entered into a shareholders' agreement will usually constitute a voting group. So will members of the same family, and corporations in the same corporate group.[16] But the definition suggests that numerous other arrangements might lead to a voting group.

Because the definition of a voting group is so murky, legal questions frequently fly. Does "ordinarily" mean always? Or just 60% of the time? And what about the phrase "continuing basis"? Although it would exclude shareholders from being a voting group if they merely voted together on one occasion, must shareholders vote together meeting after meeting? If so, can investors occasionally disagree about extraordinary matters, such as whether a company should sell a major asset, and still be regarded as voting together on a continuous basis? A related conundrum is whether the fact that two shareholders have undertaken several business ventures together creates a presumption that they will vote together in the future.

Even when there is a shareholders' agreement between investors, there may be room to dispute the existence of a voting group. A shareholders' agreement will cover major issues like the election of directors. But a shareholders' agreement will seldom encompass every matter—including proposals by shareholders and the appointment of auditors—that could come before an annual meeting. Consequently, there may still be considerable freedom for investors to dissent on a variety of issues. This fact, in turn, may allow either the government or

---

[15] It may sometimes be a mistake to rely on past voting patterns. Alignments of interest may change; antagonisms may give way to friendship.

[16] The definition of a voting group may be read in conjunction with subs. 28(2), which deals with shareholdings of associated entities. If a foreign parent company has several subsidiaries, each of which owns a small number of shares in a Canadian corporation, it cannot be argued that the shares held by each subsidiary should be treated separately for the purpose of determining the status of the Canadian corporation.

investors to assert (when doing so is in their interest) that no voting group exists.

As for personal or blood relationships, such as between father and son, they are of great significance. But such relationships may not be conclusive proof that a voting group exists. One judge worded this idea rather succinctly:

> While blood relatives may be bitter enemies, usually this is not the case. Such a case would seem to be exceptional and contrary to general experience. . . .It seems reasonably safe to say that it will not frequently happen that blood relations will be conducting business at arm's length. . . .[17]

This statement expresses a perception that lawyers for "related investors" must overcome if they wish to contend that their clients are not a voting group because of sibling rivalry.

Because almost *any* relationship may be the basis of a voting group, separating the meritorious claims from the hot air is a problem. Investors know all the facts and they may be selective when presenting them.

There is a litmus test that the government might use. If a lawyer is adamant that his or her clients form a voting group because they have been in business together for several years, it may be appropriate for government officials to suggest that those clients put their relationship on paper by entering into a written voting agreement. That suggestion should pose no problems if a solid voting group exists and may flush out some admissions if the shareholders doubt they will be voting together in the future.

(d) "Control in Fact Through the Ownership of Voting Shares"[18]

Legal control (that is, control through the ownership of a majority of the outstanding votes) is not the sole test used in the *IC Act*. There is also minority or working control.

Minority control is what the drafters were thinking about[19] when they used the phrase "control in fact through the ownership of voting

---

[17] *No. 25 v. M.N.R.*, 55 D.T.C. 331, at 332.

[18] Some articles which touch upon the concept of control in fact are: M. Pickering, "Shareholders' Voting Rights and Company Control", *L.Q. Rev.*, April 1965, p. 248; David Matheson, "Corporate Control Concepts and Tax Reform" (1972), 20 *Can. Tax J.* 45.

[19] This is obviously what the drafters were thinking about, in light of the context in

shares". Unfortunately, because they failed to explain the concept further, they left a third phrase for investors to puzzle over. (That may have been prudent since control can arise in several ways. A precise definition would have circumscribed the scope of "control".)

There are certain visible boundary lines. Because "control in fact" is restricted to control "through the ownership of voting shares", control through management and licensing agreements is excluded. In addition, "control" means "potential control". This is important when actual control and the power to control are in different hands.

Some solicitors dislike that distinction. A major foreign share-holder, they maintain, does not control if that person is passive and neither elects company directors nor issues instructions to existing directors. If these directors are also Canadians, then the company must be Canadian-controlled. (In addition, these solicitors point out that if a foreign investor who wants to buy a business does not intend to exercise actual control, that investor can have no plans for the business. Therefore, the investment cannot be of net benefit to Canada and can never be approved. To avoid this dilemma, it makes sense to interpret "control" as "actual control".)

Such contentions overlook an important point. If a shareholder in a controlling position is passive, it is because the shareholder is content with how company directors are performing. The shareholder does not have to tell them what to do because they know intuitively what is expected of them.

The authors of a study done for the Royal Commission on Corporate Concentration express the same idea in these words: "Power to control, we contend, exists independently of the actual exercise of it. Power to control, then, is the power to control if need be."[20]

If control in fact did not refer to potential control, some strange results would occur. For instance, a company equally owned by two foreign shareholders but with a Canadian board of directors that had been granted considerable autonomy, would be regarded as Canadian-controlled. Such a conclusion would fly in the face of reality, as well as the Act, which is directed at shareholder control.

---

which the phrase is used. See, for instance, para. 26(1)(c) or 28(3)(c).

[20] S. Berkowitz, T. Kotowitz, and L. Waverman, *Enterprise Structure and Corporate Concentration*, Study 17, Royal Commission on Corporate Concentration, August 1976, p. 15.

Some authors, such as Ferdinand Lundberg in *The Rich and the Super-Rich*, have concluded that "a small coterie", comparable in relative size to the owning class of a Banana Republic, "control" all important companies in the U.S.A. These authors must be using "control" to mean potential control, since they do not offer evidence that the members of the coterie actually act in concert or have strong community interests.

Fortunately, the courts, when dealing with tax statutes, have not accepted the argument that passive shareholders do not control.[21] It is, therefore, unlikely that they will reach a different conclusion when interpreting the *IC Act*.

Beyond these boundary lines, however, the ambit of "control in fact through the ownership of voting shares" is unclear. At least two interpretations are possible:

(1) *positive control*: control in fact of a sufficient number of voting shares to cause corporate decisions to be taken;

(2) *negative control*: control in fact of a sufficient number of votes to deadlock or veto decisions at the shareholder or director level.

Unfortunately, the statute gives no indication which interpretation should be favoured. Nor does it indicate what rights are "control rights" or how far the search for "control rights" should be extended.

(e) The Search for "Control Rights"

Should one look at only the documents of incorporation to find out what "bundle of rights" share ownership brings (or, if a broad interpretation is adopted, what quorum restrictions exists)? Or, can shareholders' agreements be examined as well, on the grounds that provisions which appear in a company's articles can easily be placed in a contract among shareholders?

There is no simple answer. Both the legal and economic literature stress that the power to select a majority of the board of directors is the quintessence of control. For instance, Edward Herman writes:

> Because the legal power to control corporate affairs rests with the board of directors (and ultimately the stockholders), analysis of the dynamics of the board must be the linchpin of the analysis of corporate control."[22]

However, such comments shed little light on the meaning of the *IC Act*.

One rationale for examining shareholders' agreements is to ascertain if voting shares have meaningful voting rights.[23] Another

---

[21] See, for instance, *M.N.R. v. Dworkin Furs (Pembroke) Ltd.*, [1967] S.C.R. 223. The power to elect a majority of the directors, through the ownership of more than 50% of a company's shares, is *de jure* control regardless of whether the power is exercised.

[22] E. Herman, *Corporate Control, Corporate Power*, (Cambridge: Cambridge University Press, 1981), p. 30.

[23] A legal argument in support of examining shareholders' agreements is that it is

consideration—if shareholders' agreements are excluded, a huge loop-hole exists. A foreigner could buy 49% of a company's shares and provide a loan (or technology) in exchange for the right in a share-holders' agreement to nominate a majority of the board. Yet the foreigner would not have acquired control in the eyes of the law.

During the first three years of Investment Canada's existence, solicitors were told that the agency did not examine shareholders' agreements. The statute was presented to the business community as being very simple to understand, in contradistinction to the *FIR Act*. Subsequently, the search for control rights was broadened, and share-holders' agreements are now sometimes requested (when agency per-sonnel are determining whether a transaction is reviewable or ascertaining an investor's "status").[24]

Assuming this dispute over whether shareholders' agreements can be examined is resolved, the next step in choosing a meaning for "control in fact through the ownership of voting shares" is to select one of the two interpretations mentioned above.

(f) Positive Control

At the simplest level of analysis, the issue is, does a non-Canadian shareholder have enough votes to cause corporate decisions to be taken? Control, then, is the power to do a *positive* thing. But what positive thing?

Is control in fact merely the power to elect a majority of the directors? If so, and if shareholders' agreements are outside the cur-tain of examination, the issue of control can be resolved by any eight-year-old mathematician. Given the percentage of shareholders who vote, what percentage of votes will give a minority shareholder control of the board? (*This is the narrow view.*)

But what if the curtain of examination sweeps in shareholder agreements? And if "control in fact" has a more extensive meaning, including the ability to ratify all shareholders' resolutions, even if a

---

the only way to determine if the shares owned by a Canadian meet the test of being "voting shares" (as that term is defined in the Act). If the voting rights of a Canadian are restricted in an agreement, maybe those shares are not "voting shares". Likewise, if those shares pay a dividend, but provide only for a return of paid-in capital.

[24] The courts will enforce shareholders' agreements through equitable remedies such as orders for specific performance, and mandatory and interlocutory injunctions. From a practical point of view, the terms of shareholders' agreements are, therefore, important in determining who really has control. *Greenwell v. Porter*, [1902] 1 Ch. 530; *Turvey and Mercer v. Lauder* (1956), 4 D.L.R. (2d) 225.

greater than majority vote ("a special majority") is required? (*This is the broad view.*)

In that event, the articles and by-laws of the company, its governing statute and any shareholders' agreements must be examined. The object of this examination would be to discover what rights attach to the shares and whether any special provisions exist which require unusual majorities before decisions can be taken, or which relegate decisions on specified matters to certain classes of voting shares. Once this is done and a determination made as to which rights are control rights, it may be apparent who has the power to make decisions.

Obviously, it is a question of judgment, just how much power a shareholder must possess, before there is control in fact. A foreign shareholder owning 35% of the shares of a widely-held Canadian company may well be in control. If that 35% gives him or her the right to appoint a majority of the directors, the foreign shareholder is definitely in control. If the right of appointment is in a shareholders' agreement, the legal conclusion is a little less certain. But if all that a foreign shareholder can do (under an agreement with the company) is nominate directors for election, then who knows?

(g) Negative Control

On the other hand, if "control in fact" also includes the concept of negative control, one must ask: to what degree can the investor *prevent* action being taken by deadlocking decision making?

If no vote of the shareholders of a company can be effective unless concurred in by holders of 80% of the common stock, a shareholder with 21% of the shares has substantial negative control. This shareholder will have a similar degree of control if high quorum requirements at shareholders' and directors' meetings exist.[25] By refusing to attend meetings (or by telling his or her nominee on the board not to do so) such a shareholder may prevent a quorum from being formed

---

[25] Some courts will invoke the notion of majority rule to vary quorum requirements unless they are sanctioned by statute, particularly if a company is paralyzed because a shareholder or director will not attend a meeting. See *B. Love Ltd. & Bulk Steel & Salvage Ltd.* (1982), 40 O.R. (2d) 1; *Re Routley's Holdings Ltd.*, [1960] O.W.N. 160; and *Re Copal Varnish Company Ltd.*, [1917] 2 Ch. 349. In *Re Cowichan Leader Ltd.* (1963), 42 D.L.R. (2d) 111, which involved a company with two shareholders and a quorum of two, the courts said it could not vary the quorum. When will the courts exercise their discretion? The competing policy considerations are majority rule versus upholding the original agreement between the incorporators. (In the U.S., the statutes of several states expressly permit greater than normal quorum requirements.)

and thus stymie action.[26] In both situations, a shareholder, in such a position, can prevent decisions from being made concerning employment, product innovation and other factors which the Canadian government must consider when determining if an investment is of net benefit to Canada.[27]

The diagram below summarizes the preceding discussion and the range of possibilities.

	Positive Control	Negative Control
Sh. Agr. Examined		
Sh. Agr. Not Examined		

Sh. Agr. = Shareholders' Agreement.

(h) The Case Law

Unfortunately, Anglo-American case law is of little assistance in finding a meaning for control.[28] In many cases, judges assume that the meaning is self-evident and do not even discuss the issue.

---

[26] When might a minority shareholder most effectively boycott a meeting? Imagine that a mortgage must be refinanced. The bank will want a special borrowing by-law and a special resolution approving the loan to be passed by the shareholders before funds are advanced. Another opportunity will arise if the directors want to make a fundamental change to the corporation (e.g., amalgamate or sell most of the assets). Fundamental changes must be approved by a special resolution of the shareholders, that is, a resolution passed at a shareholders' meeting by two thirds of the votes cast. *Canada Business Corporations Act*, R.S.C. 1985, c-44, ss. 183 and 189.

[27] In *Glass v. Atkin* (1967), 65 D.L.R. (2d) 501, the Ontario High Court concluded that the defendants controlled the corporation because they could deadlock decisions. In *Illinois Central Railroad Co. v. U.S.*, 263 F. Supp. 421 (N.D. Ill 1966), affd 385 U.S. 457 (1967), a U.S. court decided that the power to veto constituted control. Since only 90% of the stock was voted at shareholders' meetings, the acquiror, with 31% of the votes, could block action that required approval of two thirds of the votes. For the factors that the SEC looks at, see *Chicago Corporation v. S.E.C.*, 28 S.E.C. 463. In *R. v. Staples*, [1940] 4 D.L.R. 699, at 703, the court said that "control" was the power to do a positive thing. The ownership of one half the shares, in a company where ownership is split 50:50, does not give control. For comment, see R. Gosse, *The Law on Competition in Canada*, (Toronto: Carswell, 1962), p. 201.

Not all unanimity provisions in shareholders' agreements should detract from an argument that control in fact rests with the Canadian shareholders. An example is a provision that requires the consent of all investors before a sale of the business can take place. Such a provision is a form of investment protection. Most corporate statutes grant such protection to minority shareholders. *C.B.C.A.*, Part XV, ss. 173-92.

[28] See: *A.G. Canada v. KSC Ltd.* (1983), 22 B.L.R. 32; *Himley Estates Ltd. v. C.I.R.*, [1938] 1 K.B. 472; *I.R.C. v. J. Bibby & Sons Ltd.*, [1945] 1 All E.R. 667; *I.R.C. v. Silverts Ltd.*,

Negative control has been accepted as constituting control in several court cases dealing with other statutes. But, in general, the case law on the meaning of control is marked by an unwillingness to look behind the share register. On several occasions, the courts when interpreting the *Income Tax Act* have explicitly refused to consider constraints, such as trust agreements or the influence of one shareholder over another, on the ability of a registered shareholder to vote shares. Impressed by such jurisprudence, the Tax Appeal Board in *Rubenstein v. M.N.R.*[29] concluded that voting control of a share, as indicated in the register, is "paramount regardless of any trust or agreement existing between the registered holder and any third party".

It is doubtful whether such cases are of much use in interpreting the *IC Act*. The concepts in that Act are different from those in other statutes. In addition, statutes must be interpreted in light of their objective. The objective of the *IC Act* is to review changes in control. That objective should entail a more extensive examination of the power to control than merely asking who has legal control for the purpose of collecting taxes.

5. The Status Rules for Corporations

Once the meaning of "voting share", "voting group" and "control in fact" have been grasped, the rules for deciding whether a corporation is Canadian-controlled are easy to apply. Simply start with the first rule and if it does not fit, climb down an imaginary ladder, examining each rule in succession, until one is found which does fit. Since a set of facts may fit within more than one rule, it is important to begin at the top of the ladder.

Here is one point that confuses lawyers (and everyone else). In the definition section of the Act, the drafters declare that "Canadian" and "non-Canadian" mean: individuals, governments, corporations, partnerships, trusts and joint ventures. However, "Canadian" and "non-Canadian", when used in connection with status, refer only to individuals, governments, corporations and trustee-controlled trusts.

[1951] 1 All E.R. 703; *Barclays Bank Ltd. v. I.R.C.*, [1960] 2 All E.R. 817; *Bert Robbins Excavating Ltd. v. M.N.R.* 66 D.T.C. 5269; *M.N.R. v. Consolidated Holding Companies Ltd.* 72 D.T.C. 6007. In the *Himley Estates* case, the court refused to interpret a statute that used the words "control . . . by any other means whatsoever" as encompassing willing co-operation (or control in fact). Control, the court said, involves power, not merely reliance. Two Canadian cases that refer to *Himley Estates* are *Rous and Mann Press Ltd. v. M.N.R.* (1953), 9 Tax A.B.C. 56; and *No. 513 v. M.N.R.* 19 Tax A.B.C. 242.

[29] *Rubenstein v. M.N.R.* 65 D.T.C. 494, at 502.

Joint ventures, partnerships and beneficiary-controlled trusts, in other words, are left out. This is because of the look-through principle, hidden in subsection 27(a).

(a) The Eight Rules

RULE 1:   A corporation is Canadian-controlled if a Canadian owns a majority of the voting shares. (paragraph 26(1)(a))

COMMENT: Although the opposition in Parliament proposed a higher threshold, the government thought that majority Canadian share ownership, even if widely-held, was sufficient to protect Canadian interests.

Rule 1 means that a company will be Canadian-controlled if a Canadian owns 51% of the shares, even though a single foreign shareholder owns 49%. It does not matter that the foreign shareholder may be the sole supplier or purchaser from the company and, consequently, vital to the company's well-being. (If two or more Canadians own 51%, see Rule 5.)

Would the Canadian still control the company if the articles or a shareholders' agreement provided that all motions put before shareholders' meetings needed unanimous consent? The answer is unclear.[30]

EXAMPLE: A foreign distributor sets up a distribution company in Canada. The foreign distributor keeps 49% of the shares, sells 51% to its Canadian employee, gives the employee a loan at below current interest rates to pay for the shares and increases her salary so she can make the payments. The foreign distributor has the right to nominate one of the three company directors and (pursuant to the distribution agreement) determine the prices of the goods that are sold by the company. If the Canadian wants to sell her shares, the foreign distributor has the first right to buy them. Is this company controlled by the Canadian?

In the *KSC* case, decided when FIRA existed, a Federal Court judge said that such a company was Canadian-controlled.[31] (If a similar case were to arise under the *Investment Canada Act*, it would be even more difficult to assert the contrary.)

---

[30] For a discussion of the effect of unanimity provisions on the concept of control under the *Income Tax Act*, see Richard Miner, *Associated Corporations*, (Toronto: Carswell, 1986), pp. 49-59. One case in which a court ruled that a shareholders' agreement did not affect *de jure* control is *The International Iron & Metal Co. Ltd. v. M.N.R.*, 69 D.T.C. 5445.

[31] *A.G. Can. v. KSC Ltd.* (1983), 22 B.L.R. 32. In the *FIR Act*, control was broadly defined. Control could be exercised through a contract or "otherwise" *in addition to*

RULE 2:   A corporation is Canadian-controlled if a voting group exists and Canadian members of the voting group own a majority of the corporation's voting shares. (paragraph 26(1)(a))

COMMENT: Rule 2 applies if:

(1) a group of shareholders votes together,

(2) two or more members of this voting group are Canadians,

(3) these Canadians own a majority of the corporation's voting shares.

In other words, if there is a voting group, and Canadians who are members of that group own 50.1% of the company's shares, the company is Canadian-controlled. The presence of non-Canadians in the voting group neither taints the voting group nor affects the company's status.

EXAMPLE: A company is controlled by three shareholders pursuant to a unanimous shareholders' agreement. Two of the shareholders are Canadians; each owns 30% of the company's shares. The third shareholder, who is both a citizen and resident of Switzerland, owns the remaining 40%.

In this example, the three shareholders form a voting group. Since Canadians own a majority of the company's shares, the company is Canadian-controlled. This is so despite the presence within the voting group of a non-Canadian with a substantial interest.

RULE 3:   A corporation is not Canadian-controlled if one non-Canadian owns a majority of the voting shares. (paragraph 26(1)(b))

COMMENT: Rule 3 is the converse of Rule 1. If a foreign investor owns 50.1% of a company's voting shares, the company is not a "Canadian".

RULE 4:   A corporation is not Canadian controlled if:

(1) there is a voting group,

---

control through share ownership. Consequently, in the KSC case, FIRA officials considered the Canadian distribution company to be controlled jointly by the foreign distributor and the Canadian employee. This was because the foreign distributor was the sole supplier and, therefore, had a stranglehold over the Canadian company. Unfortunately, the Federal Court took a restrictive view and held that the Canadian's ownership of 51% of the shares left him in control. What happened when the foreign shareholder was not the sole supplier? FIRA officials examined the shareholders' agreement. If the foreign shareholder had an array of veto powers, the distribution company was regarded by FIRA as being controlled by a group that included the foreign shareholder.

(2) the non-Canadians in that voting group own a majority of the corporation's voting shares. (paragraph 26(1)(b))

EXAMPLE: One Canadian owns 48% of the shares of Nepean Ltd. Two non-Canadians, who are husband and wife, each own 26%.

Since the non-Canadians, being married to each other, will probably act in concert, they form a "voting group". Consequently, Nepean Ltd. is foreign-controlled.

RULE 5: A corporation will be Canadian-controlled if:

(1) a majority of its shares are owned by Canadians

and

(2) the corporation is not controlled in fact, through the ownership of its voting shares

(a) by a non-Canadian

or

(b) by a non-Canadian-dominated voting group, in which a non-Canadian or two or more non-Canadians own 50% or more of the total voting shares held by the voting group in the corporation. ("a majority non-Canadian voting group") (paragraph 26(1)(c))

COMMENT: Canadians do not necessarily control a company if they own more than half the voting stock. If the shareholdings of the Canadians are spread thinly among many owners, a foreign shareholder with a minority interest may have effective control. In that event, the behaviour of the company is unlikely to be any different from that of a company in which a foreign shareholder owns a majority of the shares.

EXAMPLE: ("The Influential 15% Shareholder"): Carleton Ltd. ("Carleton") manufactures electronic listening devices. A large number of Canadian and foreign shareholders own 40% and 45% of the company's shares respectively. Bill Johnson, who is the managing director of the company, owns the remaining 15%. Bill Johnson is a Canadian and is considered by everyone to "run the show". Over the last ten years, he has always been management's proxy and has put forward the slate of directors. The other shareholders have never attempted to control the company. What is the status of Carleton?

Carleton is Canadian-controlled. It has a majority (60%) of Canadian shareholders, and is not controlled in fact by a non-Canadian, or a voting group dominated by non-Canadians. As this example illustrates, the easiest way to show that non-Canadians do not control may be to demonstrate that a Canadian shareholder does control.

EXAMPLE ("49:49:2"): A company's shares are owned in the following manner:

49% by a Canadian business person

49% by a foreign business person

2% by the secretary of the Canadian lawyer who incorporated the company.

Neither business person owns a majority of the shares. Therefore, Rules 1 and 3 do not apply. If the secretary and the Canadian business person form a voting group, the company will be Canadian-controlled (Rule 2). If no voting groups exist, or if the secretary and the foreign business person or the two business people form a voting group, the status of the company must be determined under Rule 5. This rule will apply because Canadians own a majority (51%) of the voting shares. If no voting group exists, the company will likely be classified as Canadian-controlled. If the foreign business person and the secretary, or the two business people, constitute a voting group, the company will be non-Canadian.

EXAMPLE ("Control By Groups"[32]): Canadians own a majority of a company's shares. However, a voting group consisting of a Canadian and a non-Canadian (each with equal share interests) is in fact in control. Is the company foreign-controlled?

Yes! The same conclusion will be reached if the group is larger than two people, and foreigners own 50% or more of the group's interest.

EXAMPLE ("Working Control"): Canadians own 51% of a company but no single Canadian owns more than 5%. One foreign shareholder has 40%. Does control of this company rest with the board of directors through the proxy mechanism (as in all widely-held companies)?

No! Although Canadians own 51%, the foreign shareholder has *working control*. Through his mere presence, he can influence decision-

---

[32] Contrast the treatment of groups under the *IC Act* with the *FIR Act*. Under the *FIR Act*, if literally interpreted, the presence of one foreigner with a tiny interest could render a group "foreign-controlled". In practice, the group concept was interpreted more liberally. Unless the foreigner had negative control (e.g., through unanimity provisions in a shareholders' agreement), his or her presence would not affect the status of the group.

making by the board. How? Board members know that if the foreign shareholder is unhappy with what management is doing, the foreign shareholder may solicit proxies, engage in a proxy battle, and will probably win. The foreign shareholder will, therefore, get the policies (investment strategy, dividend policy) and directors he wants.

RULE 6:   If less than a majority of its voting shares are owned by Canadians, a corporation is presumed not to be Canadian-controlled. However, this is a rebuttable presumption. The presumption will be rebutted and the corporation classified as Canadian-controlled if a Canadian, despite his or her minority status, has control in fact through the ownership of voting shares, or if a Canadian-dominated voting group has control in fact. (subparagraph 26(1)(d)(i))

COMMENT: If the Canadian shareholders of a company are in the minority, or if a company cannot establish that a majority of its shares are (beneficially) owned by Canadians, because the shares are registered in the name of nominees (e.g., stockbrokers), the company will be presumed to be non-Canadian-controlled.

There are two ways to rebut this presumption. Either show that:

(1) the corporation is controlled in fact by a Canadian (through the ownership of voting shares);

or

(2) the corporation is:

   (a) controlled in fact by a voting group, and

   (b) Canadians dominate the voting group, by owning a majority of the voting interests held by the voting group. ("A majority Canadian voting group")[33]

EXAMPLE: Carleton Ltd. is widely held. Canadians own 47%. Numerous foreigners own the balance. One Canadian (Ann Brown) owns 15% and runs the company in her capacity as managing director. Can the presumption that Carleton is foreign-controlled be rebutted?

---

[33] A mind-twisting phrase in para. 26(1)(d) reads as follows: "a voting group in which a member or members who are Canadians own a majority of those voting interests of the entity owned by the voting group". This phrase refers to the voting group itself, not to members of the voting group. In para. 26(1)(d), the search is for a Canadian-dominated voting group in control of the company. In para. 26(1)(a), the search is for associated Canadians who own a majority of the company's shares.

Rules 5 and 6 both recognize that if there is no majority shareholder (everyone has a minority interest), there can be control in fact through a minority interest.

No! Ann Brown runs the company. But it would be hard to argue that she has *de facto* control *through* her ownership of just 15% of the shares!

RULE 7:   If less than a majority of the voting shares are owned by Canadians and if there is no control at the shareholder level, the company is presumed not to be Canadian-controlled. However, if two thirds of the board of directors are Canadian, the presumption can be rebutted. (subparagraph 26(1)(d)(ii))

COMMENT: Management or board-controlled companies, which have a *majority* of Canadian shareholders, are deemed to be Canadian under Rule 5. The nationality of the board of directors is irrelevant. (Apparently, the drafters of the Act thought that majority Canadian ownership was sufficient protection for Canada regardless of who was on the board. The drafters, therefore, ignored the possibility of board control when Canadians own more than 50% of the shares.)

If Canadian shareholders are *in the minority*, on the other hand, there is a presumption of foreign control even if the company is controlled by its board. However, this presumption can be rebutted by showing:

(1) that the company is board-controlled and

(2) two thirds of its directors are Canadians.

When is a company controlled by its board? Berle and Means (*The Modern Corporation and Private Property*)[34] set the dividing line at 20% stock ownership by one shareholder. A shareholder who owned between 20% and 50% of a company's stock was categorized as having minority (or working) control. R.J. Larner analyzed ownership and control in 200 corporations. Larner assumed that a minority shareholder who owned 10% of a firm's voting stock was in control.[35] (Many lawyers, however, oppose such fixed rules. They claim that each case is unique.)

Multinational companies which are controlled by their boards, like Alcan Aluminium, often want several foreign citizens to serve as directors. These foreign directors are considered better qualified than

---

[34] (New York: Harcourt, Brace & World Inc., 1968), pp. 75, 109.

[35] J. Larner, "Ownership and Control in the 200 Largest Non-Financial Corporations, 1929 and 1963", *American Economic Review*, September 1966, p. 779. Statistics Canada classifies companies as Canadian or foreign-controlled. If a person owns more than 20% of a company's voting equity, and that interest is larger than the combined percentage of the next two largest blocks, the person is deemed by Statistics Canada to have *de facto* control. Statistics Canada, *The Ownership, Control and Country of Control of Corporations*, June 4, 1987, p. 8.

Canadians to provide advice on overseas operations. Such companies should first ascertain if they can achieve Canadian status under the more relaxed test in Rule 5. If this is not possible, because Canadians own 50% of the shares or less, the total *number* of directors may have to be increased until two thirds of them are Canadians.

One interesting aspect of Rule 7 is that the foreign directors can act in concert without affecting the company's status.[36] A foreign director may even be named as management's proxy!

EXAMPLE (Board Control): Woods Ltd. ("Woods") is a widely-held, publicly-traded company. The shareholders have never tried to exercise control and have always voted in favour of management's nominees for the board of directors. At the present time, five of the six directors are Canadians.

Because no shareholder controls Woods and almost all of its directors are Canadians, Woods is Canadian-controlled pursuant to Rule 7 (subparagraph 26(1)(d)(ii)).

(i) The 50:49:1% Company

Some solicitors contend that a company with three shareholders who own 50%, 49% and 1% of the shares, is board-controlled. If the board is composed of a majority of Canadians, these solicitors then assert that the company is Canadian-controlled.

Such an interpretation is a misuse of Rule 7. This rule was intended to apply to companies with hundreds of small shareholders. In such a widely-held company, the board of directors elect themselves through their control of the proxy mechanism.

In a small private company, on the other hand, the board does not control the proxy mechanism (since there are only a few shareholders). Although the shareholders may not be involved in the daily business of the corporation, and the directors may act independently, that independence will end if a large shareholder becomes dissatisfied. A company with a 50:49:1% ownership structure is therefore controlled by its shareholders, not by its board!

(ii) Companies Controlled by Groups

Let's pause for a moment. Here, in summary form, is how to determine the status of companies controlled by a group.

---

[36] It was different under FIRA. Foreign directors of a board-controlled company could not "act in concert". Otherwise, their company might not be regarded as controlled by the Canadian directors. Because "acting in concert" was a subjective test, it was omitted from the *IC Act*.

(a) Does a Canadian or a non-Canadian own a majority of the shares? If so, this fact determines whether the company is Canadian or non-Canadian controlled (Rules 1 and 3).

(b) Do Canadian or non-Canadian members of the "voting group" own a majority of the company's shares?

EXAMPLE: A voting group consists of five shareholders. Two are Canadians who together own 51% of the company's shares. Consequently, the company is Canadian-controlled. If it is the non-Canadians in the voting group who own the 51%, the company is foreign-controlled (Rules 2 and 4).

(c) If Canadians own 51% or more of a company's shares, does a non-Canadian-dominated voting group have control in fact through its ownership of shares (Rule 5).

EXAMPLE: A company is controlled in fact by a "voting group" which owns 44% of the shares. If three quarters of the shares held by that voting group are owned by Americans, these Americans will own only 33% of the company's shares but will dominate the group. The company will, therefore, be foreign-controlled, even if Canadians own a majority of the company's shares. The point of this example is that under Rule 5, the status of the company is determined by examining share ownership *within the voting group*.

(d) If Canadian shareholders are "in the minority", does a Canadian-dominated group have *de facto* control of the company (Rule 6).

EXAMPLE: Canadians own 45% of a company's shares. A voting group (which includes some Canadians) exercises *de facto* control *through* its ownership of 60% of the shares. If those Canadians who belong to the voting group own 31% of the company's shares, they will dominate the group (since the foreigners in the group will own 29% of the shares). The company will, therefore, be "Canadian".

RULE 8:   If two persons each own 50% of the voting shares of a corporation and one is a non-Canadian, the company is a non-Canadian. (subsection 26(6))

COMMENT: Rule 8 is designed for "deadlocked" corporations with two shareholders (who may be individuals, corporations or governments), each of whom owns 50% of the shares. If one of the shareholders is a non-Canadian, the corporation is deemed to be foreign-controlled. (Here is one circumstance where the drafters of the Act clearly recognize the power of negative control. When share ownership is split 50:50, a foreign corporation can limit the opportunities open to its 50%-owned subsidiary, despite the existence of an equally large Canadian shareholder, by blocking corporate action.)[37]

Unfortunately, not all 50:50 splits are treated in the same easy-to-remember fashion. Sometimes a corporation is deadlocked because two voting groups (each made up of several persons) equally own all the shares. Or, two Canadians own half of the shares and a citizen (and resident) of a foreign country holds the remainder. Subsection 26(6) does not cover either of these scenarios.

Does this sound confusing? It is. Just do not make the mistake—as a few solicitors have done—of memorizing the "50:50 share rule" without noticing that it only comes into play when there are two shareholders. A company is foreign-controlled if a Canadian and a citizen of Malaysia each own half of the shares; but if the split is between Canadians, with 50%, and two Malaysian citizens who own the balance, there is merely a *presumption* of foreign control.

(iii) The Problem of the Casting Vote

Is a deadlocked company's status altered if its articles or by-laws provide that the chairperson of a meeting has a casting vote? (A casting vote is a second vote at shareholders' or directors' meetings whenever there is an equality of votes.)

If there is a Canadian and a foreign shareholder, each with 50% of the votes, *and* the Canadian has a casting vote, that will not transform the company into a Canadian. Rule 8 (subsection 26(6)) allows for no exceptions. However, if the division is between one Canadian and a group of Malaysian business people, the existence of a casting vote might make a difference.

The *IC Act* doesn't address the "casting vote problem". As for the case law under the *Income Tax Act*, it has vacillated.

In *Dealers Acceptance Corp. Ltd. v. M.N.R.*[38] the Tax Appeal Board ruled that a casting vote gave the holder control. In *M.N.R. v. Dworkin Furs (Pembroke) Ltd.*[39], on the other hand, the Supreme Court of

---

[37] How important can negative control be? In the 1940s and 1950s, Pan American World Airways and W.R. Grace & Co. each had a 50% interest in Panagra Airways. Pan American used its power as a shareholder to stop Panagra Airways from expanding its route to the U.S. because Pan American did not want any additional competition. *W.R. Grace & Co. v. C.A.B.*, 154 F. 2d 271; *U.S. v. Pan American World Airways Inc.*, 193 F. Supp. 18, at 39 (1961); revd on other grounds, 371 U.S. 296 (1963).

[38] 64 D.T.C. 771. Some shareholders' agreements state that a named shareholder is to be the chairperson at general meetings.

[39] [1967] S.C.R. 223. For the purposes of the association provisions of the *Income Tax Act*, it appears to be settled law that a casting vote does not confer control.

Canada described a casting vote as an adjunct of office and came to the opposite conclusion.

(b) The Imasco Exemption: A Special Rule for a Few Companies[40]

If a company is Canadian-incorporated, publicly traded and a majority of its shareholders are Canadians, but it cannot qualify under the eight rules outlined above, it may be able to take advantage of the "Imasco Exemption". This is a special provision that gives foreign-controlled companies a two-year exemption from review (except when buying or establishing cultural businesses), if their (major) foreign shareholder allows the company's directors to make their own decisions, and if the company can meet seven other objective criteria.

These criteria are set out in subsection 26(3):

(1) the company is incorporated in Canada;

(2) its shares are publicly traded (in an open market that need not be in Canada);

(3) "Canadians" own a majority of its voting shares;

(4) four-fifths of the members of its board of directors are Canadian citizens ordinarily resident in Canada;

(5) its chief executive officer and three of its four most highly remunerated officers are Canadian citizens ordinarily resident in Canada;

(6) its principal place of business is located in Canada

(7) its board of directors supervises the management of its business and affairs on an autonomous basis without direction from any shareholder other than through the normal exercise of voting rights at meetings of shareholders;

(8) the seven circumstances presented above have existed for at least 12 months preceding the application for the minister's opinion.

This is a combined Canadian ownership and autonomy test. It is not a *de facto* control test. If a company can fit itself within this eight-pronged framework, it *does not matter* that real control may lie elsewhere. If, for example, a company has a foreign shareholder who owns

---

[40] If a majority of a company's shares are owned by Canadians and the company is not controlled *in fact* by non-Canadians, it is Canadian-controlled (para. 26(1)(c)). For companies which cannot meet this test, because they *are* controlled by a foreign shareholder with a minority interest, the Imasco exemption may be useful (subs. 26(3)).

49% of the shares, and the balance are held by a multitude of Canadian individuals, the foreign shareholder has *de facto* control. But the company will be deemed Canadian-controlled for limited purposes.

Such a company is free to make almost any acquisition without having to file an application for review. However, its investment privileges are constrained in three ways:

(1) The purchase and establishment of cultural businesses are subject to the same rules that apply to all non-Canadians. In other words, the government can still review such investments.

(2) Investment Canada must be *notified* of all investments. (This is because a company with deemed Canadian status is only exempted from the review provisions of the Act.)

(3) Its special Canadian status exists for only two years, although renewals can be obtained.

In addition, a company which qualifies for the Imasco exemption is not deemed to be a Canadian with respect to shares that it holds in other companies. Consequently, its subsidiaries are considered to be owned by non-Canadians. This prevents these subsidiaries from taking advantage of the special Canadian status accorded to their parent.[41]

The decision not to extend any special status to a chain of companies was evidently made for policy reasons. It means that a company which is a deemed Canadian under the Imasco exemption cannot avoid the review process if it uses one of its subsidiaries to buy a Canadian business.

However, the same ultimate result can be achieved and Canada's review process circumvented if the parent company (that is deemed to be a Canadian) makes the purchase itself and then, through a corporate reorganization, transfers the Canadian business to a foreign subsidiary. This is because corporate reorganizations that involve no change in the ultimate controller of a Canadian business have been exempted from the Act.

To qualify for this special status, it is not sufficient for the company to self-comply. Instead, the company must satisfy the minister.

---

[41] The definition of "Canadian" makes no reference to companies that qualify for the Imasco exemption. Why? Because such companies *are* controlled in fact by non-Canadians. Since the Canadian/non-Canadian status of a subsidiary under the rules in subs. 26(1) is determined by looking at its parent (not through its parent to the shareholders), and since a foreign-controlled parent company which has qualified as a deemed Canadian under the Imasco exemption is not a "Canadian" for the purpose of the status rules set out in subs. 26(1), the subsidiaries of such parent companies are themselves "non-Canadians".

Initially, not much information need be submitted. The Act allows the minister to accept, as proof, a letter signed by all the directors of the corporation, asserting that the facts set out in the eight-pronged test exist. This letter need merely recite the factors laid out in subsection 26(3) and that the board exercises its power autonomously. If not satisfied, the minister may then make further inquiries.

Company presidents should note that paragraph 26(3)(e), which states that the board of directors must be able to exercise autonomy on a day-to-day basis, does not preclude consultation with the foreign shareholder/controller or interlocking directorships. Neither does it prevent the foreign controller from providing information to assist the Canadian board of directors in making its decision.

What it does mean is that the foreign controller cannot, between shareholders' meetings, give orders to the Canadian board of directors. In addition, the foreign controller cannot openly attempt to influence directors' decisions.[42]

To enable its Canadian associate to qualify for the exemption, a foreign controller will, therefore, need to repose considerable confidence in the directors of its Canadian company. That should not pose a problem, since most directors keep in mind who elected them.

A corporation which has satisfied the minister that it qualifies will receive a letter from the minister stating it is deemed to be a Canadian. This presumption of Canadian status is good for two years, unless substantial changes in the facts occur in the meantime. A minor variation, such as death of a Canadian director temporarily reducing the percentage of Canadian directors below the 80% level, is contemplated by subsection 26(5) and will not jeopardize the company's status.

One common concern of solicitors is fluctuations in ownership levels. Initially, for a company to receive deemed Canadian status, Canadians must own a majority of the voting stock. But what if, two months later, the Canadian ownership level has dropped to 49%? Will that nullify the company's deemed Canadian status?

It might do so. Solicitors should ask for an acknowledgement from the minister that minor fluctuations in ownership, down to a specified level, such as 49%, will not impair the company's status.

(i) Legislative History

Some lawyers ask, rather irritably, why so many conditions must be met before a company can qualify for the Imasco exemption. Here is what the drafters were probably thinking about:

---

[42] There is, however, a fine line between an order and a suggestion.

1. Companies incorporated in Canada are subject to Canadian laws.

2. Publicly traded companies must abide by the disclosure requirements of provincial securities commissions and stock exchanges. This provides a window on their ownership levels and how decisions are made.

3. Majority Canadian ownership means that non-Canadians do not have *de jure* control.

4. A high percentage of Canadians on the board of directors ensures that Canadians are, in one sense, making management decisions.

5. A predominance of Canadians at senior management levels means that the daily operations of the company are handled by Canadians. When most of the senior managers of a company are Canadians, and Canadians own a significant number of shares, Canadian interests may also be given more weight in the decision-making process.

Why is subsection 26(3) called the Imasco exemption? Because that company has been the most high-profile beneficiary[43] of the exemption.

The story goes back several years. Paul Pare, president of Imasco at the time the *Investment Canada Act* was being debated in Parliament, was a vociferous critic of Canada's Foreign Investment Review Agency. Worse still, Pare was fond of reporters. In his eyes, the negotiations that took place between foreign companies and the Canadian government were like playing "tennis in a thick fog, against an opponent who moved the lines as well as the net".[44] One government minister, in particular, aroused his ire. "The last thing we want to do is tell Herb Gray that he is a horse's 'whatever' publicly. We don't mind saying so privately."[45]

According to Paul Pare, Imasco was a "casualty of FIRA" (although most of Imasco's takeovers had been approved). He claimed that a

---

[43] Paul Pare, the president of Imasco, told reporters in March 1985 that the company was lobbying for an exemption from any review of its investments. Imasco is a Canadian company, Pare maintained, and should be allowed to grow like other Canadian companies. "Imasco Seeks Wider Investment Limits", *The Gazette*, Mar. 7, 1985, p. D8.

[44] Address to the Canadian Bar Association, Panel Discussion on FIRA, Aug. 26, 1980.

[45] Quoted by P. Best. "Why Imasco Is Getting Turned off with Canada", *Financial Post*, Aug. 14, 1982, p. 1 at 2.

substantial portion of his company's earnings were being channelled into the U.S.A. because of FIRA.[46]

Under FIRA, Imasco was considered to be foreign-controlled, although Canadians owned a majority of the shares, because B.A.T. Industries p.l.c. ("BAT") in Great Britain owned 43%. BAT, the world's largest tobacco company, did not have a single representative on Imasco's board. Moreover, all of Imasco's board members (with one exception) were Canadians and had provided FIRA with affidavits stating that they acted independently. However, because of BAT's large interest, FIRA's minister, the Honourable Herb Gray, believed that BAT was in a position to exercise control over Imasco.

The Imasco exemption is an exception to the control in fact test which otherwise governs publicly traded corporations. It may act as an incentive to a few foreign-controlled companies to "Canadianize", by achieving a higher degree of Canadian participation and autonomy. That is the hope of the government.[47]

6. Miscellaneous Provisions

Before attempting to apply the status rules, an investor should examine five miscellaneous provisions. The most important is the look-through principle. This principle explains how corporations (and other entities) are treated when they are owned by partnerships, joint ventures, and beneficiary-controlled trusts. The investor should also study how the legislation handles bearer shares, small shareholdings, and shares with fractional votes. But first, what is meant by ownership must be understood.

(a) Ownership Means Beneficial Ownership

The word "own" in the *IC Act* means beneficial ownership.[48] A registered holder of shares is not necessarily the beneficial owner, and

---

[46] R. Gibbens, "Imasco Proposal Seeks Exemption from FIRA Restrictions", *The Globe & Mail*, Feb. 12, 1982, p. B-12; "FIRA Not Hindering Firm's Growth, Gray Says", letter to the editor, *The Globe and Mail*, Aug. 25, 1982, p. 7; R. Gibbens, "Imasco Chief Bitterly Disappointed Company Not Exempted from FIRA", *The Globe and Mail*, Aug. 6, 1982, p. B3.

[47] Hon. Sinclair Stevens, House of Commons, *Minutes of the Standing Committee on Regional Development*, April 15, 1985, Issue No. 20, p. 15.

[48] See s. 3. The beneficial owners are the first Canadians or non-Canadians who are found to own an interest on their own account. Keep in mind the look-through principle (which does not apply to corporations).

unless the presumption of small holdings in subsection 27(d) can be applied, it is a mistake to assume otherwise.

A stockbroker who holds shares on behalf of a client is not the owner of the shares. Neither is a depository like Cede & Co., which holds title to shares on behalf of banks and brokers. This may give rise to complex tracing problems and is one of the disadvantages of substituting an ownership for a *de facto* control test.

Some counsel who are trying to determine the status of a corporation write to the nominee shareholders. Their letters state that there is no need to reveal the identity of the beneficial owners, merely the percentage of shares beneficially owned by Canadians and non-Canadians. Unfortunately, the nominee shareholder may not know whether the beneficiaries are "Canadian" or may not understand the status rules and the "look-through principle".

How does one determine beneficial ownership? The key is to identify the "person" who is entitled to receive the profit or advantage resulting from ownership of voting shares. That "person" may be an individual, government, corporation or a trustee-controlled trust. (See subsection 26(2)).

(b) Corporations Controlled by Partnerships, Trusts or Joint Ventures

Beneficiary-controlled trusts, partnerships and joint ventures are excluded from the definition of the term "person". When determining the status of a corporation owned by a (beneficiary-controlled) trust, partnership or joint venture, the trust, partnership or joint venture is ignored and the beneficiaries, partners, or joint venturers are treated as the owners of the shares. This is the "look-through principle", found in subsection 27(a):

> where voting interests of an entity are owned by a *partnership*, a trust, other than a trust described in subsection 26(2), or a joint venture, those voting interests are deemed to be owned *by the partners*, beneficiaries or members of the joint venture, as the case may be, in the same proportion as their respective ownership interests in the assets of the partnership, trust or joint venture. [Emphasis added.]

Similarly, the concept of a "voting group" does not include trusts controlled by the beneficiaries, partnerships, or joint ventures. Only "persons" (an "individual, a government or an agency thereof, a corporation" or a trustee-controlled trust") may be part of a voting group.

One point must be stressed. The look-through principle does not determine the status of a partnership, trust or joint venture. The rules in section 26 do that. Instead, the look-through principle is applied when determining the status of an entity whose voting interests are owned by a partnership, trust or joint venture.

What if all the shareholders of a company are Canadian-controlled partnerships?[49] The same principle still applies. The Canadian or non-Canadian status of the corporation is ascertained not from the status of the partnerships, but from the status of the partners, after calculating in what proportion they hold their ownership interests.[50]

The following three illustrations depict how the look-through principle operates in practice.

EXAMPLE 1 (Corporate Chains):

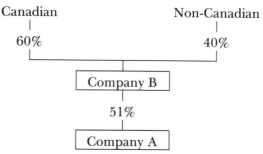

Company B is Canadian-controlled (Rule 1). Because Company B owns a majority of the voting shares of Company A, Rule 1 deems Company A to be Canadian-controlled. This example emphasizes an important point: the look-through principle does not apply to corporations in a chain of ownership.

This exclusion of corporations from the look-through principle may result in *real* Canadian ownership levels being considerably less than *apparent* Canadian ownership levels. In the previous example, Company A has an apparent ownership level of 51%, and a real ownership level of (60% x 51%) or 30.6%. Why is the corporate veil not "looked through" in order to get the true figures?

Cost is the reason. The potential for dilution of apparent ownership levels had to be balanced against the administrative costs of ascertaining the identity and nationality of shareholders in order to determine real Canadian ownership levels. (Such calculations are easier in the case of partnerships or joint ventures, because fewer participants are involved.)

---

[49] Canadian-controlled as determined by the rules in s. 26.

[50] The look-through principle does not apply to a trustee-controlled trust.

EXAMPLE 2: Beer Company is controlled by a partnership with a 51% interest. Is Beer Company Canadian-controlled?

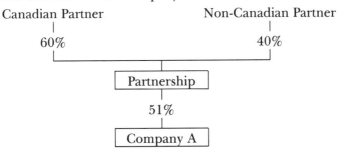

Because of the look-through principle, the Canadian partner is deemed to own 30.6% (that is, 60% × 51%) of Beer Company. The non-Canadian owns 20.4%. However, to ascertain if Beer Company is controlled by Canadians, information about the other shareholders would have to be obtained.[51]

EXAMPLE 3: Tobacco Company is controlled by three partnerships. The first two partnerships have "Canadian status" because 51% of their voting interests are owned by a Canadian. The other partnership is owned by Dutch citizens residing in Holland. Pursuant to a tight shareholders' agreement, the three partnerships must vote together on all issues and submit any disputes to binding arbitration. Is Tobacco Company Canadian-controlled?

This is the type of fact situation that unhinges lawyers and their insurance companies. One solicitor's response was that the three partnerships formed a voting group, on account of the tight shareholders' agreement. Since two of the partnerships were Canadian-controlled,

---

[51] If the owners of companies are hidden behind layers of entities and nominees, these calculations may be costly and difficult. However, the "look-through principle" is generous in one respect, in comparison with the *FIR Act*. Under the *FIR Act*, the presence of one foreigner ("non-eligible person") among the group controlling a partnership might have affected the partnership's status. In example 2, both the partnership and Company A might have been regarded by FIRA as being controlled by a group, one member of which was a foreigner. If so, both would have been "foreign-controlled".

owned (in total) a majority of Tobacco Company's shares, and were also members of a voting group, the solicitor concluded on the basis of Rule 2 (paragraph 26(1)(a) of the Act) that Tobacco Company was also Canadian-controlled. The solicitor then advised the president of the company that it could buy any business in Canada without Canadian government approval.

Unfortunately, this solicitor had forgotten something. Although a partnership is an "entity", it is not a "person". Only "persons" can be members of a voting group.

So, in law, although the partnerships voted together, there was no voting group! Because of the look-through principle, the three partnerships were deemed not to own any shares. Instead, the shares of the company were deemed to be owned by the individual partners in the same proportion as their ownership interests in the partnership assets. This meant that Canadians were deemed to own a mere 34% (51% x 66%) of Tobacco Company's shares; and the company was non-Canadian controlled under Rule 7 (paragraph 26(1)(d)). Therefore, Ottawa's approval was necessary before the company could make any major takeover.

(c) Bearer Shares[52]

The Act deems bearer shares to be owned by non-Canadians, unless the contrary can be established. A few solicitors may think: "That's odd! Canadian corporations can't issue bearer shares."

That is correct. Corporations incorporated under the *Ontario Business Corporations Act* and the federal *Canada Business Corporations Act* are required to issue shares in registered form. However, some foreign companies (such as those incorporated in the Netherlands Antilles) are allowed to issues shares in bearer form.

(d) The Presumption Regarding Small Holdings[53]

Some companies have hundreds of small shareholders. This can create a major headache for a solicitor trying to determine nationality of ownership.

---

[52] *IC Act*, subs.27(c). This "bearer share" provision may prove important when determining the status of a partnership where one of the partners is a foreign corporation.

[53] *IC Act*, subs. 27(d).

One labour-saving device in the Act may come to the rescue. Found in subsection 27(d), it allows the ownership of interests below 1% to be determined from the postal addresses that appear on the shareholders' list.

Canadian institutions are substantial minority shareholders in many companies. Sometimes it takes only a brief examination of the shareholders' list to establish that there are enough shareholders with small holdings and Canadian addresses to raise the total stake of Canadians to 51%.

However, this "presumption regarding small holdings" is circumscribed in one respect. It is restricted to the shareholdings of *individuals*. The presumption cannot be used if small numbers of shares are registered in the names of Canadian stockbrokerage firms or other corporations.[54]

Another point to note is that shareholders' addresses of record do not, *per se*, provide any information about the Canadian/non-Canadian status of a corporation. That status must be determined according to the rules laid out in the Act.

(e) Shares with Multiple/Fractional Votes

There are a few companies with shares that carry several votes each. A hypothetical example is publicly traded Contran Corp. Its Class A and Class B shares entitle holders to one and ten votes respectively. What impact does this have on Contran Corp's control status? Each of its Class B multiple voting shares is treated like ten voting shares.

This principle is set out in subsection 30(2). Its purpose is to avoid circumvention of the Act through the issuance of different classes of shares carrying unequal voting rights.

7. Partnerships, Trusts and Joint Ventures

The same section of the *IC Act* which sets out the status rules for corporations also governs trusts, partnerships and joint ventures. All of these investment vehicles are grouped together because the drafters

---

[54] This is because the address of an individual usually indicates the individual's nationality, but the address of a corporation says nothing about who owns the corporation. *Investment Canada Act: Briefing Document* (undated, released under the *Access To Information Act*), p. 58.

wanted to treat unincorporated entities in the same manner as corporations.[55]

Before seeking to determine the status of a partnership, trust or joint venture, investors should first read the definition of "voting interest" and "joint venture". If they are dealing with trusts, investors must distinguish between two types: trusts controlled by the beneficiaries, and trusts controlled by the trustees.

(a) Voting Interests

The term "voting interest", when applied to a partnership, trust or joint venture, means: "an ownership interest in the assets thereof that entitles the owner to receive a share of the *profits* and to share in the *assets* on dissolution."[56] [Emphasis added.]

It is not necessary that such an ownership interest be coupled with any voting power. The only question one need ask is: does the holder of an interest in a partnership, trust or joint venture have a right to share both in the profits and in the assets on dissolution? If so, that person has a voting interest. In turn, this means that partners, joint venturers and beneficiaries, who own voting interests and who act together on a continuing basis, constitute a voting group, even if they have no right to vote.

One important fact to remember is that if only one requirement of the definition of "voting interest" is met, the interest holder is not counted when ascertaining whether an entity is Canadian. Also, since ownership means beneficial ownership, the Act cannot be evaded by having a compliant Canadian act as a nominee.

(b) Trusts

Trusts create special problems for legislation drafters, because trusts can easily be used to skirt laws. In many real estate and energy development trusts, the trustee is often just a bare trustee who carries out the wishes of the beneficiaries and holds legal title on their behalf. For tax,

---

[55] Ibid., at pp. 4 and 6. However, corporations and unincorporated entities are not treated completely alike. For instance, the 50:50 ownership rule in subs. 26(6) applies only to corporations. The status of joint ventures and partnerships which are equally owned by two persons is determined under a different rule (i.e., para. 26(1)(d)).

[56] *IC Act*, s. 3. How does one calculate the "voting interest" of a foreign investor who has different percentage interests in the profits and assets of a joint venture (e.g., if the investor has a 45% share in the profits and a 10% share in the assets)? The Act does not say.

liability and secrecy reasons, title to a real estate project may be registered in the name of the trustee, but the trustee will have no authority to act independently. Conversely, there are certain family trusts which are created by rich Canadians to separate the beneficial and legal ownership of their fortunes and which purport to grant to the trustees uncontrolled authority over the administration of the trust property.

In the *IC Act*, Parliament has recognized two categories of trusts: those controlled by the beneficiaries, and those controlled by the trustees. Special rules have been created for trustee-controlled trusts. These will be dealt with later.

The other category of trusts, beneficiary-controlled trusts, are governed by the same rules as partnerships and joint ventures. The trust is pierced, and its status is determined by the Canadian or non-Canadian status of those who hold the voting interests (the beneficiaries). When determining the status of such trusts, solicitors should keep in mind that the interests of an income beneficiary or a capital beneficiary are not recognized in the *IC Act*. To have a "voting interest", a beneficiary must have a right to *both* income *and* a share of the assets on the dissolution of the trust. Thus, a trust can be Canadian even though an American has a right to most of the income.

(c) Partnerships

Partnerships are another type of entity recognized in the *IC Act*. The term "partnership", however, is not defined. To discover what it means, investors must look at the definition in provincial partnership Acts. Then they must read the case law which has narrowed these definitions.

In Ontario, as in the other common law provinces, a partnership is defined as: "the relationship that subsists between persons carrying on a business in common with a view to profit."[57] From this definition it is clear that two elements are essential: an intention to make a profit, and a common enterprise.

The partnerships Acts also state that co-ownership of property (an arrangement whereby two or more people own property jointly as tenants-in-common or joint tenants) does not by itself create a partnership. On the other hand, the sharing of profits is *prima facie* evidence of a partnership.[58] If two foreign investors associate to make an investment, but treat their undivided interest in the Canadian assets as

---

[57] *Partnership Act*, R.S.O. 1980, c. 370, s. 2.

[58] Ibid., s. 3.

separate property, and do not share profits or losses (just certain defined expenses), they are not partners.[59]

(d) Joint Ventures

When individuals, corporations, partnerships or trusts are making an acquisition, or establishing a business, two questions must always be asked:

1. Does a joint venture exist?
2. If so, does it have "Canadian" or "non-Canadian" status?

Investors should be wary of lurking joint ventures because the concept was intended to be a legal net or catch-all.[60] It was placed in the Act to ensure that business organizations and associations which do not constitute a corporation, trust, or partnership are caught by the legislation. Two or more non-Canadians, who have no formal agreement among themselves and who are each acquiring a minority interest in a Canadian business, may be distressed to discover that they may constitute a joint venture and that a transaction which would otherwise escape the Act is caught.

Unfortunately, the definition of a joint venture is confusing. Some legal experts think it may be flawed. The Act defines it this way:

> "joint venture" means an association of two or more persons or entities, where the relationship among those associated persons or entities does not, under the laws in force in Canada, constitute a corporation, a partnership or a trust and where, in the case of an investment to which this Act applies, all the undivided ownership interests in the assets of the Canadian business or in the voting interests of the entity that is the subject of the investment are or will be owned by all the persons or entities that are so associated;[61]

When used to determine the Canadian/non-Canadian status of a company, this definition performs as intended. Only one precondition need be present for a joint venture among several shareholders to exist, namely, an association. It is not necessary that an agreement be entered into or that the participants in the joint venture vote together.

The real problem arises if a Canadian business is being acquired. In such circumstances, it becomes more difficult to determine if the

---

[59] *Robert Porter & Sons Ltd. v. Armstrong*, [1926] S.C.R. 328.

[60] *Investment Canada Act: Briefing Document* (undated, released under the *Access To Information Act*), p. 8: A joint venture "is an all-embracing term for every association or unincorporated group, whether or not a legal entity, other than a corporation, partnership or trust as defined under Canadian law".

[61] *IC Act*, s. 3.

investors constitute a joint venture because then the definition has two prongs.

The first prong, the prerequisite for an "association", is easily met. A common purpose on the part of two or more investors, such as an intent to invest in a company, is probably sufficient by itself to give rise to such an association.

In addition, this association need only exist for a fleeting moment in time—when the deal closes. It is of no importance if, a few days later, the investors are fighting like cats and dogs.

The second prong of the definition, the requirement for un-divided ownership in assets or shares, is not so easily satisfied. Because of muddled wording in this portion of the definition, and to the delight of the Bay Street legal fraternity, a joint venture may not always be created in law when two or more parties come together to purchase a Canadian business or establish a new business. However, this is a cloudy area, about which many legal practitioners disagree.

Some solicitors have suggested that a joint venture will never exist unless each joint venturer directly owns an undivided ownership interest in each asset or share that is being acquired and, in addition, the joint venture owns 100% of the assets or shares of the business that is the target of the investment. If three joint venturers are purchasing a com-pany, there must be common or joint ownership of all the shares. Needless to say, such a narrow interpretation would create a large loop-hole. Many transactions by groups of investors would not be caught.

If a joint venture agreement has been executed for the purpose of making an investment in a company, there should be little difficulty in finding that a "joint venture" also exists within the meaning of the *IC Act*. There will be an association: the participants will own all the shares that are being purchased (that is, "the subject of investment"), although the joint venture itself may own less than all of the shares of the business; and each joint venturer will usually have an undivided ownership interest in whatever the joint venture owns in the percent-age that is set out in the joint venture agreement. (Many joint venture agreements used for the purchase of commercial property state that the participants will own the project as tenants-in-common in the same proportion as their respective ownership interests.)

When there is no formal joint venture agreement, the situation is more complex. There may be a common purchase agreement. Some-times there may be only an oral agreement to invest together in the same business. In such circumstances, it is easy to find the requisite association. But will the courts be imaginative enough to conclude that the parties have an undivided interest in the shares each is purchasing? If not, the concept of a partnership may have to be stretched to catch some unincorporated associations that would otherwise escape.[62]

The concept of a joint venture replaces the notion of a group found in the old *FIR Act*. Because of the reference to Canadian laws in the definition, a (limited) partnership, corporation or trust in a foreign jurisdiction will be treated as a joint venture for Investment Canada purposes unless Canadian law also recognizes the association as being a (limited) partnership, corporation or trust.

Unfortunately for solicitors, this creates another concern. Would the offshore limited partnership, which wants to buy a Canadian business, be considered a limited partnership under Canadian laws as well? If not, is it a "joint venture"?

8. The Status Rules for Partnerships, Trusts and Joint Ventures

The status of partnerships, trusts and joint ventures are determined by rules similar to those governing corporations. These rules must be read in sequence.

RULE 1:   A partnership, trust or joint venture is Canadian-controlled if a Canadian owns a majority of the voting interests.

COMMENT: This rule has important implications for a 50:50 joint venture between a Canadian and a foreign business person.

EXAMPLE: Under a joint venture agreement between a Canadian company and a Romanian state company, decisions will be made by a management committee to which each party will appoint the same number of representations. How can the joint venture be rendered Canadian-controlled?

The answer is simply to give the Canadian company a 50.1% equity interest. Indeed, because of the definition of "voting interests", the joint venture will still be Canadian-controlled even if the Romanian company is granted all of the voting rights at management committee meetings!

---

[62] For a discussion of the distinction between a partnership and a joint venture, see David Birnie, "Partnership, Syndicate and Joint Venture: What's the Difference?", in *Report of Proceedings of the Thirty-third Tax Conference*, (Toronto: Canadian Tax Foundation, 1982), p. 182.

RULE 2:   A partnership, trust or joint venture is Canadian-controlled if there exists a "voting group", and Canadian members of the voting group own a majority of the "voting interests" in the partnership, trust or joint venture. (paragraph 26(1)(a))

COMMENT: Within a partnership of many members, it may be possible to find some Canadians who "by contract . . . personal relationship . . . or otherwise" may be expected to act together on a continuing basis. If so, they form a voting group.

Note that the definition of a voting group is restricted to "persons". A person is defined to include "an individual, a government or an agency thereof or a corporation" and a trustee-controlled trust. The definition makes no mention of partnerships.[63] Consequently, if a joint venture is composed in part of one or more partnerships, a solicitor who is attempting to ascertain that joint venture's status must look through the partnership and find a "person". The solicitor should then decide whether that "person" is part of a voting group.

RULE 3:   A partnership, trust or joint venture is not Canadian-controlled if one non-Canadian owns a majority of the voting interests. (paragraph 26(1)(b))

RULE 4:   A partnership, trust or joint venture is not Canadian-controlled if:

(i) there is a voting group

(ii) the non-Canadian in that voting group owns a majority of the voting interests in the partnership, trust or joint venture. (paragraph 26(1)(b))

RULE 5:   A partnership, trust or joint venture will be Canadian-controlled if:

(a) a majority of the voting interests are owned by Canadians, and

(b) the partnership, trust or joint venture is not controlled in fact through the ownership of its voting interests:

(i) by a non-Canadian, or

---

[63] Section 3 defines the word "person"; subs. 27(b) states that "a trust described in subs. 26(2) is deemed to be a person for the purpose of the definition of a 'voting group' in s. 3".

When evaluating the status of partnerships, trusts and joint ventures solicitors should also keep in mind the look-through principle. This principle, discussed previously, springs into operation when (for instance) a partnership is owned by another partnership, trust or joint venture.

(ii) by a non-Canadian dominated voting group in which a non-Canadian or two or more non-Canadians own one-half (50%) or more of the total voting interests owned by the group in the partnership, trust or joint venture. ("a majority non-Canadian voting group") (paragraph 26(1)(c))

COMMENT: Rule 5 is complex. To understand it, imagine a large partnership in which Canadians own a majority of the partnership interests. If no voting group exists and the partnership is not controlled in fact by a foreigner, the partnership will be Canadian-controlled.

On the other hand, if some of the members of a partnership are related by blood and marriage, or are associated together in other business ventures, they may form a "voting group". If non-Canadians dominate this voting group, because they own a majority of the voting group's interest in the partnership, it must be established that this voting group does not exercise *de facto* control over the partnership. Otherwise, the partnership is foreign-controlled. Similarly, if *de facto* control over the partnership is exercised by a voting group of two people, which is deadlocked because each owns 50% of the voting group's interest in the partnership, the partnership will not be Canadian-controlled if one of the members of the voting group is a non-Canadian.

RULE 6:   A partnership, trust or joint venture will be presumed not to be Canadian-controlled if less than a majority of the "voting interests" are owned by Canadians. However, this presumption can be rebutted. The partnership, trust or joint venture will be Canadian-controlled if it can be established that:

(i) one Canadian exercises *de facto* control through the ownership of voting interests, or

(ii) a voting group exercises *de facto* control (through the ownership of voting interests) and Canadians dominate the voting group through their ownership of a majority of the voting group's interest. ("a majority Canadian voting group") (paragraph 26(1)(d))

COMMENT: A joint venture in which Canadians have a minority interest and which is controlled by a "voting group" made up mostly of Soviet citizens is Soviet-controlled. But if this voting group has a Canadian member, who holds a majority position *within* the voting group, the joint venture suddenly becomes Canadian-controlled.

EXAMPLE (An Accounting Firm): A partnership of accountants is composed of twenty partners. However, the partnership is in fact controlled by a voting group made up of five senior partners who together hold a total of 40% of the partnership interests. If two of those senior partners are Canadians and together own 25% of the partnership interests, these two Canadians own a majority (62.5%) of the group's 40% interest in the partnership. Accordingly, the test in the second part of Rule 6 has been met.

It may seem difficult to prove that five partners form a voting group which controls a large partnership. The history of voting patterns at partnership meetings would provide some evidence.

EXAMPLE (The 50:50 Partnership): Sovinflot, a Soviet company, enters into a partnership with a Canadian company. Each company has an equal interest. Is the partnership Canadian?

The partnership would be presumed to be controlled in the U.S.S.R. (The chance of rebutting that presumption is minimal.)

(a) Widely-Held Voting Interests

Sometimes the voting interests of a general partnership or joint venture are widely held and a management committee runs all operations. Nonetheless, for Investment Canada purposes, it is pointless to argue that the partners or joint venturers are not in control.

The *IC Act* recognizes that control may lie elsewhere than among the holders of voting interests. But that recognition is limited to just three types of business organizations: limited partnerships, trusts and corporations.

(b) Limited Partnerships

Most statutes governing limited partnerships state that a limited partner loses his or her limited liability if he or she participates in control. The *IC Act* operates on a different premise. It treats limited partners and general partners in the same fashion when ascertaining the locus of control.

This is one consequence of the statute's preoccupation with ownership interests. Because both limited partners and general partners can share in assets and profits, they both have a voting interest, which is the statutory basis for determining control. The other terms in the limited partnership agreement do not matter.

Treating general and limited partners equally makes most sense when there is only one or two limited partners. Such arrangements can be seen in the resource sector. A limited partner who holds all of the units in such a limited partnership will probably be pulling the strings behind the scenes. In such cases, equity ownership and effective control coincide.

The same rationale does not apply when partnership interests are widely held. But there is another consideration.

Many limited partnership agreements drafted by U.S. lawyers contain voting rights (apparently included on the assumption that the limited partners will not lose their limited liability). Limited partners under these agreements may have the right to approve borrowings, contracts, expenditures and the transfer of assets in the ordinary course of business. Alternatively, the limited partners may elect an "advisory board", which "supervises" the general partner by approving or vetoing certain decisions. In addition, the statutes of a few American states permit limited partners to "advise" the general partner and to have the right, by vote, to remove the general partner.[64] Such powers eliminate most of the distinctions between limited and general partners.

The first six rules governing the status of partnerships, also apply to limited partnerships. For example, if a single foreigner owns a majority of the partnership units, the limited partnership will be non-Canadian controlled, even if the general partner is a Canadian.[65]

The reverse is true as well. Kohlberg Kravis Roberts & Co. ("KKR") raises its pool of capital for future leveraged buy-outs through limited partnerships of institutional investors. KKR is the general partner and has complete authority to use the money. Nevertheless, because KKR's financial contribution is often less than 1%, the status of the limited partnerships will depend upon the status of the limited partners (and will be Canadian if the institutional investors are Canadians).

There is a special rule reserved for limited partnerships which are widely-held and not controlled by the partners.

RULE 7:   If less than a majority of the partnership interests are owned by Canadians, and there is no control in fact by the partners (through the ownership of their voting interests) the limited partnership is presumed *not* to be Canadian-controlled. However, if the general partner is a Canadian,

---

[64] Don Augustine *et al.*, "The Liability of Limited Partners Having Certain Statutory Voting Rights Affecting The Basic Structure of the Partnership", *The Business Lawyer* (1976), p. 2087.

[65] Para. 26(1)(b). Under the *FIR Act*, the general partner was usually considered to be in control. Consequently, the status of a limited partnership depended upon who controlled the general partner.

this presumption can be rebutted. (subparagraph 26(1)(d)(ii))

COMMENT: When less than 50% of the units of a limited partnership are held by Canadians (and the other rules in section 26 do not apply), the limited partnership is presumed to be controlled by foreigners. However, the limited partnership can qualify as a Canadian if:

(1) the unit holders are not in control, and

(2) the general partner is a Canadian or a Canadian-controlled company. (If there are three general partners, two thirds must be Canadian).

There is no counterpart to Rule 7 for general partnerships or joint ventures. No matter how widely held their interests may be, the *IC Act* does not recognize that control may reside elsewhere than among the general partners or joint venturers.

Rule 7 represents yet another attempt by the drafters of the Act to treat all entities like corporations.[66] Both limited partnerships and corporations in which foreigners have a majority interest, and which are not controlled through voting interests, are Canadian-controlled if two thirds of the general partners or two thirds of the directors, respectively, are Canadians.

(c) Trusts

There are two different kinds of trusts recognized in the *IC Act*: beneficiary-controlled trusts and trustee-controlled trusts. Most trusts are beneficiary-controlled, and their status is determined by looking at the status of the beneficiaries. Trustee-controlled trusts are the other kind of trust. A special rule exists just for them.

RULE 8: Where it can be established that a trust is not controlled in fact through the ownership of its voting interests . . . the trust is a Canadian-controlled entity where two thirds of its trustees are Canadians. (subsection 26(2))

COMMENT: This is a useful provision when foreigners are the beneficiaries of a trust, but do not control it. If two thirds of the trustees are Canadians, the trust itself is a Canadian.

What kinds of trust are controlled by the trustees? Pension plan trusts are one example. Others are trusts for people (such as grandchildren) who have not yet been born, or trusts where beneficiaries do

---

[66] Under the *FIR Act*, corporations and partnerships were treated differently.

exist but none are fully entitled because none of the beneficiaries have reached the age of majority or have rights without contingencies.[67]

One reason why the Act recognizes two categories of trusts is because participants in pension plan trusts do not have a voting interest as that term is defined in the Act. These participants, in other words, do not have beneficial ownership interests that entitle them to receive a share of the profits of the pension plan and to share in the assets on its dissolution. This is because the law restricts the ability of employees to treat, as their own property, contributions made by themselves or their employer to a pension fund. For instance, pension benefits cannot be assigned[68], and a deferred life annuity cannot be surrendered during the lifetime of the employee.[69] What the employee does have is the right to receive periodic payments upon retirement, or to receive a repayment of his contributions. Neither of these rights fully coincides with the definition of "voting interest".

A second reason for having a special category for trustee-controlled trusts centres around problems of calculation. If participants in pension funds were considered to have "voting interests", it would be difficult to determine what percentage interest they owned in the assets of the pension fund.

(d) Family Trusts

There may be disputes between solicitors for the wealthy and the Canadian government over whether certain family trusts are controlled by the trustees or the beneficiaries. (Family trusts are trusts, the majority of the capital of which is not to be delivered to the beneficiaries until the death of the settlor, and most or all of the beneficiaries of which are related to the settlor. Often the settlor is the trustee.)

Family trusts are frequently set up by Canadian business people who want to put their control block of company shares in a trust for their children. Hundreds of privately held companies are currently owned in this fashion, as is The Seagram Company Ltd. (whose major shareholders are family trusts). As the children who are the beneficiaries of these trusts grow older, some may leave Canada. If the Canadian business people can successfully argue that they control the trusts in their capacity as trustees, then the trusts and the companies the trusts control will remain Canadian-controlled.

---

[67] In brief, subs. 26(2) allows the status of the trustees to be the determining factor when there are no beneficiaries in being or none without contingencies.

[68] *Pension Benefits Standards Act*, R.S.C. 1985, c. P-7, para. 10(1)(b); *Pension Benefits Act*, R.S.O. 1980, c. 373, cl. 20(1)(b).

[69] *Pension Benefits Standards Act*, para. 10(1)(c); *Pension Benefits Act*, subs. 20(2).

Because the scope of inquiry under the *IC Act* is not "control in fact through any means" but is restricted instead to "control in fact *through* the ownership of voting interests", some family trusts may qualify as trustee-controlled. Any determination will depend on what strings the beneficiaries hold over the actions of the trustee and whether they can break the trust. The case for trustee-control will be strongest if the beneficiaries do not have the right in the deed of trust to remove the trustees (or where these rights are severely restricted) and if the trust document provides for the forfeiture of the interest of a beneficiary who seeks to contest the decision of the trustees.

9. Canadianization Through Trusts

When FIRA was in existence, there were a number of attempts to "Canadianize" companies through voting trust arrangements. Under these arrangements, foreign shareholders of Canadian companies transferred their voting rights to Canadians, who were granted the power to vote the shares as they wished. In the view of FIRA, such voting trust arrangements did not shift the locus of control of a Canadian business.[70] Observers believe Investment Canada will probably come to a similar conclusion.

One reason is because a trust can often be revoked by the beneficiaries despite language in the trust agreement to the contrary. There are two legal principles which have an important bearing on this point:

1. Generally, the granting of power of attorney, or the appointing of one person as an agent of another can be revoked, regardless of the express terms of the agreement, unless the donee is a purchaser for value, or the agency was created to secure an interest of the agent. Any "irrevocability" clause merely protects third parties dealing with the donee and does not in any way add to the rights of the donee.[71]

2. In many jurisdictions, the case law allows beneficiaries of a trust who are over the age of majority and of sound mind, and entitled to the whole interest, to combine and break the trust. This is often called the rule in *Saunders v. Vautier*[72] and constitutes a rather potent influence over the behaviour of the trustee.

---

[70] For a discussion of FIRA's treatment of voting trusts, see: K.B. Potter, "Recent Developments in the Application of the Foreign Investment Review Act to the Oil Industry" (1977), *Alta. L. Rev.* 494.

[71] *Re Parks, Canada Permanent Trust Co. v. Parks* (1956), 8 D.L.R. (2d) 155, at 161.

[72] For a discussion of this case, see: D. Water, *The Law of Trusts in Canada*, (Toronto: Carswell, 1974), p. 813.

(a) A Hierarchy of Owners

When solicitors experience difficulties in applying the status rules, these difficulties usually involve companies that are controlled by several different types of entities.

If a corporation is owned by a chain of other corporations, the status rules must be applied in serial fashion to each corporation, all the way up the chain, until one or more individuals or governments is encountered who/which is in control within the meaning of the status rules. When the Canadian business sits at the bottom end of a tree of corporations, partnerships, trusts and joint ventures, some of which form voting groups, the determination of its status is a nightmare for lawyers. When faced with such a tree, solicitors should follow this procedure:

(1) Ascertain the status of those shareholders who are individuals, corporations and subsection 26(2) trusts (i.e., trustee-controlled trusts).

(2) Apply the look-through principle to the partnerships, joint ventures and beneficiary-controlled trusts. Calculate the deemed shareholdings of the partners, joint ventures and beneficiaries.[73]

(3) Examine the relationship between the shareholders. Decide whether there is such a strong degree of association between the shareholders that they constitute a voting group. Keep in mind that a trustee-controlled trust is deemed to be a person for the purpose of the definition of a voting group. Conversely, a partnership, a joint venture, and a trust controlled by its beneficiaries cannot be part of a voting group.

(4) Peruse the status rules seriatim in order to find the one that fits.

Determining the status of a Canadian business would be easier if one could look straight to the top, pick out the *de facto* controller, then ascertain that person's nationality. That was the procedure during FIRA days. Replacing the uncertain and discretionary *de facto* control test of FIRA with a more precise ownership-based test has its advantages, but there are trade-offs, including the need, in complex cases, for many more details about the ownership tree of a Canadian business.

10. Mutual Insurance Companies

An example of how the status rules operate can be illustrated by considering how mutual life insurance companies are treated. These

---

[73] If an entity is owned by a chain of partnerships, trusts or joint ventures, ascend the chain, applying the look-through principle.

are companies that are owned by the policy holders. In the 1950s, Canadian-owned life insurance companies became the target for take-overs by foreign interests. To prevent this, the federal insurance legislation was amended to permit Canadian life insurance companies to buy up their own shares and become mutual companies. As a result, there exist at least 13 Canadian mutual life insurance companies in Canada, such as the Manufacturers Life Insurance Company and Sun Life Assurance Company. A few of these mutual companies have a large number of policyholders residing outside of Canada.

Under the *IC Act*, if the majority of the participating policyholders of a mutual life insurance company are Canadians, and if there is no voting group[74] among the policy holders, or no control by the policy holders, the company is deemed to be Canadian-controlled.[75] If less than the majority of the policy holders are Canadian, the company is deemed to be *non*-Canadian controlled. However, a mutual life company in this position can rebut the presumption by demonstrating that the company is controlled by its board, not its policy holders, and that two thirds of the members of the board are Canadians.

11. Rebuttable Presumptions and the Burden of Proof

The role of rebuttable presumptions in the status rules has been mentioned several times. Investors ask: "What degree of proof is necessary to rebut them?"

Rebuttable presumptions shift the burden of proof. Such burdens of proof are important in the Anglo-American system, which is an adversary system and, therefore, an evidentiary system.

Presumptions were put into the *IC Act* because it is the foreign investor who is in the best position to know the facts.[76] Presumptions force investors to establish the contrary. After that is done, the burden of proof shifts to the government.

Presumptions cannot be rebutted by establishing an equally probable state of affairs. On the other hand, the investor need not prove his

---

[74] A voting group would come into existence if policyholders organized to oppose a management proposal.

[75] Para. 26(1)(c). Most mutual life insurance companies have a majority of Canadian policy holders and should be able to fit within this paragraph.

[76] Presumptions were put into the *FIR Act* and the *Foreign Takeovers Review Act* for the same reason. Their use was subject to impassioned debate. See, for instance, House of Commons, *Minutes of the Standing Committee on Finance, Trade and Economic Affairs*, June 20, 1972, Issue No. 24, pp. 58–60.

or her case beyond a reasonable doubt. Rather, the same test is used as in all civil cases: a preponderance of evidence.[77] The investor must convince the government, and the courts if necessary, that his assertion about where the locus of control lies is more probable than not.

12. Summary of Status Determination Rules in the Investment Canada Act

Corporations Share Ownership Profile	Ownership status	Status vis-à-vis the Act
—majority ownership by one Canadian	Canadian	exempt
—majority ownership by a Canadian voting group	Canadian	exempt
—majority ownership by Canadian plus no control in fact by non-Canadians	Canadian	exempt
—majority ownership Canadian plus publicly traded plus control in fact by non-Canadians	non-Canadian	if subsection 26(3) criteria met, most acquisitions exempt from review
—less than 50% ownership by Canadians	non-Canadian	must comply with Act
unless		
— i) control in fact by one Canadian or a Canadian-dominated voting group	Canadian	exempt
or		
ii) no control in fact with board two-thirds Canadian	Canadian	exempt
—majority ownership by one non-Canadian	non-Canadian	must comply with Act
—majority ownership by a non-Canadian voting group	non-Canadian	must comply with Act
—50:50 split: two shareholders (one Canadian, one non-Canadian)	non-Canadian	must comply with Act

---

[77] *Miller v. Min. of Pensions*, [1947] 2 All E.R. 372, at 374; *Smith v. Smith and Smedman*, [1952] 2 S.C.R. 312, at 331.

CHAPTER 4

THE EXISTENCE OF A CANADIAN BUSINESS

If an investor is a non-Canadian, the next legal issue is whether the non-Canadian will be acquiring or establishing a "Canadian business". "Canadian business" is defined in the Act. If an operation does not qualify, a foreigner can buy it without worrying about Ottawa's reaction.

Students of economic history may notice that the definition of "Canadian business" is tighter than during the FIRA era (1974–85). One result is that slightly fewer "businesses" legally exist. This change reflects a different view of the type of purchases that should be reported to government officials.

1. The Meaning of "Business"

A business is defined to "include any undertaking or enterprise capable of generating revenue and carried on in anticipation of profit".[1] Two components, a revenue-generating *capability* and a profit motive, must therefore be present before a business can legally exist.[2] Also, there must be some minimum level of activity.

This third component (minimal activity) is implicit in the phrase "carried on". A purely passive investment would not qualify as a business.[3]

---

[1] *IC Act*, s. 3.

[2] The word "includes" suggests that an operation may still be a business in the absence of a revenue-generating capability and a profit motive. "Business" was defined in *Smith v. Anderson* (1880), 15 Ch. D. 247, at 258, as "anything which occupies the time and attention and labour of men for the purpose of profit".

[3] *The Investment Canada Act: Briefing Document* (released under the *Access to Information Act*), states on p. 4: "The use of the term 'carried on' indicates that a business involves active operations as opposed to the mere ownership of real or personal property as a passive investment."

Can an enterprise be a business if it has never earned a penny in revenue or made a profit? It certainly can (provided it is *capable* of generating revenue).

(a) Capability of Generating Revenue

An operation that is actively generating revenue obviously satisfies the first component of the definition. As for operations that do not produce revenue, investors will have to predict how widely the courts are likely to stretch the concept of capability. Narrowly interpreted, this concept can be restricted to operations that are able to produce goods or services at the turn of a switch. A business that is closed because of a strike has this type of capability.

But suppose an undertaking is not operational, simply because a supply contract has yet to be negotiated or employees hired. If such essential elements can be obtained in the market-place within a reasonable length of time, is the undertaking "capable of generating revenue"? Such a question will be answered affirmatively under a broad view of "capability".

The minister has adopted the narrower view.[4] According to Interpretation Note No. 4, a business must:

> . . . be actively earning revenue or be in a present position to produce revenue-earning goods or services . . . . If it is in a pre-operational state due to the lack of an essential asset, source of supply or manpower, it is not considered to be a business.

Interpretation notes are not law. However, they are published under the authority of the Act. It is unlikely that a court would allow the minister to blatantly disregard them, particularly if the investor has relied on them to his or her detriment.

Activities that are not "businesses" are market surveys and exploration activities (unless the results will be sold to several clients). These activities are carried on in anticipation of profit, but they are not capable of generating revenue. Such activities are not intended to be caught by the Act because they do not produce goods or services.

Consequently, a foreign company like Sweden's Trelleborg can send its geologists to Canada to explore for minerals without having to

---

[4] Interpretation Note No. 4 states that an undertaking is not capable of generating revenue and, therefore, is not a business if it "is in a pre-operational state due to the lack of an essential asset, source of supply or manpower". This suggests that a non-Canadian would not be purchasing a business if an undertaking is acquired that is "pre-operational" because a source of supply has not been contracted for! Non-Canadians who wish to sail this close to the law should seek the comfort of an opinion from Investment Canada.

tell Investment Canada about its presence. Likewise, a foreign company that is planning to export to Canada need not advise Investment Canada when it hires Canadians to conduct a market survey. (The definition of "business" when FIRA was in existence did not include a "capability of generating revenue" test. Foreign companies that wanted to explore in Canada had to receive prior government permission to establish a "new business".)

(b) Profit Motive

The second prerequisite for the existence of a "business" is that the undertaking be carried on *in anticipation of profit*. It is not essential that a profit be made. An enterprise that is suffering losses is still a business. But there must at least be an intention to make a profit. Obviously, a charity is not a business.[5] Most undertakings of a religious or educational nature will not be businesses either.

One important issue is whether this element of anticipation should be assessed subjectively or by using a more objective standard, such as that of the mythical reasonable man. For example, is the optimism of the wild-eyed gambler sufficient for there to be an "anticipation of profit"? Also, how remote must the profit be?

Unfortunately, lawyers cannot look to case law for the answer. The concept of "anticipation of profit" is unique to the *Investment Canada Act* (and its predecessor), and has not been interpreted by the courts.

Some research projects may meet the profit motive test, but they are unlikely to be considered as "capable of generating revenue".

2. One-Shot Deals

The term "business" and the phrase "carried on" imply some continuity of commercial operations, and not merely an isolated transaction. There are several cases that state this.[6]

Investors who wish to undertake a short-term contract or project in Canada should discuss with Investment Canada where the line is to

---

[5] An enterprise "carried on with a charitable or other non-profit objective" is not a business, according to Interpretation Note No. 4. However, it should not be assumed that the minister will always agree with the views of other governmental departments on what a charitable objective is. A few charities pay big salaries to the administrators who run them, and their "charitable" status may one day be questioned.

[6] See, for example, *Tara Exploration and Development Company Ltd. v. M.N.R.*, 70 D.T.C. 6370.

be drawn. A single three-month contract to assist in the building of a plant is not a business. But if an intention exists to seek additional contracts, the first contract will represent the establishment of a business[7] and a notification should be forwarded to Investment Canada.

3. Defunct Businesses

The purchase of the assets of a defunct business is not subject to the Act. This is because the implicit requirement in the definition that there be some level of activity before a business exists cannot be met. But when does a business become defunct? The day a decision is taken to wind it down? As soon as most employees have left? Or several months later, when there are cobwebs on the windows and the plant floor is cold?

The minister's views are set out in Interpretation Note No. 1. A business which has been permanently closed because of unprofitability is defunct. So is a business which has been permanently abandoned or discontinued—because of depletion of reserves (a mining business) or because of obsolete plant, equipment, technology or product lines.

On the other hand, a business which has been temporarily closed is still a "business". Such a temporary closure may occur because of a labour dispute, shortages of raw material, a short-term decline in demand or temporary financial difficulties. However, in the minister's view, the operation has not lost its basic identity.[8]

4. Bankruptcy and Receivership

Also, a business is not defunct merely because it has gone bankrupt. If the trustee in bankruptcy or a receiver-manager is carrying on the operations with a view to selling the business as a going concern, the business still retains its basic character. However, if the trustee has

---

[7] When the *FIR Act* was in force, an interpretation note was issued stating that work done on a contract of less than 12 months' duration would usually not be considered as constituting the establishment of a new business. This issue is of little importance under the *IC Act*, since few new businesses are (potentially) subject to review.

[8] Interpretation Note No. 1. Investment Canada's Guidelines and Interpretation Notes were published in Part I of the *Canada Gazette* in 1985. They do not have the force of law because they are not statutory instruments (as defined in the *Statutory Instruments Act*). However, the government will be estopped from asserting that an investment is reviewable if an investor relies upon the guidelines and interpretation notes and they are interpreted in a reasonable fashion.

closed down the operations because they can no longer be carried on or sold as a going concern, and is selling the assets on a piecemeal basis,[9] the operations have ceased to be a business.[10]

5. "Canadian Business" Defined

Even if a non-Canadian will be carrying on a business in Canada, or acquiring one, that business may not come within the jurisdiction of the Act for another reason: it may not be a"Canadian business". To be a "Canadian business", an operation must meet a three-pronged test. It must have:

(1) a place of business in Canada,

(2) an individual or individuals in Canada who are employed or self-employed in connection with the business, and

(3) assets in Canada used in carrying on the business.[11]

Note that the concept of a Canadian business is not restricted to businesses owned by Canadians. If the business is located in Canada, it is a Canadian business even though it is owned by foreigners.

In most cases, it is easy to determine if these three requirements are present. However, because intricate problems sometimes arise, each of these requirements is separately considered below.

To be a Canadian business, there must be assets in "Canada". This requirement excludes Canadian-incorporated companies whose only assets are located in the United States. A takeover of such a company is not subject to the *IC Act*.

"Canada" extends beyond the two coasts to include the territorial seas[12] of Canada, the sea-bed, and subsoil, and "all other areas beyond the territorial seas of Canada where Canada has or claims jurisdiction".[13] This broad compass allows Ottawa to claim jurisdiction under the *IC Act* over offshore drilling and sea-bed mining.

---

[9] If a trustee is selling a business in a piecemeal fashion, but a part being sold is capable of being carried on as a separate business, that part may be a "Canadian business". See subs. 31(2).

[10] Interpretation Note No. 1.

[11] S. 3.

[12] The territorial seas of Canada are determined in accordance with the *Territorial Sea and Fishing Zones Act*, R.S.C. 1985, c. T-8.

[13] Without this extended definition, Investment Canada would have no territorial jurisdiction beyond the 12-mile offshore limit. A foreigner who set up a drilling rig on the continental shelf without a coincident business onshore would not even have to file a notification.

A "Canadian business" must have at least one employee or self-employed person. Sole proprietorships and corporations with one employee are therefore *included* in the definition. Companies with assets and a place of business in Canada, but with no employees on their payroll, also qualify as Canadian businesses if they have arranged for people to handle their affairs and perform the usual functions of employees.

These arrangements are "caught" because the definition merely requires that individuals be "employed in connection with the business". Classic examples are companies which obtain their manpower by entering into service contracts with a management corporation, or where parent or sister companies provide the employees.

Because the definition of a Canadian business requires the presence of employees, a company which operates through independent contractors escapes from the purview of the Act. However, if the independent contractor in turn has employees, such a company may still qualify as a Canadian business. This is because the employees of a third party contractor could be regarded as being employed in connection with the business.

The difference between independent contractors, agents and employees is therefore crucial when determining if a Canadian business legally exists. It is a difference that is not easy to decipher, particularly since the category of agent can overlap the other two. In other words, an agent, who has the power to bind the principal contractually, may also be an employee or an independent contractor.

The distinction is always one of control. An employee has a contract *of* service; an independent contractor has a contract *for* service. An independent contractor has his or her own business, but his or her principal tells the contractor what to do. An employee is told not only what to do, but how to do it. In each case, it is necessary to determine what type of relationship exists. Some assistance may be obtained from the many reported cases which deal with this issue, in the context of whether a principal selling in a territory through an agent should be regarded as carrying on business there.

The third element of the definition of "Canadian business" is a place of business in Canada. An office or construction site obviously qualifies. It is possible that a hotel room used by a travelling sales person may also be a place of business.

The Act uses the phrase: "has a place of business in Canada". The wording was deliberately left vague in order to take care of title problems. A non-Canadian certainly "has a place of business" if he or she owns or leases space. But less tenuous relationships are possible as well.

EXAMPLE: A foreign airline has landing rights in major U.S. cities, but none in Canada. The foreign airline wishes to employ a Canadian resident as its representative. She will be responsible for visiting travel agents and trying to encourage Canadian travellers to use the airline. She will not issue tickets, nor will she have any authority to contract on behalf of the foreign airline. Has the foreign airline established a Canadian business?

The foreign airline will have an employee in Canada and probably assets. But there would not appear to be a place of business in Canada, which is the third factor that must be present before a Canadian business can exist. In addition, since the airline's presence in Canada is incidental to its operations elsewhere, and since no revenue will be generated in Canada, no "business" exists.

Sometimes a business may be carried on partly in Canada and partly in another country. A sales distribution business, for example, may earn only 10% of its revenue in Canada. A trucking company may haul cargo between points in the U.S. and Canada. Do these operations constitute a Canadian business? Subsection 31(1) provides the answer. This section states that "a Canadian business shall be deemed to be carried on in Canada notwithstanding that it is carried on partly in Canada and partly in some other place". Clearly, a business need not be carried on entirely in Canada in order to be covered by the Act.[14]

(a) Holding Companies

The incorporation of a holding company in Canada to hold the shares of a foreign operating company does not constitute the establishment of a business in Canada.

EXAMPLE: Sparrow Inc. ("Sparrow"), is a Canadian holding company that is owned by Americans. It hopes to carry out a primary distribution of its shares and obtain a listing on the Vancouver Stock Exchange. The funds from the primary distribution will be used to finance its U.S. operating subsidiary. The only physical evidence of its presence in Canada will be its corporate seal and minute book.

This holding company is not a "Canadian business" because there are no business assets in Canada. It is not even "a business" since there

---

[14] According to one interpretation of the Act, the acquisition of that portion of a Canadian business that is located outside Canada, even if it were to constitute a separate Canadian business in accordance with subs. 31(2), would not fall within the jurisdiction of the Canadian government. This is because the three-pronged definition of a Canadian business would not be met.

is nothing in Canada that is capable of generating revenue. An administrative rationale for excluding Sparrow from the category of "Canadian business" is the difficulty of applying the "net benefit" criteria in the event it is purchased by foreigners. These assessment criteria are directed at goods- and service-producing businesses *in Canada*.

Holding companies which carry on a business in the U.S.A. are frequently listed on the Vancouver Stock Exchange. They like the V.S.E. because of its relaxed regulatory rules, and because that exchange is a magnet for investors interested in high technology or research-oriented ventures. Except in unusual fact situations, foreigners can purchase control of such V.S.E.-listed companies without being concerned about the *IC Act*.

(b) Parts of a Business

Foreign investors who are purchasing assets should be wary of subsection 31(2). It can trip them like a rope. This subsection states: "a part of a business that is *capable* of being carried on as a separate business is a Canadian business if the business of which it is a part is a Canadian business".

A division of a company is obviously a separate business. However, the purchase of *any* part of a business that is capable of being carried on as a separate business will fall within the ambit of the Act as well.

(c) Excluded Business Activities

Because of the three-pronged definition of Canadian business, many business activities carried on in Canada are *excluded* from the jurisdiction of Investment Canada. For example, an American company may send sales people or consultants to Canada to visit clients. If these sales people stay in hotels and report to their client's office, there will be no assets in Canada, as required by the definition of "Canadian business".

Foreign companies may also perform a limited degree of "after-sales service" without being considered to have established a "Canadian business". For example, a foreign company which sells computer equipment to Canadians may keep an employee and supply of parts in Canada in order to fulfil its warranty obligations. In such circumstances, all three requirements of the definition of "Canadian business" will have been met, but the after-sales service by itself will not satisfy the definition of a "business".

(d) Cultural Businesses

Because the establishment of most new businesses and most acquisitions are not liable to be reviewed under the *IC Act*, these distinctions are of little significance. The one exception is when a business proposal involves a "cultural business" such as book publishing. Then it is essential to determine exactly what activities can be performed in Canada without a "Canadian business" being established.

EXAMPLE: An American publishing company sells its books in Canada by mailing catalogues to Canadian customers. As a convenience to these customers, the American firm arranges with a retired Canadian, Colonel Blimp, to answer the phone in the name of the American firm, store the books in his Montreal warehouse, and fill the orders. Colonel Blimp is renumerated on a percentage fee basis. However, all billings are done from the U.S. In addition, ownership of the books, while they are stored in Canada, remains with the American firm. Has a Canadian business been established by the American firm?

Unfortunately, the answer is unclear in the absence of further details. The degree of supervision and control that the American firm exercises over the Colonel will determine whether he should be classified as an employee or an independent contractor. If he is an employee, the American firm will have established a Canadian business, since the other two attributes of a Canadian business are present. On the other hand, if Colonel Blimp is an independent contractor, the American firm does not have a business in Canada unless the Colonel in turn has his own employees, in which case his employees might be attributed to the American firm.[15] If a "Canadian business" has been established, the Canadian government will have the option of ordering a review since book distribution is a cultural business.

6. "Business" and the Oil Patch

The thrust of the *IC Act* is directed towards Canada's manufacturing sector. For this reason, it is hard to delimit its impact on the oil patch.

Interpretation Note No. 4 states that undeveloped potential oil and gas properties (that is, exploration properties) are not a business. On the other hand, if:

---

[15] If Colonel Blimp is classified as an employee, the warehouse that he leases or owns would be the place of business in Canada of the American publishing company. But if he is an independent contractor, his warehouse could not be attributed to the American company, even if the other elements of the "Canadian business" test have been met.

(1) production of oil or gas is occurring, or

(2) economically recoverable quantities of oil and gas have been determined to exist[16]

—and—

the drilling of a well to recover such oil and gas for the purpose of production has commenced,

then the property is a business.

This emphasis on production marks a change from the FIRA era. Back then, the government reviewed the purchase of *proven* oil, gas and mineral reserves (that is, reserves which had been discovered and determined to be recoverable) even when production had not commenced and wells had not been drilled in order to begin production.

Now, property containing substantial reserves on which preliminary drilling has taken place can change hands without government review. An example might be reserves in isolated parts of Canada where no producing wells have been drilled because of a lack of delivery facilities.

This change is not just one of policy, but of law. A "business" was defined under FIRA as being "an undertaking carried on in anticipation of profit". To that definition the framers of the *IC Act* added the phrase "capable of generating revenue" in order to narrow the scope of what a "business" is.

Proven oil and gas reserves are not "capable of generating revenue" (at least in the short term). Until initial steps are taken to commence production, there is, therefore, no "business".

If wells have been drilled and reserves discovered, which are capable of production, but the property has been temporarily "shut-in", then the legal conclusion is different. The property *is* a business. The transfer of land on which the wells have been capped will therefore be subject to the *IC Act* if the purchaser is a non-Canadian.

A net profits interest and a net carried interest are both assets. However, neither is capable of meeting the definition of a "Canadian business".[17] Such interests can be purchased by a foreign investor without Ottawa's approval.

---

[16] What is "economically recoverable" in light of fluctuating oil prices, and the appropriate time frame, are issues the drafters of the Interpretation Note steered clear of. Can an oil well be a business one week, but not the next week because a dispute among oil-producing nations leads to a drop in oil prices?

[17] This conclusion assumes that no unusual contractual arrangements exist, such as the owner of a net profits interest or net carried interest having control over producing oil and gas properties.

The ownership of a royalty interest is not a business either.

Sometimes, when a number of oil and gas leases cover a reservoir, they will be combined into a unit. All of the various working and royalty interests will be pooled, with each owner relinquishing his or her interest in a particular tract of land in exchange for a percentage interest in the unit. To govern their relationship, the parties will execute a unit agreement and a unit operating agreement. This process, aptly called unitization, permits a more efficient management of the reservoir.

For Investment Canada purposes, it may be possible to conclude that the entire unit is a Canadian business, owned by a joint venture composed of all interest holders. The significance of this conclusion is that if a foreign investor buys a 100% interest in one of the underlying leases, provided the lease has a unit participation factor of less than 50%, there will be no acquisition of a Canadian business and, therefore, no way that Ottawa can prevent the sale. (On the other hand, Ottawa may assert that an individual lease in a unit is a separate business, particularly if the vendor is the operator, and, therefore, has employees and a place of business.)

Could one isolated producing well be a "Canadian business"? Certainly, if the three-pronged definition is satisfied.

CHAPTER 5

ESTABLISHING A NEW CANADIAN BUSINESS

Even if a non-Canadian is establishing a "Canadian business", it may not be a "*new* Canadian business". If so, the investor need not notify Ottawa.

A notification takes two minutes to complete. Why would an investor not want to file one? Some want to avoid attracting the attention of competitors. Others resent government interference in their business affairs. A few may be laundering money or circumventing their countries' tax or foreign exchange laws. (For a variety of reasons, potential investors from South America and the Middle East are more concerned than U.S. investors about providing information to governments.) For these investors, and those establishing cultural businesses, it is important to know how a "new Canadian business" is defined.

1. The Meaning of "New Canadian Business"

For the purpose of the *Investment Canada Act*, a business is a new Canadian business[1] if:

(1) the non-Canadian has no other businesses in Canada; or

(2) the proposed business is unrelated to any other business being carried on in Canada by the non-Canadian; or

(3) the proposed business is culturally sensitive (in other words, it is "prescribed as being related to Canada's cultural heritage or national identity"); in this case, it is irrelevant whether the investor is carrying on a related business.

At the present time, the government has placed four different groups of activities on the "cultural heritage and national identity" list.

---

[1] "New Canadian business" is defined in s. 3.

111

In brief, these activities are the production, distribution or sale of books, magazines, periodicals, newspapers, or music; and the production, distribution, sale or exhibition of film and video products, and audio or video music recordings.[2]

> EXAMPLE (The Non-Canadian with an Existing Business): Stripes Inc. is a Canadian subsidiary of an American company. If Stripes sets up a new operation in Canada, must it notify Ottawa?
>
> Stripes does not need to file a notification if it:
>
> (1) *expands* its existing business in Canada, or
>
> (2) sets up a different business provided:
>
> > (a) the proposed business is not culturally sensitive, and
> >
> > (b) the proposed business is *related* to the business Stripes is already *carrying on* in Canada.

What if Stripes wants to become a book publisher in Canada? Then it must file a notification even if book publishing is related to Stripes' current business in Canada. This is because book publishing has been designated as culturally sensitive.

2. Three Obscure Concepts

Three concepts mentioned above need further explanation.

(a) "Carrying on a Business"

Sometimes, a question arises as to whether an investor currently has a business in Canada. (If the investor does not, the new business obviously cannot be an expansion of or related to the existing business, and a notification will have to be filed.) The investor's lawyer must then determine what constitutes the "carrying on" of a business.

The cases on this point (decided under other statutes) are legion. In each case, the issue is what degree of contact with a jurisdiction is required to persuade the courts that a person is carrying on business there? Unfortunately, the courts have come to a variety of decisions. Nonetheless, a few general principles have been formulated:

> 1. Incidental activities in another jurisdiction do not constitute the carrying on of a business there.[3] If soliciting orders is all

---

[2] The categories of activities which the government has identified as being related to Canada's cultural heritage or national identity are set out in Schedule IV of the regulations.

[3] *Grainger and Son v. Gough*, [1896] A.C. 325, (1896), 3 T.C. 462, at 467 (H.L.); *London (City of) v. George Watt & Sons* (1893), 22 S.C.R. 300; *Linde Canadian Refrigerator Co. v. Saskatchewan Creamery Ltd.*, (1915), 51 S.C.R. 400.

that is done in a particular country, a merchant is not carrying on trade in that country. Storing stock-in-trade in Canada, or installing a product in Canada that has been manufactured and shipped from a foreign country is, therefore, unlikely to constitute the carrying on of a business in Canada.

2. Carrying on of a business involves a continuity of operations and not an isolated transaction.[4] The business must also have been operated for more than a month or two. Obviously, an investor cannot claim to be carrying on a business in Canada if the business has been shut down, unless the closure is of a very temporary nature.

3. In the case of a business person who sells goods, business is being carried on where the contract is made.[5]

4. When a foreign company sells its goods in Canada through an agent, it is a question of fact whether the "principal" is carrying on business through the agent, or the "agent" is carrying on his or her own business, using the goodwill, trademark or product or the "principal". The degree of control retained by the "principal", the role and powers of the intermediary, and the relationship between the parties are relevant.[6] However, if no contract for the sale of goods is entered into in Canada, it would seem that no business is being carried on in Canada.

(b) Relatedness

The meaning of relatedness is not set out in the Act.[7] However, "Related Business Guidelines"[8] have been published and should be examined by the aspiring investor.[9] Since these guidelines define relatedness in extraordinarily broad terms, there will probably be few

---

[4] *Tara Exploration and Development Company Ltd. v. M.N.R.*, 70 D.T.C. 6370; *Smith v. Anderson* (1880), 15 Ch.D. 247; *Re the Sherbrooke Land Co.* (1914), 27 W.W.R. 244 (Alta. S.C.).

[5] *Maclaine v. Eccott*, [1926] A.C. 424 (H.L.).

[6] *Firestone Tire and Rubber Company of Canada Ltd. v. C.I.T.*, [1942] S.C.R. 476; *Halifax (City of) v. McLaughlin Carriage Co.* (1907), 39 S.C.R. 174.

[7] There is no definition of "relatedness" in the *IC Act*, nor in its predecessor, the *FIR Act*.

[8] These "Related Business Guidelines" have been abridged from those published under the *FIR Act*. However, since the concept is the same in both Acts, investors may wish to consult the guidelines issued under the *FIR Act*. "Relatedness" can often be established on the basis of backward and forward integration, import or product substitution, and similar technology. Also, a new business is related to an existing business if the former produces products or services that result from R&D carried out by the latter, or if both businesses are in the same three-digit S.I.C. classification.

[9] Since the guidelines are neither law nor exhaustive, an investor's own arguments may be presented on the meaning of the word "related".

new businesses which *established* investors would want to set up that will be unrelated to their existing businesses. (This makes Investment Canada's database of new businesses established by foreign investors less comprehensive than it otherwise would be.)[10]

(c) Expansion

The expansion of an existing business is not subject to the Act. Consequently, there is no need to inform Investment Canada.

Unfortunately, the Act does not define what an expansion is. If a new operation is substantially similar to an existing business—from the perspective of the goods and services produced, the inputs, and the marketing channels—it probably constitutes in law an expansion of the existing business.This is the position that the minister takes in the "Related Business Guidelines".

In most cases, nothing much of consequence flows from the distinction. However, in culturally sensitive sectors, the issue is crucial. For instance, suppose a company which distributes French language books wants to open a retail store to distribute English language books and magazines. Because book and magazine distribution has been designated as an activity which affects Canada's cultural heritage, Ottawa can review and veto the opening of this store if it is categorized as a new business, but can do nothing if it is just an expansion.

EXAMPLE: (Expansion v. New Business): Easy Living Company ("Easy Living") is a foreign-owned wholesaler and retailer of home entertainment products. In Canada, it has been selling audio and video cassettes since 1972. It now wishes to add pre-recorded video tape cassettes to its product lines. The new products will be marketed through existing distribution channels and no substantial change in the manner that Easy Living conducts its business is anticipated. Is Easy Living expanding its business or establishing a new business?

There is an obvious similarity between blank and pre-recorded cassettes. Consequently, the addition of pre-recorded tape cassettes to

---

[10] Why is the "related business" concept in the Act when it serves such a minor function? The concept was left in to prevent the Act from imposing obligations on investors that went *beyond* those set out in the *FIR Act*. During the FIRA era, a foreign investor could establish a new related business without Ottawa's prior approval (and therefore, without informing FIRA). If there was no related business concept in the *IC Act*, an investor would have to tell Investment Canada when a new, related business was established. That would have imposed upon the investor a minor obligation not required by FIRA.

Easy Living's product line probably constitutes an expansion of its current business. However, Easy Living should request a binding opinion from Investment Canada on this point.

What are the consequences if the additional product line is categorized as a new distribution business (instead of an expansion)? Since the distribution of video products is a culturally sensitive activity, a notification will have to be filed even though the new business will be related to Easy Living's current business. The federal government will then have the option of reviewing (and preventing) Easy Living from adding pre-recorded video tape cassettes to its product line.

CHAPTER 6

ACQUIRING CONTROL

If a "non-Canadian" wants to invest in a "*Canadian business*", the first two pillars for federal government jurisdiction are present. The third pillar will exist if the non-Canadian is acquiring *control*.

The *Investment Canada Act* sets out thresholds for determining this issue. If the interest that a non-Canadian is buying falls below the appropriate threshold, the non-Canadian is deemed not to be acquiring control even if he or she will be "calling the shots". (This may happen, for example, in a widely-held company if an investor buys a 30% interest. The purchase of a 30% interest is deemed not to be an acquisition of control.)

1. Acquisition of Control Rules

The rules defining *how* an acquisition of control can occur and the thresholds setting out *when* "control" is acquired are found in section 28 of the Act. These rules are all-inclusive. In other words, if control is being acquired in a manner not mentioned in section 28, the Canadian government has no jurisdiction.

Upon examining these rules, the reader's first impression will be that the drafters went to considerable pain to state the obvious. Almost every combination of routes by which control can be acquired (e.g., the purchase of a Canadian company's shares) has been elaborately described.

However, there is a reason for this precision. The Canadian government was perturbed by American and European critics of FIRA who claimed that Canada was interfering in offshore mergers (whenever one of the merged companies owned a Canadian business). Consequently, when the *IC Act* was being drafted, the Canadian government took care to distinguish between direct and indirect acquisitions.

A useful scheme for organizing the "acquisition of control" rules is presented below. This scheme is built around the target of the purchase. Foreign investors should first ask themselves whether they will be purchasing shares, assets, or an interest in a partnership, trust or joint venture. Then they should turn to the appropriate section (there are five sections that follow).

(a) Share Purchase—Canadian-Incorporated Company

A non-Canadian who buys voting shares of a Canadian-incorporated company which:

(1) carries on a Canadian business,[1] or

(2) controls[2] another Canadian-incorporated company (Canadian-based partnership, trust or joint venture) which carries on a Canadian business,[3]

must examine three statutory presumptions or rules ("the acquisition of control rules") to determine if the buyer is acquiring control. These rules (which appear below) are based on ownership thresholds and make no distinction between private and publicly-traded shares.

(i) *The Acquisition of Control Rules for Corporations*

1. *Deemed acquisition of control*: the acquisition of 50.1% or more ("a majority") of a corporation's voting shares.[4]

2. *No acquisition of control*: the acquisition of less than $33^1/3$% of a corporation's voting shares. (deemed non-acquisition of control).[5]

3. *Rebuttable presumption of acquisition of control*: the acquisition of $33^1/3$% up to and including 50% of a corporation's voting shares.[6]

A foreign investor who is buying between $33^1/3$% and 50% of a corporation's voting shares is presumed to have acquired control. To escape from federal government jurisdiction, the investor must rebut this presumption by proving that:

---

[1] Para. 28(1)(a).

[2] Directly or indirectly.

[3] Canadian parent—-Canadian subsidiary (or other entity). See subpara. 28(1)(d)(i).

[4] Para. 28(3)(a).

[5] Para. 28(3)(d).

[6] Para. 28(3)(c).

(1) control in fact of the corporation will not change, or

(2) the investor will not alone be able to control the corporation in fact (through the ownership of voting shares).

The first proposition is often easy to establish. If one shareholder (or a voting group) *presently* controls the company, and will still be in control *after* the foreign investor has completed the purchase, then the statutory presumption has been rebutted. Even if the locus of control will change to one of joint or "shared" control, the foreign investor can sidestep the *IC Act* by demonstrating that he or she will not be controlling the corporation alone. This is of great significance in a 50:50 split. It also marks a major shift in policy from the FIRA era.[7] When FIRA existed, a foreign investor who moved into a position of shared control was subject to the legislation.

These propositions are easy to state. If "control in fact through the ownership of voting shares" is given a narrow interpretation, they are just as easy to apply. Control, in that event, lies with those share-holders who have sufficient votes (as indicated in the share register) to elect the board of directors. Determining the locus of control is then a mathematical exercise which children can handle.

This may have been what the legislators intended. The parliamentary debates indicate they wanted a simple statute which would seldom require legal interpretation.

If simplicity was the goal, perhaps the drafters should have been more precise, because, as pointed out in Chapter 3, "control in fact through the ownership of voting shares" can also be interpreted in a broad fashion. If this broader interpretation is adopted, the entire bundle of rights that a shareholder acquires by owning shares has to be examined (to find the "control rights"). In this event, the content of shareholders' agreements and corporate by-laws are of critical importance.

Moreover, "control in fact" can be interpreted to mean either positive or negative control (e.g., through high quorum requirements). This complicates the analysis further.

EXAMPLE (The Deadlocked Company): A Canadian company has two equal shareholders. A Polish citizen buys the 50% interest belonging to one shareholder. With it comes the right in a share-holders' agreement to equal representation on the board and the power to veto anything. Need a filing be made?

---

[7] During the FIRA era, a foreign investor who purchased 50% of a company's shares was considered to have acquired control, even when share ownership was equally divided between two shareholders.

The citizen of Poland can block any proposal put forth by the Canadian. Nevertheless, the acquisition of a 50% interest in a "dead-locked company" is not subject to the Act. Why? Because it can be shown that the citizen of Poland only shares in control and does not control the company alone. Investment Canada need not even be told that the purchase has occurred. (However, the status of the company will change from Canadian-controlled to foreign-controlled.)[8]

If the shareholders' agreement gives the Polish citizen the right to elect a majority of the company's directors, will that make a differ-ence? It certainly will make a difference, provided "control in fact through the ownership of voting shares" is interpreted broadly. In that event, the shareholders' agreement can be examined and the transac-tion will fall within the jurisdiction of Investment Canada.

(ii) Companies That Control Companies

If a foreign investor wants to buy a holding company that owns an interest in an operating company, a second calculation must be made. Using the "chain of control" presumptions, it must be determined if the holding company controls the operating company. If it does not, there is no acquisition of a Canadian business (even if the investor buys all of the shares of the holding company).

When does one company control another? The statute contains three presumptions:

1. Presumption of Direct Control[9]

    (a) Majority Ownership: A company that owns 50.1% or more of another company's voting shares is in control.

    (b) Minority Control: A company which owns between 33 ⅓% and 50% (including 50%) of the voting shares of another

---

[8] Subs. 26(6). Why did FIRA administrators want to catch purchases of a 50% interest in a deadlocked company? Because the foreign investor could, potentially at least, veto everything that the Canadian shareholder wanted to do ("negative control"). Using the fiction that a "new" group composed of the foreign and Canadian share-holders had acquired joint control, FIRA administrators asserted jurisdiction. By con-trast, *The Investment Canada Act: Briefing Document*, op. cit., p. 66, states: "The control in fact test used in para. 28(3)(c) does not encompass the concept of negative control that was used in the *FIR Act*". This is probably because the drafters wanted to encourage joint ventures and other "sharing" arrangements. (As an aside, the F.T.C.'s pre-merger notification and reporting rules promulgated under the Hart-Scott-Rodino Act define control as the holding of 50% or more of the shares of an issuer. In the case of a 50:50 split the F.T.C. considers that there exists dual control, that is, each holder of a 50% interest may exercise control.)

[9] Para. 28(2)(b). The concept of indirect control in the *IC Act* is narrower than in the *FIR Act*. Under the latter Act, indirect control could arise through a contract, trust, share ownership or otherwise.

company controls the second company, if the first company has control in fact through share ownership.

(c) Partnerships, Trusts and Joint Ventures: A company that owns a majority interest (50.1% or more) in a partnership, trust or joint venture directly controls that partnership, trust or joint venture. (Because a voting interest is defined in terms of a right to share in the profits and the assets on dissolution, a company can be "in control" of a partnership without having any voting power!)

Who is in control if a foreign company owns a 49% interest in a partnership and everyone else has tiny interests? It is *not* the foreign company. The drafters of the Act recognized minority control within a chain of companies, but ignored that possibility when a company controls an unincorporated business such as a partnership.

EXAMPLE: Pierre Richard is a citizen of France who wants to purchase 50% of the voting shares of Moose Company. Moose Company has a 45% interest in Gatineau Corp. Two other shareholders own the remaining 50% interest in Moose Company. Does Investment Canada have jurisdiction?

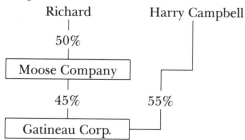

Pierre Richard faces a rebuttable presumption that he will be acquiring control of Moose Company.[10] Since (with a 50% interest) he will be the largest shareholder, let us assume that the presumption cannot be rebutted.

The next issue is who controls Gatineau Corp. Is Moose Company, with a 45% interest, in control? Since there is another shareholder with a 55% interest, Moose Company cannot be in control.[11] Consequently, Investment Canada has no jurisdiction.

2. Presumption of Indirect Control:[12] A company that directly controls another company (partnership, trust, joint venture) is

---

[10] Para. 28(3)(c).

[11] Subpara. 28(2)(b)(ii).

[12] Para. 28(2)(a).

deemed to control indirectly any entities that the other company (partnership, trust, joint venture) directly or indirectly controls.

Why is this presumption needed? It ensures that a foreign investor cannot escape the purview of the Act simply because the company being purchased controls a Canadian business through several layers of other companies.

This objective is achieved through the intermeshing of the two "chain of control presumptions". After it has been ascertained (using the "presumption of direct control") that the company being purchased controls a second company, the "presumption of indirect control" then swings into play with respect to companies further down the chain.

3.   The Associated Entities Presumption:[13] Corporations[14] that are controlled by the same parent are deemed to be associated with each other and the affiliated corporations that each of the other controls. When associated corporations own interests in the same corporation, the *associates* may be treated as a whole for the purpose of deciding who controls the second corporation.

EXAMPLE: A foreign investor buys all three subsidiaries of Holdco. Each of these subsidiaries has an interest in Beaver Corporation, but not a large enough interest to exercise control. Together, however, all three companies clearly control Beaver Corporation. Is the foreign investor acquiring control of Beaver Corporation?

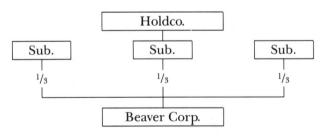

If there was no "associated entities presumption", the foreign investor could demonstrate that control of Beaver Corporation had not been acquired. As proof, that investor would point out that none of the three subsidiaries purchased can control Beaver Corporation by owning one third of its shares.[15] Fortunately, the "associated entities

---

[13] Paras. 28(2)(c) and 28(2)(d).

[14] Or other entities. Whenever appropriate, replace the word "corporation" by the word "partnership", "trust", or "joint venture".

[15] See the presumption of direct control. Subpara. 28(2)(b)(ii).

presumption" allows the Canadian government to treat all three subsidiaries as one company and assert jurisdiction.[16]

(b) Offshore Share Purchase: Foreign Company with Canadian Subsidiary[17]

When control of a Canadian company changes hands, because its parent (or grandparent) company has been purchased, an indirect acquisition is said to have occurred. Under the *FIR Act*, the government reviewed all indirect acquisitions. When the parent company was located outside Canada, this review caused considerable controversy. In Washington and European capitals, politicians thundered that Ottawa was interfering in other nations' commercial affairs. The Canadian government sought to mollify these critics when it drafted paragraph 28(1)(d) of the *IC Act*.

Paragraph 28(1)(d) distinguishes between indirect acquisitions that involve foreign corporations and those that affect only Canadian corporations. When a foreign investor purchases a foreign corporation which owns a Canadian subsidiary,[18] the threshold for review is higher than if a Canadian company with a subsidiary is purchased. (Beginning in 1992, if the purchaser is an American, there will, in most cases, be no review when a foreign corporation with a Canadian subsidiary is acquired.)

(i) How This Provision Works

A foreign investor who wants to buy a corporation incorporated outside of Canada should read subparagraph 28(1)(d)(ii). The key elements in this subparagraph are:

(1) a foreign-incorporated company,

(2) which controls an entity (corporation, partnership, trust, or joint venture) *in Canada*.

If these key elements are present, the investor must examine both the "acquisition of control rules" (to determine if *control* of the foreign-

---

[16] The "associated entities presumption" serves another purpose. If a foreign business person, who controls several companies, causes them to purchase varying interests in a Canadian business, the several companies can be visualized as one purchaser. (Because the companies will be "associated", a "joint venture" will exist. The joint venture will be the purchaser.)

[17] Foreign Parent Corporation with a Canadian Subsidiary (or with a controlling interest in a Canadian-based Partnership, Joint Venture, or Trust). See subpara. 28(1)(d)(ii), and para. 28(2)(a). The only exceptions are branch businesses.

[18] Or other entity.

incorporated company is being acquired) and the "chain of control presumptions" (to ascertain if that foreign-incorporated company controls an "entity" in Canada).

EXAMPLE: An Australian entrepreneur, buys 60% of the voting shares of The Brush Company, which has been incorporated in the U.S. The Brush Company has a 50% interest in an operating Canadian company ("Can Sub."). Has the Australian acquired control of a Canadian business?

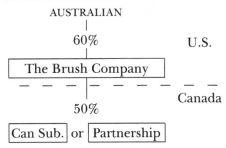

The only issue in this example is whether The Brush Company controls Can Sub. (See the "chain of control presumptions" for the answer.)[19] If it does, the Australian will be deemed to have acquired control of Can Sub.

Let's change the facts. The Brush Company has a 50% interest in an Albertan partnership (instead of a company). Although the Australian is still obtaining a 50% share of a Canadian business, he or she is deemed not to be acquiring control of the business.[20]

(c) Offshore Share Purchase: Foreign Company with Canadian Branch Business

The purchase of a foreign corporation which carries on a branch business in Canada is neither reviewable nor notifiable. If the foreign corporation controls the unincorporated ("branch") business indirectly,[21] the law remains the same.

This is a significant exclusion, since some of Canada's largest mining operations are carried on by foreign companies as branch businesses. Substantial branch businesses are also found in the oil and gas, retailing (food and department stores) and financial service sectors of the economy. In total, there are at least several hundred unincorporated branch businesses in Canada.

---

[19] Subpara. 28(2)(b)(ii).

[20] Para. 28(2)(b)(i).

[21] Through other foreign corporations, partnerships, joint ventures and trusts.

Why does Investment Canada have no jurisdiction over such transactions? To explain the legal reasoning we must return to fundamental principles. There exist two main ways that a foreign company can carry on business in Canada: create a branch business (by buying all the assets in its own name) or incorporate a Canadian subsidiary.

Subparagraph 28(1)(d)(ii) establishes the legal basis for Canadian government jurisdiction when a foreign investor purchases an offshore company with a Canadian subsidiary (or other entity). The five elements are:

(1) an acquisition of voting shares[22]

(2) of a corporation incorporated outside of Canada

(3) which controls (directly or indirectly)

(4) an entity in Canada

(5) which carries on a Canadian business.

An "entity" is defined to mean a "corporation, partnership, trust or joint venture". A branch business was deliberately not included in that definition. Therefore, subparagraph 28(1)(d)(ii) cannot be used by the government to assert jurisdiction when a foreign company with a Canadian branch business is purchased.

There is no other section of the Act that might cover indirect acquisitions of branch businesses. Only if substantially all of the assets of a branch business are *directly* purchased by a foreigner does the net of Investment Canada descend.

Why are indirect takeovers of branch businesses not covered by the *Investment Canada Act*?

Such takeovers were reviewed by FIRA for several years. Suddenly, in October 1983, the practice ceased. Solicitors who expressed surprise were told that the Department of Justice had opined that such takeovers were not subject to the Act.

Statutes can often be interpreted in two or more reasonable ways.[23] FIRA administrators had one interpretation; Department of Justice officials obviously had another. FIRA's interpretation eliminated an anomaly. However, the views of the Department of Justice coincided with Parliament's intent when it passed the *FIR Act*.[24]

---

[22] "Voting interests" is defined to include shares.

[23] This allows those who administer legislation to expand or narrow their jurisdiction.

[24] The *Foreign Takeovers Review Act*, introduced and withdrawn in 1972, was identical in major respects to the *Foreign Investment Review Act*, which was passed by Parliament in

Picture a foreign company with a branch business in Canada. Then imagine that a second foreign company buys the shares of the first foreign company. All that has happened, Liberal government officials told Members of Parliament in 1972, is that there has been a change in ownership of a foreign company but no change whatsoever in the title to the assets in Canada that constitute the branch business. In such circumstances, an order of divestiture cannot be enforced. Only when physical property used in carrying on a business in Canada is sold is there "a basis for making the Canadian writ run, vis-à-vis that acquisition of control."[25]

The Conservative government in 1985 clearly did not want to broaden the *Investment Canada Act* by including transactions that FIRA did not review. Otherwise, the wrong message would be sent to foreign investors. The problem of enforcing a "Canadian writ" was no doubt another concern. Consequently, "branch business" was omitted from the definition of "entity".

EXAMPLE 1: A Saudi Arabian prince purchases 75% of the shares of a U.S. company which carries on an unincorporated "branch" business in Canada. Since this transaction is not subject to the *IC Act*, the investor need not tell Ottawa that the Canadian business has a new owner.

EXAMPLE 2: Company A has a 100% interest in a partnership that has been organized under the laws of Colorado (or another foreign jurisdiction). The partnership carries on a Canadian business that is not incorporated. Does John Steiner (a European industrialist) acquire control of a Canadian business when he buys 60% of Company A?

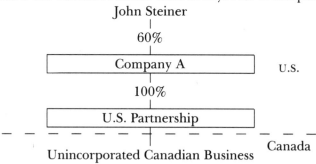

John Steiner
|
60%
|
Company A   U.S.
|
100%
|
U.S. Partnership
— — — — — — — — —+— — — — — — — — —
Unincorporated Canadian Business   Canada

Read subparagraph 28(1)(d)(ii) carefully. For this subparagraph to operate, a foreign corporation (or other entity) must control an "entity

---

1973. Government officials repeatedly stated in 1972 that the proposed *Foreign Takeovers Review Act* did not cover the acquisition of control of a U.S. company with a branch business in Canada. The branch business issue was not debated by M.P.s in 1973, because it had been fully discussed in 1972. (House of Commons, *Minutes of the Standing Committee on Finance, Trade and Economic Affairs*, June 20, 1972, Issue No. 24, pp. 80-81, 85-86.)

[25] Id., p. 80.

in Canada" that carries on a Canadian business. The phrase "entity in Canada" could be interpreted in two ways (incorporation or presence). However, only one interpretation is consistent with the principles of statutory construction.[26]

An "entity in Canada" means "incorporated in Canada" or "organized under the laws of Canada". A partnership that has been formed under the laws of a foreign country is not an "entity in Canada" even if it has a business presence in this country.

In the example above, the U.S. partnership has a place of business in Canada. However, because it has been organized under U.S. law, it is not an entity in Canada. When John Steiner indirectly buys the unincorporated Canadian business, he need not inform Investment Canada, even if that business is a cultural business.

(d) Asset Purchase[27]

A foreign investor, who buys all (or substantially all) of the assets of a Canadian business, has acquired control of that business. It is of no relevance that the assets purchased may belong to a branch business. This is because the distinction between branch businesses and subsidiaries, so crucial to determining federal government jurisdiction when the shares of a foreign company are sold, is not a factor when assets are purchased.

This creates an anomaly! Foreign investors who buy all of the *assets* of a foreign-based multinational company, including its Canadian branch business, are subject to the Act. Those who do essentially the same thing, by purchasing the *shares* of the same multinational company, avoid the statute completely.

This distinction often confuses non-lawyers. They should ask themselves one question: Will title to the Canadian assets change hands?

When a branch business is being purchased directly, the real estate and vehicles will be registered in the name of the new owners. By

---

[26] The phrase "entity in Canada" in para. 28(1)(d) has not been qualified by language that restricts its ambit to Canadian-incorporated companies. Might it mean "carrying on business in Canada"? If so, it would include foreign-incorporated companies, and would give Ottawa jurisdiction over the acquisition of a foreign-incorporated company which controls a second foreign-incorporated company which carries on a branch business in Canada. However, such an interpretation would create a redundancy (and an anomaly). Para. 28(1)(d) would then read in part "the acquisition of voting interests of. . . an entity carrying on business in Canada carrying on the Canadian business". One principle of statutory construction is that a statute should not be presumed to contain redundancies.

[27] Para. 28(1)(c).

contrast, title to those assets remains unchanged when the shares of the foreign company which owns those assets are purchased.

Many multimillion dollar asset purchases fall outside the scope of the *IC Act* for another reason. "All or substantially all of the assets" of the business are not being purchased. Unless that high watermark is attained, a business is not being acquired (at least within the meaning of the statute), and Investment Canada need not be informed that a sale has taken place.

To decide whether he or she is purchasing "substantially all" of the assets of a business, an investor must perform several calculations. Here are the steps:

1. List the assets of the business and the assets that are to be purchased.

2. Using both the qualitative and quantitative tests (to be explained later), determine whether, on the basis of either test, the proposed purchase involves substantially all of the assets of a business.

3. If the answer to Step 3 is no, consider whether the assets being purchased constitute "part of a business capable of being carried on as a separate business".

4. If a "separate business" exists, use the quantitative and qualitative tests to ascertain if all or substantially all of the assets of that separate business will be purchased.

To perform these steps, the investor must first discover what the lawmakers meant by "assets". Next the investor must ascertain the meaning of "substantially all of the assets" and "part of a business".

The word "assets" is defined to include "tangible and intangible property of any value".[28] Licences, goodwill, patents, trademarks, accounts receivable and leasehold interests are all intangible property. So is a customer list.[29] These are all "assets" that the investor must include when listing the assets of the business and the assets the investor wants to buy.

Because of the wide definition of "assets", the purchase of a business that leases its assets is "captured" by the *IC Act*. A foreign investor

---

[28] S. 3.

[29] A customer list may be valuable intangible property if accompanied by a restrictive covenant from the vendor not to solicit orders from the customers on the list. In the case of a fuel oil business, a customer list will constitute "substantially all of the assets" of the business if "substantially all" is interpreted (qualitatively) to mean the essential assets. See para. 28(1)(c).

who takes assignments of leases from the vendor is accordingly in no better position than a purchaser of the underlying assets. However, rights granted to a Canadian business under a licence agreement are not "assets" since a licence passes no interest.

(i) Meaning of "Substantially All" of the Assets

"Substantially all of the assets" can be construed either quantitatively or qualitatively.

If the quantitative test is the correct one, the issue is whether a very large portion (e.g., 85%) of the assets of a business are being acquired. This calculation is easy to perform. The investor lists the business' assets, determines their book value (see the regulations) and figures out what percentage of those assets will be acquired.

On the other hand, if "substantially all of the assets" has a qualitative meaning, the conceptional problems are less easy to resolve. The investor must then decide what is the essence ("the essential assets") of the business, and whether substantially all of those essential assets will be purchased.

In the case of a trucking business, the "essential asset" may be a transport licence and one vehicle. For a manufacturing operation, it may be the major equipment, an important patent or a constituent of goodwill, such as a trade-mark. Obviously, a qualitative interpretation will trigger the notification/review mechanism of the *IC Act* at a much lower level than the quantitative test. Indeed, these "essential assets" might well amount to less than 50% of a business' total assets.

No judicial ruling on the meaning of "substantially all of the assets" (in the context of the *IC Act*) exists. An identical phrase is found in provincial corporations statutes, and has been given a qualitative interpretation by the courts. In *Re 85956 Holdings Ltd. v. Fayerman Brothers Ltd.*, the court said "substantially all" means an asset sale that would effectively destroy the corporate business".[30]

In that case, the Saskatchewan *Business Corporations Act* was under consideration. The purpose of that statute, the court noted, was to

---

[30] *Re 85956 Holdings Ltd. v. Fayerman Brothers Ltd.* (1986), 25 D.L.R. (4th) 119, at 124; *Re Martin and F.P. Bourgault Industries Air Seeder Division Ltd.* (1987), 45 D.L.R. (4th) 296; *Lindzon v. International Sterling Holdings Inc.* (1990), 45 B.L.R. 57, at 76; *Re Olympia & York Enterprises Ltd. and Hiram Walker Resources Ltd.* (1987), 37 D.L.R. (4th) 193, at 215; *Herrmann v. Canadian Nickel Co. Ltd.* (1929), 64 O.L.R. 190; *Burnaby Paperboard Ltd. v. M.N.R.* (1967), 68 D.T.C. 12. These cases indicate that the test is whether the vendors are abandoning the business or whether the sale will destroy the business. For a discussion of U.S. litigation over the meaning of "all or substantially all" the assets in corporations statutes, see Richard Elliott, "Corporations - Disposition of Corporate Assets" (1965), 43 *N. Carolina L. Rev.* 957.

protect shareholders from a fundamental change in the business of a corporation.

If "substantially all" in the *IC Act* has the same meaning as in *Re 85956 Holdings Ltd.*, the purchase of 80% of the assets of an oil company (e.g., Shell Canada) is not an acquisition of control, provided the vendor company remains in operation. (For instance, even with just 20% of its current asset base, Shell Canada would remain an operating company of significant size with many employees.)

However, statutes are construed in light of the objects they are designed to achieve. For that reason, the courts may disregard judicial pronouncements dealing with provincial corporations statutes, and declare that "substantially all" has a quantitative meaning in the *IC Act*.

Because there is no clear-cut definition of "substantially all", it is difficult (in comparison with share purchases) to ascertain what degree of property acquisition by a foreign investor constitutes control. Each purchase, and the surrounding circumstances, must be examined attentively. If a foreign investor is buying most of the goodwill and has extracted a non-competition covenant from the vendor, the purchaser is acquiring "substantially all of the assets" from the perspective of both tests. When the purchase involves technology alone or not enough of a company's operating assets to change the company's nature, solicitors, who must give an opinion to their clients on whether "control" is being acquired, may have to respond equivocally.

Investment Canada has published an interpretation note that provides its views on the meaning of "substantially all".[31] The note emphasizes that both the quantitative and qualitative tests must be considered. According to this interpretation note, if an essential asset is not being purchased, even though all the remaining assets are being sold, no business is being acquired.[32]

---

[31] Interpretation Note No. 3. What are the consequences if the courts rule that "substantially all" does not have a qualitative meaning? One consequence is that a foreign investor will be able to buy the key or essential asset of a Canadian business without notifying Investment Canada (assuming that the essential asset of the business is not "substantially all" of the business in the quantitative sense). The qualitative test becomes important when a foreign investor is buying some of the assets of a business, but not its major equipment or goodwill.

[32] One way to acquire control under the *FIR Act* was to buy "substantially all of the property" of a Canadian company. FIRA officials thought this wording created a loophole. They were concerned that a foreign investor could purchase crucial property from a Canadian company, such as its trade-mark or brand name or key technology, without government approval. FIRA officials also worried that a foreign parent company, which had licensed a key trade-mark to its Canadian subsidiary, might sell its (the parent company's) rights to another foreign owner without the transaction being review-

The note also indicates that liquid assets (cash, promissory notes and investment portfolios) are not usually considered assets essential to the continuance of a business. If these liquid assets are excluded from the total assets of a business, what remains is principally the operating assets. These operating assets would probably meet both the quantitative and qualitative tests (since the operating assets are "essential" property and would most likely constitute substantially all of the business in a quantitative test in the absence of any liquid assets).

A wise investor will ponder both the quantitative and qualitative aspects of "substantially all the assets" when trying to decide if a purchase is subject to Canadian government jurisdiction. If the purchase is caught by one interpretation but not the other, the investor should seek the solace of a written opinion from Investment Canada.

(ii) Undivided Interests in Assets

When a non-Canadian is purchasing an undivided interest in an unincorporated business, the same enigma reappears. An undivided interest is what tenants in common or joint tenants have when they purchase a piece of property without dividing it up into separate portions.

Using the qualitative test, a 100% interest in the *essential* assets of the business would have to be purchased before control is acquired. An investor who purchased less than the total undivided interest in the essential assets would not meet this test. On the other hand, with the quantitative test, the issue is whether the non-Canadian will obtain most of the total undivided interest in the business.

Practically speaking, these high watermarks are only available when the target is a sole proprietorship and the non-Canadian wishes to form a partnership or joint venture with the owner. If a partnership or joint venture already exists and the non-Canadian wants to buy in, another provision in the Act applies.[33] This provision gives the Government of Canada jurisdiction over the acquisition of a partnership or joint venture *at a much lower threshold* (namely, the purchase of "a majority of the voting interests") than if the test of "substantially all of the assets" were to be applied.

---

able. The next step in this scenario had the new foreign owner terminating the licence agreement prematurely. To widen the scope of the Act, FIRA officials said that "substantially all" referred to a company's essential property. Nonetheless, the *FIR Act* was never amended specifically to include "essential property", apparently because government officials believed too many transactions would end up in court. Sheldon Gordon, "Westinghouse Case Shows Problems on Trade-Marks", *Financial Post*, Nov. 8, 1975, p. 28.

[33] Para. 28(3)(a).

A non-Canadian can, therefore, buy a large interest in a one-owner operation without filing a notice or an application for review. Indeed, before the "substantially all" test can be met, the non-Canadian may have to purchase an 85% or 95% undivided interest. If a mining operation or a large manufacturing concern has a single corporate owner which wants to bring in a foreign partner (or joint venturer), that foreign partner will have to buy a huge interest in percentage terms before Investment Canada can examine the transaction.

By structuring a transaction as an asset purchase, instead of a share acquisition, it may, therefore, be possible to escape review. If a foreigner wants to purchase a business operated by a company, control will be deemed to have been acquired by the foreigner if he or she buys more than 50% of the company's shares. However, if an un-divided interest in the assets of the business is purchased, the for-eigner can own a much higher interest without being subject to Canadian government scrutiny.

It is quite possible for an *entire* unincorporated business to be taken over without the *Investment Canada Act* coming into play. A foreign investor who acquires a 60% interest (undivided or otherwise) in the assets of a sole proprietorship would not be acquiring substan-tially all of the business' assets.[34] If a second foreign investor, in an unrelated transaction, later bought the remaining 40% of what would now be a partnership or joint venture, his or her purchase would also be exempt. (This investor would not bump up against the floor for government jurisdiction over the acquisition of partnerships or joint ventures, because that floor is 50.1%.)

(iii) Part of a Business

A foreign investor who buys some (but less than substantially all) of the assets of a business is obviously not acquiring control of the complete business. However, the investor must still determine whether the vendor operates two or more "separate businesses".

Subsection 31(2) of the Act defines a "separate business". This subsection states: "a part of a business that is capable of being carried on as a separate business is a Canadian business if the business of which it is part is a Canadian business". The concept of a separate business was put into the Act to remove an enormous loophole. With-out it, the *IC Act* would not cover the purchase of a corporate division as well as many operations with a less formal structure.

Unfortunately, no one can agree on what the concept means. The only consensus is that "separate" is not synonymous with "independ-ent". An operation can be a separate business although it is incapable of "standing on its own feet".

---

[34] At least not "substantially all" in a quantitative sense.

Investment Canada has issued Interpretation Note No. 2 which suggests some factors for determining when a separate business exists. However, this interpretation note is written in "general terms" and is, therefore, of limited assistance.

What should be done if an investor can identify a separate business? The investor must then apply the qualitative and quantitative tests to determine if substantially all of the assets of that separate business will be acquired.

(e) The Delaware Merger Anomaly

Here is a summary of the rules up to this point:

Transaction	Target	Investment Canada Act
asset acquisition	branch business	applies
share purchase	Canadian corporation	applies
share purchase	foreign corporation with *branch* business	does *not* apply
share purchase	foreign corporation with Canadian subsidiary	applies

One type of transaction that does not fit neatly within these rules is a Delaware merger. In a Delaware merger—which has no exact counterpart in Canadian law—one U.S. corporation continues to exist after the merger while the other U.S. corporation disappears (i.e., is swallowed up).

If the merged corporation (the one swallowed up) carries on a Canadian branch business, a classification problem arises. Should the transaction be regarded as an asset acquisition (that is "caught" by the *IC Act*) or a purchase of the shares of a foreign company with a Canadian branch business (in which case the *IC Act* does not apply)?

EXAMPLE (Delaware Merger):[35] Eagle Inc. is a Delaware corporation that has a Canadian branch business. Texas Corp. is another American company that wishes to acquire the business of Eagle Inc.

To achieve this goal, Texas Corp. creates a subsidiary called New Texas Corp., which enters into a plan of merger with Eagle Inc.

---

[35] In a merger, the separate identity of all constituent corporations, except the one into which they merged, ceases. In a consolidation, a new corporation emerges with all the rights and liabilities of the constituent corporations.

Subsequently, New Texas Corp. and Eagle Inc. merge, the separate existence of Eagle Inc. ceases and New Texas Corp., as the
surviving corporation, succeeds to all the property of Eagle Inc.
including the Canadian branch business. Immediately after the
certificate of merger is issued, the shareholders of Eagle Inc.
exchange their shares for shares in Texas Corp.

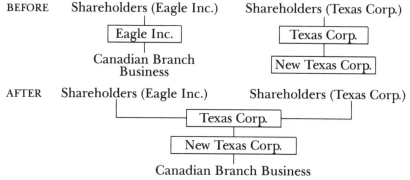

Note: Assume the original shareholders of Texas Corp. remain in
control of Texas Corp. after the merger and, therefore, become the new controllers of the Canadian branch business
that was previously owned by Eagle Inc. (If there is no change
in the ultimate controllers of the Canadian branch business,
the transaction would be described as a "corporate reorganization exempt from the Act" under paragraph 10(1)(e).)

A Canadian court wrestled with a similar transaction in the *Dow
Jones* case.[36] After noting that the merged corporation (Eagle Inc.) had
ceased to exist and its shares had been cancelled by law, the court
characterized a Delaware merger as an asset acquisition. (In the example above, New Texas Corp. would be visualized as acquiring the assets
of the Canadian business from Eagle Inc. Depending upon the size of
the Canadian business, New Texas Corp. might need the prior approval of the Canadian government.)

What if the merged corporation (Eagle Inc.) owns a Canadian
subsidiary instead of a branch business? Under the rule in the *Dow
Jones* case, the foreign investor would be *directly* acquiring the shares of
the Canadian subsidiary. (The review threshold for direct acquisitions
in the *IC Act* would, therefore, apply.)[37]

---

[36] *Dow Jones & Co. Inc. v. A.G. Can.* (1980), 113 D.L.R. (3d) 395; affd (1981), 122
D.L.R. (3d) 731 (C.A.).

[37] The *Dow Jones* case involved a transaction known in the U.S. as a "triangular
merger" or a "forward triangular merger". In a "reverse triangular merger", on the
other hand, the U.S. corporation which owns the shares of the Canadian company does
not disappear. Instead, it survives the merger, and becomes a wholly-owned subsidiary of
the acquiring U.S. corporation. A reverse triangular merger is, therefore, distinguish-
able from the *Dow Jones* case, and constitutes an indirect acquisition of the Canadian
company.

(f) Partnerships, Trusts and Joint Ventures

Non-Canadians who buy an interest in a Canadian or offshore partnership, trust or joint venture that:

(1) carries on a business in Canada,[38]

(2) controls[39] a Canadian-based partnership, trust, joint venture or corporation that carries on a business in Canada,[40]

may have to comply with the *Investment Canada Act*. To find out, non-Canadians should read the *"acquisition of control rules"* (set out below) to determine if they are acquiring control.

(The jurisdiction in which the partnership, trust or joint venture has been organized is irrelevant. Subparagraph 28(1)(b)(ii) of the Act makes no distinction between Canadian and foreign-based partnerships, trusts or joint ventures.)

The *"acquisition of control rules"*[41] for partnerships, trusts and joint ventures are similar to those for corporations, but easier to remember:

deemed acquisition of control: purchase of a 50.1% voting interest

no acquisition of control: purchase of anything less.[42]

The *"chain of control presumptions"* are also similar. A partnership, trust or joint venture (hereinafter collectively called a "partnership") controls another entity under the following circumstances:

---

[38] Subpara. 28(1)(b)(i).

[39] Directly or indirectly.

[40] *(Foreign or Canadian) Partnership, Trust, Joint Venture—-Canadian Partnership, Trust, Joint Venture.* See subpara. 28(1)(b)(ii). The partnership, trust or joint venture that is the target of the acquisition may be Canadian or foreign-based. Note that there must *not* be a corporation in the chain of control if subpara. 28(1)(b)(ii) is to be used as the legal basis for jurisdiction.

(Foreign or Canadian) Partnership, Trust, Joint Venture—Canadian Subsidiary, Partnership, Trust, Joint Venture If a Canadian subsidiary carries on a business or if there is a Canadian-incorporated company in the chain of control, see subpara. 28(1)(d)(i).

(Foreign or Canadian) Partnership, Trust, Joint Venture—Canadian Partnership, Trust, Joint Venture. If there is a foreign-incorporated company in the chain of control, the transaction falls under subpara. 28(1)(d)(ii).

[41] See paras. 28(3)(a) and (b). The drafters of these rules obviously looked at the acquisition of a partnership from an equity perspective rather than as a purchase of the underlying assets. Hence, a "voting interest" is defined as an ownership interest entitling the owner to share in the profits and (upon dissolution) in the assets of the partnership.

[42] FIRA treated these transactions differently. When a foreign investor bought an interest of less than 50% in a partnership, FIRA administrators sometimes asserted jurisdiction by claiming that a "new" group consisting of the foreign investor and the original partners had taken control.

(1) Presumption of Direct Control

  (a) Majority Ownership: the partnership owns 50.1% or more of another partnership's voting interest or a corporation's voting shares;

  (b) Minority Ownership—Corporation: the partnership owns between 33 1/3% and 50% of a corporations' voting shares and in addition has *de facto* control of the corporation (through the ownership of those shares);

(2) Presumption of Indirect Control: a partnership which controls another entity is deemed to indirectly control any entities that the other entity controls;

(3) Associated Entities Presumption: same rules as for corporations.[43]

EXAMPLE: A New Zealander buys a 49% "voting interest" in partnership A (which may be organized under the laws of Canada or a foreign country). Partnership A has a 60% interest in Partnership B, which again may be Canadian or foreign-based. Partnership B carries on a business in Canada. Does the *IC Act* apply?

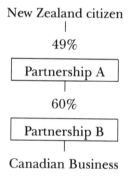

New Zealand citizen
|
49%

Partnership A
|
60%

Partnership B
|
Canadian Business

Because the New Zealander is buying less than a majority interest in the first partnership, the Canadian government cannot exercise any jurisdiction. However, Partnership A clearly controls Partnership B and if the New Zealander were to purchase a 50.1% interest in Partnership A, either a notification or an application for review would have to be filed.

Sometimes, minor differences in the structure of a business can yield dramatically different legal consequences. There are two business structures involving partnerships and branch businesses, which foreign investors can acquire without Investment Canada having any jurisdiction whatsoever (these business structures are not common).

---

[43] Subs. 28(2).

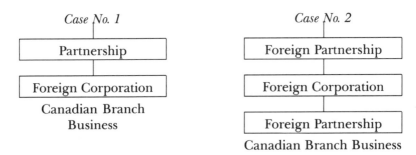

Case No. 1

| Partnership |

| Foreign Corporation |
Canadian Branch
Business

Case No. 2

| Foreign Partnership |

| Foreign Corporation |

| Foreign Partnership |
Canadian Branch Business

In the first case, a partnership (joint venture, trust) controls a foreign corporation with a branch business in Canada. An indirect takeover of a Canadian business owned in this manner is not snared by subparagraph 28(1)(d) because those who drafted the statute (for reasons explained elsewhere in this chapter) did not include a branch business in the definition of an "entity". Consequently, from a legal perspective, there is no "entity in Canada" carrying on a business. (Non-lawyers sometimes have difficulty understanding this particularly when the business is located on their city's main street.)

In the second case, a foreign-incorporated company controls a foreign partnership which operates an unincorporated Canadian business. Paragraph 28(1)(d) is again of no use if Investment Canada wants to review the transaction, since there is no "entity in Canada". As for paragraph 28(1)(b), Investment Canada cannot ground its jurisdiction on that paragraph because there is a corporation in the chain of control.

On the other hand, suppose a partnership (trust, joint venture) owns a Canadian branch business directly, rather than through a foreign corporation. The legal result is then reversed. An acquisition of that partnership (trust, joint venture) will fall within Investment Canada's domain.

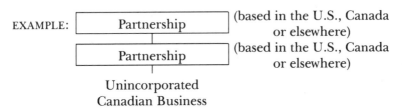

EXAMPLE: | Partnership | (based in the U.S., Canada or elsewhere)

| Partnership | (based in the U.S., Canada or elsewhere)

Unincorporated
Canadian Business

Why, in this example, does Investment Canada have jurisdiction if either partnership is acquired? See paragraph 28(1)(b). (There is no corporation in the chain of control; the nationality of the partnership is of no relevance; and although the subparagraph refers to an entity that "controls . . . another entity carrying on a Canadian business", there is no stipulation that the second entity be *in Canada*.)

(g) Limited Partnerships

There is no special treatment given to limited partnerships in the *IC Act*, although limited partnerships differ from general partnerships in fundamental ways. To determine if a foreign investor has acquired control, the same yardstick that is used for all other business organizations—the percentage of voting interests purchased—applies.

> EXAMPLE: Slater Inc. ("Slater") is the general partner in a limited partnership. Slater manages the affairs of the partnership but owns only 5% of the partnership units. A European company buys the 5% interest held by Slater and assumes Slater's obligations and liabilities under the limited partnership agreement. Is the European company now in control?

No. Even though it will now be *managing* the limited partnership, the European company has not acquired control. It can do so only by acquiring 50.1% or more of the partnership's units.

Conversely, a foreigner who purchases a majority of the units in a limited partnership is deemed to have acquired control. This is so despite the fact that, under Canadian law, a limited partner has no power to bind the partnership and will jeopardize his limited partnership status if he helps to run the business.[44]

These are, at first glance, anomalous legal results from a statute supposedly directed at changes in control. Why, investors ask, did Parliament not make an exception for limited partnerships and focus on actual control instead of equity interests?

One reason is that the drafters of the Act (like musicians in a band) wanted to give their creation some harmony. Treating all investment vehicles in the same fashion was their way of doing it. Another apparent reason is that the ownership of a large equity interest and the ability to control are often closely intertwined.

Some limited partnerships are composed of just two parties: a limited partner who owns all the units, and the general partner. Although the limited partner has no right to control the limited partnership, the weight of his or her massive interest will act like reins over the general partner. If, in addition, the limited partner has a contractual right to remove the general partner without cause, the

---

[44] However, to become liable to creditors for the debts of the partnership, a limited partner has to exercise a blatant degree of "control" (e.g., by participating in the day-to-day management of the business). This "control test" is far narrower than what Parliament was thinking of when it passed the *IC Act*. For further details see Lyle Hepburn, *Limited Partnerships*, (Don Mills: Richard De Boo Publishers, 1989), pp. 4–15 to 4–28.

limited partner is in a similar position to that of a sole shareholder of a corporation who, at his or her discretion, can throw out the board.

The converse arises when limited partnership units are widely-held and no limited partner holds a substantial interest. Real control then lies with the general partner, whose position might be compared to that of the board of directors of a widely-held company. (Good examples are some drilling funds.)

2. Trusts and Contracts

There are three types of transactions which seldom occur, but when they do, puzzle investors who are trying to understand the "Investment Canada implications". These are: acquistions *of* trusts and *by* trusts, and acquisitions of control of a Canadian business through a contract.

3. The Acquisition of a Trust

Why do investors use trusts? Trusts offer a flexible alternative to incorporation. Compared to a partnership, they provide greater protection for the capital contribution of investors through the interposition of an independent third-party intermediary. Finally, trusts offer the advantage of a flow-through of income and depreciation allowances to the beneficiary.

Trusts are sometimes employed when investors want to explore for minerals or buy commercial real estate. A group of persons will provide funds to, and receive units in, a trust, which then purchases an office building. The trust property is the building, and the income of the trust is the rent. Investors who wish to subdivide and develop land may also use a trust.

Foreigners who want to buy an interest in such a trust must examine the same "acquisition of control rules" that govern partnerships and joint ventures. If a trust carries on a business, control of that business is acquired by the purchase of either the trust property (e.g., the office building) or a majority of the units[45] in the trust.

What happens if a foreign trustee replaces a Canadian one? Nothing (as far as Investment Canada is concerned). The foreign trustee does not acquire control of the trust since he or she does not receive any units ("voting interests") in the trust.

---

[45] The "voting interests".

When a trust controlled by non-Canadians buys a Canadian business, that purchase will be subject to the *IC Act*. If the trust is terminated several years later and the foreign beneficiaries acquire the business in their own name, that event will not constitute another acquisition of control since the beneficial ownership of the business has not changed.

The outcome is different when a Canadian business person whose children have chosen to become U.S. citizens, creates an *inter vivos* trust for them, and transfers his or her Canadian business to the trust. Since the trust will usually be controlled by the Canadian business person as trustee (see subsection 26(2)), the transfer will have no immediate Investment Canada implications. However, when those children finally acquire the Canadian business under the terms of the trust documents, their acquisition of control will be subject to the *IC Act*. (Although the transfer of a business in accordance with instructions contained in a will is exempt from the Act, that exemption does not apply to an *inter vivos* trust.)

4. Acquisition By Contract

More common than the acquisition of a trust is the acquisition of effective control of a Canadian business through a contract. Following an escrow closing, for instance, a foreign investor may operate a business for a brief period of time, pending the fulfilment of a condition such as regulatory approval. Another example is the operation of a Canadian business, such as a hotel, by a foreign-controlled management company. Needless to say, franchise agreements also give foreign companies substantial power over the affairs of Canadian businesses.

Contracts can be strait-jackets, as some Canadian franchisees have discovered. Nevertheless, according to the *Investment Canada Act*, a foreign business person cannot acquire control of a Canadian business through a contract.[46] Canadian and foreign companies can, therefore, enter into tight distribution and supply contracts, and financial agreements replete with negative covenants, without government approval.

Sometimes, such relationships turn sour. The foreign company then exercises its powers and the Canadian business person complains bitterly to Investment Canada. A commercial litigation lawyer should be consulted instead.

---

[46]Thus, a contract by which a foreign investor obtained the right to control the voting rights attached to shares (e.g., an irrevocable proxy) would evidently not be caught by the legislation. There is no provision in the *IC Act* equivalent to para. 3(6)(c) of the *FIR Act*.

5. Other Provisions

Several provisions in the Act give further meaning to the concept of control. One of those provisions helps investors who have a contractual right to buy more shares. Two other provisions—dealing with step transactions and multi-voting shares—hit out at avoidance schemes. The remaining provision is directed at takeovers of Canadian businesses operating on both sides of the Canada-U.S. border.

(a) Absolute Contractual Rights

Some investors who provide equity or debt financing to a Canadian company are contemplating an eventual takeover. The usual pattern is for these investors to buy a few shares and simultaneously acquire an option on a controlling block. Others advance funds under a convertible debenture. One object of this strategy is risk reduction. These investors want a window on the company before they invest any more money.

If these investors are "non-Canadian", they face a disturbing possibility: when the time comes for them to take control, Ottawa may block them for doing so. A few foreign investors can escape from this uncertainty. If they have an absolute right to buy voting shares or assets, subsection 30(1) allows them to pretend that they have already exercised their right and now own the shares or assets.

If this election places them in deemed control of a large Canadian business, they can file an application for review immediately and discover whether their takeover plans face a green light. On the other hand, if the Canadian company is small in size, the investors can notify Investment Canada of their "deemed" acquisition of control. Years later, when the small company has become one of Canada's multinational enterprises, they can take it over without worrying about Ottawa's reaction.

Unfortunately for foreign investors, there are two restrictions: their right to acquire more voting shares must be both absolute and contained in a written contract. Conditional options and rights of first refusal do not qualify.[47] Convertible non-voting preference shares may

---

[47] A right of first refusal is a contingent right, not an absolute right. If the grantor of the right is prepared to accept an offer to sell an interest in a business to a third party, the holder of the right has an option to purchase the interest on the same terms for a certain number of days. *Canadian Long Island Petroleums Ltd. v. Irving Industries (Irving Wire Products Division Ltd.)* (1975), 50 D.L.R. (3rd) 265, at 277. Also see Arthur Corbin, *Corbin on Contracts*, (St. Paul: West Publishing Co., 1963), sec. 261, at p. 472. This book describes a right of first refusal as a right to "be given an option to purchase before O makes a contract to sell to another". Citing *Corbin on Contracts*, FIRA administrators used

conceivably qualify. (Although a convertible share is a chose in action, a conversion right may be considered to be a right under a contract.)[48] Warrants to purchase shares, and convertible debentures, on the other hand, definitely meet both branches of the test, provided they can be exercised *immediately*.

Rights of first refusal and buy-sell provisions are found in the majority of shareholders' agreements. Many investors are disappointed to learn that these are not absolute rights. They complain about the uncertainty they must live with, not knowing whether they will be permitted to exercise their rights.

This was one aspect of the trade-off when subsection 30(1) was drafted. On the other side of the scale were the public funds that would have to be spent to review takeovers that might never occur or that might occur years hence when the economic climate (and sometimes the target company itself) had substantially changed.[49]

There was a third consideration. How long does an approval last? It is unlikely that an approval would last forever. The *IC Act* must be interpreted in light of its purpose. An approval probably lasts for two or three years. After that, economic circumstances have changed so greatly that a new application and set of plans should be submitted.

---

to argue that a right of first refusal is not even a contingent right to acquire, but a right to have a right.

[48] All shares are choses in action (i.e., intangible moveables). Stewart, J.L. and M. Palmer, *Company Law of Canada*. (Toronto: Carswell, 1962), p. 180. The real issue is whether a "conversion right" is a contractual right or a proprietory right attaching to the share. In support of the "contractual rights argument" is the theory that the articles of incorporation of a company constitute a contract between the shareholders and the company. If this theory is correct, rights attaching to shares (which are set out in the articles of incorporation of a company) would be contractual rights. In the memorandum of association system, on the other hand, the memorandum and articles of association are clearly contractual in nature. *The Theatre Amusement Co. v. Stone* (1915), 50 S.C.R. 32, at 37. In the U.S., the courts have stated that the relationship between a corporation and its shareholders is contractual. Part of this contract is found in the articles of incorporation of a company and the company by-laws. *American Jurisprudence*, (Rochester: The Lawyers Co-operative Publishing Co., 1985), Vol. 18A, sec. 731.

Suppose a Canadian has a "put" allowing him to force a foreign business person to buy his shares. Does that put qualify as an absolute right under subs. 30(1)? No, because the put is not a "right" that belongs to the non-Canadian.

[49] The review of "deemed" takeovers that never actually occurred happened when FIRA existed. Under the *FIR Act*, a foreign investor who had obtained a *contingent* right to purchase sufficient shares to control a company was *deemed* to have acquired that company, and had to seek *immediate* government approval. In a memo addressed to the minister and dated June 10, 1986, the president of Investment Canada explained the problem this caused: "The government was being asked to make a decision on very little information as in most cases, the investor, being a minority shareholder, would not have the ability to access any of the corporate records." (Memo released under the *Access to Information Act*).

What if a non-Canadian investor desperately wants an immediate government review of his or her takeover plans? When the contingent rights clauses are being drafted, the Canadian vendor and the non-Canadian can insert an unfettered option or other absolute right into the agreement, but at a price so high that it will never be exercised (or if it is exercised, the Canadian will be delighted). It might be wise to put in a time limit on the exercise of this right. The non-Canadian can then take advantage of section 30, and receive a decision by the minister without delay.

(b) Step Transactions

An alternative strategy exists for buying a Canadian business over time. Instead of purchasing an option, some investors make a number of small equity investments as profits grow.

This nibbling is brought within federal government jurisdiction by subsection 29(2). This subsection catches acquisitions of control that result from a series of linked transactions by collapsing them into one transaction.

EXAMPLE: In 1990, a Brazilian industrialist bought 35% of the voting shares of a Canadian company. He subsequently buys an additional 20%.

The purchase of a 20% interest is deemed not to be an acquisition of control. However, because of the step transaction provision, the 20% and 35% interests can be totalled to determine if control has changed hands.

EXAMPLE: A non-Canadian purchases 75% of a company's *non-voting* shares. Subsequently, the company's capital structure is re-organized. Because the non-Canadian has agreed to provide additional debt financing, the other shareholders agree to amend the rights attached to the company's non-voting shares to include the right to vote. As a result, the non-Canadian ends up with 40% of the company's voting rights. Does the step transaction provision cover this series of events?

Possibly. This is a grey area of the law.

A few investors make their takeovers through a combination of direct and indirect purchases. First they buy shares in their own name, then they purchase a corporate shareholder of the Canadian business.

EXAMPLE: A company from Taiwan buys 25% of a Canadian corporation. Subsequently, the Taiwanese company buys a British company which owns 30% of the shares of the Canadian corporation. What can Ottawa do?

Subsection 29(2) snares such circuitous takeovers by allowing the federal government to agglomerate the direct and indirect purchases. Is such a takeover direct or indirect? That is a key question since the review threshold for indirect acquisitions far exceeds the threshold for direct acquisitions. (Beginning in 1992, subject to exceptions, indirect takeovers by Americans are not reviewable at all.)

According to subsection 29(2), an acquisition is deemed to occur at the time of, and in the manner of, the last step. The Taiwanese company is, therefore, considered to have made an indirect acquisition.[50]

Might subsection 29(2) be abused? Could an American in 1992 make a direct purchase followed a few hours later by an indirect purchase, and succeed in scaling a large Canadian company without review? Such a scheme would be contrary to the intent of subsection 29(2), but would not be illegal. It could, however, collide with one of the anti-avoidance provisions in the Act.

(c) Canadian Multinationals

Another miscellaneous provision is aimed at the takeover of Canadian multinational companies. Subsection 31(1) states: "A Canadian business shall be deemed to be carried on in Canada notwithstanding that it is carried on partly in Canada and partly in some other place." A company like Northern Telecom, with operations in the U.S or Europe, is, therefore, a "Canadian business".

What if only the U.S. operations of a Canadian company are acquired? And these operations constitute substantially all of the company's assets? Does Canada's screening legislation apply?[51] That is a moot point. If they have a client contemplating such a transaction, some solicitors will ask for an opinion from Investment Canada. Others advise the vendor to restructure the business before the sale so that the U.S. and Canadian assets are owned by sister companies.[52]

---

[50] Subs. 29(2) has worried a few lawyers. It reads as if the "control in fact" test of FIRA days has been reintroduced. If so, two purchases of 15% might constitute control. This, however, is too narrow an interpretation. Subss. 29(2) and (3) must be read together. When this is done, it is clear that "control in fact" is not the yardstick. The purchases that are combined by subs. 29(2) must exceed the 33 ⅓% tripwire (in subs. 28(3)), before an "acquisition" can possibly occur.

[51] If the "U.S. assets" constitute a "separate business", the three-pronged definition of Canadian business would not be met. But *quaere* whether subs. 31(2) can be used as a "shield".

[52] Have these lawyers thought about the statute's "anti-avoidance provisions"? (See Chapter 15.)

(d) Shares with Multiple Votes

The last of the miscellaneous provisions in the Act zeros in on shares with more than one vote. Multi-voting shares are not rare. The participating preferred shares of Power Corp., for instance, carry ten votes per share. A holder of just over 9% of Power Corp's shares would control 50% of the votes.

Since the "acquisition of control rules" in the *IC Act* are based upon the number of shares purchased, the existence of multi-voting shares raised the spectre of a gigantic loophole. Subsection 30(2) closed this loophole by deeming a single share with several votes to be equivalent to several voting shares.

6. Buy-backs and Involuntary Acquisitions

It is unclear whether the statute catches buy-backs and involuntary acquisitions. Section 28, which describes how control can be acquired, seems to require some action by the non-Canadian (e.g., a purchase). On the other hand, the step transaction provisions in section 29 might be used as a pillar for federal government jurisdiction.

This problem can arise in the context of a joint venture agreement which provides for the development of a mining project and which contains dilution provisions. If one joint venturer fails to pay its share of the costs, its interest will be automatically reduced, and the interest of the co-participants will be increased. If one of these participants is a foreign company, it may be shocked to discover that it has gained control of the joint venture.

Buy-backs pose a similar dilemma. Imagine that a company with Canadian and foreign shareholders redeems one class of its shares or purchases them in the open market. If the shares purchased were held by Canadians, a foreign shareholder might find himself in control of the company.

7. A Summary: The Acquisition Rules

Acquisition of	*Basis of Jurisdiction*
1. all or substantially all of the assets of a Canadian business, including a branch business	paragraph 28(1)(c)
2. the voting shares of a Canadian corporation which carries on a Canadian business	paragraph 28(1)(a)
3. the voting shares of a foreign-incorporated company which carries on an unincorporated Canadian business	no jurisdiction—a branch business

4. the voting interests of a partnership (based in Canada or elsewhere) which carries on a Canadian business

paragraph 28(1)(b)(i)

5. the voting shares of a Canadian-incorporated company which controls another Canadian-incorporated company that carries on a Canadian business

subparagraph 28(1)(d)(i)

6. the voting shares of a foreign-incorporated company which controls a Canadian-incorporated company which carries on a Canadian business

subparagraph 28(1)(d)(ii) Note: the higher thresholds in section 14 may apply

7. the voting shares of a foreign-incorporated company which controls another foreign-incorporated company that carries on an unincorporated Canadian business

branch business—no jurisdiction

8. the voting shares of a foreign-incorporated company which controls a partnership in Canada which carries on a Canadian business

subparagraph 28(1)(d)(ii) Note: the higher thresholds in section 14 may apply

9. the voting shares of a foreign-incorporated company which controls a foreign-based partnership that carries on a Canadian business

branch business—no jurisdiction; subparagraph 28(1)(d)(ii) does not apply, because there is no entity in Canada; paragraph 28(1)(b) is of no use, because a corporation is being acquired

10. the voting interests of a partnership (based in Canada or elsewhere) that controls another partnership (based in Canada or elsewhere) which carries on a Canadian business

subparagraph 28(1)(b)(iii); there must be no corporations in the chain of control; the presence of an entity *in Canada* is not necessary

CHAPTER 7

THE EXEMPTIONS

Even when federal government jurisdiction over a takeover appears incontestable, there is one remaining question to ask: does one of the exemptions apply? There are eleven statutory exemptions in the Act. If the transaction can be squeezed into one of them, a foreign investor can proceed without notifying Ottawa.

All of these exemptions have been lumped together in section 10 of the Act. Why they exist and how they work is explained below.

1. Stockbrokers' Exemption[1]

A trader or dealer in securities which, in the ordinary course of its business, acquires a company's voting shares (or interests in a partnership, trust, or joint venture) does not have to comply with the *Investment Canada Act*.

This exemption is designed for foreign-controlled financial intermediaries which engage in underwriting or block trading. In the course of their business, they may acquire as principal, but for the purpose of resale, more than 50% of a Canadian company's voting shares. Usually, ownership of these shares will be transferred quickly. Most new share issues that are being underwritten have already been presold to institutions and are held by the underwriters for only a few days.

Without the stockbrokers' exemption, foreign-controlled investment dealers who underwrite major share offerings by large Canadian companies would need approval from Ottawa before doing so. This is because the underwriters would be deemed to have acquired control of the Canadian companies whose shares they are reselling.

---

[1] Para. 10(1)(a).

147

2. Venture Capitalists' Exemption[2]

Venture capitalists are individuals or institutions which provide "seed money" in the form of equity and loans to budding entrepreneurs with a promising idea but no cash. They may also invest in companies that are experiencing financial difficulties, if they believe that the companies can be reorganized and rendered profitable. If the venture capitalists remain satisfied with the company's progress, they do not exercise day-to-day control. Instead, they provide management advice and sell their interest after the business has become successful.

Parliament has decided[3] that foreign-controlled venture capitalists should be exempt from the Act. However, Parliament gave the minister the power to impose conditions.

These "terms and conditions" have been published in the *Canada Gazette*. They set out the circumstances under which an investor is considered to be in the business of supplying venture capital in Canada. Briefly, the investor must have made venture capital available in Canada for *two years preceding* the transaction in question and should have done so principally through the purchase of voting interests or other unsecured investments. In addition, the investor must not normally acquire a majority of a business' voting interests and must usually sell the voting interests within ten years.

These conditions prevent a newly-incorporated venture capital company from qualifying for the exemption. But suppose the company's shareholders have been providing venture capital to Canadian companies for several years. Does this make a difference? Although the foreign shareholders of such a company will argue it should make a difference, their past lending practices are not taken into consideration.

However, foreign-controlled venture capital companies which do not qualify for the exemption almost never complain. Their investments are usually in struggling companies that are too small for government approval to be needed if control changes hands.

---

[2] Para. 10(1)(b). This exemption is not often used by non-Canadian venture capitalists. This is because acquisitions of less than 33% of a company's voting shares are excluded from the Act, as are temporary acquisitions for financing purposes.

[3] The history of this exemption goes back to 1972, when the *Foreign Takeovers Review Act* was being debated. Venture capital firms argued that compliance with the new law would be too time-consuming in their line of business. The Liberal government agreed but did not exempt the entire industry because government officials could not adequately define it. House of Commons, *Minutes of the Standing Committee on Finance, Trade and Economic Affairs*, Issue No. 24, June 20, 1972, p. 24:45.

3. Lenders' Exemption[4]

A foreign lender who makes a bona fide loan and obtains a security interest in a Canadian business can enforce that security interest without being subject to the Act. In other words, if the borrower defaults, the lender may foreclose or send in a receiver without notifying Ottawa.

The lender is also free to resell the business. However, the *IC Act* will apply if the purchaser is a non-Canadian.

If this exemption for lenders did not exist, some Canadian businesses might be in dire financial straits. They would be unable to obtain loans from the many foreign banks operating in Canada because the banks would be uncertain whether they could enforce their security.

There is no requirement in the lenders' exemption that the loan must be made to the company that grants the security. Therefore, a foreign lender can make a loan to an individual who wants to buy a company in Canada, and then take the assets of that company as security. The exemption will also apply if a loan is made to a foreign company that is a member of a corporate group, and a *sister* company in Canada grants the security. If the foreign company defaults, the foreign lender may seize the assets of the Canadian sister company without its seizure being subject to review or notification.

Surprisingly, there is no stipulation in the exemption that the security be granted to safeguard the rights of the lender. A foreign institution which guarantees the repayment of a loan made by another party, and receives a pledge of the shares of a Canadian business as *collateral security*, may take advantage of the lenders' exemption when realizing upon that collateral security.

It is not even essential that money change hands. Paragraph 10(1)(c) merely refers to security "for a loan or other financial assistance". "Other financial assistance" could be a line of credit. A foreign supplier, who grants trade credits and receives a pledge of assets or shares in exchange, can shelter under the exemption if proceedings to enforce the security should prove necessary. (This puts foreign and Canadian suppliers on an equal footing in this respect.)[5]

---

[4] Para. 10(1)(c). The taking of security (in the form of a chattel mortgage, floating charge, debenture) does not amount to an acquisition of control because there is no transfer of beneficial ownership.

[5] Here is the usual sequence of events. A Canadian customer falls into financial

In brief, the lenders' exemption covers all commercial transactions in which security is given. However, the financial assistance that is extended must be for a legitimate business purpose. If two parties enter into an agreement with the intention that the Canadian party will default, the exemption will not apply. Should a lender make no attempt to sell the seized security, this may be some evidence that the transaction was not *bona fide*.

4. Financing Exemption

An exemption exists for a non-Canadian who wants to acquire temporary control of a Canadian business for the purpose of facilitating its financing. However, control must be given up within two years (or such longer period of time as the minister may allow).[6] Otherwise, the notification/review provisions of the statute will apply.

This exemption allows a non-Canadian to take over a Canadian business, rearrange its capital structure by reducing or lengthening the debt burden and increasing equity, and then sell the now solvent business without having to comply with the Act. It is a particularly useful exemption when a supplier or franchisor wants to take control of a *failing* dealership or franchise. This sometimes happens in the automotive industry.

The Ford Motor Company, for example, will take over a dealership in difficulty and operate it until a new dealer can be found. Such temporary acquisitions were exempted from the Act, because no purpose would be served by reviewing them.[7]

Sometimes, a foreign franchisor will get control of a Canadian business because the Canadian owner has breached the franchise agreement. Or a foreign vendor who has sold a business to a Canadian will recover possession after the purchaser has defaulted on his or her mortgage payments. The financing exemption does not apply in either of these cases because financing the business is not the motive for the acquisition.

What distinguishes the financing exemption from the lenders' exemption? In the case of the former, control is acquired when the

---

difficulty. Its foreign supplier demands and gets a debenture or other security on assets to secure the outstanding trade credits. Eventually, if the Canadian customer does not pay, the foreign supplier may have to realize upon its security.

[6] Para. 10(1)(d). If any condition is not complied with, the exemption does not apply. See subs. 10(2).

[7] The Ford Motor Company will put up capital, take shares of the dealership as security and, thus, acquire control. The new Canadian dealer later buys the shares.

financial assistance is given. With the lenders' exemption, beneficial ownership of the pledged assets or shares remains with the borrower until default.

5. Corporate Reorganization

Amalgamations, mergers, consolidations and corporate reorganizations that do not result in a change in the ultimate controller of a Canadian business are excluded from the ambit of the *IC Act*.[8] This provision makes sense in light of the intent of the legislation, which is directed at changes in control.

This exemption is not restricted to changes in the organization of corporations, although at first glance, that may seem to be the case. The reference to "Canadian business" expands the compass of the exemption to include restructurings that involve partnerships and other entities.

When making inquiries to determine if a corporate shuffle will change the ultimate locus of control, there are two points to note. First, control is determined through the ownership of voting interests, not through contracts or loan agreements. Secondly, within that band, it is *de facto* control that must be considered.

A non-Canadian may exercise *de facto* control over a business without owning a majority of its shares, particularly if the other shares are widely held. For example, an American corporation may own only 45% of the shares of a Canadian company but exercise control because the interests held by the remaining shareholders are very small. In such circumstances, the American company can transfer the Canadian business to one of its (the American company's) affiliates without running afoul of the *IC Act*.

Reorganizations have been the subject of many requests for opinions from Investment Canada. In addition to providing evidence as to where ultimate control presently lies and will lie after the reorganization, an applicant for an opinion should also indicate the purpose of the reorganization. This is to satisfy the government that the reorganization is not being undertaken in order to evade the statute.

---

[8] Para. 10(1)(e). The ultimate locus of control is determined through the ownership of voting shares. This will usually be the last shareholder at the top of the chain of control. Some widely-held corporations are controlled by their board of directors, not their shareholders. Those who drafted the exemption ignored this possibility.

6. "Agent of the Crown" Exemption[9]

Sometimes, it can be important who the vendor is. If a business is being carried on by an agent of Her Majesty in right of Canada or a province, or by a Crown corporation within the meaning of the *Financial Administration Act*, a non-Canadian buyer has hit it lucky. His or her acquisition of the business will be exempt from the Act.[10]

The rationale for this exemption appears to be based on a "living creature" analogy. The government is assumed to be a body with many appendices and one directing mind. Accordingly, the government would be reviewing itself if it examined the sale of a business by Canada Post or Canadian National Railways under the *Investment Canada Act*.[11]

Like all Crown corporations, Canada Post and C.N.R. are wholly owned by the government. Under the *Financial Administration Act*, they are responsible to Parliament. Any acquisition of a Crown corporation requires at least the issuance of an order in council.

But what about a corporation which is partly owned by the federal or a provincial government, or by one of their Crown corporations? Does the "agent of the Crown" exemption apply if a foreigner wants to take over the entire business? It appears that the exemption cannot be used in such circumstances.[12]

---

[9] Para. 10(1)(f).

[10] Crown corporations are accountable to Parliament. Their acquisition by non-Canadians requires the issuance of an order in council. The sale of de Havilland Aircraft of Canada Ltd. to Boeing had to be reviewed under the *IC Act* only because the union owned one share.

[11] According to the living creature analogy, one part of the government knows what the other parts want. Of course, the reality is very different. Other arms of the federal government are unlikely to consider all the factors in the *IC Act* when deciding whether to sell a business to a foreigner. A well-publicized example of this occurred during the FIRA era. In 1984, Japan's Sumitomo Corporation entered into an agreement with government-owned Petro-Canada and others to earn an interest in British Columbia's Monkman Project. The agreement violated Canadian government policy dealing with the degree of foreign ownership in the resource industry. As a result, the Canadian Cabinet (actually the Governor in Council) issued an order under the *FIR Act* turning down the transaction. The ensuing public battle pitted the Canadian Cabinet and the Department of Energy, Mines and Resources against a Crown corporation (Petro-Canada). This battle probably confused the Japanese. (Eventually, new arrangements were negotiated and the transaction approved.)

[12] Because of a drafting deficiency, the issue is not free from doubt. The Canadian business must be "carried on by an agent". Unfortunately, "carried on by" is not defined. Does this phrase refer to jointly operated businesses? Is active participation in the management of the business necessary? These theoretical questions become real when a

Wholly owned subsidiaries of parent Crown corporations are also subject to the framework for control in the *Financial Adminstration Act*. Consequently, the "agent of the Crown" exemption extends to them as well. Since a parent Crown corporation cannot dispose of a wholly owned subsidiary unless authorized by an act of Parliament, the drafters of the Act evidently thought this extension of the exemption made sense.

The task of determining whether a Crown corporation falls under the *Financial Administration Act* is easy. There is a list of Crown corporations in the appendices to that act.

If the name of the corporation does not appear there, the investor must then determine whether the corporation is an agent of a provincial or the federal Crown. In the case of statutory corporations, that is, companies established pursuant to a separate statute (and not under the *Canada Business Corporations Act* or its provincial equivalents) the enabling legislation often states that the corporation is a Crown agent. If the vendor is a federal corporation, the investor should also look at the *Government Companies Operation Act*,[13] which declares that certain corporations are agents of Her Majesty.

Sometimes, there is no relevant statutory provision. The non-Canadian must then examine the common law to determine whether an agency relationship exists. One factor of importance is the degree of independence that the directors of the corporation have.[14] If it is clear that a corporation is subject to the control of the government, then the courts will usually rule that the corporation is an agent of Her Majesty. On the other hand, if the directors of a corporation have considerable discretionary power, the courts may decide that the corporation is an independent public authority, and not an agent.

EXAMPLE: A businessman borrows money from the Federal Business Development Bank. He subsequently fails to meet his monthly payments

---

Crown corporation with a "passive" 45% interest in an operating company wants to sell its interest. In the case of Air Canada and Petro-Canada, the question is academic since total foreign ownership is restricted to 25%. See the *Air Canada Public Participation Act*. *The Investment Canada Act: Briefing Document*, p. 18, (released under the *Access to Information Act*) states explicitly: "Partly-owned Crown corporations or agents are not exempt from the Act". That document appears to express the intention of the drafters.

[13] R.S.C. 1985, c. G- 4.

[14] See, for instance, *Radych & Manitoba Power Commission*, [1942] 1 D.L.R. 445; affd [1942] 2 D.L.R. 776 (C.A.); and *R. v. Ont. Labour Relations Bd., Ex parte Ont. Food Terminal Board*, [1963] 2 O.R. 91, at 95. In *North and Wartime Housing Ltd. v. Madden*, [1944] 4 D.L.R. 161, the court ruled that a company wholly owned by the Crown was a private company. In that case, the court did not use the control test but looked at the nature of the services performed.

and the bank seizes the assets of his business. Can a citizen of Taiwan buy the business from the bank without approval from the Investment Canada minister?

Yes, because the Federal Business Development Bank is listed in the appendix to the *Financial Administration Act*, the "agent of the Crown" exemption will apply.

7. "Non-Profit Corporation" Exemption[15]

The acquisition of businesses that are exempt from paying tax under paragraph 149(1)(d) of the *Income Tax Act* are also exempt from the jurisdiction of Investment Canada. To qualify for this exemption, the business must be carried on by a corporation, commission or association in which the federal, provincial or a municipal government owns 90% or more of the shares or capital. In addition, only a Canadian governmental authority may have a right or option to acquire the shares or capital. (This latter stipulation, found in paragraph 149(1)(d) of the *Income Tax Act*, is designed to discourage a province from financing a project behind the facade of a Crown corporation, and then allowing the shares to be acquired by someone else under an existing right or option.)

Obviously, there is some overlap between the "non-profit corporation" exemption and the "agent of the Crown" exemption.

8. Bank Exemption[16]

A number of transactions involving banks have been excluded from the jurisdiction of Investment Canada. These excluded transactions are:

1. The acquisition of control by a non-Canadian of:

   (a) a bank, or

   (b) a foreign bank subsidiary.

2. the establishment by a non-Canadian of a new business that is:

   (a) a bank, or

   (b) a foreign bank subsidiary.

---

[15] Para. 10(1)(g).

[16] Para. 10(1)(h). Section 307 of the *Bank Act* removes certain transactions from the *IC Act* and makes them subject to the *Bank Act*.

3. The (direct or indirect) establishment or acquisition by a foreign bank of a Canadian business whose principal activity in Canada consists of providing:

   (a) banking services,

   (b) fiduciary services,

   (c) insurance services, or

   (d) services normally performed by an investment dealer, investment counsellor or stockbroker.

4. The acquisition of control of a Canadian-incorporated company by a foreign bank subsidiary or by a corporation that the foreign bank subsidiary (directly or indirectly) controls.

This exemption is discussed further in Chapter 18, "The Bank Act and the Investment Canada Act".

9. Devolution of Estate Exemption[17]

Owners of businesses who die without a will have their estates distributed in accordance with provincial laws dealing with intestate succession. A citizen of Malaysia or some other foreign country, who acquires a Canadian business as a result of such an intestacy, does not have to comply with the *IC Act*. Instead, the Malaysian citizen benefits from the exemption in the Act for the involuntary acquisition of control of a Canadian business on the devolution of an estate.

Non-Canadians who acquire Canadian businesses under a will benefit from the same exemption. This is because the phrase "devolution of an estate" appears to cover a disposition of property pursuant to a will as well as a devolution by law as a consequence of an intestacy.

A few individuals and families in Canada control sizeable businesses. The devolution of estate exemption may one day be a major blessing to this group.

The devolution of estate exemption also covers involuntary acquisitions that occur "by operation of law". The principal target of this provision is joint tenancies.

The most important incident of a joint tenancy is the right of the survivors, upon the death of a joint tenant, to have their interests proportionately increased. If two or more people, one of whom is a foreigner, own a business in joint tenancy, the foreigner may acquire

---

[17] Para. 10(1)(i).

the entire business if he or she outlives the others. Such an acquisition will not be subject to the Act.

At common law, a joint tenancy could not exist between an individual and a corporation because corporations do not die. However, many provinces now have legislation which puts corporations and individuals on the same footing and allows corporations to hold property with individuals in joint tenancy. If the corporation is dissolved, its interest passes to the other joint tenant. Transfers of this nature also fall within the exemption.

Transfers of property through *inter vivos* trusts are excluded from the devolution of estate exemption. This may cause concern to a few wealthy Canadians. Canada's multimillionaires like to put their corporate empires into family trusts. These trust documents customarily state that the trust property is to be delivered to the beneficiaries when the settlor, or the last income beneficiary, dies. If the grandchildren are the capital beneficiaries, and they have since become citizens of some sunny southern land, they, or the trustees, may have to comply with the *IC Act*. If the trust property is a major Canadian business, Ottawa could potentially block the transfer.

Most business people whose children are foreign citizens need not worry, however. Only transfers of large businesses are reviewable.

10. Insurance Company Exemption[18]

Two categories of insurance companies do business in Canada. These categories are:

1. Canadian-incorporated insurance companies

   (a) Canadian-controlled stock companies,

   (b) foreign-controlled stock companies,

   (c) mutual insurance companies;

   · and

2. Foreign-incorporated insurance companies

   (a) foreign-controlled stock companies, or

   (b) mutual insurance companies

---

[18] Para. 10(1)(j). This exemption is consistent with the treatment accorded to mutual insurance companies under the Canadian/non-Canadian status rules. Under these rules, a mutual insurance company is Canadian-controlled (and its activities exempt from review) if a majority of the participating policy holders are Canadians and no voting groups exist. In such circumstances, investments made by the mutual insurance company can be regarded as being for the benefit of Canadian policy holders.

(Foreign-incorporated insurance companies which operate in Canada conduct their business through branches.)

An example of a company in the first category is Excelsior Life, which is a Canadian-incorporated subsidiary of the U.S.-based Aetna Group. Metropolitan Life, which is the Canadian branch operation of a U.S. mutual life insurance company, fits into the second category.

Unlike foreign-controlled, Canadian-incorporated insurance companies, non-resident insurance companies with branches in Canada must vest certain of their assets in trust. This stipulation, which is found in the *Foreign Insurance Companies Act*,[19] is to ensure that they can meet their liabilities to their Canadian policy holders.

When FIRA was in existence, foreign-owned insurance companies had to comply with it. They were not happy about this and publicly said so.

Probably as a result of their lobbying, paragraph 10(1)(j) was placed in the Act. This paragraph exempts investments by non-Canadian-controlled insurance companies, when those investments are for the ultimate benefit and on behalf of Canadian policy holders. The effect of this provision is to treat foreign-owned and Canadian-owned insurance companies in the same fashion when making investments.

However, this exemption cannot be used by all insurance companies. It is only available to:

(1) Canadian-incorporated insurance companies (that are foreign-controlled) if they are registered under the *Canadian and British Insurance Companies Act*, and if they include the investment income from the Canadian business acquired in computing their taxable income under subsection 138(9) of the *Income Tax Act*. This condition, which identifies property held for their Canadian account, is necessary because some Canadian-incorporated insurance companies have businesses in other countries.

(2) non-resident mutual or stock insurance companies, registered to carry on business under either the *Foreign Insurance Companies Act* ("*FICA*") or the *Canadian and British Insurance Companies Act* ("*CBICA*"), if the revenue from the Canadian business that is purchased is included in computing taxable income under subsection 138(9) of the *Income Tax Act*. In

---

[19] R.S.C. 1985, c.I-13, s. 2, 14 and 20. Assets may be deposited with the Receiver General of Canada or with a trust company provided the trust agreement is approved by the Minister of Finance.

addition, the shares or assets of the Canadian business must be vested in trust pursuant to the provisions of the applicable Canadian insurance company legislation. The purpose of these two conditions is to restrict the exemption to investments that are for the benefit of or held against liabilities to Canadian policy holders.

(3) Canadian-incorporated subsidiaries that are wholly owned by either a non-resident insurance company or a Canadian-incorporated but foreign-controlled insurance company, provided one further condition is met: when it purchases assets or shares of a Canadian business, the subsidiary must vest those assets or shares in trust pursuant to the *CBICA* or the FICA.

This third exempting provision clearly had a dual purpose. It was designed to allow certain foreign insurance companies (a) to purchase Canadian businesses through a holding company (or other subsidiary), and (b) to structure joint ventures with Canadians, without the insurance company having to notify Investment Canada or seek government approval in either case. (A joint acquisition with a non-Canadian is still subject to the Act.) Unfortunately, because of a drafting error, this third provision does not work. (Neither government lawyers nor the insurance industry noticed the faulty drafting when the legislation was before Parliament.)

The error is in the "vesting in trust" condition in subparagraph 10(1)(j)(iii). Under the *CBICA* and the *FICA*, only companies incorporated *outside* Canada that carry on the business of insurance can vest assets in trust.

These vesting provisions, in other words, are restricted to the direct investments of foreign insurance companies. There is no procedure for a Canadian-incorporated company or a company not in the insurance business to do so, even when such a company is controlled directly or indirectly by a foreign insurance company.

From a policy perspective, this result is perfectly understandable. Foreign insurance companies must deposit assets with the Receiver General or vest assets in trust with a corporate trustee to ensure that they can meet their Canadian liabilities. There was no reason for the drafters of the insurance legislation to permit voluntary vesting of assets by other types of insurance companies.

This has created a dilemma. To qualify for the exemption in the *IC Act*, Canadian subsidiaries of non-resident insurance companies, and subsidiaries of Canadian-incorporated but foreign-controlled insurance companies must vest assets in trust under the *FICA* or the *CBICA*. But neither Act allows this.

EXAMPLE: A Canadian-incorporated holding company owned by Metropolitan Life (or another non-resident insurance company) buys Canada's Stelco Steel Company. Does this transaction need government approval?

Yes. The holding company is Canadian-incorporated and not in the business of insurance. Therefore, it cannot vest the shares of Stelco Steel in trust under the *FICA*.[20] This means the exemption in subparagraph 10(1)(j)(iii) cannot be used.

11. Farm Exemption[21]

Foreign investors can purchase farms in Canada without having to advise Investment Canada. In the words of the Act, "the acquisition of control of a Canadian business the revenue of which is generated from farming carried out on the real property acquired in the same transaction is exempt".

The term "farm" is not defined. However, the dictionary definition refers to the raising of crops or livestock. Obviously, all activities that involve tillage of the soil, dairying, fruit growing and poultry or livestock raising constitute farming. The acquisition of a ranch, which is merely a large farm for raising horses or beef cattle, also falls within the exemption. The status of fish farming is less clear.

The exemption stipulates that revenue from farming must be generated from the property acquired. This means that the presence of revenue from other sources will taint the transaction and render the exemption inapplicable.

A farmer who has built a four-unit motel on his property, which is managed in his spare time, has taken the business outside of the exemption. A dude ranch, which is a vacation resort offering activities such as horseback riding, is also not covered by the exemption (particularly if guests are lodged on the ranch). However, the purchaser of an agribusiness, such as an automated factory-like operation for raising poultry on a small piece of land, can take advantage of the exemption, even though such an operation lacks many of the attributes of a farming business.

It is not essential that all the real property be actively used for farming. If part of the farm consists of raw or vacant land, the exemption still applies since vacant land is not a business. However, if a

---

[20] An alternative is to transfer the shares of the Canadian business from the holding company to the parent insurance company and then vest these shares in trust pursuant to the *FICA*. The exemption in subpara. 10(1)(j)(ii) of the *IC Act* would then apply.

[21] Para. 10(1)(k).

foreigner buys only assets and machinery and no land, the exemption cannot be used.

This exemption for farmers gives greater force to section 33 of the *Citizenship Act*. Under the *Citizenship Act*, passed in 1976, Ottawa delegated to the provinces the authority to prohibit or restrict foreigners from buying land within provincial boundaries.[22]

Prior to that date, the provinces had the constitutional authority to regulate the acquisition of land on the basis of residency but *not* citizenship or nationality. They could, in other words, restrict the sale of land to non-residents (including Canadian citizens who were residents of other provinces) but could not enact legislation aimed solely at foreigners (since under Canada's constitution, only the federal government has legislative power with regard to aliens).

That state of affairs was of great concern to some provincial governments, especially those in western Canada. During the 1970s, foreigners were buying large tracts of land which inflated farm prices. This, in turn, was preventing young farmers from purchasing farms.

In response, Parliament in 1976 allowed the provinces to regulate the ownership of land by aliens. Unfortunately, this did not completely solve the problem (at least from the provinces' perspective). Effective regulation by the provinces was still frustrated because farms were businesses and the Foreign Investment Review Agency reviewed takeovers of businesses by foreigners.

Consequently, an exemption was put in the *IC Act* for farming businesses. This eliminated most of the overlap between Canada's law governing foreign investment and section 33 of the *Citizenship Act*.

Now *only* the provinces can control the purchase of agricultural land. In addition, since far fewer transactions by foreigners are subject to review under the *Investment Canada Act*, compared with the *Foreign Investment Review Act*, the extent to which the provinces can regulate the acquisitions of land-based businesses (such as tourist camps, golf courses) has been increased.

The *Citizenship Act* does not require the provinces to regulate land ownership by foreigners. Moreover, the power of those provinces (like Alberta[23]) which choose to do so is subject to certain limitations.

---

[22] For a discussion of the background to section 33 of the *Citizenship Act* and the factors affecting foreign ownership of land, see: Environment Canada, *Foreign Ownership of Land and Real Estate in Canada*, (Ottawa: Minister of Supply and Services Canada, 1984).

[23] Alberta bars non-residents of Canada and foreign-controlled corporations from

In particular, their power to regulate cannot be applied to any transaction that has been approved the federal government under the *IC Act*. For instance, if West Germans buy a landholding and development company, Canada's provinces cannot directly control the transfer of the lands if the purchase by the West Germans was reviewed under the *IC Act*. Without this restriction, a province could deny approval to the acquisition of the real estate portion of a business and frustrate a transaction that in the federal government's view is of benefit to Canada.

One consequence of exempting farms from the *IC Act* is that there is no way of knowing how many farms are being purchased by foreign investors.

12. Some Non-Exempt Transactions

(a) Sale-Leaseback

There is no exemption in the statute for sale-leasebacks. What is that? A sale-leaseback occurs when a purchaser buys a business from its owner, then leases it back on a net basis. The purchaser-lessor receives a return on its investment in the form of rent, and the original owner, who is now a lessee, continues to operate the business.

A sale-leaseback is often just a form of financing, an alternative to placing a mortgage on a property. When such transactions came before FIRA, they were excluded from review. The explanation given by FIRA administrators was that control of the business had not changed.

The *Investment Canada Act* focuses on ownership interests rather than control in fact. It, therefore, "catches" sale-leasebacks. Does this really matter? Perhaps not. Many of the foreign-controlled lending institutions which enter into sale-leaseback arrangements are insurance companies. They can use the "insurance company exemption" to avoid review.

---

owning more than 20 acres. Manitoba, Prince Edward Island, Quebec and Saskatchewan impose restrictions on residents of other provinces and countries. See: Alberta: *Agricultural and Recreational Land Ownership Act*, R.S.A. 1980, c. A-9 ss. 1(a), 2, 3, 4 and Alberta Foreign Ownership of Land Regulations, Alta. Reg. 160/79 as amended by 2231/79. Manitoba: *Farm Lands Ownership Act*, Re-enacted R.S.M. 1987, c. F-35 s. 4. P.E.I.: *Prince Edward Island Lands Protection Act*, S.P.E.I. 1982, c. 16, s. 4. Quebec: *An Act Respecting the Acquisition of Farm Land by Non-residents*, R.S.Q. 1977, c. A-4.1. Saskatchewan: *The Saskatchewan Farm Security Act*, S.S. 1988–89, c. S-17.1. Extracts from these Acts are in P. Hayden, *Foreign Investment in Canada*, (Scarborough: Prentice-Hall), Vol. 2.

(b) Rental Real Estate

The Act also contains no exemption for rental real estate. Consequently, foreigners who purchase apartment buildings, office complexes and shopping centres must file either a notification or an application for review. (An astounding number of lawyers who act for foreign investors do not realize this. Neither do some lawyers for the banks which finance the transactions.)

Until third reading of the *Investment Canada Act*, rental real estate was exempt. During third reading, an opposition Member of Parliament (Lloyd Axworthy) introduced an amendment to eliminate the exemption. In a surprise voice vote, called when most Conservatives were absent from the House of Commons, 15 New Democratic Party and Liberal M.P.s cheerfully passed the amendment.

Investment Canada could have administratively restored the exemption through interpretation notes and written opinions that finessed the definition of a "Canadian business". But to do so would be to defy an express decision of Parliament.[24]

---

[24] It is often difficult to establish that the purchase of rental real estate by foreign investors benefits Canada. To avoid reviewing hundreds of such transactions, FIRA officials created their own "administrative law" to exclude them. This was done through vague guidelines based upon size and purchase price ($10 million), and through the application of an active-passive distinction. The ownership of real estate was conceptionalized as being separate from its management. If a foreign purchaser contracted out all management activities to an arm's-length Canadian property management company, FIRA officials concluded that control of a business had not been acquired. Such artificial distinctions are not regarded as being available under the *IC Act*. Asset size can never be conclusive as to whether a business is being carried on. In addition, there is a closer conceptional link between ownership and control in the *IC Act*, and the definition of business has been expanded to include a revenue-generating capability. A democratic reason for not exercising administrative discretion is that Parliament has specifically addressed its mind to the issue.

CHAPTER 8

IS THE INVESTMENT REVIEWABLE?

The *Investment Canada Act* contains provisions for automatic review and a reserve review power. However, in the great majority of cases, the acquisition of control of a Canadian business will not be reviewable. This is because the legislation permits the government to examine only large takeovers (and takeovers of any size and new businesses if they fall within a special class of investments related to Canada's cultural heritage).

1. Preconditions

If a "non-Canadian" wants to:

(i) "acquire control" of a "Canadian business", or

(ii) "establish" a "new Canadian business",

and no exemptions apply, Investment Canada has jurisdiction. At least a notification will have to be filed, and perhaps an application for review.

For an investment to be reviewable, one further precondition must be met. Either,

Reserve Review: the business being established or acquired must be designated in the regulations as being related to Canada's cultural heritage and the Governor in Council must issue an order for review; or

Automatic Review: the Canadian business being acquired must own assets with a book value in excess of $5 million (direct acquisition) or $50 million (indirect acquisition). If the investor is an American or buying an American-controlled business, these thresholds (subject to certain exceptions[1]) rise to:

---

[1] Oil, gas, uranium, transportation, and financial services businesses (except for insurance services).

Year	Direct Acquisition	Indirect Acquisition
1990	$ 50 million	$250 million
1991	$100 million	$500 million
1992	$150 million	no review
1993+	$150 million plus adjustment for inflation	no review

Note: The higher thresholds for Americans do not apply to five types of businesses: oil and gas, uranium, cultural, transportation and financial services businesses (except for insurance services), ("the sensitive business exemptions").

In this chapter, the requirements for review will be examined at length. But first, here is a summary of the questions investors must consider.

Is the acquisition direct? All direct acquisitions of Canadian businesses with a book asset value of $5 million or more are reviewable, unless the investor is either an American or buying an American-controlled business.

Non-American Investors	Americans/American-controlled Businesses[2]		
$5 million	1991	:	$100 million
	1992	:	$150 million
	1993	:	$150 million plus inflation adjustment

Is the acquisition indirect? All indirect acquisitions of Canadian businesses are reviewable if their book asset value exceeds:

Non-American Investors	Americans/American-controlled Businesses		
$50 million	1991	:	$500 million
	1992	:	no review[3]

An indirect acquisition is the acquisition of a Canadian company (or other entity) through the purchase of the shares of its parent (or grandparent) company located outside Canada. (An indirect acquisition can occur in no other way.)

Is the indirect acquisition predominantly a Canadian transaction? If there is an offshore transaction, and the book asset value of the Canadian business exceeds 50% of the asset value of the global transaction, the threshold for review *returns to* $5 million. (If the investor is

---

[2] Exceptions: "the sensitive business exemptions".

[3] Exceptions: "the sensitive business exemptions".

an American, or buying an American-controlled business, the threshold for direct acquisitions applies.)

Is the new business or acquisition culturally sensitive? The list of culturally sensitive activities is in the regulations. If a new business or acquisition is culturally sensitive, the Canadian government can order a review, regardless of the size of the business. However, the government must issue the order for review within 21 days after the investor submits a "notification" to Investment Canada.

Is the investor an American? If so, will the acquisition involve cultural, oil, gas, uranium, transportation or financial services businesses? These economic subsectors were excluded when the Free Trade Agreement raised the threshold limits for American buyers. In these cases, the general thresholds of $5 million and $50 million still apply.

Is the business being purchased American-controlled? Investors of any nationality can shelter under the higher thresholds granted to Americans if the business they are purchasing is controlled by Americans. (As pointed out above, these higher thresholds do not apply to cultural, oil, gas, uranium, transportation and financial services businesses.)

2. A Classification Scheme

The automatic review provisions are complex. To simplify them, a classification scheme is presented below. (Assume in each case that the non-Canadian investor is "acquiring control".)[4]

(a) Share Purchase: Canadian-Incorporated Company[5]

"Trigger" Elements: (a) non-Canadian,

(b) purchase of voting shares,

(c) acquisition of "control",

(d) Canadian-incorporated company,

(e) carries on a Canadian business directly, or indirectly controls another Canadian-incorporated company (or a Canadian-based partnership, trust or joint venture) which carries on a Canadian business.

---

[4] The "acquisition of control" rules are in Chapter 6.

[5] Para. 28(1)(a); subpara. 28(1)(d)(i); paras. 14(1)(a), 14(1)(b) and 14(3)(b).

Threshold: Non-American $ 5 million
            investors:

                                      Year
            American/American- :   1992 : $150 million
            controlled businesses   1993 + : $150 million
                                              plus adjustment
                                              for inflation.

Calculation: See the consolidated financial statements of the Cana-
              dian company.

(b) Offshore Share Purchase: Foreign-Incorporated Company with Canadian Subsidiary[6]

"Trigger" Elements: (a) non-Canadian,

                     (b) purchase of voting shares,

                     (c) acquisition of control,

                     (d) foreign-incorporated company which con-
                          trols[7] a Canadian-incorporated company (or
                          a Canadian-based partnership, trust or joint
                          venture) that carries on a Canadian business.

This type of transaction will be reviewable if *either* of the following two thresholds are met.

Threshold #1: Threshold 1 has two requirements. Both requirements must be satisfied before a transaction is reviewable.

(i) The 50% + proportionate test: the book asset value of the "Canadian assets" (that is, the assets of the entity carrying on the Canadian business and all other entities in Canada that it directly or indirectly controls) exceeds 50% of the book asset value of all entities directly or indirectly acquired in the international transaction.

If the foreign company being purchased keeps its accounts on a consolidated basis, and the book asset value of its Canadian subsidiary[8] constitutes more than 50% of the book asset value

---

[6] Subpara. 28(1)(d)(ii); para. 14(1)(c); subss. 14(2), 14(3), 14(4).

[7] Directly or indirectly.

[8] Or its Canadian partnership, trust or joint venture.

that appears on the parent's consolidated balance sheet, the "50% + proportionate test" has been met.

and

(ii) The book asset value of the Canadian business is $5 million or more (American purchasers/American-controlled business— 1992: $150 million; 1993 + : $150 million plus adjustment for inflation).

Threshold #2: An investment is reviewable if the book value of the "Canadian assets" is $50 million or more (American purchasers/ American-controlled businesses: 1992 + : no review).

In summary, if an offshore transaction by a non-American leads to the indirect acquisition of a Canadian business with a book asset value of $50 million or more, an application for review must be filed. However, if the Canadian business has a book asset value of less than $50 million, only a notification need be submitted unless the "Canadian assets" constitute more than 50% of the value of the global transaction and the book value of those "Canadian assets" is $5 million or more.

In addition, the Governor in Council may decide to review an indirect acquisition of *any size* if the Canadian business carries on an activity that is related to Canada's cultural heritage or national identity.

(i) Offshore Indirect Acquisitions — The Reason for Their Special Treatment

Why are indirect purchases of Canadian businesses, when they occur offshore, treated so differently from direct purchases? The explanation is rooted in the history of the *Foreign Investment Review Act*.

One of the major criticisms of the *FIR Act* was its alleged extraterritorial impact. Under that Act, the review mechanism was activated when one foreign company acquired another foreign company which carried on a Canadian business. When this happened, FIRA examined the acquisition of the Canadian company on the grounds that its ultimate controllers had changed. This annoyed FIRA's critics, who complained that the agency was interfering with takeovers in foreign countries.

These critics were wrong in their choice of language. The government of Canada never claimed nor wanted the authority to review acquisitions of foreign businesses by other foreigners. Canada's foreign investment review process had an extraterritorial effect just as an increase in Canadian income tax, which reduces the ability of Canadians to purchase foreign goods, has an extraterritorial effect. But it did not constitute the extraterritorial application of Canadian law. In the words of the Federal Court of Appeal in the *Dow Jones* case (which arose because control of a Canadian business changed hands through the merger of two U.S. companies), Canada's screening legislation,

> . . . did not seek to affect extraterritorial activity but is enforced only in relation to the Canadian business. The provisions of the Act were not applied extraterritorially although Parliament has power to enact legislation that will have such effect.[9]

During FIRA's reign, all indirect acquisitions were subject to review, regardless of the size of the Canadian business. If the new foreign owners could not demonstrate that their indirect acquisition of the Canadian business was of significant benefit to Canada, they had to relinquish control.

This seldom happened. When it did, either the business was sold, or a Canadian partner was found who took a controlling interest. FIRA's critics seized on this. There was no diminution in the level of Canadian ownership when one foreign controller replaced another. So why, they asked, should indirect acquisitions be reviewed?

The framers of the *Investment Canada Act* responded to this criticism. Canada's screening legislation, they concluded, should not apply when the indirect acquisition of a Canadian business is merely an incidental or a small part of an international transaction, unless the Canadian business is very large.

As a result, they created two special rules. If the proportionate size of the Canadian business compared to all the businesses that a non-Canadian is acquiring in one international transaction is 50% or less, the Canadian business is probably not the central focus of the takeover. There should consequently be no review, with one exception (for very large businesses). If the Canadian business being indirectly acquired has a book asset value of $50 million or more, the takeover should still be reviewed, even if the Canadian business is merely an insignificant part of a huge world-wide transaction.

On the other hand, if the book value of the Canadian business is more than 50% of the book value of the foreign parent's consolidated operations, the Canadian business being indirectly acquired is probably the major target of the offshore takeover. In such circumstances, the same threshold used for direct acquisitions should apply.

EXAMPLE: In 1992, Texas Motors Inc. buys Homes Inc. ("Homes"). Both are American companies. Homes has a balance sheet asset

---

[9] *Dow Jones & Co. Inc. v. A.G. Canada* (1980), 113 D.L.R. 395, at 401; affd (1981), 122 D.L.R. 731. This case was decided under FIRA.

value of $200 million which includes a value of $160 million attributed to its Canadian subsidiary. Is Canadian government approval necessary?

This is an indirect acquisition, normally not reviewable in 1992 and afterwards if the purchaser is an American. However, the American is in for a surprise. Because the "Canadian assets" constitute a majority of Homes' assets, the threshold for direct acquisitions applies. In 1992, that threshold (for Americans) is $150 million. Texas Motors Inc. will therefore need Canadian government approval before it completes the takeover.

Curiously, Parliament has not treated all indirect acquisitions in this same lenient fashion. The higher thresholds for indirect acquisitions apply when a non-Canadian buys a foreign corporation with a subsidiary in Canada. The higher thresholds do not apply when a non-Canadian buys a foreign partnership (trust or joint venture) which owns a Canadian corporation.

Is this distinction logical? Maybe not, but it is understandable. Parliament addressed American complaints of interference by FIRA in U.S. corporate mergers. The Americans never mentioned partnerships (trusts or joint ventures).

(c) Offshore Share Purchase: Foreign-Incorporated Company with Branch Business

Investment Canada has no jurisdiction over transactions involving branch businesses.[10] Neither a notification nor an application for review need be filed.

This result perplexes American lawyers. "Do you mean", they ask, "that if my clients set up a branch business in Canada, they must notify Ottawa, but if they purchase a U.S. company with a Canadian branch business, they need file nothing?" Yes.

---

[10] Para. 28(1)(d) refers to an entity that controls an entity in Canada. A branch business is not an "entity" as that term is defined in the Act.

(d) Asset Purchase[11]

"Trigger" Elements: (a) non-Canadian,
               (b) asset purchase,
               (c) purchase of all or substantially all,
               (d) Canadian business.

Threshold: Non-American investors: $ 5 million

		Year		
American/American-	:	1992	:	$150 million
controlled businesses		1993	:	$150 million plus adjustment for inflation

Calculation: Aggregate the value of all assets acquired (as shown on the financial statements).

Cash and Accounts Receivable: Suppose that only the plant and equipment of a business are being acquired (and that these assets constitute substantially all of the business' assets, which means there is an "acquisition of control"). Do cash, accounts receivable and inventory have to be included in calculating asset value?

It appears (from the regulations) that the answer is no, even if the exclusion of cash, inventory and accounts receivable renders the transaction non-reviewable!

(e) Purchase of a Partnership, Trust or Joint Venture[12]

"Trigger" Elements: (a) non-Canadian,
               (b) acquisition of voting interests,
               (c) Canadian or foreign partnership, trust or joint venture,
               (d) carrying on the Canadian business.

Threshold: Non-American investors: $ 5 million

		Year		
Americans/American-	:	1992	:	$150 million
controlled businesses		1993 +	:	$150 million plus adjustment for inflation.

<hr>

[11] Paras. 28(1)(c) and 14(1)(a); subs. 14(3).

[12] Subpara. 28(1)(b)(i); para. 14(1)(a); subs. 14(3).

Calculation: Aggregate asset value. See the consolidated financial statements for the partnership (trust or joint venture) that is carrying on the Canadian business, and all other entities in Canada which it (directly or indirectly) controls.

The rules for calculating a business' "value" are best illustrated through an example. Imagine that a U.S.-based partnership directly carries on a Canadian business with a book asset value of $4 million, and also owns other assets, such as an unincorporated business in the U.S., with a book asset value of $200 million. If the partnership is sold to a group of Americans in 1993, must an application for review be filed with Investment Canada?

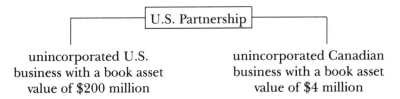

| U.S. Partnership |

unincorporated U.S. business with a book asset value of $200 million

unincorporated Canadian business with a book asset value of $4 million

The answer depends upon the book asset value of the U.S. partnership since that is the entity which carries on the Canadian business. In this example, that figure is $204 million, which is the total book asset value of both businesses.[13] Consequently, if an American (or other foreigner) buys the partnership (and thus, indirectly, the Canadian business), the takeover is reviewable under Canadian law.

This is a bizarre result. The point to note is that book asset value is determined at the *entity* level, not by examining the book asset value of the Canadian business. (An unincorporated business is not an entity.)

The legal consequences may be different if a U.S. partnership owns a Canadian company. Consider a purchase by a foreign investor of a Canadian or foreign partnership, trust or joint venture, which carries on a Canadian business *through* an intermediary.[14]

| Canadian or Foreign Partnership |

| Canadian Company |

---

[13] In the words of subs. 14(3), "the assets of the entity carrying on the Canadian business" are $204 million although the Canadian business itself is worth only $4 million.

[14] Subpara. 28(1)(d)(i); para. 14(1)(b); subs. 14(3).

"Trigger" Elements: (a) non-Canadian,

(b) acquisition of "voting interests",

(c) Canadian or foreign-based partnership, trust or joint venture,

(d) intermediary (corporation, trust, partnership or joint venture),[15]

(e) business in Canada,

(f) carried on directly through the intermediary or indirectly through a chain of intermediaries,

(g) any corporation that is an intermediary is Canadian-incorporated.

Threshold: Non-American investors : $ 5 million

Americans/American- : 1992 : $150 million
controlled businesses   1993 + : $150 million
plus adjustment for inflation.

Calculation: From the consolidated financial statements, determine the value of the assets of the intermediary that is carrying on the Canadian business (and all other entities in Canada the control of which is directly or indirectly acquired).

Unlike the example on the previous page, involving a U.S. partnership where there was *no* corporation in the chain of control, the foreign partnership in the diagram above is not *directly* carrying on a business in Canada. The partnership's offshore assets are therefore of no concern in calculating asset values. If, for instance, the partnership owns an unincorporated U.S. business with a book asset value of $200 million, that business can be ignored for valuation purposes. (Thus, there is no "bizarre result", unlike in the preceding illustration.)

EXAMPLE: A joint venture based in the Netherlands owns a Canadian-incorporated holding company with an operating subsidiary in Canada. The book asset value of the joint venture (from its consolidated financial statements) is $206 million. This figure includes the $6-million book asset value of the Canadian holding company.

---

[15] Or chain of intermediaries.

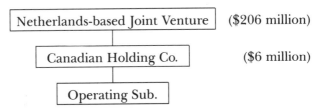

If a French citizen buys the joint venture, only the $6-million asset value of the holding company is relevant (when determining reviewability under the *IC Act*), not the $200 million in other assets which the joint venture owns.

If a foreign investor purchases a Canadian or foreign partnership, trust or joint venture which carries on a Canadian business *through* a foreign-incorporated company as one of the intermediaries, more complex rules apply.[16]

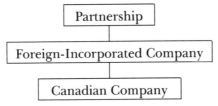

"Trigger" Elements: Same as above, except that a foreign-incorporated company is an intermediary[17] between the partnership and the Canadian company (or other entity).

The presence of a foreign-incorporated company as one of the intermediaries is the switch that activates the special rules for offshore acquisitions (discussed under category 2). This transaction will be reviewable if *either* of the following two thresholds are met:

Threshold #1: (i) The 50%+ proportionate test: the book asset value of "THE CANADIAN ASSETS"[18] exceeds 50% of the book asset value of all entities[19] acquired in the global transaction.

and

---

[16] Subpara. 28(1)(d)(ii); para. 14(1)(c); subss. 14(2) and (3).

[17] Or a member of a chain of intermediaries.

[18] The assets of the entity carrying on the Canadian business and all other entities in Canada that it directly or indirectly controls.

[19] Directly or indirectly.

(ii) The book value of the assets of the Canadian business is:

Non-Americans	:		$ 5 million
Americans/American-controlled businesses	:	1992 :	$150 million
		1993 + :	$150 million plus adjustment for inflation.

Threshold #2: The book value of the assets of the Canadian business equals or exceeds:

Non-Americans	:		$ 50 million
American/American-controlled businesses	:	1992 + :	no review.

3. Thresholds and Asset Values: Some Questions

Here are some questions that foreign investors sometimes ask:

Purchase Price: Why is purchase price not the test? Or fair market value?

A purchase price test would have required a set of rules to deal with non-arm's-length relationships. Moreover, when the final amount to be paid for a business depends on future events (i.e., earn-outs), the actual purchase price is unknown. What about a fair market value test? Purchasers would have needed appraisers so instead, a test based on balance sheet asset value was chosen.

Unfortunately, this test has some deficiencies. Fixed assets are recorded on financial statements at historical costs. Deductions are subsequently made for depreciation (and depletion). Intangible assets, like goodwill, may not appear on the financial statements at all.

As a result, there is frequently no relationship between a company's balance sheet asset value and fair market value. Usually, a company's fair market value is much higher than the book value of its assets. However, if a company is bankrupt, its book value (assets minus liabilities) and fair market value may be nil, but its balance sheet asset value may be in the millions. An anomaly of a different nature is presented by an engineering company with a high market value but a negligible asset value.

One asset which frequently distorts the numbers is goodwill. Goodwill is the excess of the purchase price over the amount allocable to assets other than goodwill. If a business, which has expanded through acquisitions, is compared with a business of equivalent size, which has expanded through internal growth, the book value of assets will be remarkably different.

Increase In Asset Value: At the end of its last fiscal year, a company's book asset value was just below the threshold for review. However, two months ago, it mortgaged its remaining assets and purchased a $12-million plant. Does Investment Canada now have jurisdiction over a takeover of the company?

No. Increases in asset value since the last completed fiscal year are irrelevant for the purpose of determining if a takeover needs government approval.

Reduction in Asset Value: A company's balance sheet lists $155 million in assets. However, two months after the balance sheet was prepared, the company sold a building for $10 million and used the proceeds to reduce bank debt. Has this sale reduced asset value for threshold purposes?

No. Asset value cannot be readjusted to reflect events (such as the sale of an asset or the payment of a dividend) that occur after the financial statements have been prepared. Why not? Vendors might declare dividends merely to assist purchasers who want to evade the *IC Act*.[20]

GAAP: A Japanese company is selling its world-wide operations including its Canadian subsidiary. Unfortunately, the financial statements have been prepared in accordance with accounting principles that are somewhat different from those accepted in Canada. Need the financial statements be redone in accordance with Canadian principles?

No. The regulations merely state that financial statements must be prepared in accordance with generally accepted accounting principles ("GAAP"); the words "in Canada" were deliberately omitted. Financial statements prepared in a foreign country can be used provided they are in accord with GAAP in that country.

Liabilities: Can liabilities be deducted from asset value?

No. Asset value is net book value, net of depreciation but not liabilities. Why? Because the *IC Act* is directed at control over assets, not the means of financing them.

---

[20] The regulations passed under the *Competition Act* adopt a different approach. They state that a company's asset value *shall* be adjusted to reflect a major event (e.g., payment of a dividend, a purchase financed with borrowed capital) that occurs after the audited financial statements have been completed. Is this a better way of handling the issue? Not necessarily. Either approach may operate to the advantage or disadvantage of an investor.

Audit: Why must financial statements be audited?

That ensures that generally accepted accounting principles have been used in their preparation. However, the regulations allow un-audited statements to be used if financial statements for the most recent fiscal year have not yet been audited.

Statements Not Prepared: "I am purchasing a Canadian business on January 5. Its fiscal year-end is December 31 and its accountants have not yet audited its financial statements. Can I use last year's statements?"

No! According to the regulations, audited financial statements can be used only if they cover the immediately preceding fiscal year. In other words, if they are more than 12 months old, they are out of date. However, unaudited statements can be used.[21]

Shareholders' Equity: An investor is paying $2.3 million for the shares of a V.S.E.-listed company with a book asset value of $6.6 million. This purchase price represents, roughly, the difference between the company's assets and liabilities. What is the value of the company for Investment Canada purposes?

It is worth $6.6 million. Asset value, not purchase price, is the test.

Slicing a Transaction: A company has several divisions, each of which is capable of being carried on as a separate business. One division has a book asset value of under $5 million. Another division operates a mechanized farm, the acquisition of which is exempt from the Act. Can these two divisions be "sliced off" (i.e., ignored) when determining the company's asset value?

The legislation is imprecise on this point, but any argument that a business can be sliced up to avoid review will likely be resisted by Ottawa.

Horizontal and Vertical Chains: How is asset value calculated if an investor is acquiring a vertical or horizontal chain of entities?

EXAMPLE (Vertical Chains): Aztec P.L.C. is a company based in Great Britain. Aztec owns a holding company in Canada ("Aztec Canada") which in turn has an operating subsidiary called Beaver Corp. A non-Canadian investor wants to buy Aztec P.L.C. or Aztec Canada. What is the procedure for determining "asset value"?

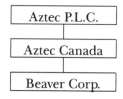

---

[21] The *Competition Act* regulations allow the use of working notes.

To calculate asset value, eliminate Aztec Canada's "long-term investment" in its subsidiary, and inter-company loans and receivables. Then add together the assets of Beaver Corp. ("the entity carrying on the Canadian business") and the assets of Aztec Canada ("all other entities in Canada, the control of which is acquired directly or indirectly"). Alternatively, take this aggregate figure directly from the consolidated financial statements for Aztec Canada. (That is much easier.)

EXAMPLE (Horizontal Chain): A parent company owns several subsidiaries each of which operates a grocery store. A foreign investor purchases the shares of each subsidiary (either by executing one master agreement or by signing seven separate agreements).

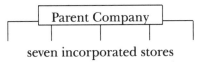

seven incorporated stores

The purchaser may argue that the businesses are distinct and cannot be combined to determine reviewability. However, Ottawa will probably assert that the seven purchases constitute a single "investment"[22] and that their asset values must be aggregated. (Alternatively, since a "business" is not a finite concept but may be both a business by itself and part of a larger business,[23] the seven grocery stores may be one grocery "business".)[24]

What if the subsidiaries each carried on distinct businesses, such as a grocery store, an auto body shop, and a hairdressing salon? Then the purchaser could argue with greater conviction that several Canadian businesses exist.

---

[22] See s. 14.

[23] Subs. 31(2) suggests that an operation may be a business by itself and part of a larger business.

[24] A technical difficulty confronting the proposition that seven entities can carry on one grocery business is the use of the singular in para. 14(3)(b). This paragraph states that an investment is reviewable where the "value of the assets of the entity carrying on the Canadian business is $5 million or more". However, since the *Interpretation Act* states that words in the singular include the plural, the word "entity" in para. 14(3)(b) may be replaced by "entities".

Counsel for the non-Canadian would probably argue that the assets of the remaining six subsidiaries should not be combined with the assets of the first subsidiary. Counsel would point out that the phrase in subs. 14(3), "all other entities in Canada the control of which is acquired directly or indirectly", cannot embrace the six other subsidiaries since they were acquired separately and not in the course of, or through the purchase of, the first subsidiary. If a court should agree, what the public would view as one $7-million transaction would in law be seven $1-million transactions.

4. Guarding Canada's Culture

Culturally sensitive businesses[25] occupy a special place in the legislative scheme. Regardless of size, the establishment or takeover of a "cultural" business may be reviewed if the government so wishes. This is the government's "reserve review power".

(a) The Public Interest Test

The Canadian government decides whether to exercise this power based upon its view of the public interest. After a notification is filed, the government (in reality, the Governor in Council) has 21 days to decide.

Foreign investors bemoan the uncertainty created by the reserve review power. They would like to know in advance whether a "sensitive" investment is reviewable.

However, the discretion given to the government has its advantages. Activities at the periphery of the cultural sector can be excluded from review. So can small, inconsequential investments.

The list of culturally sensitive businesses is not found in the statute. Instead, Parliament gave the Governor in Council the authority to establish the list by regulation. Why? Regulations can be amended more easily than a statute. This permits greater flexibility in defining culturally sensitive sectors. Changes due to new technology and other developments of a cultural nature can also be more rapidly reflected in the list of sensitive activities.

Of course, this means that the government of the day can add or subtract from the list with relative ease. This possibility concerned many organizations that made representations to the committee considering the draft legislation. The term "cultural heritage" had some precision but they worried that "national identity" was a concept broad enough to encompass many areas of the economy.

However, foreign investors need not fear that they will execute an agreement of purchase and sale and then learn that the rules for review have been altered. Any changes to the list of sensitive activities must be tabled in both Houses of Parliament and then referred to a Standing or Special Committee of each House for study. Moreover, a

---

[25] S. 15. Why was the phrase, "specific type of business activity", used in section 15 instead of "industrial sector"? Parliament wanted to force future governments to be precise when specifying culturally sensitive activities. (Otherwise, the protected "cultural sector" might be larger than it need be.)

change cannot come into force until 60 days after it has been made.[26] Parliament will therefore have the opportunity to scrutinize any changes and foreign investors will be forewarned of amendments that are in the pipeline.[27]

As of the present time, the Canadian government has identified four groups of business activities as being culturally sensitive:

1. The publication, distribution or sale of books, magazines, periodicals, or newspapers in print or machine readable form.

2. The publication, distribution, sale or exhibition of film or video products.

3. The publication, distribution, sale or exhibition of audio or video music recordings.

4. The publication, distribution or sale of music in print or machine readable form.

One activity on this list is newspaper publication. A takeover of a small newspaper will not lead to an automatic review, but the government has the option of ordering a review.

Book and magazine publishing is also "culturally sensitive". Why? Principally because there is evidence of a link between the ownership of publishing companies and the number of Canadian authors whose works are printed. For a somewhat similar reason, distributors of video products and music recordings and stores that sell books and periodicals are snared as well. From a legal perspective, they are caught because "distribution" includes both wholesaling and retailing.

The electronic media is not designated as "culturally sensitive"[28] but this is not an oversight. The electronic media was omitted because the Canadian Radio and Television Commission regulates the ownership and control of radio and television stations under the *Broadcasting*

---

[26] Subs. 35(2).

[27] The existence of this specific procedure for changing the list of sensitive businesses may act as a restraint in another way. If a foreigner wishes to take over a culturally sensitive business that is not on the list, it may be politically difficult for any government to threaten retroactive legislation.

[28] The telecommunications sector is not designated as sensitive either. Telecommunications carriers under federal jurisdiction are regulated under the *Railway Act*, although there are currently no ownership restrictions. Because of the large size of telecommunications carriers such as CNCP Telecommunications, any proposed takeover by foreigners would be reviewable under the Act in any event.

Act. This Act states that the nation's broadcasting system should be owned and controlled by Canadians.[29]

Suppose a foreigner wants to establish a convenience store (such as a Mac's Milk). Is this a culturally sensitive activity? It may seem ludicrous, but because convenience stores usually have magazine racks and sell video products, technically, they are part of Canada's "cultural heritage". (To date there have been no orders issued to review the establishment or acquisition of a convenience store.)

The following are some more issues that may puzzle solicitors acting for investors:

What does "production (and) distribution . . . of film and video products" mean?

To solve such interpretative problems, investors should look at the dictionary, case law and the Standard Industry Classification Manual ("S.I.C. Manual") published by Statistics Canada. This manual contains a codification of economic activity.

According to S.I.C. Codes 9611, 9612, 9613 and 9619, the production and distribution of film and video products includes motion picture and television production, film leasing and renting.

What percentage of a company's operations need its cultural activities be in order to trigger the government's reserve review power? Above 50% of the company's gross revenue? Above 5%?

The regulations do not say, but if the cultural activities of a company are merely incidental to its main activities, an attempt to obtain a binding opinion from Investment Canada that the company does not carry on a cultural business might be successful.

The regulations speak of "distribution" and "sale". Is the renting of video film products covered?

A foreign film-maker may want to argue that "distribution" and "sale" refer to activities at the wholesale and retail levels and that "renting" is not caught. Nevertheless, the better view is that "distribution" encompasses the supplying of products in any manner to the public.[30]

---

[29] The *Broadcasting Act*, R.S.C. 1985, c. B-9, as am. by the *Canadian Radio-television and Telecommunications Commission Act*, R.S.C. 1985, c. C-22, ensures Canadian ownership of the broadcast industry. According to a direction issued by the Governor in Council to the Canadian Radio and Television Commission ("C.R.T.C."), under the authority of the *Broadcasting Act*, the C.R.T.C. must not grant broadcasting licenses to persons who are not Canadian citizens or eligible Canadian corporations.

[30] See, for instance, *R. v. Sudbury News Service Ltd.* (1978), 18 O.R. (2d) 428 (C.A.). Since "distribution" includes distribution to the public, the solution is for a foreign producer of films or video products to rent them through Canadian agents, rather than to do so personally. (A foreign producer cannot buy a theatre chain in Canada and then show the films since, by selling tickets, the theatre chain would be "exhibiting" the films.)

If "distribution" includes "renting", why did the drafters of the regulations mention "sale" as a separate activity?

The reason is because a single "sale" does not in law amount to a "distribution".[31]

The Auto Trader is a magazine which displays only advertisements by car owners wishing to sell their cars. Are such magazines part of Canada's cultural heritage?

Car buffs may think so, but that is presently not the law. A magazine is a periodical containing articles, stories or poems. A magazine which contains only advertisements is not a "cultural" business. Nevertheless, if articles were subsequently published, a "new business notification" would have to be filed (if the magazine was foreign-owned). Ottawa would then have the option of reviewing and blocking publication of the magazine. (In the cultural area, any new business is a "new Canadian business" even if it is related to an existing business.)

What about a "tele-shopping service"?

A "tele-shopping service" creates video products promoting the sale of consumer goods and airs them on cable television. This is probably not a culturally sensitive activity since the principal business activity is selling consumer goods; the videos are merely a vehicle for doing so.

(b) The Reserve Review Power and Government Cultural Policy

The reserve review power is just one of many instruments used by Ottawa to promote Canadian culture. Other instruments include regulation by the Canadian Radio and Television Commission; government grants and subsidies and public ownership of cultural institutions such as the Canadian Broadcasting Corporation.[32]

The advantage of the reserve review power is its flexibility. It offers a case-by-case approach for achieving cultural sovereignty goals.

---

[31] *Marino & Yipp v. The King*, [1931] S.C.R. 482; [1931] 4 D.L.R. 530; affd (1931), 56 C.C.C. 136. Also *R. v. Fraser, Harris and Fraser Book Bin Ltd.* (1965), 51 D.L.R. (2d) 408 (C.A.).

[32] When the Investment Canada bill was being debated in Parliament, opposition M.P.s (e.g., Axworthy, Angus) suggested that the reserve review power be extended to the high technology, defence and natural resources sectors. The Conservative government did not agree. Consequently, the businesses designated as "sensitive" account for less than 1% of Canada's gross domestic product. House of Commons, *Minutes of Proceedings and Evidence of the Standing Committee on Regional Development*, April 15, 1985, Issue No. 20, p. 20:14; Issue No. 23, pp. 23:19, 23:22 and 23:32.

Among these goals are increased Canadian ownership, an increased supply of cultural products, and greater Canadian distribution of those products.[33]

5. Acquisitions—Canada's Oil and Gas Sector

Acquisitions in Canada's oil patch pose unique problems for lawyers trying to determine if a transaction is reviewable. These problems arise because the *IC Act* was drafted in general terms. Its principal focus is the manufacturing sector, not the country's resource industries.

In 1991, the minister issued "Guidelines—Acquisitions of Oil and Gas Interests". These guidelines describe how the Act is being administered when transactions occur in the oil and gas industry. However, some solicitors still find the guidelines issued when FIRA guarded the gate to be instructive as well.[34] Guidelines do not have the force of law (although principles of estoppel may apply), and neither version covers all possible scenarios.

The FIRA guidelines make it clear that parties who enter into farm-out, joint operating, pooling[35] or unitization agreements are not acquiring a business. This is so even when the property which is "pooled" or "unitized" is at the production stage. By contrast, the sale of an oil and gas property, which is at the production stage and which can be operated separately, *is* the sale of a business (and needs government approval if the review threshold is exceeded).

Investment Canada's guidelines do not mention farm-outs *per se*. Instead, they distinguish between the acquisition of working interests in exploratory property (not a "business") and working interests in property containing recoverable reserves (usually "treated as the acquisition of an interest in a business").

---

[33] For a description of government involvement in Canada's cultural industries, see Steven Globerman, *Cultural Regulation in Canada*, (Montreal: The Institute for Research on Public Policy, 1983); and Paul Audley, *Canada's Cultural Industries*, (Ottawa: Canada Institute for Economic Policy, 1983).

[34] The "Guidelines Concerning Acquisitions of Interests in Oil and Gas Rights" issued on Jan. 5, 1976 under the *FIR Act* may be helpful because of similarities between the two statutes. Despite their brevity and imprecision, the FIRA guidelines were the fruit of lengthy government–petroleum industry consultations.

[35] Pooling is a form of sharing arrangement. The owners of neighbouring oil and gas properties combine their interests to form a spacing unit. By doing this, they comply with oil and gas conservation legislation and achieve more efficient production. Since each party to a pooling arrangement retains the working interest in each respective tract, the parties have not really disposed of a business. Contrast that with a sale.

Farm-outs are a daily occurrence in western Canada. An owner of land (or an exploration permit) will do some geophysical work, then offer a second party (the "farmee") an opportunity to earn a "working interest" in the property. This interest is earned by the farmee providing financing or doing exploratory drilling. Since such a farm-out is not an acquisition by the farmee, what will happen if a foreign farmee earns a majority interest in a property, and then buys out the Canadian farmer? Since the foreigner will already be in control, the Canadian government will not be able to block the sale (even if the property is by that time producing oil or gas).[36]

Theoretically, even a single oil well can be operated as a separate business and its acquisition may therefore be reviewable. However, if the well is marginal and operating costs exceed revenues, the existence of a business is debatable. (These debates focus on whether the oil well is "capable of being carried on as a separate business". See subsection 31(2).)

Normally, the federal government has jurisdiction over the acquisition of a 100% working interest in a producing property (since the "substantially all" test has been met). One exception may arise if the property and that of several other owners has been unitized.[37] Unitization is the term used when a number of leases, usually covering an entire reservoir of oil or gas, are combined. The reserve can then be operated as if it were a single unit.

If two or more properties have been unitized, the entire unit is perceived by Investment Canada to be a business carried on by a joint venture. Control of a joint venture can only be acquired through the purchase of a majority interest. If a 100% interest in a single producing property is being purchased, but that property constitutes 50% or less of the unit, Investment Canada has no grounds to exercise jurisdiction. If the property being purchased and several others are subject

---

[36] However, the *Canada Petroleum Resources Act*, S.C. 1986, c. 45, governs exploration for and production of petroleum on frontier lands (in the far north and offshore). This Act states that a production licence may not be issued to a licence holder unless it is at least 50% Canadian-owned.

[37] When unitization occurs, each person with an interest in a parcel of land in effect disposes of that interest, and acquires an interest in the entire reservoir. For more information about unitization, see David Lewis and Andrew Thompson, *Canadian Oil & Gas*, (Toronto: Butterworths, 1990) Vol. 1, Part VI. In order for Investment Canada to consider unitized property to be a joint venture, all the various royalty and working interests must be regarded as being equivalent to voting interests as defined in the *IC Act*.

to a joint operating agreement,[38] then the same perception will likely prevail. Investment Canada will usually regard the joint operating agreement as evidence of a joint venture (see the guidelines) and conclude it has no jurisdiction if the property being acquired amounts to less than 50% of the joint venture.[39]

As a result, many sales of oil and gas assets are not examined by Investment Canada. The following are not subject to review:[40]

(1) the purchase of a minority interest[41] in a producing property owned by two or more companies (since their relationship qualifies as a "joint venture");

(2) the purchase of a 50% or lesser interest in a number of producing properties[42] that are subject to a joint operating agreement or a unit agreement (a "joint venture");

(3) the purchase of a number of producing properties provided each has a book asset value of less than $5 million and provided they are not subject to a joint operating or unit agreement. (If such an agreement exists, see (2) above);

(4) the purchase of exploratory properties;

(5) the purchase by a foreign investor who already owns more than a 50% interest in a producing property of a greater interest.

---

[38] There is some justification for perceiving a unit as a joint venture. Under a unitization agreement, each party has a vote based on percentage interest. Issues are decided on the basis of a majority vote or whatever percentage vote is specified in the agreement (which will depend on the type of decision). However, this joint venture analysis works less well in the case of a joint operating agreement. Under such agreements, decisions are not made on the basis of percentage of ownership. Instead, joint decisions must be unanimous. Other decisions can be made by independent action. For instance, any participant may drill a well. If the other participants do not want to join in, they suffer a financial penalty (a loss of a share in the production from the well).

[39] Exception: A legal argument exists for classifying each producing property owned by a joint venture as a "separate business". See subs.31(2). Assuming this is "correct law", the purchase of a majority working interest in one of several properties owned by a joint venture will be subject to the Act. Investment Canada has sometimes treated each producing property owned by a joint venture as a separate business. (To political scientists, this is another illustration of the flexibility of so many laws and the discretion this gives to administrators to arrive at whatever legal conclusions they choose.)

[40] Purchasers need not notify Investment Canada either. (Exception: a purchase described in (iii)).

[41] Investment Canada assumes that a "working interest" is equivalent to a "voting interest". (With respect to a joint venture, a person has a voting interest if entitled to share in profits and in assets on dissolution.)

[42] On the other hand, if the minority interests being acquired represent all or substantially all of the oil and gas business of the vendor, there will be an acquisition of control of the vendor's business, and the transaction will be subject to the *IC Act*.

An additional requirement, in the first three cases, is that the properties being purchased do not constitute substantially all of the assets of the vendor's business.

The existence of these "exemptions"[43] helped U.S-owned Amerada Hess Corp. buy 80% of the assets of Canada's financially healthy Placer Cego Petroleum Holdings Ltd.[44] They also explain why the *Calgary Herald* sometimes reports that a foreign company has bought a small interest in a large number of properties yet the article makes no mention of approval under the *Investment Canada Act*.[45]

One feature of the Act that surprises oil industry executives is that different legal results occur depending upon the number of owners of producing property. The acquisition of a "sole proprietorship" can only occur through the purchase of substantially all its assets. The purchase of a 60% working interest in producing property owned by one company will not meet that test.[46] On the other hand, if there are two owners, a joint venture or partnership will exist. The purchase of a 60% interest will then need Ottawa's blessing—if the book asset value of the producing property ("business") is over the review threshold.[47]

Sometimes investors face a daunting problem in determining what this book asset value is. They cannot consult the balance sheet for the (oil and gas) joint venture, or for the unit because no balance sheet exists.

Operators of oil and gas properties do keep an account of production costs, operating costs and revenues. However, each participant in

---

[43] Like many of the so-called "rules" governing oil and gas transactions, the "exemption" in (ii) above is not explicitly stated in the statute. It arises out of a liberal interpretation given by government administrators to the definition of joint venture in the Act, so that it applies to unitized properties. See n. 37. Private sector lawyers refer to this process as "making law through policy statements".

[44] Alan Bayless, "The Door Opens to Foreign Takeovers in the Oil Patch", *Financial Times of Canada*, Feb. 4–10, 1991, p. 1.

[45] Gordon Jaremko, "Oil & Gas Properties Worth $100 Million Change Hands", *Calgary Herald*, Dec. 2, 1987, p. B7.

[46] This assumes the property is neither subject to a joint operating agreement nor part of a unit.

[47] How should the Canadian government treat the acquisition of a changing interest? Imagine that a Canadian is part of a joint venture searching for oil and has financed most of the drilling costs. The Canadian has an 85% working interest until payout, after which the interest drops to 45%. Prior to payout, and the drop in the interest, the Canadian sells the interest to an American. Assuming that control is being acquired (there are legal difficulties in concluding that control is being acquired, because of the definition of a "voting interest"), a case can be made for government approval of the sale, since foreign control will automatically drop over time.

the unit or joint venture carries the assets on its own books at values that may vary considerably between the participants.[48]

A foreign investor may not be able to find out what these book values are. Some of the participants may not want to reveal this information. Moreover, the *IC Act* does not compel them to do so. Even if they are willing, there may be 50 or more participants in a unit. Contacting all 50 (in order to determine the aggregate value of their individual interests) would be quite a task.

What should the foreign investor do? In such circumstances, Investment Canada will accept an estimate arrived at by extrapolation that is based upon a few known book values,[49] (such as the book value of the vendor's property). However, the investor who uses this method should make any errors on the side of caution.

> EXAMPLE: A Texan is buying a 10% interest in each of five different Canadian oil and gas joint ventures. (The vendor has many other oil gas interests.) Should the asset value of the five joint ventures be totalled?

No. Control of neither a joint venture nor the vendor's total business is being acquired. Investment Canada need not even be told about the purchase. On the other hand, if five 51% interests are being purchased, the Texan is acquiring control of the joint ventures. Since the transaction should probably be viewed as one "investment" (not five "investments"), the Texan should do some adding (to determine if the $5-million threshold for review has been exceeded).

When a foreign investor purchases shares in a resource company which carries on no business activities itself but owns working interests in producing properties, the investor must ask two questions:

1. Is control of the company being acquired?

---

[48] Participants in an operating joint venture may have acquired their interests at different points in time—-some before, some after—-the drilling of the well. Even if well costs are the same, different accounting policies between participants (and therefore the amount of depletion and depreciation expenses claimed) will result in different book values.

[49] What should be done if an investor is buying an interest in a joint venture and cannot find out the book asset value of the interests of the other participants? Read subs. 13(1) and subs. 18(1) of the Act. These subsections state that a notification or application is complete if the investor provides the reason for his or her inability to provide any missing information. In such circumstances, if the vendor is selling a 25% interest, Investment Canada will usually *accept* a value for the business which is four times greater than the book asset value of the interest being purchased. However, while this will result in a complete notification if the asset value is under $5 million, *quaere* whether the investor is "off the hook" if the actual asset value is higher and an application for review should have been filed.

2. Does the resource company control the producing properties?

To answer the last question, the "chain of control rules"[50] must be examined. If a resource company has a 10% interest in several producing properties, it does not control the joint ventures which carry on those businesses. In such circumstances, the acquisition of control of the resource company may not be the acquisition of a business. This, however, is a grey area of the law.

Does it matter, in oil and gas acquisitions, who is the operator of producing properties? Or what the operating agreement states about the percentage of voting interests needed for decisions? That is not a consideration if the statute is interpreted as accentuating ownership interests to the exclusion of a broader conception of control.

6. The Reviewability Matrix: American Investor in 1992 Acquiring Canadian Company

Question	Answer	Significance
(a) Where are the shares acquired?	In Canada	Direct acquisition. Reviewable if $150-million threshold exceeded.
	Outside Canada	Indirect acquisition; proceed to (b).
(b) Does the "Canadian Content" of the global transaction exceed 50%?	Exceeds 50%	Treated like a direct acquisition. Reviewable if $150-million threshold exceeded.
	50% or less	Indirect acquisition; not reviewable.
(c) Is a cultural business with a book asset value under $5 million being purchased?	Yes	Direct-indirect distinction irrelevant; submit notification form; will be reviewable if government issues order for review.

---

[50] See Chapter 6.

CHAPTER 9

OBTAINING AN OPINION

The *IC Act* is a complex statute. Fortunately, investors need not become bogged down in legal complexities. They can get a written opinion from the government.

There are two types of opinions, status and non-status. Status opinions deal with whether a person or an entity is a Canadian or an American. Non-status opinions encompass everything else.

Status opinions are issued by the minister on the advice of Investment Canada. Non-status opinions are issued by the president of Investment Canada, pursuant to an authorization from the minister.

According to the statute, this authorization must refer to a person by name, not by position. This means that each time a new president is appointed, another authorization must be executed.[1]

Should investors seeking opinions request copies of this authorization? That would make no sense unless they are aware that an irregularity exists. Otherwise, there is no need to examine the internal workings of government.[2]

1. Legal Effect of an Opinion

Some investors hesitate to apply for an opinion. A negative opinion, they worry, might prejudice their rights. This concern is unfounded. In any dispute, the court is the final arbitrator.

---

[1] Must a new authorization be executed if there is a change of ministers? According to the case law, where a statute authorizes delegation of authority, the previously existing authority continues in full force even if there is a change of ministers. This is because the delegation represents the authority of the office, not the authority of the minister as a person. Consequently, another authorization is not needed. *Re Putnoki and Public Service Grievance Board* (1975), 56 D.L.R. (3d) 197 (Ont. Div. Ct).

[2] In addition, a person dealing with an agent is entitled to assume that the agent has the authority which persons in that position normally possess.

189

The advantage of obtaining an opinion is that it binds the minister responsible for Investment Canada. An investor can use a favourable opinion as a good defence should the minister bring a legal action asserting the contrary.[3] Another benefit is that an opinion does not expire. It remains in effect for as long as the material facts on which it is based remain substantially unchanged.[4]

However, investors must ensure that all the pertinent facts are provided. An opinion based on half-truths is not half as valuable; it is probably worth nothing.

What should an investor who has received a favourable opinion do, if the details of the proposed transaction change? There are two choices: either seek a new opinion or request confirmation that the original opinion is still valid.

2. The Procedure

Opinion requests are made by letter. Only information, not opinions, can be obtained by telephone. One hapless accountant did not understand this. He received some information by telephone which he construed as an "opinion". A few weeks later, he was furious to learn that the "opinion" was not binding, and that he had been speaking to a clerk. Worse still, his clients' multimillion-dollar deal was reviewable.

When writing a letter requesting an opinion, investors should identify the parties by their legal names and fully describe the proposed transaction. If suspicions may arise that a reorganization or other transaction is being undertaken to evade the Act, the commercial reasons for the transaction should be set out.

For status opinions and opinions on whether a voting group exists, relevant evidence may include: documents of incorporation, shareholders, voting trust and other agreements, annual reports, and corporate minutes. A description of the company's capital structure, the distribution of voting shares, and information regarding the beneficial owners of those shares is also necessary. To avoid additional questions, a few solicitors provide sworn declarations.

---

[3] The Act states that opinions are binding on the minister. It does not mention the Governor in Council. Some lawyers have wondered: "After the minister has opined that the buyer of a culturally sensitive business is a Canadian, might the Governor in Council come to a different conclusion and issue an order for review?" Technically, that may be a possibility, but practically, foreign investors are safe in assuming that an opinion from the minister binds the government as a whole.

[4] Subs. 37(3).

To show that a voting group exists, persuasive evidence of an association between two or more persons should be presented. It may be helpful to provide particulars of any blood or marital relationship between the persons and a description of any agreements, understandings or other business or personal relationships that may exist between or among them. If the persons in the alleged group have acted in concert in the past, this may also be a relevant factor.

Sometimes, an applicant for an opinion wants to prove that control of a widely-held company lies not with its shareholders but with its board of directors. To establish this fact, the applicant must demonstrate that a minority shareholder is not in control. The evidence to do this may be obtained by examining voting patterns at past shareholders' meetings, the relationship between shareholders, and any links between large minority shareholders and the company directors. Although the largest shareholder in a widely-held company may only have an 8% interest, the largest ten shareholders may own 30% or 40% of the votes. They could form a compact enough group to control the company. Other circumstances when a minority shareholder will have effective control arise when few shareholders return proxies or a strong link exists between the minority shareholder and company directors. In the latter event, the board of directors will vote the proxies it receives in support of the wishes of the minority shareholder.

Among the information that should be provided to establish board control is: the number of shares outstanding at the date of each annual meeting; the number of shares represented in person or by proxy; and the number of shares represented by proxies held by management. Details of the percentage of shares voted in favour of management proposals, and of any proxy battles, as well as the outcome of any proposals put forward by people other than management, should also be provided to Investment Canada. A declaration by a director that, to the best of his or her knowledge, the shareholders named in the declaration (and who together could control the company) do not form a voting group, is usually part of any submission.[5]

The shares of many companies are held by nominees such as trust companies. An applicant for an opinion cannot force the trust company to disclose who is the beneficial owner of the shares. However, the

---

[5] Sample wording: "To the best of the Applicant's knowledge, X, Y and Z do not act in concert with respect to the voting rights attached to their shares and are not a voting group".

If the directors are unaware of a person or group holding a sufficient number of shares to be in a position to control the company, that may be sufficient evidence to establish board control.

trust company will usually reveal whether a large block of shares are owned by a Canadian or a non-Canadian. Past voting patterns at shareholder's meetings may then show if that block is a control block.

Minutes of shareholders' meetings may also indicate whether there is a sweetheart deal between three shareholders to vote together. If so, this may be the evidence a foreign investor needs, who has acquired 35% of a company's shares, to rebut the presumption that control has been acquired.[6] On the other hand, if the company is management-controlled, the foreign investor can discharge the same presumption by demonstrating that management, through the proxy solicitation process, successfully solicits a larger block of shares than the foreign investor owns.

Can an opinion be obtained if a company intends to sell its shares to the public, and the underwriters expect that a large number of foreigners will each make small purchases? A better question is: why bother obtaining an opinion? Investment Canada can issue one, but it will be heavily caveated. Small purchases have no Investment Canada ramifications. However, when the identity of the foreign purchasers is unknown, there is no way of knowing in advance how strong the links between the purchasers will be. Some of them may form a joint venture or partnership which could acquire control.

> EXAMPLE: The owners of a Canadian petroleum company intend to transfer the company's business to a limited partnership in exchange for units in the partnership. Additional capital will subsequently be obtained by selling a number of the units to Kuwaiti investors. No foreigner is expected to acquire a majority of the partnership units. What can be done to assure potential investors in Kuwait that Ottawa will not force them to sell their unit interests?

There is no "acquisition of control" when individuals purchase less than a majority of the units of a partnership.[7] However, if two or more of the Kuwaiti investors should consciously or unintentionally form a joint venture or a partnership (either among themselves or with the original Canadian owners), there may be a reviewable transaction.

The solicitor for the limited partnership should endeavour to determine if a potential problem exists. One way is to have each

---

[6] One problem is if the other shareholders have recently acquired their shares, evidence that they vote together may not be available until two shareholders' meetings (and, therefore, two years) have passed.

[7] However, the status of the partnership could change; it could become a "non-Canadian".

purchaser warrant on the subscription form that (to the best of her or his knowledge) no association exists between that purchaser and any other purchasers.

3. Refusal to Issue an Opinion

May the minister refuse to issue an opinion? Yes, if the request is for a non-status opinion. The giving of non-status opinions is discretionary.[8]

Only if the request is for a status opinion (that is, whether an investor is an American or a Canadian) has the minister a statutory duty to provide an opinion. Even in these circumstances, the minister can legally decline to do so, if the minister concludes that insufficient information has been received.

What if the minister should categorically refuse to issue a status opinion? Or, if the minister should issue a negative opinion after failing to consider relevant facts?

Such behaviour would not be lawful. The Trial Division of the Federal Court could grant relief. In the terminology of administrative law, the minister would have acted wrongfully by "declining jurisdiction".

---

[8] *IC Act*, s. 37. Subs. 37(1) ("status opinions") and 37(2) ("non-status opinions") use the verbs "shall" and "may" respectively when referring to the obligation of the minister to render an opinion.

CHAPTER 10

FILING A NOTIFICATION

If a non-Canadian is establishing a Canadian business or buying one, and the transaction is neither reviewable nor exempt, a notification must be filed. This simple form demands skeleton information and takes two minutes to complete. Should the investor be a company, there is no requirement that the owner be identified[1] (although this information is often provided voluntarily).

1. The Purpose of a Notification

Why does Ottawa want these notification forms? The principal reason is to collect economic data. The purpose of a notification is to provide information on the level of foreign investment and to help federal and provincial governments design their investment promotion activities. Politically, it is also important for the government to be seen as monitoring the extent and form of foreign investment.

Lists of investments for which notifications have been received are published by *The Globe and Mail*.[2] They are useful to Canadian business people who are seeking new customers or sources of supply.[3] In

---

[1] An example of a press release: "Million Corporation (Toronto, Ontario) to Establish a New Business at Toronto, Ontario, a Holding and Investment Company". The press release will name the controller of the business if that information is provided.

[2] Publication is not required by the Act. However, government officials believe the public should know who is investing in Canada. The date of publication may be postponed for a few weeks at the investor's request (but only if the investor has a convincing reason).

[3] By telephoning Investment Canada, a caller can obtain the name and mailing address of the person (usually a lawyer) to whom the certificate of receipt is sent. (Although all information provided to the agency is confidential, subs. 36(4) of the Act

addition, compiled data on investments in terms of size, industry and location may be helpful to researchers.

2. When Required

(a) New Canadian Business

A notification usually must be filed when a new business is being established. However, there are two major exceptions. Together, these exceptions exclude hundreds of new businesses being established by foreign investors from this data collection exercise. Specifically, no notification need be filed if:

(1) the new business is merely an expansion of the investor's existing business in Canada, or

(2) the new business is related to an existing business that the investor is carrying on in Canada. (However, if the new business will be carrying on an activity that is related to Canada's cultural heritage or national identity, a notification must be filed in any event.)[4]

If the notification is complete, an investor will receive a certificate of receipt. Usually, that ends the matter. However, if a new business is culturally sensitive (that is, "related to Canada's cultural heritage and national identity"), Ottawa has a reserve review power. A foreign investor can be ordered to file an application for review if Ottawa issues an order for review within 21 days after the notification is certified complete.[5]

(b) Acquisitions

The reserve review power also hovers over acquisitions of culturally sensitive businesses. This creates uncertainty for a few foreign investors. If they want to buy a film distribution or publishing company with an asset size that is below the normal review threshold, they must file a notification and wait 21 days before learning if they face a government review.

3. Time For Filing

Investors need not rush to submit a notification. The legislation states that it can be filed up to 30 days after an investment has been

---

permits Investment Canada to disclose any information that appears on this certificate.) Lawyers sometimes complain about the amount of "junk mail" they receive (e.g. brochures from real estate agents), which they are asked to forward to their foreign clients.

[4] See the definition of "new Canadian business" in s. 3.

[5] See subs. 13(b) and s. 15.

implemented.[6] Since an investment is implemented when it is established, this means that the 30-day clock does not start ticking unless there is a place of business in Canada, employees, and assets used in carrying on the business.[7]

What happens if a notification is submitted a year late? No penalty has ever been imposed on account of a late notification.[8]

When a transaction is subject to the "reserve review power" and, thus, possibly reviewable, the investor is still allowed to implement the investment and thereafter file a notification, but he does so at his risk.[9] The risk is that the government may order a review and turn down the transaction.[10] Unless a non-Canadian investor is certain that the investment does not come within the list of activities related to Canada's cultural heritage or national identity, it is wise to file the notification before proceeding with the investment.

4. Certificate of Receipt

After the notification is received in Ottawa, a number of events may occur. If:

(1) the notification is deficient, or

(2) the investor has mistakenly filed a notification instead of an application for review,

the investor will be contacted.[11] Otherwise, if the notification is complete, the investor will be sent:

(1) a letter (called "a certificate of receipt") stating that the investment is not reviewable,[12] or

(2) if the investment involves a cultural activity, a certificate of receipt informing the investor that unless Investment Canada

---

[6] S. 12.

[7] See the definition of "Canadian business" in s. 3.

[8] No penalty can be imposed. The courts can only levy a fine if the investor has failed to comply with a ministerial demand that a notification be filed. After filing a notification, even though it is a year late, an investor is safe from legal action since it is no longer possible to issue a ministerial demand. Investors who have forgotten to file a notification, therefore, need not fear doing so (*IC Act*, subss. 39 and 40).

[9] Para. 16(2)(c).

[10] In which case, the investor would have to sell control of the business.

[11] Subs. 13(2). The Act requires that all communication be in verifiable form, such as by registered mail or telex.

[12] S. 13.

sends him or her a notice for review pursuant to section 15 (the "reserve review power") within 21 days after the date of receipt of the notification, the investment is not reviewable.

5. Cultural Businesses

If an investment involves an activity designated as culturally sensitive, a lot of hectic activity occurs during those 21 days:

1. First, both the province[13] where the investment will take place and the Department of Communications (the federal government department responsible for cultural matters) are consulted.

2. Next, agency staff deliver a memo to the minister containing their recommendation on whether the transaction merits a review.

3. The minister then submits a written recommendation to the Governor in Council (in reality a committee of Cabinet) by delivering it to the Clerk of the Privy Council. (If the minister decides that no review is needed, the minister is under no legal obligation to contact anyone.)

4. The Governor in Council decides whether it is in the public interest to review the investment.

5. Finally, if the decision is to hold a review, an order is issued. Typed on the letterhead of the Privy Council, this order reads:

   HIS EXCELLENCY THE GOVERNOR GENERAL IN COUNCIL, on the recommendation of the Minister of Science, Industry, and Technology, pursuant to section 15 of the *Investment Canada Act*, hereby orders that the investment by (name of foreign investor) to acquire control of the business carried on by (Canadian company) be reviewed.

As soon as Investment Canada receives this order for review, it sends a certified copy to the foreign investor.

All of these steps must occur within the 21-day period. Otherwise, the investment is deemed not to be reviewable.[14] If the Governor in Council cannot reach a decision, or an Investment Canada official forgets to mail the order for review before the end of the 21 days or

---

[13] Ottawa is under no legal duty to consult with the provinces but does so, since the province affected by the investment would be consulted if the investment was reviewed. See subs. 15(b).

[14] Para. 13(1)(b).

sends it to the wrong address, the non-Canadian can rejoice. There will be no review.

However, the non-Canadian should wait more than 21 days after the notification has been received by Investment Canada before proceeding with his or her plans. This is because the 21-day period refers to the time within which the order for review must be sent, not the time when Canada Post delivers the order by registered mail.

Should the Governor in Council order a review, can the foreign investor appeal?[15] No, provided that the investment is subject to the Act, and the proper procedures have been followed.[16]

A certificate of receipt states that the investment is not reviewable, but suppose the investor has been careless in completing the notification form. Is Ottawa still barred from pursuing that investor?

The *IC Act* states that the information provided by the non-Canadian and relied upon by Investment Canada must have been accurate.[17] If it was not accurate, the investor is standing on a shaky platform.

Errors in reading balance sheets can be disastrous. However, precision is especially important if a new business or acquisition falls within the list of activities "related to Canada's cultural heritage or national

---

[15] The Governor in Council has the power to amend or rescind an order in council. See subs. 31(4) of the *Interpretation Act*. (The definition of "regulation" in the Act includes an order in council). Therefore, an error in the name of the foreign investor can be corrected after the order is issued.

[16] Can anything be done if the Governor in Council fails to respect common law principles of fairness? Such behavior might be open to challenge although success is unlikely. *A.G. Can. v. Inuit Tapirisat of Can.*, [1980] 2 S.C.R. 735; 115 D.L.R. (3d) 1, is a case that arose out of a C.R.T.C. decision to permit Bell Canada to increase telephone rates. The intervenors appealed the decision to the Governor in Council under s. 64 of the *National Transportation Act*. The written submissions of the parties were not presented to the Governor in Council. Instead, the Department of Communications presented a summary of the positions of the parties, and the department's recommendation. (Somewhat similar procedures are followed by Investment Canada.) The Supreme Court said that Cabinet appeals are not subject to any procedural fairness obligations. By extension, fairness principles do not apply in other instances where Governor in Council exercises its statutory powers (such as under s. 15 of the *IC Act*). See Roderick Macdonald, "The Limits of Procedural Fairness: Executive Action by the Governor in Council" (1981), 46 *Sask L.R.* 187.

Since the definition of a "federal board" in the *Federal Court Act* would include the Governor in Council when exercising jurisdiction under the *IC Act*, any challenge would be heard by the Federal Court under s. 18 of that Act. An application might also be made to a provincial supreme court if only a declaration is being sought. *Re Williams and A.G. Can.* (1983), 45 O.R. (2d) 291.

[17] Para. 13(3)(a).

identity". If the investor ticks off the wrong category of activity on the notification form or forgets to tick off anything, the government could still order a review months later. (Lawyers who make such an error might be sued for negligence.)

Since the decision as to whether an investment involves a cultural activity is a "legal determination", some investors may be uncertain about the answer. In such circumstances, the best course is to assume the worst. Indicate on the form that the business involves culture. At the same time, submit a letter expressing doubt and inviting agency officials to come to their own conclusion. By adopting this cautious approach, the possibility of error need no longer haunt the future.

Even when they are confident that an investment is totally outside the area of culture, some investors still provide Investment Canada with a full description of the business activities of the takeover target or new business. By doing so, they reason, they may have a defence if an error is discovered at a future date.

CHAPTER 11

EARLY IMPLEMENTATION—FILING AN APPLICATION FOR REVIEW

If a proposed investment is reviewable, an application should be submitted promptly. This is because the law prohibits a non-Canadian from implementing an investment until the minister has reached a favourable decision.

Solicitors call this "the non-implementation rule". It exists because of the difficulty in getting investors to relinquish control of a Canadian business after the transaction has closed.[1]

The Act contains timing rules for determining when this implementation date occurs. An investment is implemented, in the case of a new business, when it has a place of business, employees and assets. For acquisitions, the relevant date is the date of closing (not when the agreement of purchase and sale is signed).[2]

Sometimes, transactions close in escrow pending the approval of the minister. The vendor remains the registered owner of the shares but votes as instructed by the purchaser whose staff manage the business. Since an escrow closing suspends the effect of a transfer until a condition (in this case, ministerial approval) is fulfilled, it does not constitute a technical violation of the non-implementation rule.

1. Early Implementation

There are three exceptions to the non-implementation rule. "Early implementation" is possible in the following instances:

(1) hardship cases;

---

[1] Subs. 16(1). Under the *FIR Act*, a transaction could be closed as soon as an application for review had been filed.

[2] Subs. 32(2).

(2) offshore share purchases: foreign-incorporated companies with Canadian subsidiaries;

(3) the purchase/establishment of cultural businesses that are subject to notification under the Act (even in those instances where the government has issued an order for review after the investor has submitted a notification to Investment Canada).

(a) Hardship Cases[3]

In certain circumstances, the minister has the power to waive the non-implementation rule and allow a transaction to be completed before it is reviewed. However, the minister must be satisfied that a delay would:

(1) result in undue hardship to the foreign investor, or

(2) jeopardize the operations of the Canadian business.

If the minister grants a waiver, the non-Canadian then has 30 days following the purchase of the business during which to file an application for review.[4]

This waiver provision was originally designed for bail-out acquisitions and public takeover bids.[5] If the sale of a Canadian company in financial difficulty could not be completed until the minister had made a decision on net benefit, creditors might foreclose in the interim.[6] In addition, if there was no waiver provision, foreign investors would be unable to make unconditional offers for the shares of publicly traded Canadian companies. This would put them at a disadvantage in comparison with Canadian investors.[7]

A brief account of securities law is helpful in understanding the latter rationale. Canadian provincial securities legislation and the *Canada Business Corporations Act*[8] contain statutory frameworks for

---

[3] Para. 16(2)(a).

[4] Para. 17(2)(b).

[5] See the statements of the Honourable Sinclair Stevens, *Minutes of the Standing Committee on Regional Development*, April 15, 1985, Issue No. 20, p. 20:15; and April 17, 1985, Issue No. 24, p. 24:36.

[6] One circumstance exists when foreign investors can move quickly to take over a failing Canadian business without the minister's approval. The Act contains an exemption for acquisitions to finance Canadian businesses, or facilitate their financing, provided the foreign investors divest themselves of control within ten years (para. 10(1)(d)).

[7] In the absence of a waiver provision, a foreign bidder might not be able to acquire shares under an offer as early as a Canadian offeror.

[8] The takeover provisions in the Canada Business Corporations Act are intended to protect offeree shareholders of federally-incorporated companies.

regulating takeover bids. Among the rules that must be complied with are time frames during which a bid must remain open, and when shares deposited pursuant to an offer must be taken up and paid for.

Under the Ontario *Securities Act*, this minimum deposit period is 21 days. Until that time period has expired, stock deposited by shareholders for purchase by a bidder cannot be acquired ("taken up") and paid for.[9] If the stock has not been paid for within 45 days after the making of a bid, those shareholders who have deposited shares are entitled to withdraw them. In order to reduce the risk of someone else making a competing bid, most bidders ("offerors") choose the earliest possible date—namely, 21 days after the offer is made—as the last day on which shares may be deposited.

A complication will arise if the bidder is a foreigner. Unless "permission for early implementation" is received from Investment Canada's minister, the foreign bidder will want to insert the following condition in the takeover bid circular: "the offeror reserves the right not to take up the shares unless any requisite approvals under the *IC Act* have been obtained".

If this condition is not met at the end of the last day for the deposit of shares, the foreign offeror may extend the deposit period.[10] An offeror can do this for a minimum of ten (or more) days, but then shareholders who have already deposited shares gain a right of withdrawal for (the first) ten days. This might give another investor the time to make a competing offer. On the other hand, the foreign offeror can wait until the condition (approval under the *IC Act*) is fulfilled, keeping in mind that shareholders' withdrawal rights commence 45 days after the making of the bid.

Why should foreign investors who want to buy publicly traded companies not wait until they have government approval? Those who drafted the Act thought it would be unfair. A Canadian business person, bidding for the same target company, could make an unconditional offer. That offer might be more attractive to shareholders, since the Canadian could purchase their shares at an earlier date than the foreign investor.

Parliament thought all bidders should be put on an equal footing ("a level playing field"), so it gave the minister the discretion to permit early implementation.

---

[9] *Securities Act*, R.S.O. 1980 as amended, Part XIX, subs. 94(3).

[10] If the deposit period is extended, either the offeror must take up all shares tendered at that time (thus waiving any conditions not yet satisfied) or it must grant withdrawal rights to the depositing shareholders.

Sometimes, there are no competing bidders, or the Canadian company is not publicly traded. Should foreign investors still be allowed to complete their purchase prior to government approval?

That is one extension of the equality argument. If foreign investors must make their offers contingent upon approval under the *IC Act*, theoretically they must offer a higher price in comparison with Canadian investors who can submit a firm offer and close at an earlier date.[11] In addition, if the target company is publicly traded but there are no competing bidders, the right of the shareholders to withdraw their shares may commence before the minister has rendered a decision. This might be detrimental to the possibility of the bid succeeding (unless the price is raised).

However, Parliament did not intend to put everyone on a completely level playing field. Otherwise, it would not have passed the *IC Act*.

The procedure for obtaining a minister's waiver is simple enough. The investor sends a letter to Investment Canada setting out the details of the proposed transaction and the reason for the request. The investor must also agree to:

(1) file an application for review within a specific period of time (usually 30 days);

(2) divest himself or herself of control of the Canadian business if, following the completion of the review process, the minister is not satisfied that the investment is likely to be of net benefit to Canada;

(3) make no material changes to the business without the minister's permission until the minister has made a decision on the issue of net benefit.

If the Canadian business is in financial difficulty, the investor may wish to take prompt action to save it. That may be a valid reason for not giving the third commitment regarding material changes.

When a request for early implementation is received, agency staff prepare a briefing note for the minister containing an analysis and a recommendation. After the minister decides, agency staff contact the foreign investor or the investor's counsel by telephone. This is followed up by a letter signed by the president of the agency officially informing the investor about the decision.

The minister's busy timetable can cause timing problems. The investor may want to announce his takeover offer within the next two

---

[11] In reality, purchase agreements for privately owned businesses contain so many contingencies that one more probably has no price consequences.

or three days, but the minister may be out of the country when the request is submitted. If timing is critical, a phone call to ascertain the minister's schedule may be worthwhile.

Set out below is a sampling of situations where an investor's request for "early implementation permission" should receive serious consideration.

No Time to File—International Transaction May Collapse: A Japanese businessman wishes to purchase the world-wide assets of a foreign company. Included in these assets are the shares of a Canadian subsidiary. This transaction is scheduled to close in a few weeks and the purchase of the shares of the Canadian company is a condition precedent to the completion of the entire transaction. If there is a delay, the financial arrangements for the entire transaction will be put in jeopardy since the lender's letter of commitment expires shortly.

Canadian Business Being Harmed—Goodwill Being Dissipated: The newspapers have reported that a Canadian company is to be sold. Since then, competitors have been taking advantage of the employees' apprehensions by offering them employment. In addition, these competitors have been telling the company's customers that the new foreign owners may be unable to assure continuity of supply and quality. The customers are then urged to change suppliers. As a result, the value of the Canadian company's goodwill is deteriorating.

Canadian Business in Jeopardy—Parent Has Financial Problems: Cat Ltd. ("Cat") is a Canadian construction company. Its parent is a U.S. company, which is in serious financial difficulty and wants to sell Cat in order to raise funds. The major creditor of the U.S. company is threatening bankruptcy proceedings. If the U.S company becomes involved in bankruptcy proceedings, the approval of a court may be necessary before it (the U.S company) can sell the Canadian business. In the meantime, the Canadian business lacks the funds to keep its heavy equipment in good operating order.

(b) Offshore Share Purchases

The second exemption to the non-implementation rule permits indirect acquisitions to be completed in advance of approval. If a non-Canadian wishes to buy a foreign company which has a Canadian subsidiary, an application for review can be filed up to 30 days after the acquisition has occurred.[12] This provision is designed to prevent

---

[12] Paras. 16(2)(b) and 17(2)(b). Instead of a Canadian subsidiary the foreign company may own another entity in Canada.

Canada's review mechanism from complicating or delaying international transactions.

(c) Certain Cultural Businesses

A notification must be filed if a non-Canadian wishes to establish a cultural business or purchase a cultural business *with a book asset value under $5 million.* The government then has 21 days to order that the transaction be reviewed.

The non-Canadian does not need to wait until the end of this 21-day period. He can accept the risk of possible review and rejection, and complete the transaction immediately.[13] According to an Investment Canada briefing document, this is:

> . . .because initially, at least, these investments are subject to notification only, and there is no certainty that each investment of this type will actually be made subject to review.[14]

2. The Risk

An investor who takes advantage of one of these three exceptions and proceeds with the investment takes an obvious risk. If the minister does not approve the transaction, the investor will be forced to sell control of the business. Consequently, investors should consult senior agency staff before making a decision.

There are no automatic fines or other punitive provisions for violating the non-implementation rule. In this respect, "Investment Canada law-breakers" are treated better than car owners who ignore "no parking" signs.

The minister's only remedy is to issue a demand requiring that an application for review be filed forthwith (or requiring the investor to explain why the Act has not been contravened).[15] If the demand is not complied with, a court may impose penalties that could include a fine.

What can a solicitor do if a client wants to close a purchase before ministerial approval can be obtained? If the purchase agreement is being drafted, a provision might be inserted providing for a transfer of

---

[13] Para. 16(2)(c).

[14] *Investment Canada Act: Briefing Document* (undated, released under the *Access to Information Act*), p. 36.

[15] Para. 39(1)(b).

control on an interim basis. This alternative is available because the *IC Act* only regulates the purchase of assets and shares. It does not restrict a foreign investor from obtaining operating control by contractual means. The owner of a business can, therefore, transfer cheque-signing or managerial powers to a foreign investor without government approval.

3. Filing An Application For Review

Three points should be kept in mind when completing an application for review.

First, if a chain of companies (or other entities) is being acquired, it is not sufficient to merely provide the name of the company at the top of the chain. Instead, all operating subsidiaries and other entities that meet the test of being Canadian businesses must be identified.

Secondly, the number of employees of each subsidiary must be given as well as the various locations where business is carried on. Too many solicitors just provide aggregate figures. Because Investment Canada must consult with each province in which employees are located, the application will be stalled if the figures are not broken down.

Finally, an application cannot be submitted on behalf of a company to be incorporated. It is not a legal entity.

If an investment by a non-existent company was approved, the company might later refuse to adopt the plans and undertakings that had been submitted without its authorization.[16] In such circumstances, the government could not rely on the indoor management rule since the lack of authorization would be apparent on the face of the application.

What, then, should be done if an investor wants to make an investment through a company but the company has not been incorporated? The best approach is for the investor to submit the application in his own name and explain what he intends to do. The investor should also undertake to cause the company to co-sign any commitments he gives.

---

[16] The *Canada Business Corporations Act* (subs. 14(2)), allows a company to adopt a pre-incorporation contract but the company is not compelled to do so.

There is no risk that a refusal by the government to certify an application by a non-existing company as complete will lead to a deemed approval. The regulations require an application to be signed by an investor or an authorized person. A non-existent company can give no authorization.

If the company is incorporated before the review is completed, a replacement application can be faxed to Ottawa. If the incorporation takes place after the minister has approved the investor's proposal, a letter should be requested confirming that the change in the identity of the investor is not a material change to the proposal.

Foreign investors engaged in hostile takeovers often have difficulty in getting the data needed to complete an application. However, this should not delay a filing. Parliament has graciously provided a solution. The Act states that an incomplete application will be considered complete if reasons for the inability to obtain the required information are given.[17]

It is not necessary that the government be satisfied with those reasons. However, inability is not synonymous with unwillingness. If the investor has the information but does not want to provide it because "it is none of Ottawa's business", the test has not been met.

The answer is the same where the information can be obtained with a little effort. (Although the term "inability" is not defined in the Act, the courts would probably interpret it with reference to the concept of reasonableness.) On the other hand, an investor is not required to hire a private detective in order to get information.

Investment Canada officials cannot sit on an application. The Act states that if no notice of deficiencies is sent within 15 days after an application has been received, the application is deemed to be complete. If this happens, Investment Canada must send the applicant a certificate of receipt[18] no matter how inadequate the application may be.

4. Confidential Information

Applications may contain information that foreign investors do not want their own governments, competitors or even Revenue Canada to know about. How confidential is it? Ottawa wanted to encourage frankness so there is a provision in the IC Act stating that all information obtained about an investment proposal is privileged.[19]

---

[17] Subs.18(1).

[18] Subs.18(3). Investment Canada Act: Briefing Document, op. cit., p. 40., states: "The purpose of the fifteen-day time frame is to ensure that the Government cannot unduly delay taking action on applications concerning a non-Canadian's investment, while providing a reasonable time in which deficiencies in application may be cleared up without resort to formal written procedures".

[19] Subs. 36(1).

There are exceptions, of course. If there were none, Investment Canada could not operate. These exceptions permit information to be communicated to other government departments and the provinces if it is for a purpose related to the administration of the Act.[20] Also, information contained in acknowledgements of receipt—such as the name of the investor and the target company—may be made public.[21] This allows a press release to be issued after the minister has approved the investment. But otherwise, only persons who are "legally entitled" may see the information.[22]

Who are legally entitled? Those who administer the Act, such as the minister and agency employees. Also entitled are employees of other government departments and those provinces which are contacted during the review process (as well as the courts, if legal proceedings are commenced).[23]

The phrase "legally entitled" would also include anyone authorized by another federal statute. However, investors can relax, Revenue Canada and the R.C.M.P. are not in this category.[24]

In the agency's eyes, the shroud of confidentiality extends not only to the contents of an application, but to its existence. The agency will not disclose that an application has been filed, or that an applicant's solicitor has completed his or her representations.[25]

---

[20] Para. 36(3)(b).

[21] Subpara. 36(4)(e)(i).

[22] Para. 36(3)(f).

[23] A court of competent jurisdiction is within the phrase "except to a person legally entitled". *Ship v. The King* (1949), 95 C.C.C. 143, at 155. So, presumably, are secretaries hired on a temporary basis through private agencies. (Other statutes, such as the *Income Tax Act*, extend their confidentiality provisions to persons engaged by the Crown as well as those employed by it.)

[24] If the R.C.M.P. were to show up with a subpoena, they would be "legally entitled". However, an application would have to be made immediately to set aside the subpoena on the grounds that it was wrongfully issued. Statistics Canada has a right to information under s. 13 of the *Statistics Act* but any information that Statistics Canada receives retains its privileged character under s. 17 of that Act.

[25] The conclusion that the existence of an application is privileged information is premised on the belief that the confidentiality provision in s. 36 swings into gear the moment an application is received. (S. 36 of the *IC Act* is very similar to s. 14 of the *FIR Act* which was taken from what is now s. 241 of the *Income Tax Act*. The jurisprudence under the *Income Tax Act* might be consulted for further guidance.)

CHAPTER 12

THE REVIEW PROCESS: PROCEDURE AND DEADLINES

After an application has been received by Investment Canada, it is forwarded to an investment review officer, who then prepares an evaluation based upon those factors outlined in section 20 of the Act.

During this stage, additional information is obtained through discussions with the investor ("applicant"), and consultations with federal government departments. A photocopy of the application is also sent to those provinces that will be significantly affected by the investment for their comments.

After all the information has been assembled, the review officer drafts a memo to the minister, setting out the background to the application and merits of the proposal. The memo will also contain the agency's recommendation on whether the investment should be approved.

After the memo has been studied by senior officials in Investment Canada, it is forwarded to the minister. It is then up to the minister to decide whether the investment is likely to be of net benefit to Canada.

1. Time Limits

The *IC Act* imposes strict time limits on this review procedure. If any time limit is overlooked, the investment is deemed to be approved. This causes some stress on agency officials, none of whom want a major takeover to be automatically approved because of a missed deadline.

How long can the review process take? Unless the investor otherwise consents, the maximum time period during which the minister must make a decision is 105 days.[1] This may seem like a long time, but

---

[1] After an application has been certified complete.

it is better than no time limit at all, which was virtually the case under the previous legislation. Of course, the applicant and the minister can agree to an extension of time beyond 105 days, and sometimes do. A few cases have dragged on for months, but do not always blame the government for this. Applicants can be dilatory too.

The initial statutory time period is 45 days.[2] In most cases, the minister reaches a decision during these 45 days and a letter is sent, informing the applicant that the minister is satisfied that the investment will likely be of net benefit to Canada. If nothing is sent and the 45-day clock expires, the Act states that the minister is deemed to be satisfied. This means that the investment is approved as a matter of law[3] ("the deemed approval guillotine").

If the minister is unable to complete his or her consideration of the investment before the end of the 45-day period, the minister must send a notice to that effect ("the extension notice") to the applicant.[4] This resets the clock and gives the minister an additional 30 days (from the date of the sending of the notice). This 30-day period can be extended for a longer period of time if the applicant and the minister agree.[5]

Should the minister reach a favourable decision during the extended period of time, a letter is sent to the applicant. If the clock runs out without any letter being sent, the minister is deemed to be satisfied. In other words, if the minister has not reached a decision after 75 days, the applicant can proceed with the investment.[6]

The minister cannot turn down an investment proposal without giving the investor the opportunity to make further representations. The Act states that if the minister is not satisfied that an investment is likely to be of net benefit, the minister must advise the applicant of

---

[2] Subs. 21(1).

[3] Subs. 21(2).

[4] Subs. 22(1). A notice stating that the minister is unable to reach a decision (and extending the time for 30 days) is issued by Investment Canada, not the minister. No specific delegation of authority is required for Investment Canada to do this. Under subs. 24(2) of the *Interpretation Act*, words empowering a minister to do an act include the minister's deputy. (For the same reason, no specific authorization is necessary for the agency to issue a demand under s. 39.)

[5] The "extension notice" states: "This is to advise you that the Minister is unable to complete the consideration of your investment within the 45-day period referred to in subsection 21(1) of the *Investment Canada Act*. As prescribed in subsection 22(1) of the Act, this is to notify you that within 30 days from the date of this letter, or within such further period as may be mutually agreed upon, the Minister will complete the consideration of your investment."

[6] Subs. 22(3).

that fact by letter.[7] The applicant then has 30 days (or more, if the applicant and the minister mutually agree) to make further representations and give additional undertakings in order to convince the minister that the investment will benefit Canada.

This explains how the minister can gain up to 105 days' time before rendering a decision. First, the minister must exercise his right to extend the review process by 30 days. Then the minister must advise the applicant that he is not satisfied the investment is likely to be of net benefit to Canada. This results in another 30 days being tacked on to the total.

Usually, the maximum time period during which an applicant can force a decision to be made will be shorter than 105 days. This is because the 30-day extension periods run from the date of the sending of the notice.

2. The Deemed Approval Date

Because of the deemed approval guillotine,[8] it is important for agency officials to accurately calculate time limits. If a government employee makes an error in arithmetic and a major takeover is automatically approved, not only will the employee's boss be angry, the whole country may be as well.

If the last day for sending out a notice resetting the clock falls on a holiday, agency officials may send it out on the following day. Their authority for doing so is section 26 of the *Interpretation Act*.[9]

To compute the day on which the minister (if no notice is sent) is deemed to be satisfied, the day on which the application is certified

---

[7] Subs. 23(1). The letter (telex) reads as follows: "This is to advise you that the Minister responsible for Investment Canada has reviewed your application and is *not* satisfied that your proposed investment is likely to be of net benefit to Canada. This telex constitutes a notice under section 23(1) of the Act that you, as applicant, have the right to make representations and submit undertakings within 30 days from this date or such further period of time as may be mutually agreed upon."

[8] It is risky for Canadian embassy employees to accept notifications or applications because of the "deemed approval guillotine". An embassy employee could create the impression that he or she is authorized to receive the document on behalf of Investment Canada. This could cause a court to conclude that Investment Canada was deemed to have received the document at the same time the embassy employee did. The results are potentially disastrous. The clock would start ticking immediately and a deemed approval (if the investment is reviewable) or the elimination of the government's option to issue an order for review (in a case involving a cultural business) could be the result.

[9] R.S.C. 1985, c. I-21.

complete must be excluded. Subsection 26(4) of the *Interpretation Act* is clear on that point.

Can an investment receive automatic (or "deemed") approval on a Sunday or a statutory holiday? The answer is not absolutely clear. The better view is that, since deemed approval is by operation of law, it can only happen on a juridical day. A juridical day is defined in *Black's Law Dictionary* as a "day on which court is in session" (that is, a day on which the courts are open for business).

Ontario's Rules of Civil Procedure, (made under the *Courts of Justice Act*)[10] state that Saturday and Sunday are holidays, and that court offices are closed on these days. Obviously, the courts cannot be in session when their offices are closed,[11] so there can be no deemed approvals on Saturday or Sunday.[12]

Sometimes, the last day that the minister can send a notice extending the time for a decision falls on a Friday. When this happens, what is the "deemed approval" day (if no extension notice is sent)? Applying the principles set out above, the minister would be deemed to be satisfied on the next juridical day, namely, Monday.[13]

---

[10] S. 26 of the *Interpretation Act* states: "Where the time limited for the doing of a thing . . . falls upon a holiday, the thing may be done on the day next following that is not a holiday". In s. 35, "holiday" is defined to include Sunday and other named days and "in any province . . . any day that is a non-juridical day by virtue of an Act of the legislature of the province".

S.O. 1984, c. 11. Rule 3.04 regulates court office hours. "Holiday" is defined in rule 1.04.

[11] Alternatively, if one equates the "deeming" effect of subs. 21(2) with the "doing of a thing" under s. 26 of the *Interpretation Act* and applies the extended definition of holiday (which includes a non-juridical day) in s. 35 of the *Interpretation Act*, one would come to the same conclusion, namely, that deemed approval cannot occur on a Saturday or Sunday.

[12] The General Rules and Orders of the Federal Court also state that Saturdays and Sundays are holidays.

[13] When Canada Day falls on a Saturday, the banks and government offices are closed on Monday, July 3. However, July 3 is never a legal holiday. See the *Holiday Act*, R.S.C. 1985, c. H-5. One day this fact may cause an unpleasant surprise for an administrator at Investment Canada.

CHAPTER 13

THE REVIEW PROCESS: ASSESSING THE APPLICATION

The investment review process is intended to be fast, friendly and efficient. Investors can simply fill out the application for review, include a plan to make the business better, then sit back and wait for the decision.

Many investors, however, want to know how to prepare a good application, that anticipates problems and requests for information and meets the concerns of the government. To do this, they must understand internal agency procedure plus the six factors, consisting of some twenty sub-factors, which the minister may consider before rendering a decision.

1. Preparing an Application

Investors who are preparing applications should ensure that government officials understand four elements. These are:

(1) the transaction,

(2) the nature of the business,

(3) how the business fits into the economy,

(4) how Canada will benefit if the transaction takes place.

Experienced legal counsel often attach an addendum in which they discuss each of these elements.

Investors who are at this preliminary stage sometimes ask government officials:

1. Is a prefiling meeting needed?

2. Should undertakings be included with the application?

(a) Prefiling Meetings

A prefiling meeting is not necessary. One is arranged only if the foreign investor requests it. Most do not, although the agency officially encourages such meetings in its Guidelines on Administrative Procedure.

The advantage of a meeting, or a telephone conversation, is that agency officials may mention a government policy which should be addressed in the submission, or may highlight industry-specific factors which are of particular concern. This may result in a better application and quicker processing. (In many straightforward cases, even in the resource sector, no meetings are ever held. Such cases are handled entirely over the telephone.)

(b) Undertakings

In the days of FIRA, investors routinely gave undertakings. Often lawyers attached them to an application as a matter of course. Many of these undertakings were just boilerplate.

Investment Canada has a different attitude. The agency encourages investors to put as much detail as possible into their plans in order to reduce the need for undertakings.

As a result, very few undertakings are received; and generally, they are confined to sensitive cases. When they are given, they address one or two significant issues, such as Canadian equity participation, reinvestment in oil and gas exploration, or expenditures on R&D.

The best advice for investors is to wait until they have discussed their application with an investment review officer. Then they can decide whether to submit undertakings.

Why are undertakings needed at all? Who should sign them? These are issues of contract law. However, investors should think about them because the format of an undertaking and its manner of execution may influence the weight given to its contents.

(c) The Formalities of Undertakings

Undertakings are specific plans which the investor has bound himself to fulfil if the minister approves the investment. They strengthen the investor's case and add to his credibility. (Undertakings are easier to enforce than plans worded in more general terms. For this reason, they provide greater certainty that the investor will carry out his promises.)

Undertakings should be addressed to Her Majesty in right of Canada. Some investors address them to Investment Canada but that is improper. Investment Canada is an agent of the Crown and has no power to contract in its own name.

Undertakings should also be executed under seal. However, if they are not and the minister approves an investment, that would be sufficient consideration to create an enforceable contract.

Who should sign the undertakings? There are four possibilities:

(1) the foreign investor,

(2) the vendor,[1]

(3) the Canadian company that is being purchased (the "target Canadian company"),

(4) the foreign investor's controlling shareholder (if the investor is a corporation).

Government officials might want the target Canadian company to sign an undertaking for three possible reasons. First, the Canadian company that is being purchased is within the jurisdiction of Canadian courts and has assets in Canada. The undertaking is, therefore, easy to enforce. Secondly, if an offshore company owned by a foreign investor is the only signatory, the investor might evade his responsibilities. This could be done through a corporate reorganization that turns the offshore company into a shell.[2] Finally, if the Canadian company is sold, the undertaking would be among the liabilities assumed by the new purchaser.

A related issue is whether there should be a clause in the agreement of undertakings making it binding upon "successors and assigns". If such a clause is included, it will indicate that the investor intends the undertaking to be assignable (even if it would otherwise not be) and that a subsequent buyer of the business should agree to perform the undertakings. (The foreign investor will remain bound as well, in the absence of a novation agreement.)[3] Except in unusual

---

[1] There are very few undertakings that a vendor could give. One possibility is an undertaking regarding the manner in which the proceeds from the sale would be utilized. A vendor might also agree to maintain a certain level of activity or employment at the vendor's other businesses.

[2] How might this happen? Imagine that the Canadian business has been purchased by a subsidiary of a foreign company, and that only the subsidiary signed the undertakings. The foreign parent might transfer the assets of the Canadian business to another subsidiary and wind up the first subsidiary. Such a corporate reorganization would be exempt from review since there would be no change in the ultimate controller.

[3] If there is a "successors and assigns clause", what would happen if a Canadian later buys the assets of the business but does not assume responsibility for performing the undertakings? In theory, the Canadian might be open to suit by the federal government for inducing breach of contract if the Canadian knew about the undertakings prior to the purchase.

circumstances, solicitors for foreign investors and government representatives will probably decide not to include a "successors and assigns" clause in the agreement.[4]

How long does an undertaking endure? Most undertakings (e.g., to sell shares to Canadians within five years) have an obvious termination date. However, some undertakings are silent on when they end (e.g., to develop a particular technology in Canada). In the absence of express or implied wording to the contrary, an undertaking probably exists forever.[5] However, the continued enforceability of such an undertaking is another question.

A *force majeure* clause should be included in all undertakings, as well as a clause making performance of the undertakings conditional on ministerial approval (or actual implementation) of the investment. To preclude continued liability in the event of a subsequent sale, the undertakings can be made contingent upon the investor remaining in control of the business. Linking performance of the undertakings to sales volume, profitability or similar factors is another way of controlling liability.[6]

However, this is not always a good idea. If an undertaking is too vague or has too many caveats, it may be given little weight. To avoid this dilemma, some investors restrict undertakings to matters over which they have complete control, such as expenditures on research and development.

2. The Net Benefit Test

The heart of the review process is the net benefit test. This is the test used to evaluate a proposed investment. Section 20 lists the factors which the minister may consider in determining benefit.[7] These are:

---

[4] It may be desirable for subsequent purchasers to be released from the undertakings that a foreign investor has given. If the business is sold to a non-Canadian and the transaction is reviewable, new undertakings can be obtained.

[5] Whether a contract is of permanent duration depends upon its construction. There is no longer a presumption of permanence. See *Halsburys*, 2nd ed., Vol. 9, para. 528, and the cases referred to therein.

[6] Solicitors handling major commercial transactions must ordinarily prepare several attestation documents—the usual ones being affidavits of execution, certificates of incumbency, and a legal opinion that all documents have been executed in accordance with the by-laws of their corporate clients. When FIRA was set up, the same formalities of execution were at first demanded by the government of Canada, but were soon dropped. Attestation documents are not required by Investment Canada.

[7] These new benefit factors are the same as those in the *FIR Act*—with one addition

(a) the effect of the investment on the level and nature of economic activity in Canada including, without limiting the generality of the foregoing, the effect on employment, on resource processing, on the utilization of parts, components and services produced in Canada and on exports from Canada;

(b) the degree and significance of participation by Canadians in the Canadian business or new Canadian business and in any industry or industries in Canada of which the Canadian business or new Canadian business forms or would form a part;

(c) the effect of the investment on productivity, industrial efficiency, technological development, product innovation and product variety in Canada;

(d) the effect of the investment on competition within any industry or industries in Canada;

(e) the compatibility of the investment with national industrial, economic and cultural policies, taking into consideration industrial, economic and cultural policy objectives enunciated by the government or legislature of any province likely to be significantly affected by the investment; and

(f) the contribution of the investment to Canada's *ability to compete* in world markets.

It is not necessary for the investor to address all these "net benefit factors" in the application. Some will not be relevant. For example, the purchase of a shopping centre complex will have no effect on Canada's exports.

Foreign investors who want to purchase Canadian manufacturing operations can usually align their proposals with most of the assessment factors. Fewer factors will be relevant when the target is a resource-based or service-oriented company. At times, there will be only one factor around which to structure a recommendation for approval, namely, the compatibility of the investment with government policy.

For the investor building a case, there are two considerations. First, what combination of factors must be present in order to meet the net

---

(ability to compete in world markets). They can be classified into short-term factors (employment, investment); medium-term factors (new products, transfer of technology); and long-term factors (level of exports, utilization of Canadian parts). The last-mentioned factors have their historical roots in the truncation problem discussed in the *Gray Report Foreign Direct Investment in Canada*, (Ottawa: Information Canada, 1972). Note that most of the factors are performance oriented.

benefit test? Secondly, what evidence should be presented to establish that the benefits claimed will be realized?

Unfortunately, little guidance can be offered on these points. When Parliament passed the Act, it simply prescribed the factors to be taken into account. Parliament did not define the meaning of net benefit. Nor did it state what weight should be attached to each factor.[8] That was left to be determined by policy, not law.

Not much has changed since then. Ottawa has provided little information to flesh out the skeleton of these assessment factors, or their respective weights. As for the provincial governments, they have been even less explicit. Most of them have few "enunciated" industrial, economic and cultural policies.

As a result, the net benefit test is quite fluid. There are no predetermined performance levels. Each case is evaluated individually. This creates uncertainty for an investor and, presumably, for the minister, since Canada has no national industrial strategy[9] or comprehensive set of industry-specific performance standards within which investment proposals can be judged. This lack of certainty was one of the complaints voiced by business spokespeople when the legislation was being debated in Parliament.

But the opposite approach—predetermined standards—would have been either arbitrary or unfair.[10] The conditions for approval of a takeover of a bankrupt company that is already foreign-owned and located in a depressed region must differ immensely from the conditions that would have to be met if the company was profitable, Canadian-owned and a recipient of government grants.

For this reason, no weights are attached to the twenty assessment factors. Instead, the weight of each factor goes up or down depending upon the nature of the transaction. The argument is that the benefits to Canada of, say, new foreign technology depends upon the industry

---

[8] Any system of weights would need to be complex. For instance, the weight attributed to a transaction's job creation potential would vary depending upon where the jobs were to be located, the degree of job security, and other aspects of job quality.

[9] In 1978, the Science Council complained (in reference to FIRA) that in the absence of a national industrial strategy, almost every proposed takeover was likely to promise benefit. The Science Council claimed that FIRA influenced foreign investment only in the short term. In the Council's view, this was ironic, since foreign investment brought advantages in the short term and disadvantages in the long-term. John Britton, and James Gilmour, *The Weakest Link: A Technological Perspective On Canadian Industrial Underdevelopment*, (Ottawa: Science Council of Canada, 1978).

[10] For a discussion of the benefits of a fixed-rule scheme, see: David Anderson, *Foreign Investment Control in the Canadian Mineral Sector: Lessons from the Australian Experience* (Kingston: Centre for Resource Studies, Queen's University, 1984).

sector affected. As for job creation, there will be more direct and indirect benefits if it takes place in Cape Breton, where unemployment is high, than in Toronto during an economic boom.

The imprecision of the net benefit test is, therefore, its strength. It allows for flexibility in the application of policy, sector, and regional considerations which are not static in themselves. But there exists an important trade-off that investors do not like: a lack of transparency and predictability.

Despite these limitations, some comments can be offered on the net benefit factors and their ambit. These factors are examined below.[11]

(a) Economic Activity[12]

The first assessment factor is the investment's effect on the level of economic activity in Canada. That effect will depend upon the investment's size.

Foreign investors planning a takeover usually think they are making a huge investment. They count the purchase price, liabilities assumed, and all amounts they plan to spend to expand or modernize the business or to contribute to working capital.

Unfortunately, the government cannot use this aggregate figure. The price paid for the business merely represents the replacement of the vendor's investment. Only those funds spent after the transaction has closed can be considered when determining its economic impact.

For this reason, it may be helpful for an investor to provide information on the target company's planned expenditures. Any incremental increase arising from the investor's plans can then be quickly calculated.

---

[11] This discussion is of a general nature. How cases are actually assessed (e.g., which factors are emphasized, whether a dynamic or static approach is adopted) will depend upon the views of the people employed as investment review officers at the time in question.

In practice, the depth of the analysis naturally varies. A takeover in a sensitive sector (such as high tech) or a takeover involving layoffs may be studied in great detail (e.g., industry studies, meetings with executives of the corporate investor and the Canadian company to discuss plans). In a routine case, the information submitted by the investor may be presented to the minister with comparatively little analysis being done. No guidelines have been published outlining how cases demanding detailed analysis are distinguished from routine ones. Such decisions are probably best made on an *ad hoc* basis.

[12] Many of the benefits from an investment cannot be measured in a satisfactory way. For instance, how is greater competition or improved efficiency quantified? As for the review process itself, its effects are even more difficult to gauge. This is because a hypothetical question must first be answered: what would have happened if there had been no review process?

In most cases, details about how the investor's post-purchase expenditures will benefit Canada are not necessary. However, some investors like to highlight them. The following might be discussed:

(1) the nature of the investment. Is it for leasehold improvements, working capital, new buildings, equipment or machinery?

(2) whether the money will be spent inside or outside Canada;

(3) the form of the investment (purchase/lease), its timing and source (equity or debt capital, from within Canada or abroad);

(4) the direct or indirect effects on third parties (such as customers, employees, and suppliers).

If the government is reviewing a proposal to establish a new cultural business, the analysis will be a little different. Then, the total amount of the investment can be taken into account.

There is a small controversy among armchair economists over whether the *IC Act* should be an instrument of stabilization policy. Those who favour the idea believe the impact of a proposal on the level of economic activity and employment should be weighed more or less heavily depending upon whether the economy is in recession or overheated.

The statute does not say this. Nothing in section 20 suggests that the assessment factors should be adjusted for changes in the business cycle. Nevertheless, it is hard to imagine that any minister would overlook the current state of the economy. (Especially when the general public seems to evaluate the review process in terms of its short-term impact on employment and capital spending, instead of longer-term structural objectives.)

(b) Employment

The effect of an investment on the level of employment (its "job creation potential") is the second major factor. This effect can be evaluated in a number of ways, such as the area of Canada in which the jobs will be created, as well as the quantity, and the quality of the jobs. From the perspective of quality, the: (i) terms, levels and grades of employment, (ii) degree of job security, and (iii) provisions of any pension plans, may all be relevant. Unfortunately, while an investment's direct effects on employment levels may be clear, it is difficult to measure the indirect effects.

There are no official guidelines for applying this net benefit factor (or any of the others). However, it appears that the thought process of review officers can be broken down into four phases:

1. What is the current economic situation within the Canadian economy and the industry in question?

2. Assuming that the proposed investment is not proceeded with, what projections can be made?

3. If the proposed investment is implemented, how does this change the future projections?

4. How do the two projections compare?

This process of analysis is aimed at determining net or overall benefit rather than absolute benefit. If the vendor intends to create a certain number of jobs if the business is not sold, the plans of the foreign investor, if they are similar, may be given little weight. However, each case must be assessed on its merits. It may be that the foreign investor, but not the vendor, has the financial capability to realize those plans. (In reality, the intentions of the vendor are seldom considered.)

When analyzing the impact of an investment, a dynamic (not a static) view of events is (or should be) adopted. The significance of a dynamic approach is that it requires the review officer to estimate the difference in employment activity if the Canadian business continues under its present ownership versus the level of activity expected if the takeover is approved. If a takeover target is a solvent, efficient company in an expanding industry, one can reasonably suppose that employment levels will keep pace with levels in the industry, regardless of whether the target company is acquired. Therefore, if it cannot be demonstrated (on a theoretical level) that a foreign investor's plans will result in an increase in employment beyond what will occur in any event, there exists no net benefit in terms of the number of jobs.[13]

The displacement effect may also be a consideration. If the foreign investor intends to buy and expand a business in an industry sector where Canadian companies have sufficient capacity to meet projected demand, existing production and employment may be displaced. In such circumstances, the investor's proposal might be credited with little or no increment to employment. (On the other hand, since forecasts of future demand are often unreliable, the possibility of a displacement effect is likely to be ignored).

Examples of the displacement effect may be found in the service industry. Imagine that an investor wants to buy a Canadian restaurant chain and is promising to build additional restaurants throughout Canada. Will this benefit the country? That will depend upon the

---

[13] The other assessment factors can also be applied in either a dynamic or static fashion.

locations chosen. The only effect may be to reduce business and employment levels in nearby restaurants.[14]

However, the net benefit test is multi-dimensional. Although it may bring no net increase in employment, a proposal may receive a positive rating for other reasons.

For instance, although an equivalent number of similar jobs may be lost elsewhere, the proposed investment may create jobs in a depressed area of the country, with corresponding spill-over and multiplier effects. Or it may create a higher quality of job—one offering retraining, a profit-sharing scheme, or a pension plan. The investor should highlight these offsetting factors, if they exist.

At times, a plan merely to maintain jobs or avoid large-scale cutbacks, may be received with as much enthusiasm as job creation. An example is a rescue operation. In such circumstances, the investor should emphasize the dire consequences that may befall the vendor if the business cannot be sold. Representations from the vendor are obviously a good tactic.

Sometimes, an investment will indirectly create jobs. For instance, a foreigner who wants to buy a construction business in Canada should point out how an expansion of the business will benefit the subcontracting trades and Canadian suppliers.

A few investors are less than forthright. They extol the many jobs that their takeover will create, but never mention that they will be cutting back on employment at their existing plant in Canada. Such a lack of candour is not advisable, particularly if the investor plans to make future acquisitions.

(c) Resource Processing

Much of Canada's development in the nineteenth century occurred because there was a demand by other countries for Canada's natural resources. These natural resources were usually processed abroad. As a result, for many years, a large portion of Canada's export trade consisted of unprocessed and semi-processed raw materials.

Resource processing creates jobs and Canada, like other mineral-exporting countries, would prefer to keep some of those jobs at home.

---

[14] It is difficult to predict if there will be a displacement effect. Suppose a foreign investor is planning to buy a company and create a hundred jobs. Will jobs be lost elsewhere in Canada? There are so many variables. If an investor wants to buy a restaurant chain, then establish new restaurants which will serve ethnic dishes unavailable elsewhere, there may actually be an overall increase in employment in this economic subsector. For these reasons, Investment Canada officials are unlikely to consider the displacement effect.

A foreign investor's plan to add further value through the processing of natural resources in Canada is, therefore, a benefit. An investor who cannot afford to build a processing facility might consider whether a Canadian processor can process the materials at reasonable cost.

(d) Utilization of Parts, Components and Services Produced in Canada

Some foreign-controlled companies purchase more of their supplies and services from foreign sources than Canadian-controlled companies do. This is understandable. The managers or affiliates of foreign-controlled companies may have had a long association with foreign suppliers.

Until 1983, foreign investors often gave commitments to purchase (a certain percentage or amount of) Canadian-made goods, provided the price and quality were competitive. The U.S. objected and complained to the GATT Council. In July of that year, a panel appointed under the General Agreement on Tariffs and Trade ("the GATT panel") ruled that the practice of approving investments conditional upon commitments by investors to purchase goods from Canadian sources or goods of Canadian origin was inconsistent with Article III.4 of the GATT.

Under GATT, Canada must grant the same treatment to imported goods that it does to Canadian-made products (when enacting laws or imposing "requirements that affect their purchase"). There can, in other words, be no discrimination against foreign goods after they have been imported. According to the GATT panel, commitments ("requirements") to purchase Canadian goods provided they are competitive violated this principle because they gave a small margin of preference to Canadian suppliers.

As a result, Canada (without breaching its international obligations) cannot accept unqualified commitments to purchase Canadian-made products. However, sourcing commitments worded in more general terms are still compatible with both GATT and the Free Trade Agreement.

For instance, an investor can indicate that Canadian suppliers will be given a full and fair opportunity to participate on a competitive basis in the supply of goods and services to the Canadian business. In addition, since the GATT panel decision only covers trade in goods, Canada can still legally accept unqualified commitments to purchase services (such as advertising and engineering services) in Canada. (In practice, undertakings to purchase services in Canada are not accepted.)

How can a vague commitment to "give Canadian suppliers a full and fair opportunity to compete" ever be fulfilled? There are several ways. The investor might agree to provide technical assistance to Canadian suppliers, so that they can meet the investor's standards. Alternatively, the investor can promise to work with government officials in identifying Canadian suppliers, assign an employee to the task of identifying potential Canadian suppliers or set up a Canadian purchasing division.

(e) Exports from Canada

The export performance of foreign-owned companies in Canada has been subject to frequent criticism. Some foreign subsidiaries do not export because they lack the incentive. They were set up to serve Canada's domestic market, and that is all they intend to do. Other companies cannot export because of high production costs and short production runs. Still other companies are prevented from exporting by their multinational parents, which do not want their Canadian subsidiaries competing with other affiliates.

An investor can seldom commit himself to an absolute level of exports. If the investor is an American, the Free Trade Agreement prevents him from giving such a commitment in any event.

However, investors can indicate that they will not impose export restrictions on the Canadian business. They can offer to assist the Canadian business in its export activities. They might even promise to establish export departments (to seek markets abroad) within their Canadian subsidiaries.

Consideration could also be given to a world or North American product mandate. A Canadian subsidiary with such a mandate has the responsibility for all research, product development, manufacturing and marketing of a product (or product line) on a North American or world-wide basis.

This is a major step beyond mere rationalization. Rationalization reduces production costs through the phasing out of uncompetitive products and achieves economies of scale through specialization. A subsidiary with a world product mandate, on the other hand, does its own research and development, and its management has significant autonomy to run the business and engage in new product development.

The Canadian (and Ontario) governments first began promoting the idea of world product mandates in 1980. With tariff barriers declining, Canadian industry was facing increased international competition. World product mandates offered a way for branch plants to cope and compete in foreign markets. A publication by the Science Council of Canada entitled *Multinationals and Industrial Strategy*[15] explains other reasons for the government's support of this idea.

A world product mandate can transform a domestically oriented branch plant into an enterprise that is both export oriented and internationally competitive. The parent company benefits through realization of economies of scale (and greater profits). Canadians benefit because export-led growth leads to greater output, employment and capital expenditures. In addition, local Canadian suppliers indirectly benefit, since they are able to produce components at high volume and become cost competitive with foreign-based component suppliers.

World product mandates are not suitable for every industry. They are more likely to succeed in technologically intensive industries. Investors who are purchasing companies that manufacture machinery, electrical equipment, and aerospace products might think about them.

(f) Canadian Participation

"Canadian participation" is an assessment factor with an interesting history. The legislation which governed Investment Canada's predecessor, FIRA, was passed by Parliament in 1973 because the high degree of foreign ownership and control of the Canadian economy was causing concern. Nationalist forces, such as the Committee for an Independent Canada (disbanded in 1981), claimed that foreign ownership of Canadian industry carried with it some major costs (e.g., the payment of dividends, reduced exports, decreased R&D).

In the early years of FIRA, the prospect of increased Canadian participation and control was the most important of the benefit criteria. However, by 1978, observers noted that Canadian ownership and control had lost its priority. Instead, Cabinet was giving more weight to other factors, such as increased exports, R&D, employment and productivity. This change in emphasis, the *Toronto Star* noted, allowed the Liberal government to claim that FIRA was a success, although FIRA was doing little to increase Canadian ownership.[16] Liberal government

---

[15] Science Council of Canada, *Multinationals and Industrial Strategy*, (Ottawa: Supply and Services Canada, 1980).

[16] "Cabinet Is More Willing to Sell Businesses to Foreigners: Survey", *Toronto Star*, July 22, 1978, p. A1. The *Toronto Star* contacted 25 Cabinet ministers for this survey. This paper also mentioned what it called "the classic Canadian trade-off: Canadian control

ministers, on the other hand, argued that how control is exercised is more important than ownership.

Since the passage of the *IC Act* in 1985, this change in emphasis has continued. Underlying it is evidently the belief that Canadian ownership seldom contributes much to the economic performance of a business.

Nevertheless, increased Canadian participation remains an important objective to some Canadian nationalists. They believe that Canadian owners or managers will be more responsive to Canadian needs and policies.[17] Other benefits are more tangible. When Canadians are owners, they share in the profits created by the business. When they participate as directors and managers, they build experience and expertise.

Investors often ask what level of Canadian participation is required by the government. In most provinces, legislation requires that a majority of the directors of a company be resident Canadians. However, with that exception and a few key sectors (such as financial services, film distribution, the oil and gas sector and book publishing) there exist neither laws nor official policies. Unlike some countries, which insist that their citizens have a specified equity interest in all foreign-controlled operations, Canada has not adopted the fixed rule approach.[18] Canadian participation is just one of many factors taken into account in the review process.

---

can be fostered by restricting foreign access—but at a cost of higher prices and fewer jobs, whereas competition and lower prices, and more jobs in the short-run, can be fostered—at the cost of permitting foreign investment".

[17] How important is it that directors be Canadian? Many large companies are effectively controlled by their management, not by their Canadian directors. As for wholly owned Canadian subsidiaries of foreign corporations, a Canadian director who asserted "too much" independence would likely be removed by a resolution signed by the sole foreign shareholder.

At the time that FIRA was created, there were complaints in the press that key positions in U.S. subsidiaries in Canada had been filled by managers from the U.S. Nationalists saw the review process as a way of changing that pattern.

[18] The *Canada Business Corporations Act* and all provincial incorporation statutes with the exception of that of New Brunswick require that a majority of a company's directors be Canadian residents. The "Baie Comeau Policy" governs takeovers and the establishment of new businesses in the book publishing and distribution industry. It is designed to encourage joint ventures under Canadian control. The government's policy on "Foreign Investment in the Film Distribution Industry" states that takeovers of Canadian-owned and controlled film distribution businesses are not allowed. Both policies are administered through the *Investment Canada Act*. Copies of these policies are available from Investment Canada. In addition, there are government policies governing takeovers in the oil, gas and uranium industries.

The weight accorded to this factor, however, may vary. If a foreign investor wants to buy a company in a potential growth area or in an industry where there is already a high level of foreign ownership, the degree of Canadian participation may be of greater concern.

Obviously, in a takeover of a Canadian-controlled business by foreigners, the reduction in Canadian participation constitutes a negative factor. It must be more than counterbalanced by positive elements in order for net benefit to exist. This negative factor can be minimized by promising to appoint Canadians as directors and managers, or to make some equity available to Canadians through a stock option plan. If the employees cannot afford to buy stock, a profit sharing plan may be an alternative.

A few foreign investors go a step further and seek Canadian partners. On very rare occasions, an investor will even undertake to make a public offering of shares. However, such undertakings will naturally be hedged by a variety of conditions (e.g., satisfactory earnings record, feasibility opinions by underwriters, sale price of shares to be above a specified price/earnings ratio).

Occasionally, a foreign investor asserts: "I may not be able to hire any Canadians. There is a severe shortage of workers with the necessary skills." To strengthen the case, the investor submits a letter from Canada Employment and Immigration ("C.E.I.C.") attesting to the lack of qualified people. Such letters are not necessary. Investment Canada knows that foreign workers cannot be hired by businesses in Canada unless C.E.I.C. is convinced of the need to do so.

Foreign investors who are establishing a new cultural business (the only type of new business that may be reviewable) seem to think that Ottawa requires a particular form of business organization. "Do you want us to incorporate?" they ask. That decision is for the investor to make. However, Investment Canada prefers that a Canadian corporation be utilized.

An advantage of the corporate form is that the *Canada Business Corporations Act* and almost all provincial companies legislation requires a majority of a company's board of directors to be resident Canadians. Canadian participation is, therefore, assured. In addition, in the event of a subsequent indirect acquisition of the new business, the transaction will be subject to the Act if the business is incorporated but not if it is a branch business.

(g) Technological Development, Product Innovation and Product Variety

The industrialized countries are engaged in stiff competition for technologically based investments. This competition works to the advantage of foreign investors seeking approval under the *IC Act*, if they can transfer technology (e.g., patents, trade-marks and "know-how") to a Canadian business.

If technology is to be transferred, the investor should briefly describe it. Is it marketing strategy, design and engineering concepts, or methods of packaging or manufacturing? Why is it better than current technology? The investor may also want to explain the terms under which any technology will be transferred.

These terms are significant, because importing technology carries a financial price. Other costs might include reduced opportunities for Canadian researchers and a dependence upon foreign technology that may not be well adapted to Canadian needs.

Because of these costs, Ottawa for many years has expressed misgivings about the low level of research and development done in Canada. Multinational firms have been criticized for this state of affairs because they tend to locate their research facilities in their home countries. However, the fragmentation of the Canadian market and the small size of many Canadian firms have been contributing factors.

The level of R&D is often measured as a percentage of sales. Foreign companies should, therefore, consider whether the Canadian business they are purchasing can perform R&D on a scale that bears the same relationship to its sales as that of its new foreign parent.

This may involve a promise to establish or expand R&D facilities in Canada, or to contract out R&D to independent Canadian organizations. Details on the number of staff to be employed and the proposed budget may strengthen such a promise.

R&D expenditure plans are often key factors during the review process. So is the extent to which the Canadian business being purchased will have the opportunity to manufacture and market worldwide any products it develops.[19] This is evident from press releases that were issued following government approval of takeovers of Canadian high tech companies. (See, for example, the takeovers of Connaught BioSciences by Institut Merieux of France, and Lumonics by Japan's Sumitomo. These takeovers sparked considerable public opposition.)

(h) Productivity and Industrial Efficiency

Economists have commented adversely on Canadian productivity levels, in comparison with those of foreign countries. Perhaps this is

---

[19] A few multinational companies apparently require that their subsidiaries transfer to the parent company the results of R&D research plus the rights to patent and control it. Even if a formal transfer does not occur, the parent company obviously has indirect control. Thus, Investment Canada may be interested in knowing if a Canadian company being purchased will be able to exploit new processes resulting from its R&D efforts.

why productivity—that is, the ratio of output to the number of persons employed—is one of the factors Parliament included in the net benefit test.

How can productivity be increased? There are several means, including automation new capital equipment and technology, innovative management techniques, retraining and greater economies of scale. If improvements in productivity will come primarily from automation, and result in a loss of jobs, the investor might explain how the long-term benefits to the economy justify the short-term increase in unemployment.

Industrial efficiency is a related concept. It may be brought about through financial controls that reduce overheads, rationalization of operations that increase economies of scale, or by improved quality controls and management techniques. Such "efficiency savings" are the alleged reason for many large mergers.

The potential for improvements in productivity and efficiency is an especially important factor in the review process at the present time. This is because such improvements increase Canadian competitiveness in the new "global" economy.

(i) The Effect on Competition/Role of the Competition Bureau

As soon as an application for review is received, Investment Canada sends a written summary of the facts (called the "case summary") and a photocopy of the application to the Bureau of Competition Policy ("Competition Bureau") at Consumer and Corporate Affairs. The Competition Bureau then decides whether the proposed transaction ("merger") "is likely to prevent or lessen competition substantially".[20] This analysis is done for two reasons: to provide advice to Investment Canada and to fulfil the Bureau's own responsibilities under the *Competition Act*.

The process of analysis involves three steps:

1. The relevant product and geographic markets are determined for each of the products and services of the merging companies. [Sample issue: are cellophane and wax paper distinct product markets or do they compete?] Overlaps between the products of the merging companies and where they are sold are noted.

2. Market share data (pre- and post-merger) is obtained.

---

[20] *Competition Act*, subs. 92(1).

3. Several "evaluative criteria" such as the extent of foreign competition and barriers to entry are then considered.

Throughout this evaluation, the focus is on whether prices are likely to be higher ("a market power test") than they would have been without the merger.[21] If the merged company could impose a material price increase in a substantial part of the market for two years or more, the Bureau would conclude that competition is likely to be substantially prevented or lessened. In that event, the acquiring company may be able to meet the requirements of the "efficiency exception".

The first step—the determination of the relevant market—is described in the Bureau's *Merger Enforcement Guidelines*.[22] Both the relevant geographic market (the area in which firms compete) and the relevant product market (which is related to the degree of substitutability between products) are ascertained.[23] A number of factors, including the end use of the product, what buyers state they will do if prices rise, the cost of switching suppliers, and transportation costs may be considered. Here are two illustrations of how the process works:[24]

(1) Imagine that two airline companies want to merge. The relevant product market for determining if there is a competitive overlap between the two companies is passenger airline service. (The relevant product market is not "all forms of transportation" since a significant rise in airfares—such as 5%—will cause few, if any, passengers to switch to travel by car, bus or

---

[21] However, non-price aspects of competition such as service and innovation are also considered.

[22] Director of Investigations and Research, "Merger Enforcement Guidelines". Ottawa: Supply and Services Canada, March 1991. For commentary on similar guidelines issued by the Anti-trust Division of the U.S. Department of Justice, read: Steven Salop and Joseph Simons, "A Practical Guide To Merger Analysis" *The Antitrust Bulletin*, Winter 1984, p. 663-703.

[23] A relevant market for merger analysis is defined in terms of the smallest group of products in which the sellers, if they were all one firm, could profitably impose a significant non-transitory price increase (usually 5%, for a one-year period). This may involve asking buyers and actual and potential sellers what they are likely to do if prices of the product increases. In this way, those actual and potential sellers which constrain the exercise of market power by the merged company are identified.

[24] Crampton, P. "Relevant Market Analysis in Recent Merger Branch Decisions". Paper presented at the National Conference on the Centenary of Competition Law and Policy in Canada (Toronto: October 24-25, 1989). See also: Paul Crampton, *Mergers and the Competition Act*, (Toronto: Carswell, 1990). For an excellent discussion and critique of how relevant markets are defined, see Herbert Hovenkamp, "The Measurement of Market Power: Policy and Science" in Mathewson, F., M. Trebilcock and M. Walker, *The Law and Economics of Competition Policy*, (Vancouver: The Fraser Institute, 1990).

rail).[25] The relevant geographic market will be flights between cities of origin and destination ("O/D city pair markets"). A good reason for choosing "O/D city pair markets" is that passengers will not substitute another city as their destination, even if airfares rise by 5%.

(2) In 1989, Consumers Packaging Inc. purchased all of the assets of Domglas Inc. Both companies were major Canadian manufacturers of food and beverage glass containers. The issue in that case was whether the product market should be confined to glass containers, or whether it should include "all rigid-wall containers (that is, plastic, aluminum, steel and paperboard containers) manufactured for the food and beverage industries. Despite differences in price and product characteristics, the Competition Bureau concluded that, from the perspective of most Canadian purchasers of glass containers, the market was rigid-wall containers. One reason was that plastic and metal cans were being used to hold soft drinks. Also, paperboard cartons and plastic had taken the place of glass bottles in the milk industry and several others.[26] In the words of the press release:

> "various alternative rigid-wall packaging materials are effective substitutes for many glass end-uses. As a result, the market power of the merged firm will be constrained by the ability of purchasers to substitute over a wide range of end-use applications".[27]

As for the relevant geographic market, the Competition Bureau concluded it was (at a minimum) all of Canada.[28] Consumers and Domglas quoted prices on a national basis and competed for sales across the country.

After the appropriate market has been selected, Competition Bureau officials look at two possible anti-competitive effects of the merger. These are:

---

[25] The Competition Bureau normally uses 5% as its price test, but the price chosen can be more or less depending upon the industry under examination.

[26] Bureau officials were aware that some purchasers of glass containers—such as companies that sell wine and beer—would not switch to another container. Demand in that segment of the market was "inelastic".

[27] Consumer and Corporate Affairs Canada, *Backgrounder*: "Background Information on the Examination of the Acquisition of the Assets of Domglas Inc. by Consumers Packaging Inc." p.1. Attached to News Release NR-10188 dated April 25, 1989.

[28] The market possibly included U.S. plants located close to the U.S.-Canada border. In the words of the *Backgrounder* (cited in note 27), p. 3, "The analysis has revealed that many companies in diverse end-use market segments in Canada consider U.S. manufacturers to be viable alternate suppliers of their glass container requirements. This supply option has served as an important constraint on domestic pricing".

(1) whether the merger will result in the merged company domi-
nating the market, and

(2) whether the merger will enhance the ability of firms in an
oligopolistic market to engage in tacit collusion (in connection
with price, market share etc.)

An important consideration is the market share of the merged
company and the post-merger industrial concentration ratio.[29] In the
Consumers-Domglas case, for example, the two companies accounted
for 90% of Canadian glass container sales, but less than 25% of the
larger rigid-wall container market. (This illustrates the significance of
different market definitions.)

The *Merger Enforcement Guidelines* state that market share may be
measured on the basis of dollar sales, unit sales or production capacity.
These Guidelines also indicate that if the merged company will have
less than 35% of the market, the Director of the Bureau of Competition Policy "will not generally be concerned about the firm raising
prices in the market by raising only its own price. Moreover, where the
top four firms in the market hold a total share of less than 65 percent,
the Director will not generally be concerned about prices being raised
in the market by firms acting together. Even if the top four firms have
a share of greater than 65 percent but the merged firm will hold less
than 10 percent of the market, the Director will not generally be
concerned".[30]

According to subsection 92(2) of the *Competition Act*, even if a
merged company will have a high market share, that fact alone cannot
justify a finding that competition will be substantially lessened or
prevented. Several other evaluative criteria must be examined as well.
These criteria include:

(1) The extent of foreign competition:	If prices in the relevant market rise, will enough buyers switch to foreign suppliers to constrain the price rise?

---

[29] A concentration ratio is usually defined as the aggregate percentage share of
market sales accounted for by the four largest firms in the market. For example, if the
four largest firms each have 15% of the market, the four firm concentration ratio will be
60%.

[30] Consumer and Corporate Affairs Canada. "*Backgrounder*. Merger Enforcement
Guidelines Issued By The Bureau of Competition Policy", page 3. This *Backgrounder* is
attached to News Release NR-00184-91-09 issued on April 17, 1991.

(2) Whether the business is likely to fail:

The purchase of a firm that is about to fail cannot be held responsible for lessened competition in the market place. However, because the purchaser may obtain a greater degree of market power, other possible scenarios, such as retrenchment or purchase by another party must be examined.

(3) Substitutes:

Will the availability of acceptable substitutes constrain a price increase?

(4) Barriers to Entry:

A few examples are regulatory barriers and any cost advantages of established firms (over new/ potential entrants) arising from control over scarce resources, lower distribution costs and tariffs. If two firms merge but barriers to entry faced by new firms are minimal, any attempt to raise prices above the competitive level will not succeed, and the merger will not likely create problems.

(5) Effective Remaining Competition:

Will effective competition remain in the market after the merger (and, thus, prevent any price increase)?

(6) Removal of a vigorous and effective competitor:

The purchase of a company which engages in vigorous competition such as discount pricing, or introduces new products, may lessen competition to a greater extent than its share of the market would suggest.

(7) Change and Innovation:

Market power is more difficult to exercise in a dynamic market (e.g., a market where new firms are entering, and packaging and the distribution system is changing).

(8) Other factors:

countervailing power of buyers/ suppliers; prior history of anti-competitive conduct.

After analyzing these factors, the Competition Bureau decides whether the merger is likely to prevent or lessen competition substantially. In the majority of cases, the Competition Bureau advises Investment Canada that the transaction "does not appear to raise any significant competition issues". In those cases where the competitive impact will be positive or negative, the Competition Bureau provides reasons. The minister responsible for Investment Canada than takes that advice into account when determining net benefit.[31]

A merger can have a positive impact on competition if it improves efficiency. This may happen through long-term rationalization of the industry sector, greater consumer choice or an increased supply of goods and services with consequent downward pressure on prices. In addition, the merger of two firms doing business in Canada may increase competition if the greater financial strength of the merged company allows it to compete more effectively with larger firms in the industry.

On the other hand, a merger may lessen competition substantially if the new merged firm will have a major share of the market, and if a vigorous competitor will be eliminated, or if barriers to entry will be elevated to such a high level that new firms cannot enter the market. If a transaction will have such an effect, the foreign investor will want to stress any efficiency gains which the transaction is likely to achieve. One reason is that the Competition Tribunal cannot make an order blocking a merger:

(1) if the merger will bring about gains in efficiency that are greater than and will offset any lessening of competition; and

(2) if the efficiency gains are likely to be obtained through some other means — such as internal growth — if the order (blocking the merger) is made.

"Efficiency" is undefined in the Act.[32] According to the *Merger Enforcement Guidelines*, for a gain from a merger to qualify as an "efficiency gain", it must involve a real saving of resources. Redistributive gains, such as those which arise when the increased bargaining

---

[31] The minister responsible for Investment Canada is not bound by the opinion of the Director of the Competition Bureau. In other words, the minister can come to his own conclusion concerning the effect of a transaction on competition.

[32] Paul Crampton in his book *Mergers and the Competition Act*, op. cit. p. 509-554, discusses what Parliament meant by the word "efficiency". On page 509, he states: "the term 'gain in efficiency' should be taken to include all real resource savings . . . that permit a firm to produce more or a higher quality output for the same amount of inputs".

power of the merged company allows it to extract reduced prices from suppliers, are not considered. Production efficiencies (economies of scale, reduced inventory costs, elimination of duplication) and dynamic efficiencies (R&D synergies, superior organizational structure) are examples of legitimate efficiency gains.[33]

Might the minister responsible for Investment Canada, and the director of the Competition Bureau come to conflicting conclusions? That is a possibility.

In 1989, for instance, the minister approved the merger of Hostess Food Products Limited and the Frito-Lay Division of Pepsi-Cola Canada. About the same time, the Competition Bureau announced that it intended to file an application with the Competition Tribunal to block the transaction. (The Competition Bureau never took that step but only because the parties to the merger agreed to sell Frito-Lay's Kitchener plant and certain other assets.)

Conflicting decisions under the two statutes should be expected to happen on occasion. Although the assessment criteria they use overlap to some extent, Investment Canada and the Competition Bureau have very different mandates.[34]

This fact is recognized by section 34 of the *IC Act*. That section declares that a decision made under the *IC Act* does not affect the administration of any other Act. One consequence is that the Competition Bureau (under sections 92 and 97 of its legislation) can challenge a merger before the Competition Tribunal, up to three years after it has been completed (and, therefore, three years after approval under the *Investment Canada Act*).

---

[33] The basic goal of competition policy is to promote consumer welfare and wealth maximization. Allocative efficiency, productive efficiency and dynamic efficiency are, therefore, intermediate goals. Some authors criticize wealth maximization as a goal. Others point out that if a merger causes unemployment, human resources are being used inefficiently. However, the effect of mergers on the level of employment in Canada is not a consideration under the *Competition Act*. For a general discussion of such issues, see Dunlop, B., David McQueen and Michael Trebilcock, *Canadian Competition Policy: A Legal and Economic Analysis*, (Toronto: Canada Law Book, 1987), p. 61-71.

[34] How similar are the factors that Investment Canada and the Competition Tribunal take into account? Investment Canada considers the impact of a takeover on exports, imports and industrial efficiency, as does the Competition Tribunal when evaluating the efficiency exception. Indeed, there is so little guidance offered to the Competition Tribunal when assessing efficiency that both government bodies may end up considering: the effects of a takeover on productivity, technological development, product innovation, product variety and resource processing, as well as the contribution of the takeover to improving Canada's international competitiveness.

(j) Compatibility with National and Provincial Policies

The *IC Act* requires that the minister take into account "the compatibility of the investment with national industrial, economic and cultural policy objectives". This has led to a debate among lawyers about when a policy of a federal government department becomes a national policy. Must such a policy first have Cabinet approval? This legal issue remains unresolved.

The minister must also "take into consideration any economic, industrial and cultural policy objectives enunciated" by any province likely to be significantly affected by the investment. However, the minister is not compelled by law to consult the provinces.[35] He can do so if he wishes, or he can come to his own determination as to whether an investment is compatible with provincial policies.[36] (The intent of the legislation is to give the provinces a voice but not a veto.)

In practice, the minister, through Investment Canada, solicits the views of federal government departments with relevant expertise. Those provinces where the Canadian business has (or will have) employees are also contacted.

The minister does not request advice on the issue of net benefit. Instead, federal government departments are asked to describe any departmental policies that are relevant to the proposed investment. They are also asked to identify and describe any other considerations which Investment Canada should take into account.

The provinces, on the other hand, are asked if they consider the proposed investment to be compatible with their industrial, economic (and cultural) policies. Reasons are requested as well.

---

[35] Why is there no legal obligation on Ottawa to consult with the provinces? The explanation can be found in the Parliamentary debates concerning the *FIR Act*. (S. 20 of the *IC Act* was copied almost verbatim from the *FIR Act*.) Consultations are not required because that would have led to a major argument over what the word "consultations" meant. The federal government would have declared that it had talked to the provinces. The provinces might have insisted that that was not consultation. Consequently, the *FIR* and *IC Acts* were drafted so that the only legal obligation of the federal government is to read the stated objectives of the provinces and take them into account. Nevertheless, the *policy* of Ottawa is to consult with the provinces. House of Commons, *Minutes of the Standing Committee on Finance, Trade and Economic Affairs*, July 10, 1973, p. 39: 40. According to the Hon. Alastair Gillespie, there is an implied legal obligation to consult a province if its economic and industrial policies have been made public, op. cit., p. 39:34.

[36] According to s.20, national policies must be taken "into account"; provincial policies "into consideration". This wording is a carry-over from the *FIR Act*. It reflects the insistence of the federal government during debate on the proposed *FIR Act* that national policies should be accorded more weight than provincial policies. Note that provincial policies must have been "enunciated" in order to be given consideration. That is not a requirement with respect to national policies.

Investors, when drafting their applications, often wonder what federal and provincial government policies they should take into account. Occasionally, they cannot find out. There are few published policies. Even more frustrating is the fact that some of the published policies, left flexible to accommodate changing circumstances, are not specific enough to provide much guidance.

In many cases, government policy is clearly set out in the form of legislation. Laws designed to protect the environment and ensure a safe workplace are prime examples. In addition, there are several industry sectors (such as the oil and gas and uranium industries) that have been the subject of government policy statements.

These statements may be obtained through the Information Services division of the appropriate government department by asking for either the back issues of News Releases or policy papers presented to the House of Commons. In addition, any policy statements which have a bearing on foreign investment can be obtained from Investment Canada.

Sometimes, however, a policy or departmental objective is unavailable in written form. The only way to get an inkling of its existence is to speak with senior departmental officials.

Why do the federal and provincial governments not publicize all their policies? A common reason is that the policies are ill-defined. In addition, publication might restrict the freedom of officials to make decisions that are contrary to their general policies.

An exception are policies restricting foreign ownership. They are easy to find. Investors should examine policy statements covering book publishing and distribution, film distribution, and the oil, gas and uranium industries. There is also (provincial and federal) legislation restraining foreign ownership in the financial service industry (banks, insurance and trust companies) and in public broadcasting.

With the exception of these policies, which are aimed directly at foreign investors, the issue of whether an investment complies with government policy seldom arises. If it should be broached during discussions with government officials, foreign investors should remember to distinguish between government policies and departmental objectives (or "department positions"). Sometimes, they are synonymous. Frequently, they are not. (It might also be useful to differentiate between provincial policies that are in statutory form and those that are not).

A departmental objective may be loosely referred to as a "policy". In reality, it may merely represent the views of a few senior administrators. Investors should ask if the departmental "policy" has been publicly announced by a minister, or if official decisions have been taken, based upon this policy.

What happens if an investment proposal is incompatible with a federal or provincial government policy? The minister could still approve the proposal if there are sufficient offsetting benefits.

(k) Canada's International Competitiveness

The final factor on the net benefit check-list is the contribution a foreign investor can make to Canada's ability to compete abroad. This factor is distinct from the others which focus on the domestic economy. It was added to emphasize that international competitiveness is a key factor in the growth of the country.

How can a foreign investor improve Canada's trading position? If the investor is a corporation with a global distribution network, it might offer Canadian products greater access to world markets. A world product mandate, additional capital or new technology might also make Canada more internationally competitive. If two companies are to be amalgamated (merged), the new company may sometimes be a lower cost producer, and, therefore, a more effective competitor in U.S. and other foreign markets.

(l) Environmental and Other Factors: The Legal Parameters

There are numerous benchmarks by which an investment could be assessed that are not mentioned in the Act. Subsection 20(e), for instance, speaks of national policies that are of an industrial, economic or cultural nature. But what about environmental policies or Canadian laws? Must the minister give his stamp of approval to an otherwise attractive investment proposal, offering increased employment, 100% Canadian content, and product variety, such as a new publishing company specializing in obscene literature, if the business may violate the *Criminal Code*? Does it really matter what factors the minister considers?

It does matter. The Act sets out the factors on which a ministerial decision can be based. If the minister should consider factors other than those listed in the statute, and if an investor can prove it, a court would nullify the minister's decision.

What should the minister do, then, if it appears that an investment will contravene provincial or federal laws? The *IC Act* is silent on the point, but for a reason. Investment Canada was not intended to be used as a vehicle for enforcing other laws. If it appears that an investment will run into a conflict with another law, but the lawyers for the investor are of a contrary view, the *IC Act* should not be used to deprive the investor of his day in court. That is the position of Investment Canada staff.

That position, however, is somewhat narrower than the Act's legal parameters. Subsection 20(e) talks of policies and objectives, not laws. Nonetheless, since behind every law there must exist a policy of some sort, national and provincial laws can legally be looked at during the assessment process (provided that these laws and the policies underlying them are of an industrial, economic or cultural nature).

On the other hand, suppose, like the obscenity provisions in the *Criminal Code*, the law in question is not of an industrial or economic nature. Then the minister would have no legal right to consider its potential breach when examining an investment proposal.

There is one exception. If the plans of an applicant were clearly prohibited by the *Criminal Code* and, therefore, could never be realized, the investment could not possibly meet the net benefit test. The minister could then legally arrive at a negative decision.[37]

If a provincial or federal law would be clearly violated, must the minister automatically turn down an investment proposal? Consider, for example, Ontario's *Paperback and Periodical Distributors Act*.[38] That Act provides that if a single non-resident owns more than 10% of the shares of a company, the company cannot carry on the business of distributing periodicals in Ontario.

Suppose a foreign investor proposed to acquire 51% of the shares of a company engaged in such a business. What should the minister do? One option would be to turn down the proposal. Under the *IC Act*, the minister can consider provincial policies and, therefore, laws of an economic nature.

On the other hand, the minister could approve the proposal and let the Attorney General of Ontario decide whether to enforce the province's laws. This is because an approval under the *IC Act* is not an approval for any other purpose, and in no way prevents a province from enforcing legislation that would block foreign investment.

A similar dilemma can arise when environmental issues come to the fore. A non-Canadian may want to buy and expand a steel company that is causing air pollution or increase the size of a pulp and paper mill that is discharging poisons into a river. Because of anticipated complaints from voters, or out of concern that provincial environmental laws are deficient, the province where the investment will take place may object to the proposal for environmental reasons.

---

[37] A good argument for not considering potential breaches of laws (as opposed to clear breaches) is that investors are entitled to have their day in court.

[38] *Paperback and Periodical Distributors Act*, R.S.O. 1980, c.366, subs. 9(1).

Unfortunately, the potential for and control of environmental pollution is not specifically mentioned as one of the statutory factors that can be considered for assessment purposes. Neither does pollution control easily fall under the heading of industrial policy objectives in subsection 20(e), although some environmental laws certainly form part of federal and provincial industrial policies. So, if the only objection to a proposed investment is increased pollution, that may or may not be a factor that the minister can legally take into account.

Usually, however, pollution does have economic effects in addition to its assault on people's sense organs. For instance, the effluents from an expanded pulp and paper mill may kill crops and fish, causing farmers and fishers to suffer economic loss. The same effluents may affect the health of residents downstream, which will yield another set of economic consequences. If pollution and its economic effects can be tied together, then the minister has the legal right to weigh environmental factors when assessing proposals.[39]

The Act's silence about the environment should not discourage foreign investors who plan to install pollution control equipment in the Canadian business they hope to acquire. Their purchase of pollution control equipment will increase employment and production elsewhere in Canada and will lead to a more technologically modern plant. These are direct and indirect economic effects which the minister is fully entitled to ponder.

There is another matter not mentioned in the statute that may one day cause consternation. Will a foreign country retaliate if Ottawa turns down a series of takeover proposals by its nationals? Or (and this is more likely) will Canada's relationship with the government of that country become strained?

Under the *IC Act*, the nationality of a foreign investor is not supposed to matter. In section 20, which lists the factors that the minister can consider, there is no reference to the country of origin of the investment.

Nonetheless, if a foreign government was threatening to triple the duties on Canada's exports if another major transaction was thwarted, the minister could take that effect into account. Subsection 20(a)

---

[39] The *Canadian Environmental Assessment Act* requires an environmental review where a federal authority "is the proponent of the project" (s. 5). However, this Act does not apply to Investment Canada's review process, and does not compel Investment Canada to conduct an environmental assessment when it reviews a takeover. If a foreign investor wants to buy a chemical company, then expand its facilities, the Investment Canada minister must approve the sale. However, that does not make the minister a "proponent" of the proposed expansion of the company.

provides the minister with the legal authority to consider the impact of an investment on exports from Canada. As for the possibility of a strained relationship with a foreign government, the minister could lawfully address his mind to that outcome, but only if harmonious international relations were one of Canada's "national industrial, economic and cultural policy" objectives.

There are two important considerations not found among the net benefit factors. Yet they demand attention by their very nature. These are third party representations and alternative Canadian buyers.

3. Third Party Representations

Investment Canada is forbidden by law from disclosing information about a Canadian, non-Canadian or a business if the information is obtained in the process of administering the Act. This restriction clearly encompasses the contents of applications for review. It has also been interpreted as barring the agency from revealing the mere fact that an application has been received.

Nevertheless, third parties sometimes learn about pending foreign takeovers from other sources, such as from the industry grapevine or through the disclosure requirements of securities legislation. Then they attempt to intervene.

Interventions may come from competitors, employees, unions, managers, suppliers and municipal officials. Sometimes, they are funnelled through members of Parliament and senators. Occasionally, interveners support a proposal but usually they oppose it.

Their motives run the gamut. A competitor might allege that a foreign company engages in predatory pricing. A union might point out that the same company uses vicious strike-breaking tactics and violates labour laws in its home country.

The Act does not provide for interventions and Investment Canada does not solicit them. To do so would be to disclose that an application had been received. However, Canadians are free to communicate with Ottawa about investment proposals. And such interventions may carry weight, even though Parliament did not include them in the assessment criteria.

These third party interventions raise two legal issues. To what extent can comments of intervenors legally be disclosed to investors whose proposals are under study? Secondly, can Investment Canada forward the views of interveners to its minister?

(a) The Issue of Disclosure

The issue of disclosure revolves around the statute's confidentiality provision, and the question of whether a legal duty of fairness exists.

During the days of FIRA, solicitors from the Canadian Bar Association complained that their corporate clients did not know the case they had to meet. The government, they said, was taking into account representations from third parties even though investors were blissfully unaware that any representations had been made.

This was unfair, grumbled these solicitors, and contrary to the requirements of natural justice. In support, they pointed to the decision of the court in *Re Nicholson and Haldimand-Norfolk*.[40]

The plaintiff in that case was not a foreign investor but a probationary policeman who had been dismissed by the Board of Commissioners of Police. The significance of the *Nicholson* case was that the Supreme Court of Canada said that a duty of procedural fairness extended to some administrative bodies.

In brief, the court ruled that although persons entrusted with administrative or executive functions do not have to comply with the principles of natural justice, a court may be able to imply an obligation to act with fairness. To support its conclusion, the court quoted from an English case that an

> . . . investigatory body is under a duty to act fairly, but that which fairness requires depends on the nature of the investigation and the consequences which it may have . . . The fundamental rule is that, if a person may be . . . adversely affected by the investigation and report, then he should be told the case against him and be afforded a fair opportunity of answering it.[41]

Since the *Nicholson* case, the existence of a duty of fairness is no longer contingent upon whether the power being exercised is classified as administrative or quasi-judicial. However, the ambit of *Nicholson* and subsequent cases is not clear-cut.

Functions of a legislative nature, such as an appeal to Cabinet under the *National Transportation Act*, are not subject to the common law duty of procedural fairness.[42] Neither are many government decisions of a commercial nature.[43]

---

[40] [1979] S.C.R. (D.L.R.) 311; 88 D.L.R. (3d) 671.

[41] Id., at 682.

[42] *A.G. Can. v. Inuit Tapirisat of Can.*, [1980] 2 S.C.R. 735; 115 D.L.R. (3d) 1. But see *Re Gray Line of Victoria Ltd. and Chabot*, [1980] 117 D.L.R. (3d) 89 (B.C.S.C.); [1981] 2 W.W.R. 635 (S.C.), which dealt with an appeal to the provincial Lieutenant Governor over the refusal of a licence.

[43] *Transhelter Group Inc. v. Committee on Works and Operations* (1984), 28 Man. R. 137; 9 Admin L.R. 187 (C.A.). The purchase of a battleship would not be a subject for judicial

As for investigatory and advisory bodies, their legal position is in a state of flux. In years past, the courts said such bodies were outside the rules of natural justice because they do not make final decisions. Modern courts have been digging holes into that line of thinking. They are now willing to inquire into whether a doctrine of fairness or natural justice should apply.[44]

(b) Investment Canada and the Fairness Doctrine

Are Investment Canada and its minister subject to this legal duty to act fairly? If they are, it has major implications for agency procedure. To put it bluntly, should Investment Canada and its minister be required to exercise their statutory powers in a certain way, but do not, the minister's decision on net benefit may be quashed by the courts.

Investment Canada is an investigatory body. The minister, when making a decision to approve or not to approve an investment, is exercising an executive function. It is, therefore, unlikely that the courts will nail a duty of fairness onto the review process.[45]

Nevertheless, the agency has addressed the concerns of the court in the *Nicholson* case, at the same time balancing them against other equally pressing considerations. Topping that list is the wish not to discourage interveners, who may fear reprisals from vengeful bosses or suppliers if their names are revealed.

As a result, it is agency policy to disclose to foreign investors the gist of "unsolicited" third-party representations but not their source. The investor is then given the opportunity to submit a reply.[46] (See the "Guidelines on Administrative Procedures" issued by the minister.)

---

intervention according to the court in *M.N.R. v. Coopers & Lybrand*, [1979] 1 S.C.R. 495, at 505; 92 D.L.R. (3d) 1, at 8.

[44] Natural justice and procedural fairness are not distinct and separate concepts, according to Dickson J. in *Martineau v. Matsqui Institution Disciplinary Board (No. 2)* (1979), 106 D.L.R. (3d) 385 at 411.

Re Abel and Advisory Review Board (1980), 31 O.R. (2d) 520; 119 D.L.R. (3d) 101 (C.A.); affd (1979), 24 O.R. (2d) 279; 97 D.L.R. (3d) 304.

[45] Two writers argue that the courts would impose a duty of fairness. E. James Arnett and Robert Rueter, *FIRA and the Rule of Law*, 62 Can. Bar Rev. 121, especially pages 132 and 134. The same reasoning that Arnett applied to FIRA would apply to the *IC Act*.

[46] Foreign investors are advised of the substance of unsolicited representations from third parties. This does not include representations from the provinces and other federal government departments which are solicited by the agency.

Is this lawful, when the confidentiality provisions of the Act are so strictly worded? That depends on how paragraph 36(3)(a) is interpreted. If the paragraph is interpreted broadly, the minister does have a discretion to tell foreign investors about the contents of third party representations. There is no stipulation in the paragraph that the permission of the third party be sought beforehand.[47]

Is the agency complying with the law when it forwards the representations of interveners to the minister?[48] This is the second legal issue. Section 19 of the Act stipulates what information must be referred to the minister so that "net benefit" can be determined. This section mentions information submitted by the applicant and the vendor, undertakings, and representations from the provinces. It does not mention the comments and criticisms of Canadian citizens.

Fortunately, there is no suggestion in the statute that section 19 is all-inclusive. The agency, therefore, summarizes for the minister the comments of third parties and the response of the foreign investor.[49]

Third parties sometimes wonder why the principle of fairness does not allow them to know what foreign investors are saying to the government and what disparaging remarks those investors may be making about their (the third parties') submissions. The answer, from a legal perspective, is that third parties have no status under the Act. They are not mentioned anywhere and, therefore, cannot demand procedural rights.

---

[47] If a third party gives the agency information in confidence, on condition it not be released, the agency may be obliged not to release it without permission. See *Slavutych v. Baker* (1975), 55 D.L.R. (3d) 224.

[48] According to Montreal lawyer Jim Arnett, the minister is taking into account irrelevant evidence and acting in an *ultra vires* fashion when considering the representations of interveners. For further details, see E. James Arnett and Robert Reuter, op. cit., n. 45 at 136. (Although Arnett's comments dealt with FIRA, the same argument would apply to the Investment Canada minister.)

[49] To know the case that must be met, should an applicant be told of the facts used by the minister to determine the current state of the s. 20 assessment criteria (such as the present level of employment in Canada)? These are general facts ("legislative facts"). The courts are unlikely to extend the rules of national justice and the applicant's need to know legislative facts, even if they are obtained from third parties. Adjudicative facts, on the other hand, pertain to the parties. An example of an adjudicative fact is the likely effect of a non-Canadian's investment on employment. If adjudicative facts come from a third party, the courts are more likely to uphold the applicant's right to know and challenge them. For a discussion of this distinction, see Kenneth Davis, *Administrative Law Treatise*, 2nd ed. (San Diego: K.C. Davis Pub. Co., 1979), p. 412. (Any discussion of the law of fairness as it applies to Investment Canada must take into account the statute's confidentiality provision.)

4. Alternate Canadian Buyers

Another form of representation comes from Canadian business people who have heard about an imminent foreign takeover, and wish to buy the business themselves. Sometimes, they have already tried and are writing to complain. Within government, these Canadians are referred to as "alternative Canadian buyers" (although "potential Canadian buyers" might be more exact). Investment Canada never seeks out alternative Canadian buyers.[50] When they contact the agency they are neither encouraged nor discouraged.

Often the takeover they are calling about is too small to be reviewable. However, if government approval is needed, Investment Canada may try to determine just how serious the alternative Canadian buyer is. To do this, four questions may be asked:

1. What efforts did you make to buy the business?

2. What was the vendor's reaction?

3. Do you have any documentary evidence showing you have the financial ability to buy the business?

4. What are your plans if you buy it?

Sometimes, the "alternative Canadian buyers" are the senior managers of the company targeted for takeover. Understandably, they are worried about confidentiality (and the possible loss of their jobs). Such worries are unwarranted. The foreign investor is never told who the potential buyer is, just that one exists. Only the minister is told the name.

For a surprising reason, the minister cannot directly compare the plans of the alternative Canadian buyer and the foreign investor to see which plan is best. This is because the statute requires the minister to determine if a proposed investment by a non-Canadian is likely to be of net benefit to Canada. The minister is not instructed to grade investment proposals or rank them according to the degree of benefit. Perhaps this is why, among the assessment criteria in section 20, there is no reference to potential Canadian buyers.

---

[50] The Act does not allow the minister to actively seek out alternative Canadian buyers. They might come forth if it was disclosed that a takeover was under consideration, but the minister would then be in breach of the confidentiality provision in s. 36. In addition, the minister might (at least in theory) be sued for inducing breach of contract if, as a result of this action, the Canadian vendor broke a contract with a foreign investor in order to sell to a Canadian. (To better understand the legal perils, read about the Texaco-Pennzoil court battle. Thomas Petzinger, *Oil & Honor: The Texaco-Pennzoil War*, (New York: G.P. Putnam's Sons, 1987)).

In addition, there is one practical reason for not comparing plans. What would happen if the Canadian buyer did not do what was promised? Ottawa would have no statutory remedy.[51]

What use, then, is the information that alternative Canadian buyers may provide to the agency? According to the minister's "Guidelines on Administrative Procedures", such information can be used by the minister to evaluate what may happen if the foreign investor does not buy the business.[52]

For instance, suppose a foreign investor promises to create a hundred jobs and several alternative Canadian buyers promise to create fifty. The minister might conclude that a certain number of new jobs will be created, regardless of who owns the business. The minister may then weigh the foreign investor's commitment to increase employment less heavily.

5. Consultations: The Provincial Role

When Investment Canada receives an application it sends both a photocopy and a "case summary" to all "significantly affected" provinces. In practice, this means the province(s) in which the Canadian business (that is to be purchased) has employees.[53] This summary is forwarded to one person within the provincial government who then informs Investment Canada whether the province has any objections.

Can these provincial government employees then tell the world what they know? It appears they cannot. Like federal government

---

[51] Using identical reasoning, if two foreign investors want to buy the same Canadian business, each application must be assessed separately.

[52] The position of the Canadian Bar Association is that the minister cannot consider alternative Canadian buyers ("A.C.B.s"), since the representations of A.C.B.s are not listed in s. 19 as being among the information that the agency must refer to the minister. (Neither are representations from members of Parliament or government departments.) The counter-argument is that s. 19 is not all-inclusive. In addition, the government is free to establish, as a matter of national industrial or economic policy (see subs. 20(e)) that A.C.B.s should be taken into account in the assessment process. It can also be argued that since the minister must choose between approving and not approving a transaction, which, in turn, involves an evaluation of the likely effects of each alternative, the plans of the alternative Canadian buyer and the foreign investor must be compared.

[53] What if a province should request some information about a case even though the applicant was not going to invest in that province? That might happen if a foreign-owned Ontario company was going to buy a Quebec plant and then close its Ontario plant. In such circumstances, Ontario would be "significantly affected" and could be provided with information.

employees, they are bound by the general confidentiality provisions in the *IC Act*[54] (as well as by an agreement between Ottawa and the provinces that confidential information will not be released).

Federal government departments with relevant expertise are also sent case summaries. That means Energy, Mines and Resources, in energy cases, the Department of Communications, in cultural cases, External Affairs, if foreign governments, or bilateral issues like transborder trucking are involved, and the Bureau of Competition Policy (Consumer and Corporate Affairs) in every case. Industry, Science and Technology Canada, which houses a number of industry specialists, receives a copy in most cases (exceptions: rental real estate, oil and gas and cultural business cases). If a proposed investment will affect a number of jobs, Employment and Immigration Canada will also be contacted.

The legal right of Investment Canada, on behalf of the minister, to consult with these federal government departments cannot be found anywhere in the legislation. If it exists, it exists by implication from section 20.[55]

This right to consult, however, is a restricted right. Information about a transaction can only be divulged to federal or provincial "employees of Her Majesty" and then only in the course of administering the Act. Cabinet ministers and government employees who are not involved in administering the statute are not entitled to be told anything.[56]

Who qualifies as provincial or federal "employees of Her Majesty"? Certainly, anyone appointed under the *Public Service Employment Act*. However, the answer is not always so clear when an employee is appointed under another Act.[57] Moreover, there are some "government" employees, such as those working for the Canada Mortgage and

---

[54] The purpose of the phrase "terms and conditions" in subs. 36(3) is to give to the minister a discretion as to the amount of information to be forwarded.

[55] The drafters of the *FIR Act* appear to have thought that the provinces would forward their enunciated policies to the minister, who would then decide whether an investment was compatible with those policies. Instead, after FIRA was set up, government officials began sending photocopies of the applications to the provinces. This quickly became the established practice. (The legislative history of the *FIR Act* is important in understanding the *IC Act*, because the two statutes are identical in many respects. For instance, subs. 20(e) of the *IC Act*, which allows the minister to consider provincial policies, is the same as its counterpart in the *FIR Act*.)

[56] S. 36.

[57] Consider the case of Canadian Wheat Board ("C.W.B.") employees who are appointed under the *Canadian Wheat Board Act* ("*CWBA*"). By implication, s. 8 of the *Public Service Employment Act* ("*PSEA*") excludes people who are employed under another

Housing Corporation ("C.M.H.C.") and the Canadian Broadcasting Corporation ("CBC") who are not "employees of Her Majesty".[58]

The status of employees must always be determined on a case-by-case basis. Pertinent statutes and, on occasion, even tort law must be examined.[59] Should Investment Canada want to consult with (and, therefore, provide information to) an organization like C.H.M.C., whose employees are not employees of Her Majesty, it cannot legally do so without the prior authorization of the investor.

6. Consulting with the Vendor

A foreign investor who wants to buy a business may occasionally seek government approval, although no discussions with the business' owners have been held. After receiving approval, the investor can then submit an offer and give the owners a few days to accept it.

From the investor's perspective this is sometimes a better strategy than submitting an offer that is conditional on the minister's approval. The owners can be presented with a firm offer, and there is less time for them to find a white knight (a friendly buyer).

Unhappily, such a strategy poses awkward problems for everyone else. Investment Canada personnel may want to talk with management or the controlling shareholders of the Canadian business. Yet, without the foreign investor's consent, they cannot very well do so. (Investment Canada personnel could talk to the Canadian shareholders but they could not explain why; otherwise, they would be forced to reveal privileged information.)

There is an additional potential problem. The owners of the Canadian business might not find out about the proposed takeover of their business until they read in the newspaper during breakfast one morning that the federal government has approved it. (This has not, in

---

Act. Consequently, C.W.B. employees are not employees within the meaning of the *PSEA*. Moreover, they have not been declared employees for the purposes of the *Government Employees Compensation Act*. And the C.W.B. is not mentioned in the schedules to the *Financial Administration Act* which provides a regulatory framework covering most Crown employees. However, subs. 4(2) of the *CWBA* states that the C.W.B. is an agent of Her Majesty and, therefore, C.W.B. employees are probably employees of Her Majesty.

[58] *Canada Mortgage and Housing Corporation Act*, R.S.C. 1985, c. C-7, subs. 13(1); the *Broadcasting Act*, R.S.C. 1985, c. B-9, subs.29(3).

[59] See those cases in which people, injured by the negligence of an alleged government employee, have attempted to sue the Crown on the basis of the principle of respondent superior.

fact, happened. Foreign investors have been persuaded to allow agency personnel to talk to the business' owners.)

7. Memo to the Minister

When all the information is in, Investment Canada prepares a briefing memo for the minister. The form of this memo has naturally varied over the years. However, a good memo should outline the transaction, summarize the position of the other government departments and the provinces, describe the industry sector,[60] and the benefits to be obtained, and end with the agency's recommendation. On receipt of this memo, the minister decides if the transaction will likely be of net benefit to Canada.

To determine net benefit, the positive and negative aspects of the transaction should be offset. If there is an overall benefit, the chance that this benefit could be achieved to the same or a greater extent if the transaction does not occur, should also be considered.

In theory, the net benefit test can be met by a very slight improvement in the performance of the Canadian business that is to be acquired.

8. Ministers and the Civil Service[61]

When deciding on "net benefit", does the minister ever disagree with the recommendations of Investment Canada? Foreign investors

---

[60] The number of firms and people employed, future outlook, effect of free trade, etc.

[61] Is it fair to say that Investment Canada officials sometimes make the decisions instead of the minister? That is not a heretical idea. Several authors (e.g. MacDonald, Kernaghan) have observed that because of the complexities of modern life more matters are being decided by public servants. According to these authors, not only the House of Commons but the government (ministers) have gradually been losing control to the civil service. In the case of Investment Canada, public servants influence the minister's decisions by the way memoranda are written. The agency's recommendations are, of course, of key importance. However, certain adjectives and adverbs may have the same effect. For example, an increase in employment, involving 25 new jobs, can be described as either "modest" or "significant". Other word choices that might affect the outcome of a case include: acquisition/takeover, claim/state, and transfer of ownership/loss of ownership. (This is not a comment on what actually appears in memoranda. That information is confidential.) Flora MacDonald, "Who Is on Top? The Minister Or The Mandarins" in Fox, Paul *Politics: Canada*, 5th ed., (Toronto: McGraw-Hill Ryerson Limited, 1982) p. 471-76. Kenneth Kernaghan, "Power and Public Servants In Canada" in K. Kernaghan *Public Administration in Canada*, (Toronto: Methuen Publications, 1982), p. 227-35.

sometimes ask that question, but no minister since 1985 has made a public comment.

Whatever the current situation, civil servants obviously occupy a potentially powerful position in the investment approval process. Their potential power was recently spotlighted by some remarks made by the Honourable Donald S. Macdonald, who was a government minister in the 1970s. Referring to Investment Canada's predecessor, FIRA,[62] Mr. Macdonald said: "The FIRA staff had a very firm belief in what they were doing, and I felt very reluctant to leave to chance what might be decided within the Cabinet room".[63]

---

[62] FIRA's recommendations went to the minister, and then to Cabinet.

[63] Letter dated Mar. 20, 1991, from the Hon. Donald S. Macdonald to the author. In 1981, Mr. Macdonald told university students: "In my time, the greatest number of FIRA decisions were not determined at the Cabinet table. Cabinet's conclusion was predetermined by the manner in which individual cases were brought forward from the public service level". Hon. Donald S. Macdonald, *Notes for Remarks to: Mercantile Bank - Wilfred Laurier University M.B.A. Seminar*, Nov. 6, 1981.

Format of Memorandum to Minister

PROTECTED—INV. Act
File no.: <FILE>

INVESTMENT CANADA ACT
DIRECT ◇ (INDIRECT) ACQUISITION
Summary and Recommendation that the proposal
be ◇ (not be) approved

INVESTOR

Name and location: <INV> (<INV NICKNAME>),
                         <INV LOC>
Control: <INV NICKNAME> ◇
Activity: <INV NICKNAME> ◇
Assets: <INV ASS>
Revenues: <INV REV>

CANADIAN BUSINESS
Name and location: <CBE> (<CBE NICKNAME>),
                         <CBE LOC>
Control: <CBE NICKNAME> ◇
Activity: <CBE NICKNAME> ◇
Assets: <CBE ASS>
Revenues: <CBE REV>
Employment: <EMPL>

PROPOSAL OR TRANSACTION   ◇

BACKGROUND (opt.)   ◇

CONSIDERATION   ◇

INDUSTRY   ◇

THIRD PARTY   ◇
REPRESENTATIONS (opt.)

TIMING   The statutory review period under
                         subsection ◇ expires on <EXP
                         DATE>.

COMMERCIAL DEADLINE (opt.) ◇

PROVINCIAL POSITION(S)   ◇

DEPARTMENTAL POSITION(S)   ◇

BASIS FOR RECOMMENDATION   The investor plans/undertakes*:
                             - ◇

RECOMMENDATION   It is judged that this proposal is _____
                             _____ . If you
                             agree, please sign this summary and
                             the attached record of your decision
                             and return them to me so that I may
                             inform the investor.

                             _____
                                        President, Investment Canada

I agree with the recommendation.

                             _____
                                                    Minister

CHAPTER 14

AFTER THE DECISION

After an application for review is submitted, the average turn-around time is 35 days. If there is a commercial deadline, such as an imminent closing, this time-span can be abridged.

Sometimes, the minister is out of the country. It would be convenient on these occasions if the minister could delegate his or her power to approve or reject investments to another minister or the president of Investment Canada. However, the legislation does not allow this.[1] If it happened, the courts would quickly grant relief to a foreign investor who was disappointed with the results. (The solution adopted has been to appoint an acting minister.)[2]

When a decision has been made, a letter from the minister is sent to the foreign investor. If the decision is favourable, the letter reads:

> I have concluded my review of your application and I am satisfied that your investment is likely to be of net benefit to Canada. This letter constitutes approval of your investment pursuant to the *Investment Canada Act*.

The news is also sent by telex to the province where the investment will occur, followed by a letter enclosing a summary of the investor's plans (and undertakings).[3] A few weeks later, after several decisions

---

[1] The *IC Act* does not expressly authorize the minister to delegate the powers to approve investments. Although the courts, when deciding if a power of delegation exists, now employ a more flexible test that looks beyond the mere statutory language, there is nothing in the Act from which a power of delegation can be implied. As for the *Interpretation Act*, which contains much scope for delegation to deputy ministers, that Act is of no assistance in the face of clear instructions in the *IC Act* (that the minister shall make the decision).

[2] Subs. 24(2) of the *Interpretation Act* states that words empowering a minister to do a thing includes an acting minister.

[3] "Significantly affected" provinces receive copies of all documentation submitted with the application, but they do not always receive copies of plans submitted after the application is filed.

have been made, a press release is issued. *The Globe and Mail* always prints the full text.[4] The following are samples:

DECISIONS

323150 B.C. Ltd. (Vancouver, British Columbia), controlled by Sligo Holdings Limited (Hong Kong), to acquire control of the business carried on by the Pacific Palisades Hotel (Vancouver, British Columbia). APPROVED

Christiana Energy Ltd. (Dallas, Texas), to acquire control of the business carried on by Coseka Resources Limited (Calgary, Alberta), consisting of certain natural gas properties in the Hatton area of Saskatchewan. APPROVED

Fuji Project Co., Ltd (Tokyo, Japan), to acquire control of the business carried on by Banff Park Lodge (Banff, Alberta), a hotel. APPROVED

1. Is It Final?

How final are such decisions? After they find out, can outraged members of Parliament or coalitions of special interest groups force the minister to retract his approval? If this was possible, foreign investors who had closed their deals would be in an unenviable position. However, investors have little cause for concern.

The minister can correct an accidental mistake, such as a typing error in an official document, and can probably set aside the decision if it was obtained through fraud. But, otherwise, the minister is *functus officio*, even if new facts come to light. After the minister has exercised his discretion once and approved a transaction, the decision cannot be reversed and approval withdrawn.[5]

---

[4] *The Globe and Mail* publishes the complete list of notifications and acquisitions. Other sources are P. Hayden and J. Burns, *Foreign Investment in Canada*, (Toronto: Prentice-Hall Canada Inc.), Vol. 3, and Investment Canada's computer databank.

[5] *Pure Spring Company Ltd. v. M.N.R.*, [1946] Ex. C.R. 721; [1947] 1 D.L.R. 501, 2 D.T.C. 844, at 851 and 857. See also *Ex parte Blackburn*, [1956] 3 All E.R. 334; 1 W.L.R 1193 where the English Court of Appeal concluded that once a person who has a discretionary authority has exercised discretion, that person has no right to exercise it again. There is nothing in the *IC Act* that allows the minister to reverse a decision.

B.C. Conservative M.P. Robert Brisco and his constituents were not aware, in January 1987, of this limitation on the minister's powers. They wanted the Investment Canada minister to reverse a decision approving the 1987 takeover of West Kootenay Light and Power Company Limited by American-owned Utilicorp British Columbia Ltd. Rita Moir, "U.S. Bid for B.C. Power Company Stirs Hornets' Nest of Nationalism", *The Globe and Mail*, January 19, 1987, p. A4. This takeover, the first foreign takeover of a

2. Post-Decision Queries

As soon as they learn of the decision, successful applicants can implement their investments. Unsuccessful applicants (there have been none so far) will have to reconsider their strategy. If an unsuccessful applicant has taken the risk of buying a Canadian business or setting up a new cultural business (that the government decided to review) before the decision was announced, that applicant will now be under a legal obligation to give up control.[6]

Whichever result occurs, investors will have some questions. Successful applicants ask:

1. Will the contents of my application be made public, now that an approval has been announced?
2. Is there any follow-up or monitoring?
3. What happens if I cannot fulfil my commitments?

Unsuccessful applicants may wonder:

1. How can I find out why the minister rejected my investment?
2. Can I submit another application?

(a) The Issue of Confidentiality

After the minister has made his or her decision, the bare bones of the transaction—such as the names of the parties and the nature of the Canadian business—are no longer confidential. However, the substance of the information remains privileged, and cannot be communicated to anyone without the investor's consent.[7]

This includes the R.C.M.P. and the tax beagles at Revenue Canada. They have no legal right to an investor's file because there is no provision in their governing statutes which overrides the *IC Act*. Should an Investment Canada official decide to help colleagues in another department by slipping them some information, that official would not be doing so for the purpose of administering the *IC Act*, and would, therefore, be violating the law.

---

hydro-electric utility in Canadian history, caused an angry debate over Canadian resource sovereignty.

[6] S. 24.

[7] Under subs. 36(1) of the *IC Act*, all information received about a non-Canadian and that person's investment is privileged.

This should reassure the edgy investor who has given Investment Canada technological and marketing plans which competitors would like to see. But occasionally, an investor is still uneasy. Perhaps because money is being transferred to Canada through other than officially approved channels, an investor may be alarmed at the thought of seeing his name in a news release. Other investors have more respectable concerns. One company, which was acquiring a 45% controlling interest in another company, rightly thought that the public announcement of a takeover might mislead people and disrupt labour-management relations.

There is a simple solution to such a predicament: incorporate a company and identify it as the applicant. Then only the company's name will appear in the press release.[8] Even if an enterprising newspaper reporter investigates further, and finds the names of the company's directors (which under federal and provincial corporations statutes are a matter of public record) the identity of the foreign shareholders will remain hidden.

(b) Disclosure of Undertakings

There is one exception to the general rule of confidentiality. It concerns undertakings. An investor's plans can never be published, but the Act does allow the minister, after an investment proposal has been approved, to disclose the contents of the undertakings.[9] This means that these undertakings, or a summary of them, may appear in a news release.

Disclosure serves several purposes. It allows the public to know some of the benefits a transaction may bring.[10] It helps dispel suspicions that decisions are capricious. Finally, making undertakings public provides other foreign investors with a better understanding of how the government interprets "net benefit".

Investors who are trying to draft undertakings need not become alarmed over this. As a matter of policy, undertakings will not be

---

[8] Hartley Nathan and Clifford Goldfarb, "The Use of Nominee Corporations in Business Transactions", in Sarna, Lazar, *Corporate Structure, Finance and Operations*, (Toronto: Carswell, 1980), p. 465.

[9] Para 36(4)(b). Additional information can be disclosed, following a decision on net benefit, if the investor consents (para. 36(4)(d)). (The purpose of para. 36(3)(a), on the other hand, is to permit the agency, during the review process, with the written authorization of the investor, to discuss the case with a person named in the authorization.)

[10] Do not assume that the published undertakings explain why the application was approved. The Canadian business may have been on the verge of bankruptcy, or the investor's plans may have been the key factor.

published if doing so will damage the commercial interests of the investor. After all, there would be no point in Ottawa encouraging investors to come to Canada, if it then ruined their businesses.

Government officials are well aware that some undertakings, if divulged, could provide competitors with an advantage or disturb labour-management relationships. Consequently, during the review process, applicants are asked what undertakings can be made public if the minister approves the investment.[11]

Foreign investors sometimes have another worry: litigation. Since undertakings lose their cloak of confidentiality after the minister approves the investment, can a third party subpoena the agreement of undertakings? The answer is a qualified no. The minister is free to make the undertakings public, but cannot be compelled by a court to do so. If the minister believes that disclosure:

(1) is not necessary for the administration and enforcement of the Act, and

(2) would prejudicially affect the non-Canadian in the conduct of his business affairs,[12]

both the minister and employees of Investment Canada can decline to give evidence.[13] In other words, the undertakings will remain protected from legal process, provided the minister is on-side.

The only time when a court might order the production of confidential Investment Canada documents is when legal proceedings relate to the administration and enforcement of the Act. If, for example, the minister initiates a lawsuit to force an investor to honour his or her commitments, the curtain of confidentiality in section 36 is lifted.[14] The investor may then, by subpoena, compel a government official to bring the file to court.

---

[11] Investment Canada discloses undertakings which the investor agrees do not come within the exception in para. 20(1)(b) of the *Access to Information Act*.

[12] Why is it not a judge who determines whether the disclosure of undertakings will prejudice an investor? The Investment Canada minister can see the complete agency file. A judge cannot, unless involved in legal proceedings relating to the administration and enforcement of the Act. In addition, the minister, who must get elected, may be more sympathetic to the business community and its concerns over secrecy than certain members of the judiciary. (For an article on Canada's judiciary, see M. Crawford, "Judging Judges", *Canadian Lawyer*, May 1989, p. 18.)

[13] *IC Act*, subs. 36(2).

[14] *IC Act*, para. 36(4)(a).

Should this happen, the principles of Crown privilege, which are codified in section 37 of the *Canada Evidence Act*,[15] still apply. This section allows the Crown or any interested party to object to the disclosure of information before a court on the grounds of a "specified public interest". The court will then perform a balancing test to determine if the public interest in disclosure is more important than the "specified public interest". If the court decides that the general public interest should prevail, the court will order disclosure, although conditions may be attached.

Information relating to federal-provincial relations, such as a province's comments about a proposed takeover, is not subject to an absolute privilege. Its release will depend upon the outcome of the balancing test.

The *Canada Evidence Act* is stricter with respect to information that might injure international relations. Only the chief justice of the Federal Court or the chief justice's designate is allowed to decide whether the public interest in the administration of justice outweighs any harm that might be done to Canada's relationship with other countries.

"Confidences" of the Cabinet can be barred by the minister even from the eyes of a court. Under the *Canada Evidence Act*, they are protected by an absolute privilege. A document summarizing discussions between ministers about a pending takeover would be an example of a Cabinet confidence.

What if two companies are in the thralls of litigation or involved in a dispute before a quasi-judicial body like the Canadian International Trade Tribunal and one of them decides to subpoena an Investment Canada file?

A representative of the agency will appear in court (unless the subpoena is set aside). If the documents subpoenaed contain information constituting confidences of the Queen's Privy Council, the agency's representative will have a certificate to that effect, signed by the clerk of the Privy Council, and objecting to the disclosure of the information. Otherwise, if the information subpoenaed is privileged under section 36 of the *IC Act*, the agency employee will claim that privilege when called to testify.

Investors may be interested to learn there are no back-door routes to Investment Canada's files. A mandamus action will not work. The

---

[15] R.S.C 1985, c. C-5. The principle of Crown privilege is codified in s. 37 of the *Canada Evidence Act*. However, this privilege is far from absolute. In the past, the courts have rejected a number of claims by the Crown that a document is not producible. *Re Bais and Andras* (1973), 30 D.L.R (3d) 287; *Churchill Falls (Labrador) Corp. v. The Queen* (1972), 28 D.L.R. (3d) 493.

Access to Information Act opens no doors. Even if litigious third parties go after the foreign investor itself, that road will probably be blocked.

In *Hamilton v. A.G. Can.; Black and Decker Canada Ltd. ("Intervenor")*,[16] union leaders sought a court order to force the minister to disclose undertakings that Black and Decker had given. A few years previously, Black and Decker had received government approval to buy a plant that manufactured housewares in Barrie. Shortly thereafter, Black and Decker announced it was going to close the Barrie plant and consolidate all its operations at another plant in Brockville.

The union suspected that Black and Decker had given Ottawa a promise of continued employment for the Barrie workers as a condition of obtaining the approval. The union wanted to learn the exact terms of the undertakings.

The action failed. The court ruled that "the remedy of mandamus does not lie unless there is a clear public duty imposed on the Minister, the performance of which is not a matter of discretion".[17] The minister was under no duty to release the undertakings and could not be ordered to do so.

Third parties who pursue the investor directly are unlikely to be any more successful. *Re Camco; Canadian General Electric Co. v. G.S.W. Inc.*[18] involved a motion to compel discovery of an application and supporting documents that Canadian General Electric ("C.G.E.") had submitted to FIRA. A subsequent appeal was heard by the Ontario Supreme Court.

The court examined the confidentiality provisions of the *FIR Act* (which are virtually identical to those in the *IC Act*) and concluded that G.S.W. Inc. could not see photocopies in the possession of C.G.E. In the court's view, these documents were surrounded by a cloak of privilege that prevented the government from revealing them and also allowed the investor to refuse to produce them.

Subsection 36(3) of the *IC Act* permits the minister to provide information to a third party if the investor consents. Could a litigant get a court order compelling an investor to consent? Such a tactic has never been tried. However, the legislation gives the minister an unfettered discretion to refuse to supply information even if the foreign investor gives permission.[19]

---

[16] (1985), 28 B.L.R. 92 (F.C.T.D.). The Black and Decker case was decided under the *FIR Act*. However, the confidentiality provisions in the *FIR Act* are mirrored by those in the *IC Act*.

[17] Ibid., p. 95.

[18] (1983), 22 B.L.R. 1 (Ont. H.C.). Although this case was decided during the FIRA era, the wording of the statutory provisions on which it was based has not changed.

[19] The minister at least has this discretion during the review process. Compare the wording of subs. 36(3) with para. 36(4)(d).

What if an obstinate judge ordered the government to release the information in any event? Then the government's representative, who would probably be in court with the file pursuant to a subpoena, would have a choice to make: comply, defy the order, or ask for an adjournment in order to appeal.

Finally, there is the *Access to Information Act*. Undertakings that an investor submits to Investment Canada become accessible under that Act if:

(1) the minister does not opine under the *IC Act* that their disclosure would prejudice the investor, and

(2) no exemption in the *Access to Information Act* applies.

The opportunities presented by the *Access to Information Act* are discussed in another chapter. For now, it is sufficient to note that the *Access to Information Act* contains more exemptions than there are guards at the prime minister's residence. Confidential information is well-protected.

(c) Monitoring

"Will anyone check to see if my plans and commitments are being performed?" That is another common query. After a proposal has received government approval, a foreign investor can expect to be contacted at least once. According to the "Guidelines on Administrative Procedures", the first evaluation of performance will occur 18 months after the investment has taken place. If the investor has substantially fulfilled the commitments, there will be no further monitoring.

Section 25 gives the agency the statutory authority to perform this monitoring function. It also forces investors to submit any pertinent information. However, the Act only requires investors to submit information that is in their possession. In other words, if an investor does not have the information, there is no need to fret about it.

Investors also need not worry that Ottawa will use section 25 to disguise a fishing expedition. By law, the investor is only required to provide information that will enable Ottawa to determine if the plans and commitments are being fulfilled.[20]

3. When Investments Go Sour

Even the most astute investors make mistakes. Sometimes, a foreign investor will take over a Canadian company and then find, a year down the road, that he cannot fulfil his commitments. Sales may have

---

[20] S. 25.

declined because of a recession or new competition. As a result, the investor may be unable to maintain the employment levels he promised or do more research in Canada. If the commitment was to issue shares to Canadians, the market may have evaporated.

The agency's "Guidelines on Administrative Procedures" states: "Where inability to fulfil a commitment is clearly the result of factors beyond the control of the investor, the investor will not be held accountable".

In such cases, renegotiation is the answer.[21] The investor should contact the investment review officer who handled the original application and ask for more time or suggest substitute undertakings that will yield equivalent value in terms of net benefit to Canada. The investment review officer will prepare a memorandum for the minister containing the facts and recommendations. The minister will then make a decision.

Sometimes, an undertaking can never be fulfilled. A key contract may have been lost or the Canadian business closed. In such circumstances, the only solution may be to request a formal waiver of the undertaking. (No investor has ever been taken to court for failure to fulfil an undertaking.)

Not all commitments that cannot be fulfilled need be renegotiated. If the commitment is contingent on favourable economic conditions, it may be unenforceable.[22]

The courts will not enforce a commitment that is ambiguous or excessively vague.[23] Commitments containing phrases such as "best efforts", "insofar as possible" and "substantially" fall within this category, as do promises to:

(1) increase employment as sales increase,

(2) expand markets if demand warrants, or

(3) issue a certain percentage of shares to the Canadian public provided economic conditions are suitable.

---

[21] The Act does not specifically provide for the renegotiation of undertakings. However, consider subs. 31(4) of the *Interpretation Act*.

[22] The minister can approve or not approve an investment but he cannot issue a conditional approval (*IC Act*, subss. 21(1) and 23(3)).

[23] If an undertaking is too indefinite to support an action by the Crown for breach of contract (or has been improperly executed), it might be possible to bring an action based upon detrimental reliance. However, the Crown would have to show that the undertaking was a material factor in the granting of ministerial approval of the investment. (The defendant might then assert that there could not have been much reliance placed on the undertaking on account of its generality.)

Suppose an investor has promised to create a hundred new jobs if sales double. Instead, the jobs do not materialize because sales have declined. The government will be disappointed, but legally it can do nothing.

If the investor has given a promise to confine activities to a particular line of business (e.g., not to engage in book publishing for four years), that might not be binding for another reason. In certain circumstances, it may be in restraint of trade.

The doctrine of restraint of trade was developed by the courts for reasons of public policy. It states that provisions in contracts which constitute unreasonable restrictions on the freedom to trade and carry on business will not be enforced.

What is unreasonable? Essentially, it is a limitation of such scope and severity that it interferes with an individual's right to earn a living. The central question is always the degree of restriction. The courts are most likely to enforce a restrictive commitment that is narrowly defined or for a limited purpose.[24]

(a) Enforcing Plans and Undertakings

"By the way", investors casually ask, "what happens if someone deliberately ignores commitments or makes an investment that is different from the one described in the plans submitted to Investment Canada?" It is possible that government officials may never find out. The work of monitoring is premised on the assumption that investors will be honest in their replies. Moreover, Investment Canada has no statutory authority to conduct an investigation. This may make it difficult to ascertain the facts.

For instance, suppose the performance of an undertaking is subject to a specific level of sales being attained (or some other condition precedent). If the government wanted to establish that the foreign investor had refused to comply with the undertaking, the government would have to prove that the condition precedent had been achieved.

This may be done through section 25 and the monitoring process. But there may be times when the detailed evidence needed for a successful court application will be difficult to obtain. In that event, the absence of a right to search business premises may bring the curtain down on the government's case.

---

[24] For this reason, restrictive undertakings that have been voluntarily given would have the best chance of being enforced. The argument would be that the investor has restricted himself or herself.

However, investors should not be complacent. Most plans and undertakings—such as to modernize a plant, build new facilities, create jobs or export more—can easily be verified.

(b) Ministerial Demand

If an undertaking is not being complied with, or the actual investment is different from what was described, the minister may issue a demand. The effect of a ministerial demand is to give the investor an opportunity to have an exchange of views with the minister. If the minister is still not satisfied, a court order may then be sought.

Because undertakings are specific promises, they can be enforced individually. That is not the case with plans (described as "terms and conditions" in the Act). When deciding whether to enforce them, a court must consider the plans in their entirety.

For example, imagine that an investor has received approval to buy a Canadian business because of a plan to manufacture a new product line in Canada, which will increase employment. A minor variation to such a plan would be acceptable. But the investor will be expected to adhere to the overall plan.[25] If the investor were to import the product, instead of manufacturing it, this would be a material variation, resulting in a major loss of benefits for Canada. The government would then have the legal justification for taking action.

The minister's authority for taking such action is in paragraph 39(1)(g) of the Act. This paragraph states:

> Where the Minister believes that a non-Canadian, contrary to this Act . . . has implemented an investment on terms and conditions that vary materially from those contained in an application filed under section 17 . . . the Minister may send a demand . . .

How far in the future can the minister act? This question once intrigued a member of Parliament (when a similar provision was being discussed in 1972). The M.P. wondered what would happen if, five or ten years after receiving government approval to make a takeover, a foreign investor changed his or her method of doing business. And, if this change conflicted with the terms under which the takeover was approved. The laconic reply of a Department of Justice official was

---

[25] Para. 39(1)(c) refers to "terms and conditions . . . contained in the application" and "information or evidence provided under this Act" as the benchmark from which to measure whether the investor has done what was promised. There is no reference to plans and undertakings. This terminology may create some confusion in a court as to just what an investor must live up to.

that the lapse of time would be a matter to be considered by the court.[26]

(c) Closures and Layoffs

Every once in a while, the newspapers report that a foreign company which has received government approval to buy a business, is laying-off employees. The article will then mention that the unions are furious and the mayor of the community is upset.

Layoffs prompt the question: is the foreign investor fulfilling all of its plans and commitments? If not, and the layoffs are for non-economic reasons, the government may have grounds for legal action. However, investors always put the blame on changing market conditions. The Department of Justice then indicates it is "unclear" what the government can do.[27]

Can a foreign investor get rid of its commitments by closing the Canadian business down and moving the assets to another location in Canada? It all depends. A bona fide abandonment of a business may put an end to an investor's commitments (depending on how the commitments are worded). But if the investor were to use the assets to set up a new business, its motives would surely be questioned.

Interpretation Note No. 1 sets out the government's position. If a closure is for a purpose related to the Act—and the goal of avoiding commitments that were given during the approval process certainly falls into that category—then government officials will consider that the business is not defunct even though normal business operations have ceased. In such circumstances, the minister could commence legal proceedings beginning with a ministerial demand.

4. Investment Not Approved

What should an investor do if his investment proposal is turned down? There are several options, but first, the investor should find out why.

---

[26] This question was asked by M.P. Gordon Ritchie (Dauphin, Manitoba) when a Parliamentary committee was discussing the *Foreign Takeovers Review Act* in 1972. The latter Act had a provision which was very similar to para. 39(1)(g) of the *IC Act*. House of Commons, *Minutes of the Standing Committee on Finance, Trade and Economic Affairs*, June 21, 1972, Issue No. 25, p. 25:15.

[27] Hon. Sinclair Stevens, *Proceedings of the Standing Senate Committee on Banking, Trade and Commerce*, March 20, 1985, Issue No.4, p.4:14.

The person to contact is the investment review officer who handled the file. This officer should provide a full explanation. However, there is no statutory obligation on the officer or the minister to do so. This is because the decision on net benefit may have been based on confidential information from the provinces or other sources.

If the officer's explanation is insufficient, has the investor any right to see the memorandum that the agency sent to the minister? The answer is no. Even if the memorandum was based almost totally on information provided by the investor, it cannot be seen.

Under the common law, no one has a right to government information. Such a right may be granted by statute but otherwise the decision to release or withhold information is one of the prerogatives of power.[28]

Several years ago, Parliament passed the *Access to Information Act*, which opened some doors. However, the Act exempts the agency's case summaries and memoranda.[29]

(a) The Options

After learning what went wrong, the unsuccessful foreign investor must decide what to do. A sit-in at Investment Canada will gain publicity but is unlikely to succeed.

An appeal to the courts will not work either. In *Baril v. Min. of Regional Industrial Expansion*,[30] a judge ruled that the decision of the minister on whether an investment was of net benefit to Canada was administrative in nature, and could not be reviewed under section 28 of the *Federal Court Act*. There are, however, several constructive routes that should be considered.

(1) Restructure the investment to remove it from federal government jurisdiction. One way is to change the status of the

---

[28] de Smith, *Constitutional and Administrative Law* (Middlesex: Penguin Books Ltd., 1985), p. 149 and n. 71 on p. 142.

[29] Para. 36(3)(a) does not grant foreign investors any enforceable rights. That paragraph allows the agency, at its discretion, after receiving a written request from an investor who has filed an application for review, to forward to third parties confidential information that the investor has provided (or, in some cases, that has been obtained from outside sources). If subss. 36(1) and (3) are read together, it is clear that the reference to privileged information in subs. 36(3) does not refer to documentation prepared within Investment Canada.

[30] (1986), 26 A.C.W.S. (2d) 322 (F.C.A.). On the other hand, if the minister committed a procedural error, such as denying an investor the right under s. 23 of the Act to make further representations, the courts would quash the minister's decision on "net benefit".

investor. If the investor is a company, its ownership can be restructured, so that it becomes a "Canadian".

(2) Submit a new application. The new application should be substantially different from the previous one and should address those points that caused the government concern.

If the takeover took place, or a culturally sensitive business was established before the minister made the decision, the investor is in a more difficult position. On the other hand, there are several more choices:

(3) Sell the business to a Canadian.

(4) Sell the business to another foreign investor. (This second transaction will be reviewable).

(5) Close the business down. This happened during FIRA days. The aggrieved foreign investors made certain the media knew about it.[31]

(6) Do nothing. Simply wait and see if the government will take legal action.

The most fruitful of these options may be to submit a new application. Might it be rejected on the grounds of *res judicata*? That is the doctrine used by the courts to throw out the subsequent applications of disappointed litigants because their rights have been previously determined.

Res judicata, however, is of very limited scope in the hands of policy-oriented administrative bodies like Investment Canada which try to realize the public interest.[32] It would be out of place. As Wade remarks in his textbook, *Administrative Law*, "*Res judicata* rests on a theory of an unchanging law, whereas policy must be free to change at any moment, as public interest may require."[33]

---

[31] U.S.-owned Harper & Row shut down J.B. Lippincott of Canada in 1982, after rejecting offers by Canadians (Fitzhenry and Whiteside Ltd.) to buy the business (on the grounds that the price was too low). Twelve employees lost their jobs. Fred Lebott, "Publishing Firm Says It Bid $1 Million for Lippincott", *Toronto Star*, August 7, 1982, p. F8.

[32] *Re Fernie Memorial Hospital Society and Duthie* (1963) 42 W.W.R. 511 (B.C.S.C.); affd (1964), 47 W.W.R. 120 (B.C.C.A.). The court in this case stated that *res judicata* only applies to a judicial decision made by a judicial tribunal. Also see: *Society of Medical Officers of Health v. Hope*, [1960] A.C. 551; and *Cafoor v. ITC*, [1961] A.C. 584. A tax assessment for a previous year does not determine issues at a subsequent period of time.

[33] H. Wade, *Administrative Law*, (Oxford: Clarendon Press, 1977), pp. 234-36. A major difference between the courts and administrative tribunals is that the former focus on certainty and a final determination of issues while the latter strive to realize the

This does not mean that an investor can submit a photograph of the previous application. The agency can legally reject a second application if it is identical to the first one and if relevant economic circumstances have not changed.

But such a concurrence of events is unlikely to happen. If the difference between the two applications is more than trivial or if Canada's economic climate has changed since the minister's rejection of the first application and the submission of the second, there will be great pressure on Investment Canada (and the courts, if necessary) to conclude that the second application is different.

Economic circumstances are a key factor in this determination because an investment proposal is assessed with an eye on the state of Canada's economy and the industry sector affected. The greater the time span between the first rejection and the second application, the easier it will be to conclude that the economic milieu is not the same.

If the government refuses to examine the second application, the investor can proceed to court. In court, the judge will have to be convinced that the second application is sufficiently different from the first one and that it is legally complete. If successful, the investor can get a court order forcing the minister to review the transaction and render a decision.

On the other hand, if 45 days have passed since a complete application was submitted, a court order will not be necessary. The investment will be deemed by law to have been approved. Because of this risk, if there is a continuing dispute over a second filing which the investor will not withdraw and government officials refuse to process, Investment Canada should make a summary application to the courts for a ruling on the application's validity.

Can an angry investor stop enforcement action from ever being taken by repeatedly filing new applications? Such a harassment tactic may annoy the government clerks in the Record Office but it will not prevent legal action.

Section 24 of the Act imposes an obligation upon an applicant, who made an investment before the government rejected it, to give up control. This obligation is not contingent upon the existence or non-existence of further applications.

5. Investment Implemented Prior to Disapproval

If an investor has proceeded with his plans without waiting for the minister's decision, and that decision is unfavourable, the investor is in

---

public interest expressed in the statute which they administer.

hot water. He will probably have to sell the business or, at least, a controlling interest.

But that takes time. Will Ottawa give the investor enough time? When the *FIR Act* was in effect, that was not a concern. Under that Act, which was written to constrain any precipitous action, an order of disallowance was simply the opinion of Cabinet that an investment did not benefit Canada. An investor who had already established a business or purchased one could continue to operate it unless and until the Department of Justice got a court order.

Should an order be sought, the judiciary was instructed by the FIR Act to avoid, to the greatest extent possible, any undue hardship to persons not involved in the investment (such as employees, customers and suppliers). Accordingly, a court would probably have granted an investor several months to comply with the decision of Cabinet.

The *IC Act* is less lenient. If the minister has rejected the investment, section 24 imposes a mandatory obligation on the investor to relinquish control of the Canadian business. The implication is that the continued existence of an investment which has not been approved is detrimental to Canadians.

Section 24 has caused some apprehension among solicitors. A few have wondered whether it is intended to operate like the summary eviction provisions in the *Landlord and Tenant Act*. Laws aimed at extraordinary situations generate needless anxiety. If a foreign investor knew that the Canadian government was strongly opposed to a takeover, but baited Ottawa by going ahead, the existence of section 24 might persuade a court to grant an order that is enforceable immediately. Otherwise, the court would probably grant the investor a reasonable length of time to divest, regardless of what the section says.

In any event, such a scenario is unlikely to arise. It is hard to imagine that Ottawa would ever take precipitous action in view of the message that would be conveyed world-wide.

6. Disclosure in Unsuccessful Cases

There is one final worry that unsuccessful investors may have: will the minister make public the investor's commitments? Investors can relax; the minister is barred from doing so. It would be too great of an affront. Undertakings can only be disclosed in successful cases.

CHAPTER 15

REMEDIES AND PENALTIES

What happens if a foreign investor ignores the *Investment Canada Act*? Is there a penalty if a notification or an application for review is not filed? After the government has approved the purchase of 49% of a company's shares, can the investor buy all the company's assets instead? Disregard his undertakings? Or refuse to provide information for monitoring purposes?

An investor who has committed such a *faux pas* will be pleased to learn that no criminal penalties can be imposed. In other words, there will be no arrests.

Only if an investor has knowingly provided the government with false information may he be subject to criminal prosecution. Even then, the government's powers are circumscribed. Unless proceedings are initiated within two years after the offence is committed, no legal action can be taken.[1]

Moreover, if the investor who provided the false information is living abroad and gets a summons to appear in a Canadian court, it can be thrown away.[2] If it is a company that committed the offence, its directors, officers or agents cannot be held vicariously liable.[3]

---

[1] S. 43.

[2] A Canadian court cannot proceed *ex parte* against a defendant who is served with a summons outside Canada. *Re Shulman and The Queen* (1975), 58 D.L.R. (3d) 586 (B.C.C.A.). Consequently, if a foreign corporation is going to be prosecuted, service would have to be made upon an appropriate representative in Canada. As an aside, it should be noted that the provisions of the *Criminal Code* dealing with summary convictions (except for the six-month time limit) apply to a prosecution under the *IC Act* (by virtue of subs. 27(3) of the *Interpretation Act*).

[3] S. 42. The *FIR Act* contained a provision whereby officers, directors and agents of a corporation could be guilty of an offence committed by the corporation. This

It may comfort investors further to learn that there are no powers of search and seizure in the *IC Act*.[4] Unlike the tax authorities and the R.C.M.P., who frequently raid business premises, employees of Investment Canada have no power to do so. If an investor proceeds with his plans without observing the *IC Act*, Ottawa does not even have the statutory right to seek an immediate (*ex parte*) injunction (although a provincial superior court may grant one in reliance upon its equitable jurisdiction).[5]

Instead, should there be a breach of the statute, the minister is limited to sending out a demand. There is no time limit within which this must be done. However, no judicial proceedings can be commenced until a demand has been issued and there has been a failure to comply with it.[6]

Why are there virtually no criminal sanctions in the statute? Civil remedies, Parliament decided, would be sufficient. The Conservative

---

provision was included in that Act because a corporation might be unreachable for a number of reasons or might have been dissolved. Because of the difficulties in enforcing similar provisions in other statutes, it was omitted from the *IC Act*. *Investment Canada Act: Briefing Document*, (undated, released under the *Access to Information Act*), p. 86. However, investors should carefully read s. 42. Even if a corporation is making the investment, an officer or employee, who deliberately provides misleading information, may be held criminally liable.

How can the criminal liability of a corporation be established? By showing that an officer or employee had the necessary mental element required by s. 42, and that this person caused the corporation to provide the misleading information.

[4] Conservative M.P.s had vehemently criticized the search and seizure powers in the *FIR Act* when that Act was being debated in 1973. Edmonton M.P. Marcel Lambert saw in these powers "the familiar pattern of the bureaucratic octopus spreading out". Another M.P. spoke about the chaos that the seizure of a company's books could cause. In any event, the investigative powers in the *FIR Act* were never used, except as a threat. Perhaps this is the reason why they were not included in the *IC Act*. In most cases, evidence of a breach of the Act, such as a takeover occurring without government approval, should be easily available. But *quaere* whether the lack of an investigative power may prove to be a handicap, if Investment Canada wishes to establish that an undertaking has been breached, or that an investment has been implemented in a fashion different from the terms described in the application for approval. House of Commons, *Minutes of the Standing Committee of Finance, Trade and Economic Affairs*, July 19, 1973, Issue No. 42, p. 42:42.

[5] The *FIR Act* contained a provision allowing the government to obtain *ex parte* injunctions. Conservative M.P. Don Blenkarn called that a "police state method" (since *ex parte* orders can be obtained without the other side knowing about it). Another M.P. pointed out that corporate transactions are conducted by a battery of lawyers. Thus non-compliance with the Act was unlikely. (See the *Minutes of the Standing Committee on Finance, Trade and Economic Affairs*, July 19, 1973, Issue No. 42, pp. 48 and 49.) These are probably the reasons why the Conservative government did not include a similar provision in the *IC Act* in 1985.

[6] S. 39.

government also wanted to improve Canada's image abroad. Removing the aura of criminality from the country's foreign investment review legislation was one way of doing this.

Another way was through greater administrative fairness. The previous statute had given the government the power to obtain injunctions and certain other court orders without first giving the investor an opportunity to be heard. This was wrong, government officials clearly thought, and unnecessary.[7] The existence of such powers might also alarm foreign business people. Hence, the *IC Act* requires the minister to initiate any action by sending a demand.

This demand must be served personally or by registered mail or telecommunicated text.[8] It will indicate what the investor must do, the time period for compliance, and the nature of the court order that will be sought if the demand is ignored.

In order to comply with the demand, the investor may be required to:

(1) cease contravening the Act,

(2) remedy a default,

(3) show cause why there is no contravention of the Act, or

(4) justify why a written undertaking is not being complied with.

It is important that the minister specify each remedy being sought. (Parliament wanted to inform people who might be tempted to evade the law of the possible sanctions.) If the demand simply says that the minister will be applying to the court, it will not fully conform with subsection 39(2) and may be a nullity.

If the non-Canadian refuses to submit to the demand, judicial proceedings may be instituted by the Attorney General of Canada "on behalf of the minister of Industry, Science and Technology". These proceedings may be commenced in either the Federal Court or a provincial supreme court.[9]

In court, the onus will be on the minister. He will have to justify his reasons for sending the demand and bring forth facts proving that the

---

[7] See: Tom Barton, "Investment Canada—Farewell to FIRA", in *Investment Canada*, (Toronto: Department of Education, Law Society of Upper Canada, 1985), p. B9. Tom Barton was one of the Department of Justice officials who contributed to the drafting of the Act.

[8] S. 33. Any verifiable means of communication may be used.

[9] S. 40. The superior courts of the provinces and the federal courts have concurrent jurisdiction in relation to the civil remedies. Note that the power to determine whether legal proceedings should be commenced lies with the Attorney General of Canada, and not the Investment Canada minister. (See the *Department of Justice Act*, s. 5.)

non-Canadian has failed to comply with the demand.[10] If a takeover took place without Ottawa's blessing, such proof should be easy to provide. But evidentiary difficulties may arise if the minister must show to what degree an undertaking remains unfulfilled or to what extent an investor has failed to abide by the plans submitted with the application.

This is because all information will be in the files of the foreign investor or the company acquired. The minister has no authority to seize and examine these files. (Section 25, however, might unlock closed doors. This section compels a non-Canadian who has made an investment to provide information to Investment Canada for monitoring purposes.[11])

If the minister can make out a case, the court has several remedies available. Sections 40 and 41 list eight of them but this list is not exhaustive.[12] A court retains the discretion to do what is just.[13]

1. Scope of the Remedies

The following remedies are among those available to the court.

(a) Order of Divestiture

Sometimes an investor will buy a business before the minister has made a decision. If the minister subsequently decides not to approve the investment, section 24 of the Act requires the investor to give up control. No time period is mentioned in the Act. However, the investor would no doubt be given a reasonable length of time to do so.

---

[10] The minister must convince the court that he was justified in sending the demand. Could the minister be successful in court if he had a bona fide belief based on erroneous facts? Although subss. 39(1) and 40(2) may be read as implying that it need only be established that the minister was justified in the belief that there was a contravention of the Act, surely, no court order would be issued if the minister had made a mistake. The better view is that the onus is on the minister to show that there actually was a contravention of the Act.

[11] A court in Toronto cannot compel a company in Germany to provide information to the Investment Canada minister. However, if the German company has bought a Canadian company, the Toronto court will likely have sufficient leverage to "persuade" the German company to provide the information.

[12] The minister could, for instance, obtain an order forcing an investor who has bought a business to provide information for monitoring purposes.

[13] Subs. 40(2) gives the court the power to make such "orders as, in its opinion, the circumstances require".

If the investor does nothing, the government may get annoyed eventually and get an order of divestiture from the courts. This order would direct the investor to sell enough shares so that he is no longer in control. Such an order might also be appropriate if the foreign investor receives approval to make an investment, and then does so in a manner that bears little resemblance to what was said in the application.

For several reasons, a divestiture order may not be as fearsome as it sounds. To begin with, the courts are instructed to be just and reasonable when making such an order. This suggests they may listen to heart-string arguments. One result may be creative or unusual orders, or at least an order that affords the investor ample time to divest.

Secondly, a divestiture order can only be made against a "non-Canadian". If a Canadian and a non-Canadian have made an investment in the same company, the Canadian need not fear that a court might order him to divest as well. That could happen only if an entity (partnership, joint venture, trust) in which the Canadian was a participant, had made the investment, and if that entity was controlled by a non-Canadian.

Thirdly, even if an order is made, the non-Canadian investor can retain a sizeable minority interest. Indeed, although control would have to be given up, it might not have to be transferred to a third party. This may come as a surprise. Most people would think, if told to sell control of a business, that someone else must get control. However, this is not necessarily a requirement of the law.

Section 24 states: ". . . the applicant . . . if the investment has been implemented, shall divest himself of control of the Canadian business that is the subject of the investment". The section does not explicitly state that control must be transferred to a Canadian. Unless "control" in section 24 means negative control, a foreign investor who owns 100% of a company can give up control by merely selling 50% (not 51%). Although the company will remain "non-Canadian-controlled" under the status rules (in section 26) the investor will have complied with section 24.

This outcome is consistent with other provisions of the Act. For instance, a foreign investor who buys 50% of the shares of a business is presumed to have acquired control (paragraph 28(3)(c)). However, if the vendor retains the remaining 50%, that presumption can often be rebutted.

Perhaps this was the drafter's way of encouraging foreign investment. An investor, whose purchase has been turned down by the government, can retain 50% and hold a veto, through which the remaining interest can be protected. There are also accounting advantages. Some foreign companies cannot include a subsidiary's financial results in their consolidated financial statements unless the parent company owns 50% of the subsidiary.

(b) Injunction

Sometimes it is hard to unwind a transaction after it has been completed. Innocent parties may be seriously inconvenienced. In these circumstances, an injunction, swiftly obtained, is an appropriate remedy.[14]

An interim injunction could be sought if a foreign investor was seeking to implement an investment before the minister could review it.[15] It could also be sought if the purchase had already occurred (without the minister's consent) and the new owners were firing staff, selling assets, discontinuing a product line or taking other action that might harm the Canadian business.

On the other hand, if an investor tries to buy a business after the minister has concluded that the purchase will not benefit Canada, the proper remedy would be a permanent injunction. If an interim injunction was first obtained and the government subsequently decided to seek a permanent injunction, the wording of the Act suggests that another ministerial demand would have to be issued.

Injunctions are remedies that are not easily secured.[16] The courts will grant them only in compelling circumstances. This means that the

---

[14] The Attorney General of Canada when seeking a temporary injunction under the *IC Act*, is not required to give an undertaking concerning damages. *A.G. Can. v. Fallbridge Holdings Ltd.* (1979), 7 B.L.R. 275, at 280 (F.C.T.D.). Were it not for Fallbridge and similar cases, the Crown would be required to give an undertaking to abide by any court order to pay damages incurred by the investor as a result of the temporary injunction if the action at trial was not successful.

The court would probably grant an injunction that was conditional on the minister proceeding expeditiously to determine if the investment would be of net benefit to Canada.

[15] Could an injunction be obtained to block the transfer of shares on company registers? Referring to a very similarly worded provision in the *Foreign Takeovers Review Act*, a Department of Justice spokesperson told M.P.s in 1972 that the provision did not specifically contemplate that the courts would be asked to block the transfer of shares. (House of Commons, *Minutes of the Standing Committee on Finance, Trade and Economic Affairs*, June 7, 1972, Issue No. 18, p. 22.)

[16] See *OSF Industries Ltd. v. Marc-Jay Investments Inc. (1978)*, 20 O.R. (2d) 566 (H.C.). In that case, the plaintiff, suing a non-resident corporation on a promissory note, was unable to obtain any injunction despite fears that the non-resident corporation would remove its assets from the jurisdiction. If a plaintiff has no right which exists at law or

minister would have to demonstrate a pressing need for the injunction. In addition, it would have to be proved that the proposed acquiror was a non-Canadian, that the proposed acquisition was an acquisition of control, and that the target was a Canadian business. Should the minister fail to prove any of these elements, the court would not have the authority to grant the injunction.

Paragraph 40(1)(b) closely ties the injunction remedy to the divestiture order remedy. To obtain an injunction, the government must convince a judge that the investor's purchase of a business or discontinuance of a product line would make it more difficult for a court to effectively enforce any subsequent divestiture order.[17]

Why are the two remedies linked in this way? Those who drafted the Act evidently believed that the government would seek an injunction primarily to prevent the disposal or intermingling of assets.[18] If assets were sold or two companies were merged and their assets combined, it might be impossible to later unwind the transaction through a court-ordered sale. This "narrow" perspective is probably the reason why, in the Act, an injunction is not a "stand alone" remedy that can be used to prohibit normal business operations after an "illegal" takeover has taken place.

Suppose a takeover is completed without government approval. The new foreign owners then slash prices as part of an aggressive marketing campaign. This provokes the company's competitors who complain. Is there anything that Ottawa can do while the review process is grinding to a conclusion? Probably not. Damage to a competitor is not a factor that would prejudice the ability of a court to issue a divestiture order under paragraph 40(1)(a).

---

equity, the courts will not restrain the defendant from dealing with her or his property until the rights of the litigants are ascertained. In order to overcome this hurdle and establish a legal right, Ottawa might rely on the "non-implementation rule" in s. 16 of the *IC Act*.

[17] An injunction could be obtained to block a purchase that is taking place before government review or after the minister has decided the transaction will not benefit Canada. An injunction might also be issued if a takeover has been approved but is being carried out in a fashion significantly different from the plans submitted to Investment Canada. If the takeover has already been completed, the court might enjoin the parties from intermingling assets. All of these actions could be prejudicial to the ability of a court to effectively enforce a divestiture order.

[18] The drafters of the *IC Act* closely copied the wording of the injunction remedy in the *FIR Act*. One must therefore assume the drafters of the *IC Act* adopted the same views as those who framed the *FIR Act*. On June 5, 1973, the Hon. William Gillespie told a Parliamentary committee: "If the investment has already been completed, the minister may obtain an injunction to forestall the intermingling of assets or *any other action* which would make it difficult to frame any subsequent order rendering the investment nugatory." House of Commons, *Minutes of the Standing Committee on Finance, Trade and Economic Affairs*, June 5, 1973, Issue No. 26, p. 26:15.

Change the facts. Suppose the investor has sold the business and is trucking the machinery to the U.S. Can the investor be stopped? At this late stage, there might be no point in trying. In any event, for a similar reason to that presented above, an application for an injunction would likely fail.

(c) Order of Compliance[19]

The courts can enforce an undertaking given during the review process through an order of specific performance. If it can be obtained, this is a powerful remedy: failure to obey is contempt of court. However, there are several circumstances when the courts may refuse to grant such an order.

Undertakings that are ambiguous and uncertain are unenforceable. That is basic contract law.[20] Because of the peculiar wording of paragraph 40(2)(c), which refers to undertakings addressed to "Her Majesty in right of Canada", a literal-minded court might rule that undertakings which were not addressed to Her Majesty had not been given with a sufficient degree of solemnity.

Moreover, the remedy of specific performance, like the injunction remedy, is discretionary. That means that the clean hands doctrine applies. If the government were to rush to court the moment that an investor was in technical default in fulfilling an undertaking, the courts might be less than willing to take action. Hardship to an innocent third party is another discretionary bar to an order of specific performance.[21]

In addition, the courts would probably not order the performance of undertakings requiring judicial supervision, such as an undertaking to build a manufacturing plant. This has always been the position of the courts when applications have been brought[22] for the specific

---

[19] This remedy is in addition to an action for breach of contract.

[20] Under para. 39(1)(c), the minister can issue a demand if an investment is implemented on terms and conditions that vary materially "from any information or evidence provided under this Act". If an undertaking is "information" provided under the Act, it might still be possible for the minister to obtain a divestiture order, even though the undertaking is otherwise legally unenforceable.

[21] I.C.F. Spry, *The Principles of Equitable Remedies: Injunctions, Specific Performance, and Equitable Damages*, (London: Sweet and Maxwell, 1980), pp. 187–93.

[22] For the law on specific performance of a contract to build, see *Tanenbaum v. W.J. Bell Paper Co.* (1956), 4 D.L.R. (2d) 177, at 197. For general information, see any book on contracts, such as M. Furmston, *Cheshire and Fifoot's Law on Contract*, (London: Butterworths, 1981), p. 564.

performance of contracts. There is no reason to believe that the attitude of the judiciary would be different merely because the *IC Act* specifically provides for an order of compliance. Consequently, there may be few undertakings which an investor may contemplate giving which will be capable of an order of specific performance.

Paragraph 40(2)(c) gives the courts no discretion beyond deciding whether to issue an order to comply. Although economic circumstances can change and render absolute compliance unfeasible, the courts have not been empowered to order partial compliance or to structure substitute undertakings.

Frequently, investors submit plans and other information that are virtually analogous to undertakings but are not worded like an undertaking. Can they be specifically enforced? Since paragraph 40(2)(c) contains no reference to plans, there is no statutory basis for seeking an order of specific performance.

(d) Financial Penalty

This civil remedy is similar to that contained in U.S. anti-trust legislation, and is in lieu of any criminal sanction. If a non-Canadian has acquired the shares of a foreign-incorporated company which indirectly carries on a business in Canada, and is refusing to file an application for review where one is required by law, a financial penalty may be an effective tool. The penalty can be up to $10,000 a day, for each day that the non-Candian investor contravenes the Act.

Such a penalty cannot be imposed against a Canadian who is a party to an investment. However, if the Canadian is a member of a foreign-controlled partnership which is violating the *IC Act*, the Canadian will obviously feel an indirect blow to the pocket-book. In these circumstances, the $10,000-per-day financial penalty would be levied against the partnership (because it is considered to be the non-Canadian investor), not separately against each individual partner.

(e) Order of Revocation

An order that revokes voting and dividend rights attached to shares acquired in a direct acquisition hits at the essence of the transaction. This remedy also has the advantage of flexibility, since the suspension may be for any specified period of time. The court would probably order that all dividends declared by the Canadian business and belonging to the foreign shareholder be paid to a trustee until the Act is complied with.

(f) Order of Disposition

A disposition order, directing the non-Canadian investor to sell the assets or shares he has purchased, may be an alternative to an order of divestiture. This alternative may be particularly attractive if it is not feasible to restructure the transaction so that the foreign investor sells control but retains an interest. Although it is possibly an oversight, the Act does not instruct the court to make disposition orders on such terms that the court considers reasonable (unlike the case with orders of divestiture).

(g) Citation for Contempt

The ability to punish a foreign investor for contempt through fines and jail sentences, if he refuses or fails to obey a court order, is a potent weapon, but only if the foreign investor is within the jurisdiction of the court. If a transaction between a British and French investor (involving a Canadian business) occurred entirely offshore, a citation for contempt would most likely be unenforceable.[23] A citation for contempt in these circumstances might also be condemned abroad as an extraterritorial application of Canadian law.

(h) Vesting Order[24]

If a share purchase takes place outside Canada, obviously Canada cannot force the foreign investor to dispose of the shares. Nevertheless, a Canadian court is not helpless if an investor living in Florida shrugs off a court order. In such circumstances, the court can vest the shares (or assets) which the investor purchased in a trustee. The trustee may then be authorized to sell them.

Should a sale take place, the Canadian government cannot confiscate the proceeds. After court costs have been deducted and the fees of the trustee paid, the balance of the money must be remitted to the foreign investor.

There is one limitation on vesting orders which may cause a tenacious investor to smile. A vesting order can only be used if the foreign investor has directly purchased the shares or assets of a Canadian company. If the investor bought shares of a foreign-incorporated

---

[23] Canadian government minister Jean-Luc Pepin discussed this problem in 1972. He told members of Parliament that, in such circumstances, a court would not try to do something it could not enforce. (House of Commons, *Minutes of the Standing Committee on Finance, Trade and Economic Affairs*, June 21, 1972, Issue No. 25, p. 18.)

[24] S. 41.

company which in turn owned a Canadian business, Canadian courts have no jurisdiction to impose a vesting order. That means this remedy cannot be used when there has been an indirect acquisition. (The reason should be clear: a Canadian court cannot vest in trust the shares of a French company owned by a resident of France.)

2. Enforcement Problems and Indirect Acquisitions

Indirect acquisitions pose many other enforcement problems.[25]

EXAMPLE: A non-Canadian billionaire buys a foreign company with a large subsidiary in Canada without waiting for approval under the *IC Act*. The Investment Canada minister later decides that the transaction does not benefit Canada. The billionaire flies into a rage and refuses to sell. What can the courts do?

A judge might levy a fine of up to $10,000 a day, enjoin the investor from exercising any control over the subsidiary,[26] issue an order to the investor to cause the subsidiary to sell the Canadian business or order the investor to comply with a written undertaking. What if the investor ignores the courts? Then the courts might fine the investor, cite him or her for contempt, or issue an order of committal. However, if the investor, surrounded by burly bodyguards and sitting in the Far East, has no personal assets in Canada that can be seized, he may be amused by these courtroom theatrics.

One solution, from the government's perspective, would be to ask for the court's permission to join the Canadian subsidiary and its foreign parent in any legal proceedings. The argument for joinder would be that these companies are necessary parties in order to enforce any court order. If the Canadian subsidiary was made a party to the action, the court could then order the subsidiary to pay no dividends (or make any other payment) to its foreign parent. The subsidiary might also be ordered not to obey any instructions from the foreign parent.

---

[25] The enforcement problems which arise when a multinational company changes hands were discussed before committees of Parliament when the *Foreign Takeovers Review Act* and the *FIR Act* were being examined in 1972 and 1973.

[26] Service of a writ on a foreign investor can be effected under the rules of court. However, since an injunction is directed against a person, a Canadian court cannot enforce it in a foreign country. Since the billionaire would be outside Canada and there would be no person or thing within the jurisdiction of the court against which to enforce an order, a judge might simply refuse to grant an injunction.

It is questionable whether a court would give its assent to this. The Canadian lawyers for the billionaire would point out that the two companies had themselves done nothing to infringe the *IC Act*. Moreover, if there were any minority shareholders, they might be hurt.

3. Laches and Limitation Periods

If an investor does not fulfil his undertakings or purchases a business without approval, it may be some time before Ottawa finds out, perhaps months. Does this delay work to the advantage of the investor? Generally not. Except in extreme cases, allegations of government tardiness are no defence. Investors cannot raise the issue of estoppel based upon laches because the doctrine of laches does not apply to the Crown.[27] Moreover, should the government seek an order for specific performance (or an injunction) under section 40, this would not be an equitable remedy but a statutory or legal remedy. The doctrine of laches does not apply when legal rights (as opposed to equitable rights) are being asserted.[28]

On the other hand, if the government should procrastinate before taking action, a statutory limitation period may be relied upon in an investor's defence. This is because the old rule, that time never runs against the Crown, has been superseded by section 39 of the *Federal Court Act*. This section requires the federal government to abide by the same provincial limitation periods that all citizens must take cognizance of. (The limitation period in Ontario is six years for contracts not under seal.)

Even if a limitation period was missed, this might not prejudice Ottawa's ability to enforce an undertaking. The government could still argue that a breach of an undertaking is a continuing breach and a lawsuit can be commenced at any time.

4. Implementation and Disallowance

From the foregoing, it is apparent that the government has a rather frightening list of remedies. But for that very reason, they are

---

[27] P. Hogg, *Liability of the Crown in Australia, New Zealand, and the United Kingdom*, (Melbourne: Law Book Co., 1971), p.36. *Kennedy v. M.N.R.*, [1929] Ex. C.R. 36. For an argument that laches should bind the Crown, see H. Street, *Government Liability: A Comparative Study*, (Hamden, Connecticut: Archon Books, 1975), pp.159–61.

[28] *In re Maddever* (1884), 27 Ch.D. 523 (C.A.) at 528. This case was followed in *Anderson v. South Vancouver (Municipality of)* (1912), 45 S.C.R. 425, at 462.

unlikely to be used. The Canadian government wants to attract investors to Canada. They may decide to go elsewhere if they read in their newspapers about injunctions and vesting orders.

Notwithstanding this, if an investor has taken the risk of acquiring a Canadian business before the minister has made a decision and that decision is negative, the investor should sell the business or at least a controlling interest. If a buyer cannot be found at a reasonable price, the investor should ask Investment Canada for an extension of time.

By keeping the channels of communication open, an investor can probably ensure that legal action will never be initiated. But if that day should come, the investor who can demonstrate *bona fides* to the court, as evidenced in part by efforts to keep the agency informed, may be more likely to benefit from any exercise of judicial discretion.

5. Counter-Attack

If legal action is launched, investors are not restricted to responding; some counter-attack. Counter-attacks may not be successful. However, they will probably cause delay and possibly consternation. Since there is no appeal mechanism in the Act, such investor-initiated action is an acceptable route to judicial review.[29]

For example, suppose a major corporation and Ottawa are at loggerheads over whether the corporation is a "non-Canadian". The corporation attempts a takeover. Ottawa issues a demand (for compliance with the Act). The company could seek:

---

[29] What remedies does a dissatisfied foreign investor actually have? The powers of the minister under the *IC Act* appear to be "administrative" in nature, since they are guided by considerations of policy, not law. Hence, an investor cannot use s. 28 of the *Federal Court Act* to question them (s. 28 of the *Federal Court Act* excludes "administrative decisions"). Certiorari and prohibition cannot be used either, since these remedies are only available if a power is of a judicial or quasi-judicial nature. That leaves mandamus (but only to ensure that a power—e.g., to rule on an application—is exercised, not to review its exercise), an injunction and an action for a declaration. An investor seeking such remedies would proceed by way of s. 18 of the *Federal Court Act*. (Might a chagrined foreign investor sue the Crown for failure to properly consider the merits of the application? Any thought of a successful tort action is fanciful.)

If the Investment Canada minister and a province strongly disagree over whether a takeover should be approved, could the province seek a declaration that the transaction is not reviewable and an injunction preventing the minister from attempting to block the transaction? M.P.s asked a Department of Justice spokesperson a similar question when the *FIR Act* was being debated in 1973. The answer was no. The avenues available to foreign investors for judicial review are not available to the provinces. The Senate of Canada, *Proceedings of the Standing Senate Committee on Banking, Trade and Commerce*, Dec. 11, 1973, Issue No. 23, pp. 23:18, 23:25.

(1) a declaration of Canadian status, and

(2) an interim injunction preventing enforcement proceedings from being taken until the trial of the status issue.[30]

Such an action would be brought in the trial division of the Federal Court of Canada. The Federal Court has exclusive jurisdiction to review the decisions and other actions of a "federal board, commission or tribunal". That phrase, which is defined in section 2 of the *Federal Court Act*,[31] encompasses the minister responsible for Investment Canada.

An action against the federal government should name the minister of Industry, Science and Technology as defendant.[32] To ensure that the Crown generally is bound by any ruling of the court, it may be wise—although not strictly necessary—to add the Attorney General of Canada as defendant.

One case, decided under the *FIR Act*, arose because two companies mounted just such an aggressive defence. After receiving a formal demand for compliance from the minister, British Columbia Forest Products and Western Forest Products Ltd. asked the Federal Court for an interim and permanent injunction restraining the minister from taking any further action, and a declaration that they were not "non-eligible persons".

At the hearing of the application for an interim injunction, the court cited *Yule Inc. v. Atlantic Pizza Delight Franchise (1968) Ltd.*[33] That case reviewed some of the principles used in deciding whether an injunction should be granted. The court then concluded:

> . . . the plaintiffs have made out a fair prima facie case, have established irreparable injury for which damages cannot be compensated and the balance of convenience lies solely with the plaintiff.[34]

---

[30] Injunctive relief is not available against the Crown in right of Canada. An injunction is available against a minister of the Crown, but only if that minister is acting beyond the scope of his or her authority. *Whelan v. Min. of National Defence* (1985), 10 Admin. L.R. 200 (F.C.T.D.).

[31] R.S.C. 1985, c. F-7.

[32] Do not name Investment Canada as a defendant. Its legislation does not say it is a suable entity. *B v. Dept. of Manpower and Immigration Commission of Inquiry* (1975), 60 D.L.R. (3d) 339, at 349 (F.C.T.D.).

[33] (1977), 80 D.L.R. (3d) 725. One precondition to obtaining an injunction is proof of "irreparable harm". For the meaning of this term, see: Paul Perell, "The Interlocutory Injunction and Irreparable Harm" (1989), 68 *C.B.R.* 538.

[34] *B.C. Forest Products Ltd. and Western Forest Products Ltd. v. Min. of Industry, Trade and Commerce* (1981), 15 B.L.R. 161, at 164. On the other hand, the decision by the minister to

An interim injunction was then issued pending the determination by the court, after trial, of the eligible or non-eligible status of the plaintiffs. (The case never proceeded further.)

Similar actions for declarations are frequently pursued by "administrative law" lawyers whenever their clients and government bodies disagree over the proper interpretation of a statute. Many of these cases involve disputes over the limits on the authority of a government official, or the legal status of a company or person.[35]

Unhappily, there are several limitations on this form of relief. One problem is that interim declaratory relief is not available.[36] Another is that the granting of a declaration is discretionary. The courts have not formulated clear principles setting out when they will exercise their discretion. Finally, a declaration simply declares rights but does not require that anything be done. In theory, a tribunal or a government minister could ignore the declaration if it was not combined with a claim for other relief.

In the context of the *IC Act*, a declaration may be sought that an investor is not subject to the Act, or that the minister, by misinterpreting the scope of statutory powers, has exceeded his jurisdiction. In this way, disputes over the meaning of "control" and whether a "Canadian business" exists can be determined by the courts, hopefully before the transaction is scheduled to close.

However, an investor cannot rush to court just because he and Ottawa are having a verbal brawl. One precondition for obtaining a declaration is that a real dispute must exist. The courts will not rule on hypothetical issues. Unless the government has commenced, or at least threatened to commence, legal proceedings, the courts will likely refuse to grant declaratory relief.[37]

---

issue a demand under s. 39 is not subject to review by the courts. J. Spence and W. Rosenfeld, *Foreign Investment Review Law in Canada*, (Toronto: Butterworths, 1984), p. 210.

[35] R. Reid, *Administrative Law and Practice*, (Toronto: Butterworths, 1978).

[36] It does not seem to be included in s. 18 of the *Federal Court Act*.

[37] *Mellstrom v. Garner*, [1970] 1 W.L.R. 603 (C.A.); I. Zamir, *The Declaratory Judgment*, (London: Stevens & Sons Limited, 1962), p. 43.

Imagine that a company, about to make a takeover, asks the Investment Canada minister for an opinion that it is a Canadian. To the distress of the company, the minister issues a contrary opinion. What can the company do? Opinions do not bind the applicant, just the minister. Therefore, the company may take the risk of proceeding with its investment. Can a risk-adverse company seek a declaration from the Federal Court (Trial Division) that it is a Canadian? No, unless a ministerial demand had been

There is still a route to court in such circumstances, but the investor will need the co-operation of the Department of Justice. Under subsection 17(3) of the *Federal Court Act*, if both the Crown and the investor agree, a motion can be brought by way of stated case for the opinion of the court on a legal or factual issue.[38]

issued for compliance with the Act. The courts will not grant a declaration on the basis of contingencies that may never arise. *Fries v. Fries*, [1950] O.W.N. 661. A mere difference of opinion, which is not adversarial in nature and does not involve two parties' legal relations, is "not justiciable". E. Borchard, *Declaratory Judgments*, (Cleveland: Banks—Baldwin Law Publishing Co., 1941), p. 30.

[38] In *Dow Jones & Co. Inc. v. A.G. Can.* (1980), 11 B.L.R. 18, decided under the *FIR Act*, the parties proceeded by way of stated case.

CHAPTER 16

THE RISKS IN ATTEMPTING TO AVOID REVIEW

Despite the receptiveness of the Canadian government to foreign investment, some foreign business people still wish to avoid the review process. Because the *Investment Canada Act*, like the *Income Tax Act*, is very technical in nature, it offers possibilities for doing this by altering facts and relationships.

Under the *IC Act*, creative restructuring may turn some foreign-controlled companies into Canadian ones, gaining for these companies the benefits of Canadian status without much *de facto* control being relinquished. In addition, a degree of control over a Canadian business may be secured without an acquisition occurring within the meaning of the legislation.

Some of the arrangements for achieving these results are obvious and were intended by Parliament (which wanted to encourage foreign investment and reduce constraints affecting business people). However, there are a few arrangements which appear to comply with the mechanical rules in the Act but yield results that Parliament may not have anticipated. It is over these latter schemes that the battle between crafty Bay Street lawyers and government regulators is fought.

1. The Risks

Any strategy which gives the appearance of complying with the Act, but does not alter reality, is risky to undertake. One reason is that many concepts in the legislation are open to both a narrow and broad interpretation. In the absence of a Supreme Court ruling, investors will never be certain which interpretation is correct.

Adding to this risk are the anti-avoidance provisions in the Act. These lie in wait for any investor who too boldly oversteps the "acquisition of control" or "status" rules. Among these anti-avoidance provisions is the basic rapier of the step transaction,[1] and a second instrument that combines into one aggregate total, direct and indirect acquisition of shares.[2]

There is also the very malleable definition of a voting share, the definition of ownership as "beneficial" ownership, and the general authority of the minister to issue a demand if the main purpose of a transaction is to evade the Act. Sometimes called the sham transaction provision, this last-mentioned cudgel is not restricted to transactions that are contrary to the Act, but sweeps in any transaction, the primary purpose of which is "related" to the Act.[3] At present, the scope of these anti-avoidance provisions remains untested in the courts.

2. A Compendium of Ideas: Legitimate and Dubious

Presented on the following pages are 27 ideas (or "schemes") for avoiding review. Proffered by Canada's corporate lawyers at seminars, in articles and on other occasions, these ideas range from the most obvious and legitimate, such as establishing a new business, to the most "creative" and legally dubious.

Readers of the *Financial Post* and the *New York Times* will already be familiar with several of these schemes. Similar commercial arrangements have been used by well-known public corporations.[4]

---

[1] Subs. 29(1).

[2] Subs. 29(2).

[3] Para. 39(1)(g). According to some lawyers, the efficiency of this foil may be clouded by the phrase "contrary to this Act" in s.39. Before the minister can demand that a non-Canadian discontinue a scheme which is primarily intended to evade the Act, must the minister also point to some section in the Act that the scheme contravenes? (This potential impediment was first raised by Toronto lawyer John Craig at a seminar entitled *The Proposed New Investment Canada Act: A Legal and Business Interpretation*. Organized by Insight Educational Services, this seminar was held on April 22, 1985. The same point was also mentioned during the panel discussion.)

[4] E.g., Lasmo Canada, MCA/Cineplex, Ranchmen's. During the FIRA era, Trizec Corporation "Canadianized" through the legal device known as pyramiding. Jack McArthur, "Hustling to Become Canadian-Controlled", *Toronto Star*, Oct. 2, 1976, p. D10. Public companies like Cineplex must file a mound of documents with the Ontario Securities Commission. Corporate lawyers order paper copies of these documents (which describe the companies' commercial transactions) from Micromedia Limited or

The scope of these ideas/schemes emphasizes the monumental task that legislative drafters face. Only lawyers for the rich have the time to discover all the possible routes for complying with a law by avoiding its application. Nevertheless, those who draft legislation are expected to perceive these routes in advance. Then they are supposed to block those commercial arrangements that do not achieve the objectives of the legislation.

A word of caution, however. Many (perhaps most) of these schemes *may not work*. Even those that have been implemented without challenge in the past may not be successful in the future. Only the Supreme Court can make a final determination on whether a creative commercial transaction complies with the Act. Consequently, investors would be wise to obtain a written opinion from Investment Canada before proceeding with any "creative ideas".

3. The Meaning of Equity

Before these 27 ideas or schemes, and the risks attached to them are examined, there is one basic concept that must be highlighted: the meaning of equity.

Equity shares are shares which carry a residual right to participate in the earnings of a corporation and/or its assets upon winding-up or liquidation. Equity shares include all common shares, as well as preference shares, restricted voting shares, and non-voting shares, provided they have a right to participate. While it may offend federal and provincial corporation statutes to create a class of voting shares with absolutely no equity rights, there still exists ample room for lawyers to manoeuvre.

Some of this manoeuvrability is the result of the *Canada Business Corporations Act* ("*CBCA*") and provincial statutes modelled on it. The *CBCA* abolished the traditional distinction between preference and common shares. Instead, that statute merely requires that the three attributes of share ownership—the right to vote, to receive dividends, and to receive the remaining property of the corporation upon its dissolution—be attached to at least one class of shares. If a corporation has several classes of shares, these rights can be apportioned in a variety of ways.

For instance, classes of shares may be created which carry almost all or very few equity rights. In turn, these shares may be voting, non-voting, or have:

---

view the documents on microfiche. (This microfiche service is called Can Corp. This is an abbreviation of "Canadian Corporate Reports Subscription Service". In the U.S., Q-Data Corporation (St. Petersburg, Florida) provides a similar service.)

(1) limited voting rights (such as the right to elect less than 50% of the directors);

(2) restricted voting rights (the maximum number of votes that a shareholder may cast be limited to 1,000 votes, even if he owns one million shares);

(3) subordinate voting rights (which arise when there are two classes of shares with (say) one and ten votes respectively); or

(4) contingent voting rights (which attach to preferred shares when dividends remain unpaid).

Shares may also carry protective coat-tails. These allow holders of non-voting shares to get the benefit of the premium for control if a takeover offer is made for all the voting, but not the non-voting, shares.

The law is thus very flexible whenever anyone wants to spread the attributes of share ownership among several classes of shares. It is this flexibility which allows lawyers to design many of the formulae for capitalization and control which appear below.

1. *The "51:49" Company:* A company is Canadian-controlled if a Canadian owns 51% of the voting shares and one or more foreign investors own 49%.[5] There is no statutory stipulation that the Canadian and non-Canadian be at "arm's length", nor does any section of the Act expressly bar changes to the locus of control by contractual means. Through the use of unanimity requirements and provisions dealing with quorums and cheque-signing authority, lawyers may be able to give their foreign clients the power to block corporate action without affecting the company's status.

It is also conceivable that a voting trust agreement, allowing a foreign shareholder to exercise the votes attached to the 51% interest owned by the Canadian, would not affect the company's status. Since "own" in paragraph 26(1)(a) means beneficial ownership, the argument would be that the Canadian has not fettered the beneficial ownership of his shares if he is still in possession of the power to sell them. (This, however, is debatable. Moreover, if the purpose of the voting trust is to circumvent the *IC Act*, the arrangement would not comply with the law.)

Other variants of this 51:49 structure involve the creation of voting and non-voting shares.

EXAMPLE: A company's voting and non-voting shares both entitle the holder to share in the company's assets on winding-up. However, the voting shares carry no right to share in profits. As a result,

---

[5] Status Rule No. 1. See para. 26(1)(a).

all the dividends go to the holder of the non-voting "equity" shares. The Canadian and the foreign investor get 51% and 49% of the voting shares. However, the foreign investor receives most or all of the equity shares.

EXAMPLE: Both classes of shares carry voting rights. However, the holders of the Class A shares are only entitled to a fixed dividend while the Class B shares are fully participating. The Canadian gets 2,000 Class A shares, and the foreign investor, 1,000 Class B shares. The Canadian has *de jure* control, but the foreign investor has all the equity.

EXAMPLE: The Class A shares are voting; the Class B shares carry no votes. The Class A shares are entitled to a 9% preferential dividend; the Class B shares get all the remaining profits. On a winding-up, the Class A shares are entitled to a maximum of $2 per share; thereafter, all the remaining assets belong to the holders of the Class B shares. A Canadian (or a Canadian-controlled voting group) pays $2 for each Class A share. The foreign investor is the only purchaser of the Class B shares.

These capital structures will usually be supplemented by a shareholders' agreement. This shareholders' agreement may require unanimous consent for all decisions, and equal representation in the board. To ensure that *de jure* control can be acquired in the future, the foreign investor may be given an option to buy the Canadian's shares. Alternatively, the Class A shares may become redeemable by the company on a certain date.

Such structures result in a company which, its legal advisers hope, is Canadian-controlled, although a foreign investor receives most of the dividends and has an equal voice in decision making.[6]

Can such arrangements be thwarted? Government lawyers may challenge them under the sham transaction provision.[7] However, other routes of attack may encounter a few difficulties.

One obvious difficulty is in the wording of paragraph 26(1)(a). In the absence of a shareholders' agreement, there may be no legal

---

[6] Toronto lawyer Robert Donaldson states that a corporation can be structured so that it is Canadian-controlled but foreigners own 95% of the true equity. This is because of the definition of voting share in the *IC Act*. However, he recognizes the possibility of a strong legal challenge by the government. Robert Donaldson and Craig Thorburn, "The Regulation of Foreign Investment in Canada: The Investment Canada Act", in *Foreign Investment Issues in the 1990s*, (Toronto: Insight Educational Services, May 18, 1989), pp. 46, 100. If these corporate structures allow foreign investors to benefit from grants restricted to Canadian-controlled companies, further conditions could be put on the awarding of the grants.

[7] S. 39(1)(g).

foundation for taking any action. Moreover, paragraph 26(1)(a) does not even mention and, therefore, may preclude an examination of shareholders' agreements.[8] (Some lawyers disagree. Shareholders' agreements, these lawyers suggest, can be examined to determine if the shares owned by a Canadian really fulfil the requirements for being "voting shares". Unfortunately, only the Supreme Court can resolve this contentious issue.)

Another technical difficulty lies in the pliant definition of "voting shares". Shares issued to a Canadian qualify as "voting shares" if they entitle the holder to share in profits *or* assets. Both attributes, it appears, need not be present.[9] Also, the definition of voting shares only requires that the voting rights be "ordinarily exercisable at meetings of shareholders".

Government lawyers may assert that voting rights are not "ordinarily exercisable at meetings of shareholders" if there exists a shareholders' agreement requiring unanimous consent before action can be taken. Counsel for the investors will probably argue that nothing in the Act prevents a Canadian from entering into an agreement to fetter his or her control at the shareholder and board level.[10]

If there are several shareholders, the status rule in paragraph 26(1)(a) does not apply.[11] If Canadians own a majority of the shares, the status of the company will be governed by paragraph 26(1)(c). However, the principal legal issue remains the same. Does the Act

---

[8] James Arnett argues that control through a shareholders' agreement is irrelevant. In his view, if a Canadian and an American own respectively, 51% and 49% of the voting shares of a company, the company is "deemed to be Canadian-controlled notwithstanding the shareholders' agreement". E. James Arnett, "From FIRA to Investment Canada" (1985), 24 *Alta. L.Rev.* 1, at 8. James Arnett was "Special counsel to the Governor in Council in connection with Bill C-15". James Spence presents similar arguments to those of Arnett. James Spence, "Investing Without Review Under the Investment Canada Act", in, *The Proposed New Investment Canada Act: A Legal and Business Interpretation*, (Toronto: Insight Educational Services, April 22, 1985). However, statutes can frequently be interpreted in diametrically opposed ways. Other lawyers disagree with the views expressed by Spence and Arnett.

[9] How can a non-Canadian get all the equity in a company? The word "or" in the definition of "voting shares" allows such a result. By contrast, the Ontario *Securities Act* defines both equity and voting shares and catches both in its definition of a takeover bid (See the *OSA*, s.89). The definition of a voting share should also be contrasted with the definition of a voting interest in a partnership, trust or joint venture, which requires that the owner share in both the profits and the assets on dissolution. It is an odd distinction.

[10] Because of the shareholders' agreement, the Canadian and non-Canadian will probably constitute a "voting group". However, in this case, the existence of a voting group has no impact on the Canadian/non-Canadian status of the company.

[11] Assume that, despite the existence of an agreement between two or more shareholders, there is no Canadian-dominated voting group owning more than 51%.

permit government regulators to examine shareholders' agreements to ascertain if a foreign investor is really in control?

2. *Canadians Vote but the Foreign Investors Have the Equity:* A riskier variation of the 51:49 scheme is to give 100% of the votes to one or more Canadians. The foreign investor(s), who are providing all of the financing, get the equity shares (except for a few shares to keep the Canadian motivated).

One technique (also used by tax planners) is to create two classes of identical shares—except that one class is non-voting. The voting shares can be called "common shares". The non-voting shares may be termed "special participating shares" and may be convertible into common shares if they are sold at a future date to Canadians.

After the corporation is set up, the Canadian receives 100 voting shares at nominal cost. The foreign investor(s) get a large number of "special participating shares". This allows the foreign investor(s) to participate in the growth of the company as if they were common shareholders. (If the foreign investors own most of the equity, they will be virtually the only participants in that growth.)

The foreign investor(s) will want representation on the board. To achieve this, the Canadian(s), in a shareholders' agreement, may covenant to vote for the foreign investors' nominee. Alternatively, the holders of the special shares can be given the right to elect a director (although this may turn the special shares into "voting shares" and clearly destroy the scheme).

If the foreign investors want more reins over the company, additional provisions may be added to the shareholders' agreement (or negative covenants inserted in the loan documentation). These provisions may state that certain matters can only be decided with the written consent of the foreign shareholders, that by-laws and resolutions need the signatures of all directors, or that the quorum at directors' meetings is comprised of all directors.

In this way, foreign shareholders may attempt to gain the best of all worlds: a secure investment, a window on company affairs, the right of veto over major matters, and the opportunity to participate in the growth of a "Canadian-controlled" company. (The risk investors face is that Ottawa may mount a successful legal challenge.)

Since the Canadian government has the option of reviewing new cultural businesses, a few lawyers may be using similar types of corporate edifices when a new book publishing venture or other cultural business is being set up.[12] From the perspective of Canada's arts

---

[12] Kenneth Kidd, "Only Two Publishers Have Been Put in Canadian Hands", *Toronto Star*, February 8, 1989, p. F1 at F4. Kenneth Kidd, "U.S. Firm's Effort to Sell Ginn Was Not Serious, Publishers Say", *Toronto Star*, May 16, 1988, p. 12. According to this article, Gulf & Western wanted to sell 51% of Ginn, but retain 50% of the board.

community, the problem with such corporate structures is that the profits from the business may be more likely to leave the country instead of being reinvested in Canada's cultural industries.[13]

3. *Quorums, Super-Majorities and Negative Covenants:* The power of minority foreign shareholders can be magnified in many ways. From a risk assessment perspective, the issue is where the courts will draw the line between compliance and evasion of the Act.

> EXAMPLE: A company has two shareholders, one foreign and one Canadian, who own 35% and 65% of the common shares respectively. Under the status rule in paragraph 26(1)(a), such a company is Canadian-controlled. Can the foreign shareholder be given greater control?

The quorum at directors' and shareholders' meetings can be set at two persons. Nothing can then be done if the foreign shareholder does not attend.[14]

Alternatively, the foreign shareholder (or his or her designate) can be a required co-signer for all cheques, or that shareholder's approval made a prerequisite before contracts are entered into, shares issued, dividends paid, officers hired, or salaries agreed to. If the bargaining power of the foreign shareholder is great enough, a provision may be inserted in the articles, by-laws or a shareholders' agreement requiring unanimous consent or a super-majority (such as 85% of the votes) before any by-law or resolution is adopted.

4. *The "49:49:2" Company:* Sometimes a company will be structured so that a foreign investor and a Canadian each own 49% of the voting shares, and the Canadian secretary of the lawyer who incorporated the company holds the remaining 2%. If the secretary and the Canadian form a voting group, or if there are no voting groups and the concept of "control in fact" in paragraph 26(1)(c) is narrowly interpreted, the company will likely be "Canadian-controlled" despite the substantial interest held by the foreign investor.[15]

5. *The "1/3:1/3:1/3" Company:* If two Canadians and one non-Canadian each own one third of the voting shares of a company, the prospects for the company being Canadian-controlled are good. If the two

---

[13] A government publication, entitled *Canadian Cultural Industries: Vital Links*, (Ottawa: Supply and Services Canada, 1987), explains the connection between economics and culture.

[14] In *Re Cowichan Leader Ltd.* (1963), 42 D.L.R. (2d) 111, one of two shareholders was refusing to attend annual meetings. The quorum requirement was two persons. The court held that it had no power under the British Columbia *Companies Act* to direct that one shareholder be deemed to constitute a meeting.

[15] Paras. 26(1)(a) and (c).

Canadians form a voting group, by entering into an appropriately worded shareholders' agreement, the company will be Canadian-controlled.[16]

6. *Non-Voting Share:* The purchase of non-voting shares does not come within the purview of the Act. An example is British Gas' purchase of shares in Bow Valley Industries. British Gas bought 33.32% of the voting shares of the company but ended up with 51% of the equity (the balance being non-voting preference shares). Pursuant to the share acquisition agreement, British Gas also got the right to nominate a majority of the directors in the company's proxy circulars for election at shareholders' meetings.[17]

7. *"Less than One Third":* The purchase of less than one third of a company's voting shares falls outside the *IC Act.* (This is what Parliament intended.) So does the purchase of 50% or less of the voting interests of an unincorporated entity, such as a real estate investment trust.[18] Yet such purchases may give a foreign investor either *de facto* control, if the other interests are widely held, or considerable negative control (by being able to veto proposals of the other shareholders) if the company's articles, by-laws and shareholders' agreements are appropriately worded.

The existence of *de facto* control will depend upon the continued passivity of the other shareholders. If only 50% of the shareholders attend shareholders' meetings in person or by proxy, a shareholder who owns $33^1/3$% less one share will dominate shareholders' meetings and determine the fate of the company. This sometimes happens in publicly traded, widely held corporations.

If a company is closely held, on the other hand, the other shareholders are unlikely to be passive. However, a foreign investor buying a 32% interest may obtain extensive veto powers through a shareholders' agreement.

One example of a transaction in which a foreign investor acquired just under $33^1/3$% of a Canadian company's shares received extensive media coverage.[19] California-based MCA Inc. was the investor, publicly traded Cineplex Odeon Corp., the target.

According to press reports at the time, a new class of Cineplex Odeon shares were first created, called "subordinate restrictive voting

---

[16] Paras. 26(1)(a) and (c).

[17] Further details about this case can be found in the newspaper accounts (e.g., *Toronto Star*, Dec. 22, 1987, p. B1), or the *Information Circular/Proxy/Notice of Shareholders' Meeting* filed with the Ontario Securities Commission in February 1988.

[18] Paras. 28(3)(b) and (d).

[19] *The Globe and Mail*, May 13, 1986, p. B4, and May 27, 1986, p. B5. See also the *Financial Post*, Jan. 25, 1986, p. 5.

shares". These shares carried both equity and voting rights (and the right to elect four members of a fifteen-person board).

MCA then bought enough of these "subordinate restrictive voting shares" to raise its (MCA's) equity interest in Cineplex Odeon to 50%. However, the voting rights of all shares purchased by MCA were "restricted to one third less one of the votes of *all* issued Cineplex Odeon shares".[20]

The same objective can be achieved in a simpler way by using voting and non-voting shares:

EXAMPLE: A foreign company has an operating subsidiary in Canada ("Canada Sub."). The foreign company wants to take over a publicly traded Canadian company ("Quebec Corp.") through an exchange of shares.

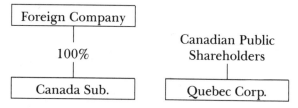

The first step is to calculate the exchange ratio. This ratio is based upon the relative net worth of Canada Sub. and Quebec Corp. Let us assume that the ratio is 60:40 (Canada Sub.:Quebec Corp.). The next step is for Quebec Corp. to issue treasury shares to the foreign company in exchange for receiving all of the outstanding shares of Canada Sub. After this exchange has been completed, the companies will be owned in the following manner:

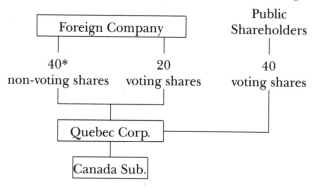

*These figures are simplified; add some zeros.

---

[20] "MCA Raises Cineplex Interest to 50%", *The Globe and Mail*, May 13, 1986, p. B4.

Normally, the foreign company would get 60 common shares for every 40 common shares of Quebec Corp. that are outstanding. (This would give the foreign company 60% of the votes.) However, to side-step the *IC Act*, the foreign company may be given 20 common shares and 40 preference shares instead.

This leaves the foreign company in a dominant position in terms of equity, with 60% of the equity pool, but just under one third (20 out of 60) of the voting shares. The balance of the voting shares are held by the public shareholders of Alberta Corp.

In the absence of special circumstances (e.g., unusual provisions attached to the non-voting shares), Ottawa may be unable to review such a transaction.[21] On the other hand, since Canadians still own a majority of the voting shares many business representatives would argue against the need to do so.

At first glance, the "one third minus one" formula is the solution for the foreign investor seeking to avoid review. However, it creates another problem: the unwanted suitor.

With just under one third of a Canadian company's voting shares, a foreign investor cannot block a corporate raider. If the company is widely held, it will be vulnerable to takeovers. (In the preceding example, a raider need only buy 31% of the equity of Quebec Corp. to take control, since just 60% of the outstanding shares are voting.)

Convertible preferred shares are only a partial answer to this dilemma. If they are convertible at the option of the investor and will give the foreign investor more than one third of the votes in a widely held company, any conversion will require prior government approval. On the other hand, if the shares are stated to be automatically convert-ible the moment a hostile takeover is made,[22] there would be an automatic breach of the statute's "no implementation without ap-proval" rule. (Any other arrangement, designed to allow an investor to block a takeover bid and maintain control in fact, would probably founder on the rock of the sham transaction provision.)

8. *The Incorporation of a Foreign-Based Partnership:* Indirect acquisitions of Canadian businesses benefit from a higher threshold for review. Under the Free Trade Agreement, indirect acquisitions by Americans will not be reviewable at all in 1992. However, for an offshore transac-tion to qualify as an indirect acquisition, there must be a foreign-

---

[21] Quebec Corp. may also retain its status as a Canadian-controlled company. However, this is less certain. The tests for "Canadian status" and "acquisition of control" are different. A Canadian company may become foreign-controlled although a for-eigner did not acquire control within the meaning of the legislation.

[22] "Poison pill" convertible shares.

incorporated company in the chain of control. (Another condition is that the "Canadian assets" constitute less than 50% of all the assets being acquired.)[23]

Suppose an American wants to buy a foreign-based partnership which controls a Canadian company. This will be treated as a direct acquisition. The review threshold for direct acquisitions will then apply.

Can the American turn this transaction into an indirect acquisition by asking the vendor to incorporate the partnership before the sale (or interpose a foreign company in the chain of control)? One paper distributed at a legal seminar discussed such a manoeuvre.[24] (The paper did not mention the risk.)

9. *Establishment of a New Business:* Instead of buying an existing Canadian business, a foreign investor may consider establishing a new business instead. Only new businesses that will carry on a "culturally sensitive" activity (like book publishing or film distribution) are liable to be reviewed by Investment Canada.

10. *Appointment of Canadian Nominees to the Board:* If a company is controlled by its board, it can easily be rendered Canadian-controlled. Simply increase the number of Canadians on the board to two thirds.[25]

What if the chairperson of the board is a non-Canadian who also controls the proxy mechanism, and can ensure the election of his or her nominees? That is not a consideration in determining if a company is Canadian-controlled.

11. *Majority Ownership by Non-Canadians:* If non-Canadians own 70% of a company's voting shares and their interests are widely held, the company may still be a "Canadian". However, the company's legal advisers would have to show that the company is controlled in fact by a Canadian (through her or his 30% interest).[26]

12. *Different Voting Rights for Different Shares:* A company is Canadian-controlled if a voting group made up of Canadians owns 50.1% or more of the voting shares. However, the waters become muddy when different voting rights are attached to two classes of shares.

---

[23] Para. 28(1)(d).

[24] See the paper entitled "Bill C-15. The Investment Canada Act Brief Analysis Submitted by Tory, Tory, Deslauriers & Binnington" in *The Proposed New Investment Canada Act: A Legal and Business Interpretation*, (Toronto: Insight Educational Services, April 22, 1985). Before proceeding with such schemes, investors should consider the statute's remedial provisions.

[25] Subpara. 26(1)(d)(ii).

[26] Para. 26(1)(d).

For instance, one class of shares, owned by foreigners, may give them a minority of the total votes but the right to select all the directors. The other class of shares, owned by Canadians, gives them a majority of the votes but denies them the right to vote for any directors. Is the company still a Canadian?

A variant of this *questionable* idea involves no restrictions on voting rights. Instead, the foreign investors are given the right of nominating for election all of the directors. (This right can be attached to the class of shares owned by the foreign investors or placed in a shareholders' agreement.)

13. *Creation of a Branch Through Dissolution or Reorganization:* The indirect acquisition of a branch business is neither reviewable nor notifiable. Naturally, this has prompted some dubious suggestions from Canada's corporate lawyers.

EXAMPLE: A European company has a Canadian and American subsidiary. The shareholders of the European company want to sell the Canadian business to a foreigner.

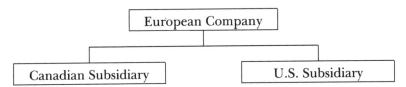

One of their suggestions is to dissolve the Canadian subsidiary. This will create a branch business. Another idea is to cause the U.S. subsidiary to purchase the assets of its sister company, the Canadian subsidiary. This purchase will not be subject to review because the European company will remain the ultimate controller of the Canadian business. However, a branch business will again be created.[27] (Is this really a way to avoid review? Investors who think so should study the Act's "sham transaction provision" closely.)

14. *Control of Partnerships Through Written Agreements:* Because the *IC Act* focuses on ownership interests, the locus of real control may sometimes be changed through contractual means.

---

[27] One author who discusses such a scheme is Warren Grover, "The Investment Canada Act" (1985) *Can. B.L.J.* 475, at 480.

The "branch business loophole" was first identified by Toronto M.P. Steven Otto in 1972 when the *Foreign Takeovers Review Act* was being debated. This loophole was left in the *FIR Act* and is now in the *IC Act*. For the explanation, see Chapter 6 of this book. (Otto's comments and the Liberal government's reply can be found in: House of Commons, *Minutes of the Standing Committee on Finance, Trade and Economic Affairs*, June 20, 1972, Issue No. 24, pp. 86–88.)

EXAMPLE: Canadians own the majority of the interests in a limited partnership. A Swedish company, which acts as the general partner, has operating authority in accordance with the terms of the partnership agreement. (The Swedish company also has a 20% financial interest.)

This partnership will be Canadian-controlled if a phrase in the status rules, "control in fact through . . . voting interests" (paragraph 26(1)(c)) is interpreted narrowly.[28] A narrow interpretation will prevent government regulators from examining the partnership agreement to determine who is actually operating the business.

15. *Testamentary Trusts:* A common form of testamentary trust leaves the income to the widow for life and the remainder to the children. Senior citizens drafting their death-bed wishes are probably unaware that this arrangement has another legal effect: neither the widow nor the children will own a "voting interest" as defined in the *IC Act.* (To own a voting interest, one must have a right to share in both income and, on the termination of the trust, in its assets.)

This means the testamentary trust will be classified as trustee-controlled. If the trustee is a Canadian, the trust will be a Canadian as well.[29]

16. *Inter vivos Trusts:* Another arrangement involving trusts, is to simultaneously incorporate a company and establish a trust, which owns all the company's shares. Canadians are the only beneficiaries of the trust, and nominally control it.[30] However, the trustee is a foreign investor who also owns all the company's non-voting shares.

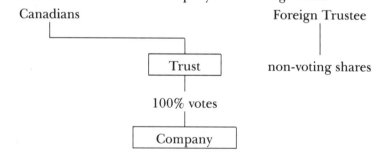

---

[28] Para. 26(1)(c). A number of lawyers maintain that the Act permits government regulators to examine shareholders' agreements. Might a legal rationale be developed to permit government regulators to examine partnership agreements? One possible basis for doing so might be to determine if the partnership units meet the definition of "voting interests" in the Act. However, this rationale would not justify an extensive examination of the agreement.

[29] Subs. 26(2).

[30] Para. 26(1)(a).

The result is that the company has Canadian status and can make acquisitions without review. An additional blessing, in the eyes of tax and corporate lawyers, is that the benefits of the company's growth accrue to the foreign investor, who likely has effective control of the company. (Alas, there is little certainty in law. Among the pitfalls the investor may stumble into is the sham transaction provision.)

17. *Combined Asset/Share Purchase:* A corporate vendor has two subsidiaries. It sells the shares of one and the assets of the other to the same foreign purchaser. Must the value of both businesses be added together to determine if the transaction is reviewable? The *IC Act* contains no provision specifically stating so.[31]

18. *The "1/3 to 1/2 Acquisition":* In certain circumstances, a foreign investor can buy up to 50% of a company's voting shares without having to notify Investment Canada. However, the investor must be in a position to establish that he or she does not control the company alone. Otherwise, it will not be possible to rebut the statutory presumption that the investor has acquired control of the company.[32]

The Ranchmen's case, where a majority interest was acquired without review, may depend upon special facts. In 1988, *The Globe and Mail* reported that a company ultimately controlled by the French government had been able to buy the control block in a profitable Canadian oil company despite a Canadian government policy forbidding takeovers of such companies. According to the newspaper, "Total Erickson will own 53% (of Ranchmen's Resources Ltd.) but by agreement with Investment Canada will only vote 44%".[33]

If a company is deadlocked, because two shareholders each own 50%, and a foreign investor buys out one of the shareholders, the presumption that control has been acquired can sometimes be rebutted. In theory, this means that a company equally owned by two Canadian shareholders could be bought by two foreigners, and the transaction would escape the Act, particularly if the two foreigners bought their 50% interests at different periods of time. (In reality, the two foreigners would probably be associated closely enough to constitute a foreign-controlled joint venture. The acquisition by such a joint

---

[31] See subs. 14(3). It appears that the drafters of the Act did not foresee all the different types of transactions that could occur. Combined direct/indirect acquisitions cause a similar problem. Another author who touches upon this matter is Brian Rose, "Review of Differences Between the Foreign Investment Review Act and the Investment Canada Act", in *Investment Canada*, (Toronto: Law Society of Upper Canada, May 3, 1985), p. A-9.

[32] Para. 28(3)(c).

[33] Dan Westell, "French Firm Finds Way to Acquire Ranchmen's", *The Globe and Mail*, May 4, 1988, p. 88.

venture of a 100% interest in a Canadian business would be subject to the Act.)

19. *Joint Ventures and Partnerships: Separating Assets and Profits:* The status of a joint venture (or partnership) depends on the Canadian/non-Canadian status of those who own "voting interests". To own a "voting interest", an investor must have an "ownership interest" that gives him a right to share in both the profits and the assets (on dissolution).

What about an investor who has a right to share in profits but *not* assets? This person does not have an "ownership interest" and, therefore, should not be enumerated when determining who controls the joint venture.

This distinction may permit a joint venture to be classified as Canadian-controlled, although a foreign investor is garnering much of the profits.[34] (If this is a correct interpretation of the law, perhaps Parliament intended this result as a way of bringing needed foreign technology and investment to Canada.)

20. *Turning a Direct into an Indirect Acquisition:* Lawyers who enjoy paper-shuffling have mused about ways to turn direct acquisitions into indirect ones. (The incentive is the potential benefits to foreign clients. If a Canadian business is indirectly acquired, the threshold for review is much higher. Moreover, most indirect acquisitions by Americans are not reviewable beginning in 1992. However, transactions that shift title to assets just to avoid the *IC Act* can clearly be challenged.)

EXAMPLE: A multinational company ("Europe Corp."), controlled by Swiss investors, has several divisions, including two separate divisions that make furniture in Canada and the U.S. The assets of the Canadian and U.S. divisions are $20 million and $300 million respectively.

An Australian entrepreneur wants to buy the world-wide assets of Europe Corp.'s furniture operations. If the assets of the Canadian division are purchased directly, the transaction will need Ottawa's approval (since the $5-million threshold will be exceeded). What might the Australian do?

If the vendor is co-operative, the Australian might structure the transaction as an indirect acquisition of a Canadian corporation. Europe Corp. would first incorporate a subsidiary ("New Eagle Corp.") to which it would transfer the assets of its U.S. furniture

---

[34] The possibility of structuring a partnership in this fashion is also mentioned in: P.R. Hayden and J.H. Burns, *Foreign Investment in Canada*, (Toronto: Prentice-Hall), para. 10028.

division. Next, the Canadian assets would be transferred to a newly incorporated Canadian subsidiary ("Canco") of New Eagle Corp.

In diagram form, here are the steps:

Initial Ownership Structure

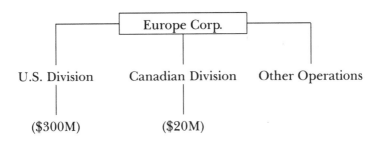

New Ownership Structure

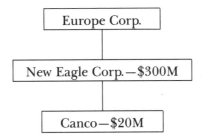

The result? If the Australian buys the shares of New Eagle Corp., he or she will indirectly acquire Canco and its Canadian assets. The higher $50-million review threshold may then apply. (On the other hand, it may not. Canadian government approval will still be needed if Ottawa successfully uses the "step transaction" provision or the "sham transaction" provision to assert jurisdiction.)

21. *Enlarging the Size of the International Transaction:* Indirect acquisitions are treated like direct acquisitions if the Canadian business is more than 50% of the global transaction (measured in terms of book asset value). This may not please a few foreign investors since direct acquisitions are governed by a lower review threshold. From the perspective of such investors, every additional regulatory requirement is an unwanted complication in a complex international transaction.

To avoid review, can the size of the international transaction be enlarged so that the Canadian business constitutes less than 50%?

EXAMPLE:

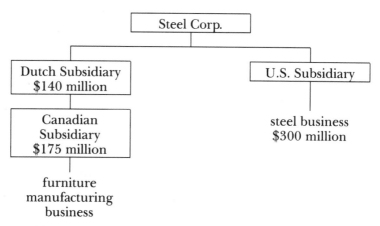

In this example, a Hong Kong business person has decided to purchase the shares of Steel Corp.'s U.S. and Dutch subsidiaries. If, for Investment Canada purposes, the international transaction consists only of the acquisition of the Dutch subsidiary, the Canadian business will constitute 55% of the entire $315-million (i.e., $140 million + $175 million) transaction. The threshold for direct acquisitions (American vendor–$150 million in 1992) will then apply. On the other hand, if the international transaction includes the purchase of both the Dutch and U.S. subsidiaries, the Canadian portion is merely a small fraction (28%) of a $615-million transaction.

Can the international transaction be increased in size, perhaps by having a master purchase agreement instead of two separate ones?

Possibly. The wording of subsection 14(2) of the Act is a bit vague.[35] It may allow investors to argue in favour of either a literal or a broad interpretation of what the international transaction consists of.

22. *Offshore Holding Companies:* Some solicitors tell their foreign clients who are establishing a new business in Canada to use an offshore holding company. One reason is that there may be some tax advantages. In addition, if the Canadian business is unincorporated, another foreign investor can later buy the holding company and thereby acquire the Canadian business without government approval, regardless of size. This is so even if it is a cultural business.[36] (If the Canadian

---

[35] Subs. 14(2) reads as follows: " . . . the transaction of which the acquisition of control of the Canadian business forms a part". The term "transaction" is not "delimited".

[36] The branch business loophole has existed in Canada's foreign investment review screening legislation since 1972. On June 20, 1972, Don Thorson, a senior government official, was questioned about it in the House of Commons. He thought this avoidance scheme would seldom be used. Many factors would mitigate against establishing a company in the U.S. to hold business assets in Canada if the only purpose was to avoid review. (For the citation, see n. 27.)

business is incorporated, the legal consequences are more complex. See Chapter 8.)

23. *To Lease or Buy:* A foreign investor can avoid the *IC Act* by leasing all the assets of a Canadian business (instead of buying them), even if the leases are long-term triple net leases which give the lessees most of the rights of an owner.

The framers of the *IC Act* were no doubt aware of this possibility. They probably believed it was too remote a possibility to worry about. However, they also wanted to tie ownership and control together. FIRA, they evidently thought, over-emphasized control. (Particularly when an investor, who owned only a small interest in a business, was sometimes regarded by FIRA as being in control.) So they omitted a provision[37] found in the *Foreign Investment Review Act,* which equated the acquisition of a leasehold interest with the actual purchase of the underlying property.[38]

Rarely, instead of buying a business, a foreign investor will just purchase the inventory and accounts receivable. The investor may then lease all of the operating equipment, land and buildings for a 15-year period. Unless the inventory and accounts receivable constitute substantially all of the business' assets, there will be no need for government approval.[39]

24. *The "Export" of a Canadian Corporation:* Companies can change residency just as individuals can. The *Canada Business Corporations Act,* and several provincial statutes, permit corporations to be "exported" to a jurisdiction outside Canada, provided the laws of the other jurisdiction permit the corporation to be "imported".[40]

There is no change in the ownership of a Canadian business when this happens. The theory is that the corporation is the same entity, which has merely changed location.

---

[37] See the *FIR Act,* para. 3(6)(c). The Hon. Jean-Luc Pepin explained its purpose in 1972 (when discussing an identical provision in the *Foreign Takeovers Review Act*). The government, he said, cannot exempt leaseholds because a company could go into the business of acquiring businesses and leasing them to foreign investors. That would be a clear circumvention of the Act. See the House of Commons Debates, July 4, 1972, pp. 3762–63. How realistic were Pepin's worries?

[38] Similarly, because the drafters of the *IC Act* wanted to link ownership to control, the Canadian/non-Canadian status of a limited partnership is determined by asking who owns the partnership interests, not by inquiring into the nationality of the general partner who runs the business.

[39] The dictionary definition of "acquire" (in s. 28) includes "to get". However, the courts are unlikely to rule that "acquiring" includes "leasing". Consequently, if Amoco had leased Dome Petroleum's assets in 1987, instead of buying them, government approval might not have been required.

[40] *CBCA,* s. 182; *OBCA,* s. 180.

However, there is one difference. Because of the change in residency, the Canadian business that the corporation owns becomes a "branch business". If the shares of the exported corporation are sold, the indirect acquisition of this branch business will not be subject to the Act, unless Ottawa invokes the step transaction provision.[41]

25. *"Window-Dressing" Financial Statements:* How can a Canadian make a business more attractive to foreign buyers? One idea is for the business owner to sell assets, then use the cash to retire bank loans. Alternatively, the owner might draw out assets as a dividend. This would reduce the business' asset value (as of its fiscal year-end), on which the threshold for review is based.

Another idea (which may appeal to accountants) is to force a change of year-end through an amalgamation. First, the balance sheet of the Canadian business is window-dressed (to reduce liabilities). Then the Canadian company is amalgamated with a new "off-the-shelf" subsidiary. The new year-end is the date of the statutory amalgamation. The amalgamated company's asset value is then determined at the end of the next month's fiscal period. (Is this strategy open to attack by government regulators? Yes, because it is clearly "for a purpose related to the Act".[42])

26. *The Potential Immigrant:* Some investors who are in the market for a Canadian business, hope to move to Canada at a later date.

> EXAMPLE: A Hong Kong investor, worried about tax reform after 1997, is moving his wealth offshore. He wishes to buy a Canadian business, but does not want Ottawa looking at his plans. The investor, or the investor's children, may eventually move to Canada. What can this investor's Canadian lawyers do?

One idea that has been suggested is to incorporate a holding company. The foreign investor then loans the purchase money to the company which then makes the acquisition. The investor also gets 49% of the company's shares. The Canadian lawyer keeps the remaining 51%, but gives his client an option to buy this 51% at any time.

On becoming a landed immigrant (and thus a Canadian), the foreign investor exercises the option. If the investor does not come to Canada but the children do, the option is assigned to them.

Where is the flaw in this scheme? The investor, not the Canadian lawyer, is probably the "beneficial" owner of the 51% interest. Consequently, the holding company will remain foreign-controlled. When it

---

[41] In certain circumstances, para. 39(1)(g) might be invoked as well.

[42] Para. 39(1)(g).

buys the business, the company must comply with the *IC Act*. (Hence the scheme does not work.)

27. *Canadianization:* Can a company with a foreign controller be "Canadianized" without the foreign controller losing control?

A few law firms think so.[43] One route is to convert the foreign controller's voting shares into non-voting, common or preference shares.[44] This leaves the Canadian shareholders with voting control. However, the foreign shareholder retains all of his equity rights (i.e., the right to participate in dividends and on a winding-up). To create a big stick with which to maintain effective control, the preference shares are made redeemable at his option.[45] This allows the foreign shareholder to demand repayment of the value of the shares if the new Canadian controllers do not perform as expected.

Variations of this format involve debentures payable on demand, convertible debentures, options, or convertible non-voting shares.[46]

4. Court Challenges

The foregoing are some of the ideas lawyers present to clients who are hoping to avoid Canada's foreign investment review legislation.

Many of these ideas are obviously a gamble to undertake. Foreign investors who are considering them should question their lawyers about the possibility of a legal challenge by the Department of Justice. Investors should also ask whether their proposed transaction will invite inquiry under Canada's *Competition Act*.

---

[43] The "blueprint" outlined above, which is available under the *IC Act*, was first put forward by lawyers working with the predecessor legislation. See the article by Ken Potter, "Recent Developments in the Application of the FIR Act to the Oil Industry" *Alta. L.R.* 494. An article by Peter Hayden, which discusses the same scheme, contains an interesting account of how Slater Walker of Canada transferred control to Canadians. Peter Hayden, "Go Canada and Avoid FIRA", *CA Magazine*, Feb. 1976, pp. 36–39. Several other lawyers have also written about ways to Canadianize companies.

[44] Preference shares provide protection against the Canadian controllers reducing dividends. However, if the preference shares should become voting because of non-payment of dividends, the foreign shareholder would be back in control.

[45] Under the *FIR Act*, it was possible to argue that if the Canadian corporation would be unable to borrow sufficient funds to redeem the preference shares, if the foreign shareholder demanded their redemption, the foreign shareholder was still in control through "the ownership of shares". This argument might not be available under the *IC Act*, which is based on control through "voting shares".

[46] *Convertible* non-voting shares are more marketable. They can be sold to a Canadian who can convert them into voting shares.

The *Competition Act* contains an efficiency defence. If a proposed transaction will have negative effects on competition, a foreign investor may want to show how the efficiency gains from the transaction will outweigh those negative effects. To do this, the investor may point to improved economies of scale and lower transportation costs, which will lead to a corresponding increase in exports or a reduction in imports.

If a transaction will bring these benefits, the investor should consider whether any concerns he may have about a review under the *Investment Canada Act* are really justified.

CHAPTER 17

THE FREE TRADE AGREEMENT AND THE AMERICAN INVESTOR

Because of the Free Trade Agreement ("FTA") between Canada and the United States, a special set of rules governs American investors in Canada. The threshold for the review of direct acquisitions is much higher than those faced by other investors; from 1992 onward, most indirect acquisitions cannot be reviewed; and the Canadian government is prevented from imposing minimum equity, forced sale and several trade-related performance requirements as a precondition to permitting an investment.

When the free trade agreement was announced, these special rules were heralded by many political commentators. Happily, for lawyers, the free trade agreement also created new layers of legal complexities.[1]

The first layer is the issue of investor status. After it has been determined that an investor is a "non-Canadian" (under the status rules discussed in Chapter 3), another question must be answered: Is the investor an American? If so, the investor benefits from the liberalized investment rules of the FTA. Foreign investors from other countries ("third country investors") do not.

1. The Definition of an "American"

The definition of an "American"[2] is an adaptation of the definition of a "Canadian" in the *IC Act*. For an individual, the test is nationality

---

[1] It is no accident that the FTA and the *IC Act* use some of the same terminology. (See the definitions of a voting interest, business, and entity.) Canadian lawyers put forward legal concepts they were familiar with, and the Americans agreed to their use in the FTA.

[2] Subs. 14.1(9).

or permanent residence. In the case of a corporation or other entity, an ownership test is used.

(a) Individuals

An American is an individual who:

(1) is a national of the United States, or

(2) has been "lawfully admitted for permanent residence" to the United States in accordance with the U.S. Immigration and Nationality Act.

American citizens are, of course, nationals of the United States. So are American Samoans (who can now purchase Canadian businesses of considerable size without approval from Ottawa).

What about an individual with dual status, such as a Canadian citizen who lives in the U.S. as a resident alien? The definition of an "American" circumvents this problem by excluding Canadians from its ambit. A Canadian cannot benefit from any right granted to American investors under the FTA.[3]

(b) U.S. Governments

The U.S. federal government, all 51 state governments and thousands of local governments also qualify for the advantages of American investor status, as do their agencies. But what agencies? Because there is no amplification of what an "agency" is, any dispute will have to be resolved by reference to statutory and common law.[4]

(c) Corporations and Other Entities

Corporations, trusts, partnerships and joint ventures ascertain if they are an "American" or not on the basis of the same rules used for determining their "Canadian/non-Canadian" status under the *IC Act*. These status rules are set out in sections 26 and 27 of the Act (see Chapter 3 of this book). By replacing "Canadian", "non-Canadian" and "Canadian-controlled" in these rules by the words "American", "non-American" and "American-controlled", a corporation (trust, partnership or joint venture) can discover if it qualifies as an "American".[5]

---

[3] The principal benefit that an American has, that a Canadian does not, is the right to sell a large business to a Japanese or third country investor without Ottawa's approval.

[4] The meaning of "agency" is discussed in Chapter 3.

[5] Subs. 14.1(10).

To save readers this effort, these American status rules are presented in Appendix B. The three examples that follow explain how the rules work.

EXAMPLE (Minority American Ownership): A company is owned 10% by Canadians and 45% by Americans. Is it an American?

Since Canadian ownership is less than 50%, the company is presumed to be controlled by non-Canadians.[6] Now substitute "American" for "Canadian" throughout the status rules. Since American ownership is also under 50%, the company is assumed to be a non-American (i.e., nationals of a country other than Canada or the U.S. are assumed to be in control).[7]

EXAMPLE (Board-Controlled Company, Canadian and American Directors): Enco P.L.C.[8] is listed on the London Stock Exchange. American shareholders own a 20% interest; British shareholders own the rest. However, the company is not controlled at the shareholder level. Five of the company's ten directors are Americans; the other two are Canadians. Does the company qualify as an American?

A board-controlled company in which Americans have a minority interest is an American if two thirds of its directors are either Americans, or a combination of Americans and Canadians. Consequently, Enco, although based in Great Britain, and majority-owned by British investors, enjoys the benefits of being an American.

A special provision (paragraph 14.1(9)(d)) was added to the *IC Act* in 1989 to achieve this result. The intent was to avoid prejudicing widely-held companies that have a combination of Canadian and American directors.[9] Without this provision, a widely held company would be an American if two thirds of its directors were Americans, but would suddenly become third-country-controlled (neither American nor Canadian) if a few Canadians were appointed to the board.[10] Such an outcome would have annoyed people in both countries.

---

[6] Para. 26(1)(d).

[7] Para. 14.1(9)(c), subs. 14.1(10) and para. 26(1)(d). However, if the company is controlled by its board, and Americans are directors, the presumption that the company is controlled in a third country (not Canada or the U.S.) may be rebutted. On the other hand, if Americans own a majority of the shares, the concept of board control is of no relevance. Instead, the rule in paras. 14.1(10) and 26(1)(c) applies.

[8] Enco P.L.C. is, of course, an imaginary company.

[9] The intent of this paragraph is obvious from its wording.

[10] In the absence of para. 14.1(9)(d), the company would not be a "Canadian", because less than two thirds of its directors are Canadians, and not an "American"

EXAMPLE (Joint Control: 50:50 Split): Imagine that U.S.-owned Dow Chemicals and Canadian-owned Olympia & York decided to form a new corporation ("Dow Olympia Ltd."), in which share ownership is evenly split. General Motors of the U.S. and Toyota of Japan then do the same thing ("General Motors–Toyota Ltd."). Which joint venture is an American?

A company in which ownership is split 50:50 between an American and a Canadian is deemed to be American-controlled.[11] Dow Olympia Ltd. is therefore an American.

Conversely, a company which is 50:50 American/Japanese is presumed not to be controlled by the American. Consequently, "General Motors–Toyota Ltd." is assumed to be controlled by Toyota (although this presumption is rebuttable).[12]

Is there an anomaly here? In both cases, there is a deadlocked company. Yet, depending on whether a Canadian is one of the two shareholders, the statute creates, in one case, a deemed presumption and, in the other case, a rebuttable presumption.[13] The FTA negotiators likely have an explanation. They were just following the structure of the existing legislation.[14]

(d) Corporations with Dual Standing

A corporation cannot be both an "American" and a "Canadian", since the definition of an "American" excludes a "Canadian-controlled entity". However, a company can be both an "American" and a "deemed Canadian". This is because the definition of an "American"

---

because less than two thirds of its directors are Americans. There is a similar provision for limited partnerships that are not controlled by the limited partners. Note that a company must first determine that it is not an "American" under para. 14.1(9)(c) before it can use para. 14.1(9)(d).

[11] Para. 14.1(10)(b). The para. is compatible with subs. 26(6). Without para. 14.1(10)(b), such a company would be neither Canadian- nor American-controlled, but instead would be regarded as an investor from a third country.

[12] Para. 26(1)(d).

[13] There is no anomaly if para. 26(1)(d) is strictly interpreted. It will then be impossible for the Japanese to rebut the presumption that they control "General Motors–Toyota Ltd".

[14] A company in which ownership is split 50:50 between a Canadian and a non-Canadian is deemed to be non-Canadian-controlled. It follows that if the non-Canadian is an American, the company should be deemed to be American-controlled. Para. 14.1(10)(b) is therefore a logical sequel to subs. 26(6). (There is no such deeming rule for a 50:50 split between an American and a Japanese citizen.)

does not exclude a company which is a deemed Canadian under the Imasco exemption.[15]

The Imasco exemption[16] (found in subsection 26(3)) was discussed in Chapter 3. It allows a Canadian-incorporated company, which is foreign-controlled but relatively autonomous, to be treated like a Canadian when making most investments.

This possibility of dual status is apparently not an oversight by the free trade negotiators. The FTA was intended to increase or, at worst, preserve the investment privileges of Americans. Certainly not to reduce them. The negotiators from both countries wanted American-controlled companies to retain all of their existing rights.[17] That included the right to be a deemed Canadian, if a company could qualify for the Imasco exemption.

Why would an American company want to be a deemed Canadian, especially since the threshold for review will be $150 million in 1992? Frankly, the idea will appeal to very few companies. On the other hand, if a company's directors are contemplating a massive acquisition or an acquisition in the oil and gas sector (where the $5-million review threshold applies), dual status may bring financial benefits.

The most significant benefit is that a "deemed Canadian" can make any takeover without getting government approval (except for takeovers in the cultural area), regardless of the size of the target business. That includes takeovers of Canadian oil and gas companies. If a foreign company becomes a "deemed Canadian", Ottawa's policy restricting foreign ownership in the energy sector can no longer be applied.[18]

2. The Advantages of Being an American

What advantages does an investor who qualifies as an "American" have? More to the point (from the perspective of the legal profession), is it worthwhile to restructure a foreign corporation that is on the verge of being classified as an American, so that it becomes one?

---

[15] Although an American company can become a deemed Canadian, it would still be considered an "American" with respect to other corporations it controls. In other words, its subsidiaries would be "Americans".

[16] Chapter 3 explains the history behind the name "Imasco exemption".

[17] This is clear from public statements made by U.S. officials and from the final text of the agreement.

[18] The American must still file a notification. FTA 1604 permits the Canadian government to ask for basic information about a transaction.

The quick answer is yes. Minor restructuring will frequently be worth the effort, because Americans have several advantages when investing in Canada.

Fewer takeovers are subject to review. There is greater freedom of sale, as well as a government buy-back obligation if an American investor indirectly acquires a Canadian cultural business and is later ordered by Ottawa to sell it. Finally, if an investment is reviewable, a number of performance requirements cannot be imposed by Ottawa. (However, the net benefit test remains the same.)

(a) Higher Thresholds

The major advantage to being an American is that the thresholds for review are much higher than those confronting third country investors. Moreover, after 1991, indirect takeovers of even the largest Canadian businesses cannot be reviewed by Investment Canada.

There are five exceptions. The higher thresholds do not affect Canada's cultural industries, or oil and gas, uranium, transportation and financial service businesses (with the exception of insurance services). Generally, however, because of the higher thresholds, Americans can buy most Canadian businesses (unless they are enormous in size) without Ottawa's approval (although Americans must still file a notification with Investment Canada).

Reducing the authority of Investment Canada in this way was a major objective of U.S. free trade negotiators.[19] Testifying before the Senate Finance Committee on April 11, 1986, U.S. Trade Representative and Ambassador Clayton Yeutter stated that the U.S. wanted to "produce a Canadian policy environment as open to inflows of foreign direct investment as our own".[20]

For direct acquisitions, the threshold for review has risen in four successive stages:

effective January 1, 1989	Cdn $ 25 million
effective January 1, 1990	Cdn $ 50 million
effective January 1, 1991	Cdn $100 million
effective January 1, 1992	Cdn $150 million
effective January 1, 1993	Cdn $150 million in constant 1992 dollars.

---

[19] U.S. officials had made it clear that a free trade agreement that excluded investment would not be acceptable. *Toronto Star*, Oct. 7, 1987, p. A26.

[20] *Hearings before the Committee on Finance*, United States Senate, 99th Congress, 2nd Session, April 11, 1986, p. 39 (No. S361–82).

Until 1992, these ceilings are in current Canadian dollars. However, the free trade negotiating teams did not overlook inflation. Each year, beginning in 1993, the threshold increases by an appropriate amount (see the formula in the IC regulations) to account for inflation.

The threshold for the review of indirect acquisitions has also increased in step fashion, but with a difference. In 1992, the review of indirect acquisitions completely ceases. After that date, an American can buy I.B.M. or the Ford Motor Company, and thus indirectly acquire their Canadian subsidiaries without Canadian government approval. (In addition, beginning in 1992, a Korean or other non-American will is free to indirectly acquire American-controlled subsidiaries in Canada of any size without Ottawa's approval.)

Here is how the threshold has changed:

effective January 1, 1989   Cdn $100 million
effective January 1, 1990   Cdn $250 million
effective January 1, 1991   Cdn $500 million
effective January 1, 1992   no review.

However, two pitfalls exist that may trap unwary investors. An indirect acquisition will not only remain reviewable after 1992, but will be reviewable at the same threshold as a direct acquisition ($150 million in 1992), if the asset value of the Canadian portion of a transborder transaction is more than 50% of the asset value of the total international transaction.[21] This is the 50.1% proportionate test. Americans who buy U.S. holding companies with Canadian operating subsidiaries should watch out for it.

The second pitfall affects "Delaware" mergers. In a "Delaware" merger, a U.S. target company that owns a (Canadian) subsidiary merges into a subsidiary of the acquiring company. Thereafter, the U.S. target company is deemed to be dissolved. That leaves the acquiring company's subsidiary (which now owns the Canadian subsidiary) as the survivor.

In American eyes, these mergers result in an indirect acquisition of the Canadian company. Canadian courts disagree. In their view, there is a direct acquisition.[22] (Direct acquisitions of large Canadian businesses need Canadian government approval.)

Canada's most "sensitive businesses"—those Ottawa considered central for generating wealth or preserving Canada's identity—are excluded from the higher thresholds. These excluded businesses are:

---

[21] Para.14(1)(c).

[22] *Dow Jones & Co. Inc. v. A.G. Can.* (1981), 113 D.L.R. (3d) 395; (1981), 122 D.L.R. 731 (C.A.).

(1) oil and gas businesses,

(2) uranium businesses,

(3) cultural businesses,

(4) businesses that provide transportation services,

(5) businesses that provide financial services (except for insurance services).

Americans who purchase one of these "sensitive businesses" are in the same position as all other foreigners. They must seek approval from the minister responsible for Investment Canada if the book asset value of the Canadian business exceeds:

(a) $ 5 million—direct acquisition;

(b) $50 million—indirect acquisition;

(c) $ 5 million—indirect acquisition, if the book asset value of the Canadian business is more than 50% of the asset value of the global transaction.

The exclusion of these "sensitive businesses" from the higher thresholds has several implications. The one trumpeted most loudly, when the FTA was announced, was that Ottawa can still review most purchases by Americans in five key sectors. Unfortunately, these exclusions, although they may solve some political problems, only add to the complications faced by lawyers.

Consider the Canadian companies that operate several businesses: the real estate companies that own oil and gas assets; the retail store chains that carry on trucking operations. What threshold applies in such cases, when an excluded business is part of a larger business? $5 million? Or $150 million? Sometimes there is no easy legal answer. It depends on whether the "excluded business"—like the trucking operation of the retail store chain—can be categorized as a separate business.

Section 31 of the *IC Act* allows Ottawa to make such distinctions. If an indirect acquisition—which will not normally be reviewable after 1991—takes place, and one of the divisions of the Canadian company that is indirectly acquired is a transportation service with assets exceeding $5 million, Ottawa can "chop off" the transportation business and review its takeover.

But what if (conceptually speaking, of course) the transportation service is so intertwined with the main business that the transportation service cannot be considered to be a separate business? Then the issue becomes one of proportions. Is the transportation operation the major activity of the business or merely an insignificant and incidental part?

Drawing such fine distinctions is not easy. If Ottawa makes a mistake, or if the Americans believe Ottawa has, it will not be a simple matter for an arbitration panel appointed under the free trade dispute settlement mechanism to resolve.

(b) Right to Sell Freely

The second advantage to being an American is a greater freedom to sell. American owners can more easily sell their Canadian businesses to British and other third country investors because such sales are subject to review on the basis of the same thresholds that apply to American investors.[23]

This was another important goal of U.S. free trade negotiators. They wanted to ensure that Canada's foreign investment screen—if its existence was to continue—did not affect the marketability and sale price of American-controlled businesses in Canada. (The FTA therefore benefits U.S. buyers and U.S. sellers.)

To illustrate how this provision works, consider an Australian in 1992 buying a company in Canada with an asset value between $5 million and $150 million. If the seller is an American multinational, the Australian will not need Canadian government permission to close the deal (unless, of course, the target company is a transportation or other excluded business). But if the business is French-controlled or, for that matter, Canadian-controlled, then the Australian will require Ottawa's blessing to proceed (because the $5-million review threshold will have been exceeded). As some commentators have pointed out, this is one advantage that puts Americans seeking a foreign buyer in a better position than Canadians. (On the other hand, if the Canadian government continues to approve all takeovers, any "advantage" will be mostly theoretical.)

However, before foreigners close deals, blithely thinking that the higher thresholds apply because the seller is an American, they should note two points. First, the business must be "American-controlled". And secondly, because the word "control" for sale purposes is qualified by the word "ultimate" and excludes the "chain of control" rules in subsection 28(2) of the *IC Act*, it may be given a slightly different interpretation than when it is used elsewhere in the statute.

Section 14.1 spells out the difference:

---

[23] Para. 14.1(5)(b) of the *IC Act*. Also para. 2(b) of FTA Annex 1607.3. The increased thresholds for review benefit companies that are not "Americans" (e.g., a German-controlled company) but only when they are buying an American-controlled business in Canada.

"controlled by an American", with respect to a Canadian business, means, *notwithstanding subsection 28(2)*,

   (a) the *ultimate* direct or indirect control in fact by an American through the ownership of voting shares, or

   (b) the ownership by an American of all or substantially all of the assets used in carrying on the Canadian business. [Emphasis added.]

Why did the drafters of the FTA exclude subsection 28(2) of the *IC Act*—which lays down simple mathematical rules for determining when one corporation controls another—and create their own set of more complex rules? They obviously thought that mathematical formulae should not be a roadblock to reality. If an American controls a business, then regardless of his or her percentage interest, the American should benefit from the "freedom of sale" provision in the FTA.

   EXAMPLE: An American corporation owns 50% of a joint venture in Canada. The rest of the interests are widely-held. Does the American corporation control the joint venture for the purpose of the "freedom of sale" provision in the FTA?

Under the "chain of control" rules in subsection 28(2) of the *IC Act*, the American corporation would *not* control the joint venture because it does not own 51% of the voting interests. However, because these "chain of control" rules have been excluded, it may be possible to demonstrate that the American corporation controls with just 50%. Even with just 30%, the American corporation might be in control.

With so many concepts of control in the statute, the process of analysis becomes confusing (to say the least). The following questions should be asked:

Question	To Find the Answer
1. Is the vendor an "American"?	1. See the status rules.
2. Is the Canadian business "American-controlled"?	2. See the definition of "controlled by an American".
3. Will the foreign investor be acquiring control?	3. See the acquisition of control rules in subsection 28(3).

Three slightly different sets of rules on the meaning of control determine the answer to each question.

   EXAMPLE: A U.S. company carries on two businesses in Canada, one through an operating subsidiary, the other as a branch. (None of these businesses involve a transportation or other excluded business.) The U.S. company is widely-held and board-controlled and all its directors are Americans. In 1995, Korea's Samsung Co. buys the U.S. company and thus gains control of both Canadian businesses. Can Ottawa block the transaction?

Koreans and other foreigners who directly buy an American-controlled business in Canada benefit from the higher thresholds that apply to Americans. Similarly, since indirect acquisitions by Americans are not subject to review from 1992 onward, indirect acquisitions by Koreans and other foreigners of American-controlled subsidiaries in Canada are not subject to review either.

In the above-mentioned example, the U.S. company qualifies as an "American" under the status rules. Its two Canadian businesses are therefore "controlled by an American". Consequently, Ottawa cannot stop Samsung Co. from indirectly acquiring the U.S. company's subsidiary in Canada.

What about the indirect acquisition of the branch business? Since the day Investment Canada was established, the agency has had no jurisdiction over such transactions.

(c) Forced Sales and Canada's Buy-Back Obligation

Being an American carries a third advantage. A provision in the FTA states that Americans cannot be required, by reason of their nationality, to sell or otherwise dispose of their investments in Canada.[24] What does this mean? Ottawa cannot bring in any new policies (such as the "Baie Comeau policy" currently governing book publishing) which make the approval of a takeover conditional on the eventual sale of the business to Canadians.

There are exceptions. This prohibition against forced sales does not apply to the financial services[25] and transportation sectors, nor does it affect investments in Canada's cultural industries. However, there is a twist. If Canada orders an American investor to sell a cultural business that has been indirectly acquired through the purchase of its U.S. parent, the Canadian government must offer to purchase it ("Canada's buy-back obligation").

This obligation is found in clause 1607 of the FTA:

---

[24] FTA 1602(3) is directed at forced sales. A minimum equity requirement was not classified by the FTA negotiators as a "forced sale". Minimum equity requirements are dealt with in FTA 1602(2).

[25] Except for insurance services.

> In the event that Canada requires the divestiture of a business enterprise located in Canada in a cultural industry pursuant to its review of an indirect acquisition of such business enterprise by an investor of the United States of America, Canada shall offer to purchase the business enterprise from the investor of the United States of America at fair open market value, as determined by an independent, impartial assessment.

This clause will apply if an American investor buys (for example) the foreign parents of McGraw-Hill, Grolier Limited or Collier MacMillan Canada Ltd. (and if the minister responsible for Investment Canada requires the sale of the Canadian company as a condition of approval of the indirect takeover).[26] "Potentially all Canadian subsidiaries of foreign book publishers could be affected by Article 1607".[27]

The Association of American Publishers lobbied Washington hard for this provision. They wanted protection from being forced to sell a Canadian book publishing company at what might be a distress price, after it had been acquired in an indirect fashion.

Their concern arose out of the Canadian government's book publishing and distribution policy, better known as the Baie Comeau policy, which had been announced on July 6, 1985. It was directed at ensuring that Canada's book publishing and distribution industry remained under Canadian control.

According to this policy, the direct purchase of Canadian-controlled book publishing companies by foreign investors would not be approved (unless the purchase was by a joint venture with Canadian control). The policy also indicated that:

(1) direct acquisitions of Canadian-based but foreign-controlled book publishing companies, and

(2) the indirect acquisition of any Canadian-based book publishing companies,

would receive a green light if the foreign investor agreed to sell control of the Canadian company to Canadians at fair market value within two years.[28]

Because of the FTA, if an American indirectly acquires a publishing company—or, indeed, any cultural business, even a recording

---

[26] McGraw-Hill Ryerson Limited is owned by McGraw Hill Inc. (U.S.); Grolier Limited by Hachette S.A. (France); Collier Macmillan Canada Inc. by Maxwell Communications Corp. (U.K).

[27] KPMG Peat Marwick, "A Study of Valuation Issues, Acquisition Activity, and the Implications of the Free Trade Agreement with Respect to the Book Publishing Industry", (October 19, 1989), p. 5.2. This study was released under the *Access to Information Act*.

[28] Two examples of companies, the "control" of which was divested to Canadians as a result of the Baie Comeau policy, are Addison-Wesley Canada and Doubleday Canada.

studio—and Ottawa orders the American to give up control, the American has a ready buyer in the wings with a good price. That buyer is the government of Canada which must offer to buy the business at fair open market value.[29] (One government document states: "The Government of Canada should not necessarily be seen as the buyer, but rather as the guarantor of a purchase price reflecting a fair open market value".)[30]

This may be something more than fair market value. One of the two countries, it appears,[31] did not like that concept. Fair market value is what would be offered in a market that might be restricted by Canadian government policy to *Canadian* bidders.[32] Consequently, the free trade negotiators settled on "fair open market value". That is the price that could be obtained if *both* Canadians and foreign bidders could participate, and is to be determined by an independent impartial assessor. This assessor will presumably be provided with briefs by the Canadian government and the divesting U.S. parent company. The assessor will then determine the price at which the U.S. company's Canadian book publishing subsidiary or other cultural business will be purchased. By saddling the Canadian government with a cash

---

[29] FTA 1607(4).

[30] Interpretative note on article 1607, attached to a letter dated Feb. 8, 1988, written by Meriel Bradford, Trade Negotiations Office (released under the *Access to Information Act*).

[31] Fair market value is a concept used in thousands of commercial agreements. Obviously one of the parties at the free trade negotiations did not like that concept (maybe the Americans).

U.S. Trade Representative Clayton Yeutter told the president of the Association of American Publishers that fair open market value ("FOMV") "makes the U.S. investor whole". (Letter dated February 5, 1988, from Clayton Yeutter to Nicholas Veliotes; Mr. Veliotes gave a copy of this letter to the author of this book.) Yeutter evidently thought that an assessment based upon fair market value ("FMV") would not make the U.S. investor whole. (Fair open market value must therefore be equal to or greater than FMV.) In his letter, Mr. Yeutter also said that "despite the general exemption for cultural industries in the FTA, we succeeded in ameliorating a key irritant for U.S. investors in publishing and cultural industries, namely forced divestiture at fire sale prices". Mr. Yeutter then added, ". . . frankly we did not obtain everything we aimed for in this area". Joel Schacter, who was a consultant to the FTA negotiators, says in his book: "the word 'open' in FTA 1607.4 ensures that the price of the business will reflect its true value as if it were being sold voluntarily and at arm's length". R. Johnson and J. Schacter, *The Free Trade Agreement: A Comprehensive Guide*, (Aurora: Canada Law Book, 1988), p. 142.

[32] See the Canadian government's book publishing and distribution policy. Copies can be obtained by contacting Investment Canada or Communications Canada. Under this policy, foreign investors who buy foreign-controlled book publishing companies in Canada must sell them to Canadians at fair market value within two years.

outlay, Washington was hoping that "forced divestitures" would be less likely.[33]

Americans who buy the assets or shares of a cultural business directly, however, are in a different boat. Should they suffer the same fate, and be forced to sell, they are out of luck. Canada's buy-back obligation does not extend to direct acquisitions.[34]

Might this buy-back obligation cause the Canadian government to become the largest book publisher and producer of music recordings in Canada? That is unlikely. Subsection 24(2) of the *IC Act* gives Ottawa the authority not only to acquire but also to dispose of any cultural business.[35]

The most likely scenario is that the Canadian government will not make an offer until the American investor has been given an opportunity to sell in the private sector, although it is hard to imagine that the American investor will not at least demand an appraisal of the

---

[33] "Publishers Heartened by Administrative Assurances on Trade Pact", *Inside U.S. Trade*, Feb. 19, 1988. Referring to para. 1607(4) of the FTA, U.S. Trade Representative Clayton Yeutter said, ". . .this paragraph makes it highly unlikely that Canada will force divestiture of an indirect acquisition. Moreover, paragraph 4 applies to all cultural industries, not merely book publishing" (quote from the letter to Mr. Veliotes, mentioned in n. 31). Since 1985, Canada has forced only four U.S companies to sell their Canadian book publishing firms. U.S government concern may therefore have reflected the political influence of a few U.S. companies, rather than the number of businesses involved.

[34] FTA 1607(4). This is why subs. 24(2) of the *IC Act* refers to para. 28(1)(d)(ii), which makes it clear that the Canadian government's offer to buy only applies to indirect acquisitions. An indirect acquisition of a cultural business of any size may be reviewed by the government under s. 15 of the Act. An indirect acquisition will be automatically reviewed if the Canadian business has a book asset value of $50 million, or $5 million if the book asset value of the Canadian business is more than half the book asset value of the global transaction.

[35] Section 91 of the *Financial Administration Act* ("*FAA*") gives most Crown corporations the power to purchase a Canadian business with Governor in Council approval, so they do not need the additional legislative authority in subs. 24(2) of the *IC Act*. However, since s. 90 of the *FAA* restricts Her Majesty from acquiring shares of a business without the authority of Parliament, there was clearly a need for a power overriding s. 90 to be put in the *IC Act*. If the government wants a Crown corporation to make the purchase, the Governor in Council must designate the corporation as its agent. Had subs. 24 simply stated that any Crown corporation has the power to buy a cultural business, all Crown corporations (e.g., Canada Post) would have had an independent authority to buy cultural businesses. Perhaps this is why subs. 24(2) does not refer to all Crown corporations.

Subsection 24(2) uses the word "may" (a power) instead of "shall" (an obligation). However, the obligation of Canada to buy a cultural business that an American has indirectly acquired, and is forced to sell (and the method for determining the price) is set out in the Free Trade Agreement. The FTA has the force of law.

business, as provided for in the subsection, to see if more money can be obtained from Ottawa. Should the business' fair open market value exceed what was offered by a private buyer, the American investor would probably ask the Canadian government to pay the difference.[36]

Suppose no private buyer steps forward in time. In such circumstances the Canada Development Investment Corporation ("C.D.I.C.") may be chosen by Ottawa to buy the business (then sell it to Canadians).[37] The C.D.I.C., which was incorporated under the *CBCA* in 1982, and is wholly owned by Her Majesty in right of Canada, has purchased Canadian cultural businesses on government orders in the past.[38]

Curiously, the buy-back clause in subsection 24(2) in the *IC Act* merely refers to an obligation by Canada to purchase control. As everyone knows, a controlling interest can be acquired by purchasing substantially less than 100%, in fact, 51%. Might an American be left with a 49% interest?

Few Americans would want to become business partners with the Canadian government (although the Canadian government may be the best partner an American could have). However, Americans need not worry. The buy-back obligation in the FTA (Article 1607-4) makes no reference to control. Ottawa would therefore have to purchase the complete interest.

The FTA left a few issues unclear. At what point in time must fair open market value be determined? Also, if a foreign buyer is given a

---

[36] An independent assessment of "fair open market value" would be influenced by what a multinational company would be willing to pay. The value of the business to a private Canadian bidder might be somewhat less. If the "fair open market value" of a Canadian publishing company is $8 million, and a Canadian bidder offers $6 million, the Canadian government would have to pay $2 million to the American vendor.

[37] The sale of a publishing company may encounter some difficulties. Canadian book publishing companies, which are owned by foreign publishing companies, make much of their income by distributing the books of their parent company. In a parent-subsidiary relationship, the contract granting these distribution rights is usually for a short term (and is extended periodically). A Canadian might not want to buy the Canadian company unless its foreign parent granted long-term distribution rights for its (the foreign parent's) books. For this reason, Peat Marwick (see n. 27) suggests it is possible that a subsidiary may be unsaleable at any price.

[38] In May 1989, the C.D.I.C. announced it would purchase 51% of both Ginn and Co. (Canada) Ltd. and GLC Publishers Ltd. from U.S.-owned Gulf and Western Inc. The Canadian government, wanting to preserve its cultural policy, instructed C.D.I.C. to make the offer. The previous year, Ottawa had made an unsuccessful bid for Ginn and Co. (Canada). At that time, Ruth Hubbard, Investment Canada's executive vice-president, said the bid had been made "in the spirit of what had been negotiated under the FTA". Renate Lerch, "Ottawa's Offer for Publisher Rejected", *Financial Post*, Mar. 4, 1988, p.4.

period of time (two years under the Baie Comeau policy) to dispose of the business, precisely when must Canada buy the business? (One view is that Canada's obligation to buy crystallizes when the deadline for a sale arrives, which is also the time when fair open market value must be determined.)[39]

The date when value must be determined is important for another reason: it will affect the estimated valuation gap. That is the "gap between the price the Canadian government would (have to) pay for companies, and the selling price of the same businesses to a Canadian purchaser".[40]

It is reasonable to expect such a gap. Canada will be paying the price that could be obtained in a global market ("fair open market value") for the cultural business and selling in a market presumably restricted to Canadian purchasers. Also, the cultural business, after being severed from its U.S. parent, will be valued on a "stand alone" basis by potential Canadian purchasers. That value will reflect the loss of any synergies (economies of scale, merged distribution systems, greater access to foreign markets) that being connected to a large U.S. company might have brought.

Although their estimate seems unduly pessimistic, Peat Marwick believes the valuation gap could be as much as 50%. In its report prepared for Investment Canada, Peat Marwick states: ". . . we believe it would be prudent for the Government of Canada, in preparing its fiscal budgets, to provide a reserve for losses of 50% of what it pays for Canadian subsidiaries affected by article 1607 of the FTA".[41]

(d) The Move Towards National Treatment

U.S. investors whose transactions are subject to review benefit in a fourth way from the FTA. Unless they are purchasing a "sensitive business"—oil and gas, uranium, financial services, transportation, or a cultural business—Canada cannot demand from them a number of performance requirements.

---

[39] Under current government policy, foreign investors who *indirectly* acquire control of a Canadian book publishing and distribution company must sell control within two years (the "Baie Comeau policy"). Fair open market value would therefore be determined at the end of this two-year period, which is when the government would be obliged to buy the business. This would allow the American vendor time to find a Canadian buyer or partner.

[40] KPMG Peat Marwick, op. cit., n. 27, p. 1.1. This study was released under the *Access to Information Act* by Investment Canada after consultation with External Affairs Canada.

[41] Ibid., p.5.5.

This was another of the compromises between American demands that U.S. investors be treated like Canadians ("national treatment") and Ottawa's concern over foreign ownership. Instead of eliminating Investment Canada as the Americans had first insisted upon, the parties agreed to "grandfather" or keep existing laws, like the *Investment Canada Act*, which treat Canadians and Americans differently, provided that, in the case of the *IC Act*, there were fewer reviews, and a reduction in the number of possible commitments.[42]

This compromise, the U.S. concluded, would be sufficient to protect its investors. As long as Canada agreed to abide by the concept of national treatment in the future, by treating American companies like domestic ones when enacting new laws or policies, Canada could keep its foreign investment screen. At least any new rules would apply equally to both Canadian and American investors, and Canada could never reimpose discriminatory laws, like the National Energy Program, or reintroduce the tougher rules of FIRA days. (National treatment should not be confused with reciprocity. Had the FTA been based on the principle of reciprocity, Canada would have been obliged to treat American investors like the U.S. treats Canadian investors, and vice versa. By contrast, the principle of national treatment allows the laws in the two countries to differ.)

However, not all investors from south of the border are legally entitled to all the benefits of the FTA, for one strange reason. There are actually *two* definitions of a U.S. investor in the Free Trade Agreement.

One, the definition of an "American", is used to determine if the higher thresholds for review apply. The other definition, termed an "investor of a party", is found in the main body of the FTA.[43] Only an investor who is an "investor of a party" is entitled to the advantages of the FTA, such as the right to national treatment, and reduced performance requirements if an investment is reviewable.

These two definitions do not completely overlap. As a result, it is possible for a U.S. investor to be an "American" but not an "investor of a party", and therefore be entitled to the advantages of the higher thresholds, *but not* the reduced performance requirements.

---

[42] The degree of discrimination between American and ·Canadian investors is frozen as of Jan. 1, 1989 (FTA 1607). This prevents Canada from amending the *IC Act* (even if the amendment is just of a technical nature) if the amendment slightly reduces the rights of Americans. The Canadian government's policies governing takeovers in the oil and gas and book publishing sectors are also exempted from the FTA's requirements of national treatment. (Note the definition of "measure" in FTA 1607.)

[43] FTA 1611.

This possibility, however, is of more academic than practical significance. The Canadian government has indicated (in its "Guidelines Under the Free Trade Agreement") that in those rare instances where a U.S. investor qualifies as an "American" but not an "investor of a party", the Canadian government will ignore the distinction. In other words, Ottawa will not exercise its right to impose trade-related performance requirements that would otherwise be excluded by the FTA.

(i) Reduced Performance Requirements

For U.S. investors who qualify, there are four types of performance requirements that they need never give (unless they are making a reviewable investment in one of the five exempt business sectors like transportation):

1. Export commitments: to export a given quantity or percentage of their Canadian production of goods or services.
2. Import substitution commitments: to substitute Canadian goods or services for imported goods and services.
3. Sourcing commitments: to purchase Canadian goods or services instead of imports or to accord a preference to Canadian goods and services.
4. Domestic content commitments: to achieve a given level or percentage of Canadian content in the final value of a product by purchasing Canadian-produced goods and services ("local content requirements").[44]

Reducing trade-related performance requirements was a goal about which American negotiators were especially keen. The U.S. administration wanted to stop its nationals from giving export, domestic content and other commitments which, in its view, were distorting trade patterns, creating unemployment in the U.S., and harming American industry.

The U.S. knew that Investment Canada (unlike FIRA) was asking for few commitments from American investors. However, the U.S. wanted to stop *all* countries from imposing trade-related performance requirements. Preventing Canada from imposing such requirements in the future was just one step towards this objective.

The U.S. was so insistent on this point because of its enormous trade deficit. When countries require a foreign company, as a condition of establishing a business, to purchase some components domestically ("local content requirements"), imports from third countries

---

[44] FTA 1603. These "special rules" that apply as a consequence of the FTA are restated in the "Guidelines Under the Free Trade Agreement" (written by the author) and issued by the minister responsible for Investment Canada. These guidelines can be found in the consolidated edition of the Act.

(such as from the U.S.) may be reduced. A stipulation by other countries that a certain proportion of a company's output be exported can also damage U.S. trade. The effect of such performance requirements is to shift the benefits of investment across national borders, thereby transferring unemployment from one nation to another (e.g., to the U.S.).

The U.S. presented the same arguments at the Uruguay round of GATT. Trade-related performance requirements, the U.S. maintained, were similar to quotas, which restrict imports and force goods to be exported regardless of price. When a country, such as Brazil, India or Mexico demands that a foreign company purchase locally all of the components that add value to its product, that is equivalent to a zero import quota. According to the U.S., such requirements are like quotas in another way. They are contrary to the principles of GATT (non-discrimination among trading nations).

Even though Canada, because of an adverse GATT panel ruling in 1983, had long ceased demanding strict sourcing commitments, it appears the U.S. still wanted a provision in the FTA dealing with that aspect. The GATT panel decision was not legally binding on Canada and in any event did not cover services.

Critics in Canada viewed the matter through different glasses. With trade-related performance requirements gone, the critics complained, Canada could no longer force U.S. subsidiaries to pursue important Canadian economic goals, such as increased Canadian exports or greater use of Canadian parts and components.

The FTA states that Ottawa cannot "impose" any of the four trade-related commitments. It also cannot "enforce" them if such commitments are voluntarily given. Should an American put a prohibited commitment in a business plan, obtain Canadian government approval to his investment plans, and then promptly default on that commitment, Canada can bring neither an action for specific performance nor divestiture.[45]

But what about similar commitments of an exhortatory nature? For instance, since the adverse GATT panel ruling against stringent sourcing commitments in 1983, Canada has been asking some investors to give Canadian suppliers "a full and fair opportunity to participate on a competitive basis in the supply of goods and services to the

---

[45] FTA 1603(2) and (3). Since such performance undertakings cannot be enforced even if voluntarily given, they would probably not be considered by the minister in determining whether a takeover is of net benefit to Canada. Unless an American can establish net benefit in another fashion, the FTA could, paradoxically, put U.S. investors at a theoretical disadvantage in comparison with other foreign investors.

Canadian business".[46] Commitments like this still appear to be possible in the era of free trade.

(ii) Equity and Reinvestment Commitments

Two other types of commitments that Americans need not give are:

5. Equity commitments.[47]

6. Commitments to reinvest profits in Canada.[48]

An equity commitment is an undertaking to sell a minority equity interest in a business to Canadians. Since the early days of FIRA, these commitments have been fulfilled by the foreign investor floating shares in its Canadian subsidiary to the Canadian public or by locating a Canadian partner.

Because of FTA 1602, Ottawa cannot insist upon minimum Canadian ownership in a Canadian business being purchased by an American investor. (A few sectors, such as oil and gas, uranium and cultural business have been exempted from this provision.) An American wanting to take over a steel company in Canada, such as Dofasco, can own 100% of it.

This is another minor irritant to the FTA critics. Minority Canadian shareholder participation in major U.S. subsidiaries, they insist, gives Canadians some influence over decisions made in U.S. corporate head offices. FTA defenders reply that Canadians can still buy shares in U.S. parent companies. Moreover, Canada's past practice has been to focus on securing commitments for Canadian equity participation in the cultural and resource industries. That is still permitted under the FTA.

The imposition of commitments to reinvest in Canada is also forbidden. That would be contrary to one of the pillars of the FTA: the freedom to repatriate profits, royalties, interest, and other earnings. Why is such a provision in the FTA? Neither Canada nor the U.S. has ever imposed restrictions on the remittances of earnings.

---

[46] A few years after FIRA (1974–85) was set up, U.S. government officials began voicing objections to commitments given by U.S. investors to purchase Canadian goods, export a specific quantity of production, or manufacture in Canada goods which would otherwise be imported. In 1983, a GATT panel upheld Canada's right to impose export commitments, but said Canada was acting contrary to GATT when it tried to force investors to use Canadian-manufactured goods regardless of price and other considerations.

[47] FTA 1602(3).

[48] FTA 1606.

Both countries obviously wanted to ensure that such restrictions were not imposed in the future. In addition, the U.S. apparently wanted a "freedom to repatriate profits" provision in the FTA as part of its campaign against "trade-distorting performance requirements" imposed by other countries.[49] Some countries, especially in the Third World, prevent foreign companies from repatriating earnings unless these companies meet specified import substitution or export targets. That in turn affects U.S. and world trade.

One consequence is that if an American corporation buys a Canadian business, Ottawa cannot demand, as a condition of approval, that a certain amount out of profit be reinvested in Canada. Likewise, Ottawa cannot ask for or enforce an undertaking that a newly acquired Canadian company will not send dividends back to its U.S. parent for five years (or some other period of time).

Does the "freedom to repatriate profits" provision also bar commitments to spend a sum of money—if the commitments are not directly tied to future profits? That interesting possibility may still be open.

One intriguing feature of the FTA affects the obligations of investors outside North America. Ottawa cannot impose export, substitution, sourcing and domestic content commitments on an investor from a third country if such a commitment will have a significant impact on Canada-U.S. trade.[50]

That does not preclude Canada from demanding that a French company, buying a Canadian business, give a pledge to cause the Canadian business to export to the U.S. or world-wide; the adjective "significant", which qualifies the word "impact", allows for some flexibility in this regard. But if the U.S. considers that the outcome will be significant, it can invoke the disputes settlement mechanism.

Should such a disagreement come before an arbitration panel, the U.S. would have to show—not that the export commitment from the French company would definitely affect Canada-U.S. trade—but that

---

[49] U.S. views are clearly expressed in the speeches of U.S. delegates to the Uruguay round of GATT. The bilateral investment treaties, which the U.S. has negotiated with a number of countries, also contains a "freedom to repatriate profits" clause.

[50] FTA 1603(2). "Investment Canada negotiates commitments or 'undertakings' with foreign investors in approximately 11% of the cases it reviews. The agency does not negotiate undertakings relating to local content. As the FTA prohibits the use of export requirements, Investment Canada does not negotiate undertakings relating to export requirements in connection with acquisitions by U.S. investors. For non-U.S. investors, the agency only rarely negotiates undertakings relating to export requirements." (Untitled document released under the *Access to Information Act* in 1991.)

it *may* do so. In other words, the onus would be on the United States to prove its case on a balance of probabilities (not beyond a reasonable doubt).

(iii) Permitted Commitments

Are there any commitments that Ottawa can still impose on American investors? Actually, there are quite a few, including commitments related to:

(1) world product mandates (however, since export commitments are prohibited, an American investor cannot be required to export a minimum percentage, quantity or value of production);

(2) research and development;

(3) technology transfer;

(4) employment and the use of Canadian employees (because of FTA 1603(c), Canada cannot demand that "independent contractors" used by an American investor be Canadians);

(5) improvements in productivity;

(6) new investment.

The U.S. probably agreed to exclude such commitments from the list of prohibited performance requirements because they are not directly "trade-distorting". Nevertheless, Canada's ability to demand such commitments constitutes a departure from the general principle of national treatment granted to Americans.[51]

(iv) Forced Sales

One restriction on Canada has already been referred to—no forced sales. Except for the financial service, cultural and transportation sectors, Ottawa cannot issue an approval conditional on an American selling the Canadian business in a few years. If Ottawa is insistent on Canadians owning a particular business, it has just one option: refuse to approve the takeover.

Forced sales are still possible for other reasons. An American breaching the *IC Act* can be forced to sell the Canadian business that

---

[51]The FTA applies only to business enterprises. This allows the provinces to discriminate against Americans who buy cottage property. On the other hand, although a farm is a business, Saskatchewan's law restricting foreign ownership of farms remains enforceable because it predated the FTA. (The obligation to accord national treatment to Americans covers future, not existing laws. But non-conforming laws that predate the FTA cannot be made more restrictive.)

was acquired. The *Competition Act* can also be used to compel divestiture. Competition policy is non-discriminatory and thus does not violate the principle of national treatment.

One point not well understood by Americans, is how the FTA affects existing commitments. Since 1974, when FIRA was born, Americans have been giving plans and promises to the Canadian government. There is now quite a collection. Most have been met or are outdated but some are awaiting fulfilment.

In the minds of certain American business people, the FTA prevents Canada from enforcing any of the prohibited undertakings—such as export commitments—listed in the FTA. That is incorrect. The FTA applies to contractual commitments given after the FTA came into force (January 1, 1989). Those submitted in the past remain enforceable.[52]

3. Excluded Businesses

Five key businesses are (partially or totally) excluded from the investment chapter of the FTA.[53] These are oil and gas, and uranium businesses, cultural businesses, financial service businesses (except for insurance services), and transportation businesses.

The higher thresholds do not apply to takeovers of these businesses. Neither does the ban on Ottawa imposing trade-related performance requirements (and certain other commitments) prior to approving a takeover.

However, not all operations within these business sectors are "protected". If the definitions are examined, it will be seen that, although Canada protected what it thought was essential, the excluded business sectors are actually smaller than they appear to be.

That is a point many American investors are unaware of. How these five excluded business sectors are defined (and the impact of the FTA on these sectors) is therefore examined below.

---

[52] FTA 1603 lists four prohibited undertakings which cannot be "imposed" on an investor. However, enforcing an undertaking given before the FTA came into effect is not "imposing" it. (See FTA 1603-3 which refers to undertakings given after the agreement came into force.) A second argument that might buttress Canada's case would be that FTA 1607 "grandfathers" existing measures. "Measure" is defined to include a requirement. The argument would be that existing performance requirements are measures, which are grandfathered.

[53] The investment chapter is Chapter 16. See articles 1601, 2005 and Annex 1607.3 for details about the exclusions.

(a) Oil, Gas and Uranium Businesses

The FTA "grandfathered" (a fancy name for "kept") Canada's published policies on non-resident ownership in the oil, gas and uranium-mining industries.[54] These policies are set out in an exchange of letters between Canada and the U.S.

Briefly, these letters state that takeovers of healthy Canadian-controlled oil and gas companies with assets of $5 million or more will not be approved. However, the purchase of the same companies, if they are in financial difficulty, may be permitted and the direct or indirect acquisition of foreign-controlled companies will normally be permitted.

The ban against Ottawa imposing minimum equity (FTA 1602-2) and "trade-distorting performance requirements" (FTA 1603) does not apply to these businesses. Consequently, Ottawa can make its approval of a takeover contingent upon an American purchaser selling a minority equity interest to Canadians.

On the other hand, Ottawa cannot force the sale of either a controlling interest or part of an oil and gas business ("an asset sale"). The FTA does not permit policies of forced divestiture (FTA 1602-3).[55] This is a significant restriction. Prior to the FTA, an American buying a Canadian oil and gas company might offer to sell either a major portion of the shares or certain assets to Canadians.[56]

Could an American voluntarily undertake to sell assets as a condition of approval? There is nothing in the FTA prohibiting the voluntary acceptance of such undertakings, but there may be a question (in light of FTA 1602-3) about their enforceability. The FTA also prohibits undertakings requiring the reinvestment of earnings or profits (FTA 1606-1). However, Ottawa's policy of extracting commitments to reinvest a certain amount out of profit (or a percentage of cash flow) in further exploration and development of oil and gas properties was grandfathered (retained) by the FTA.[57]

---

[54] FTA Annex 1607.3(4) and subs. 14.1(8) of the *IC Act*.

[55] Why can there be no forced divestiture (the sale of a controlling interest) in the oil, gas and uranium-mining sectors? Because FTA 1602(3) is not among the exclusions listed in FTA Annex 1607.3 (4).

[56] For instance, in February 1985, Chevron undertook to sell its 60% controlling interest in Gulf Canada to a Canadian at a fair price. On May 23, 1985, the government of Canada announced that Olympia & York had bought Chevron's interest.

[57] FTA 1606 provides for the free flow of dividends and the repatriation of earnings. FTA 1607.3 (4) excludes the oil, gas and uranium industries from the provisions of the FTA that deal with thresholds, performance commitments and minimum equity

Of what significance is this? In 1987, Ottawa approved Amoco's takeover of Dome Petroleum. In return, Amoco Canada agreed to offer 20% of its equity to Canadians, spend $2.5 billion on exploration and development in Canada, and not send any dividends back to its U.S. parent for five years.[58] American oil and gas companies can still be required to give similar commitments today.

To qualify as an exempt business, it is not sufficient for a company to own proven oil or gas reserves. The company must also be engaged in activities involving development or production. This is because of the combined ownership and activity test that Ottawa used to define an oil and gas business.[59]

Canadian government officials chose this two-cylinder definition because they wanted to review only the acquisition of producing properties. Purchases and sales of other types of properties, they obviously thought, should be encouraged since the government's policy was to promote investment.

Some Canadians, whose holding companies own "passive" interests in oil and gas properties, are probably pleased by that choice. Their holding companies are more marketable and, therefore, worth more since they can be sold to Americans without restriction. (Arguably, there has been no change in the law. The term "business" in the *IC Act* contains an implication of activity. A pure holding company is inactive and can be bought and sold outside the framework of the statute.)

A similar ownership/activity test has been used in defining exempt uranium businesses. The takeover of a business that owns an interest in an uranium property *and* is engaged in the production of uranium continues to be governed by the $5-million (direct acquisitions) and $50-million (indirect acquisitions) thresholds for review.

This double-headed test makes it clear that an American in 1992 need not obtain Canadian government approval before buying a uranium exploration business with proven but undeveloped reserves that

---

commitments. FTA 1606 is not referred to in this exclusion. However, the letters exchanged between the Canadian and U.S. governments indicate that reinvestment commitments can still be imposed. (For an example of commitments extracted in the past, see "Good Deal Gained from Amoco", *Calgary Herald*, Dec. 27, 1987, p.D4.)

[58] Kevin Cox, "Investment Canada Backs Proposed Amoco-Dome Deal", *The Globe and Mail*, Dec. 22, 1987, p. B3.

[59] A legal reason for having a combined activity and ownership test is that the mere ownership of proven reserves is not enough to make a company a "Canadian business" within the meaning of the *IC Act*. A practical reason is that, without a combined test, it would be difficult to sever oil and gas businesses from other businesses.

have a book value below $150 million.[60] But that does not mean a U.S. buyer can get around Canada's uranium policy, limiting non-resident ownership to 49% at the production stage. Ottawa can still enforce that policy by refusing to grant an export permit.

(b) Financial Service Businesses

Laws and policies affecting businesses that provide financial services (other than insurance services) have been excluded from the investment chapter of the FTA. This means that an American who wishes to buy a business in Canada's financial sector must abide by the $5-million and $50-million thresholds for direct and indirect acquisitions respectively. In addition, Canada can impose trade-related performance requirements. However, this exclusion is largely irrelevant, since other legislation governs the acquisition of many businesses in this sector.

For instance, the *Bank Act*, not the *IC Act*, governs the acquisition of banks. Under the *Bank Act*, no individual (resident or non-resident) can own more than 10% of a Schedule I bank's shares.

As for federally regulated Canadian-controlled loan, trust and insurance companies, foreigners have been prohibited in the past from acquiring such companies by the "10/25" rule. This rule prevents any single non-resident from buying more than 10% of the shares of these companies. Total non-resident ownership is limited to 25%.

U.S. residents (firms and nationals) have been exempted from this rule by the FTA. In theory, this means that Investment Canada could review the acquisition by U.S. investors of federally regulated loan, trust and insurance companies (if a company's book asset value exceeds the review threshold). However, proposed new legislation governing loan and trust companies is presently before Parliament. The legislation states that all takeovers of loan and trust companies require the approval of the Minister of Finance. Before it is passed, this legislation may be amended to oust the jurisdiction of Investment Canada when a U.S. resident is the purchaser.

The financial sector takeovers that Investment Canada normally reviews are mainly the takeovers of financial service businesses that grant credit and finance instalment sales. Some examples are pawn

---

[60] If a company explores for uranium, but has no interest in a producing property, does the *IC Act* even apply? Probably not. The company does not have a "business" as defined in the Act. (When the Act was being drafted, the government apparently did not want to restrict foreign ownership in companies that were merely exploring for minerals, and oil and gas.)

brokerage operations, cheque cashing services, the financial service arms of automobile manufacturers, and the credit granting businesses of department stores (like Sears), provided their book asset value exceeds $5 million.[61]

Businesses engaged in the underwriting and selling of insurance policies have not been excluded from the investment chapter of the FTA. This means that the higher thresholds apply and Ottawa cannot impose the four prohibited types of performance requirements.

(c) Transportation Service

Transportation services are the fourth category of excluded businesses. Consequently, small Canadian transportation companies (airlines, trucking firms, rail, bus and marine transport companies) remain protected by the $5-million and $50-million review fence.

Are tour boat operations or pipelines "transportation services"? There is no definition in the *IC Act*. The Governor in Council can define the term through regulations, but has not done so.

The exclusion of transportation services from the investment chapter of the FTA was not done to preserve the review mechanism in the *National Transportation Act* ("*NTA*"). Like the *Competition Act*, the *NTA* applies to Canadians and foreign purchasers and is therefore non-discriminatory in nature.

(d) Cultural Businesses

Culture was the most politically sensitive topic for the Canadian government during the free trade negotiations. At the time, foreign books and periodicals accounted for 84% and 71% of Canada's domestic market share. Almost 98% of films shown in Canada were foreign imports. In the area of sound recordings (vinyl records, prerecorded tapes, compact discs), ten foreign-controlled firms (e.g., WEA Music, A & M Records) accounted for 90% of the industry's revenue. The Canadian public and the media were clearly worried that closer commercial ties with the U.S. would further threaten Canada's cultural identity and uniqueness.

Supporters of free trade were equally concerned that if culture was not excluded from the agreement, Canada's attempt to get secure

---

[61] The Canadian government may conceivably have excluded a few American takeovers of these businesses from the $5- million thresholds as well. How? The definition of "financial services" in the *IC Act* refers to services provided by financial institutions. See subs. 14.1(9).

access to U.S. markets would be jeopardized. They were aware that the Laurier government had negotiated a draft agreement with the U.S. in 1911 for the reciprocal lowering/elimination of tariffs, then lost the ensuing election. Part of the reason for Laurier's defeat was the fear of Canadians that they would lose their cultural, economic and political sovereignty.

Before they could exempt culture from the FTA, however, Canadian and American negotiators had to define it. Was culture merely a nation's music, literature, artwork, and forms of dance? That is what some Americans thought. They could not understand why the Canadians wanted the sale of video cassettes or foreign magazines to be classified as "cultural businesses". Finally, however, U.S. negotiators conceded the point and agreed to the following categories:

(1) the publication, distribution or sale of books, magazines, periodicals or newspapers in print or machine readable form, other than the sole activity of printing or typesetting of books, magazines, periodicals or newspapers;

(2) the production, distribution, sale or exhibition of film or video recordings;

(3) the production, distribution, sale or exhibition of audio or video music recordings;

(4) the publication, distribution or sale of music in print or machine readable form; or

(5) radio communication in which the transmissions are intended for direct reception by the general public, any radio, television and cable television broadcasting undertakings and any satellite programming and broadcasting network services.[62]

Americans who purchase a business involved in one of these activities face an automatic review at the usual $5-million and $50-million thresholds. In addition, Ottawa has the option (under section 15 of the Act) of reviewing the establishment or takeover of cultural businesses under that size.

---

[62] This list of cultural businesses is in the FTA 2012. An almost identical list appears in the regulations to the *IC Act* and applies to other foreign investors. Can Ottawa further protect Canadian culture by adding an Eskimo carving business to the list in the regulations? It can do so, but the new category will only affect third country investors, not Americans. This is because what is culture, and therefore exempt from the FTA, is defined in the FTA. An Eskimo carving business is not mentioned in the FTA. In addition, although FTA 1607 grandfathers the *IC Act*, the *IC Act* cannot be made more restrictive.

Investment Canada gets no cases in the radio communications area because they are dealt with under the *Broadcasting Act*.

Printing and typesetting *per se* are not cultural activities. A company that prints books and newspapers under contract for several publishers can therefore be sold to an American without Canadian government permission (unless the company is very large). Will this console an American who is barred from purchasing a Canadian publishing company? At least the American can still do the company's typesetting.

If Canada introduces new legislation to protect its cultural industries, the Americans can retaliate with measures of equivalent commercial effect (if the legislation would have violated the FTA had culture not been exempt). This worries some Canadians. Might the U.S. retaliate by placing a duty on an unrelated industry, such as Canadian fish exports? Despite this possibility, the United States' power of retaliation (in clause 2005 of the FTA) actually leaves Canada in a better position than in pre-FTA days. Back then, there was no limit to possible U.S retaliation. Moreover, the U.S. cannot retaliate against the "Baie Comeau policy" on book publishing since that policy predates free trade.

4. The Dispute Settlement Mechanism

The FTA offers major financial advantages to qualifying companies. It also uses obscure language. This explosive mixture provides fertile ground for disputes.

Altercations may spring from many sources. Is an investor an "American"? Is Ottawa misapplying the oil and gas policy? Are prohibited commitments being imposed in a different form? Has a business activity been improperly categorized as a transportation service?

A general dispute settlement mechanism has been set up to resolve quarrels over the interpretation of the FTA. Known as the Canada-United States Trade Commission, it is sometimes referred to as a tribunal, although it is not a court. If a dispute arises, the U.S. or Canadian governments may request consultation with each other. Thereafter either party may apply to the commission to resolve the dispute.

If the commission is unsuccessful in its mediation efforts, either government may request that the issue be heard by a panel of experts, whose decision is not binding. Alternatively, if all members of the commission are in agreement, a dispute may be referred to a five-member arbitration panel for a binding ruling. (The U.S. apparently wanted compulsory arbitration of all investment disputes, but did not achieve that goal.)

One matter can never be challenged before the commission: a decision by the minister responsible for Investment Canada not to approve an investment by an American. However, all other contentious issues arising from the investment chapter of the FTA may be brought to the commission for a hearing.

This dispute settlement mechanism operates on a government-to-government basis. Private parties have no rights. If a U.S. company is angry because Canada has refused to categorize it as an "American", it must petition the U.S. government (under section 301 of the Trade Act of 1974) to commence an inquiry.

Will U.S. government action depend upon the merits of the case or the company's political clout in Washington? That remains to be seen. However, one advantage of this government-initiated procedure is that there are no costs to the private parties involved.

Appendix A

"Investor of a Party"

There is a distinction in the FTA between an "American" and an "investor of a party".[63] An "American" benefits from the higher thresholds for review. An "investor of a party" is entitled to the "other advantages" of the FTA.

These "other advantages" include the provision that prevents Canada from imposing trade-related performance requirements as a condition of approving an investment. An "investor of a party" is also entitled to national treatment (that is, to the same treatment as Canadians under future laws and policies when establishing, buying, operating or selling a business).

These two definitions do not completely overlap. In exceptional circumstances, an investor may be an "American", but not an "investor of a party". In such circumstances, Canada has the right to impose otherwise prohibited performance requirements.

Ottawa has indicated it will not do this. However, investors may still want to know what their precise legal rights are. The chart that follows explains how the two terms differ.

---

[63] The acquisition rules in the FTA (see the definition of "acquisition") also differ from those in s. 28 of the *IC Act*. The FTA refers to the acquisition of "ultimate direct or indirect control" while the *IC Act* relies on percentage-based rules. In addition, the FTA definition includes leasehold interests; the *IC Act* does not. However, this should cause no anomalies since the FTA definition is broader than its IC equivalent, and therefore any acquisition under the *IC Act* would also be an acquisition for the purpose of the FTA (and the provision covering performance requirements). Under the FTA (unlike the *IC Act*), an "acquisition" may occur if an American acquires less than a one-third interest.

American	*Investor of a Party*
"American" is a term used in the *IC Act* and the FTA.	"Investor of a Party" appears in the main body of the FTA. It is referred to in the "Guidelines on Administrative Procedures" issued under the *IC Act*.
Test: (1) An ownership test is used except when a company is widely-held, in which case there is a board control test; (2) uses the expression "control in fact through ownership of voting interests".	*Test:* (1) An ownership test is used throughout; (2) uses the expression "ultimate direct or indirect control in fact . . . through the ownership of voting interests".
Consistency: Identical with "Investor of a Party" except if a company is widely-held. However, if the courts interpret "ultimate control" in a different fashion from "control in fact" the two definitions will diverge in other ways.	*Consistency:* Identical with "American" except if a company is widely-held. However, if the courts interpret "ultimate control" in a different fashion from "control in fact" the two definitions will diverge in other ways.
Differences: A widely-held company (not controlled by its shareholders) is an American if two thirds of its directors are Americans, or if two thirds of its directors are Americans and Canadians.	*Differences:* The same company is not an "investor of a party" unless 51% of its shares are owned by Americans. Accordingly, a company may be an American but not an investor of a party. (For technical reasons, the reverse is not possible).
Implications: Americans benefit from the higher thresholds.	*Implications:* In theory Canada could impose prohibited performance requirements on an American that does not qualify as an "investor of a party".

EXAMPLE: Americans own 49% of a widely held board-controlled company and make up two thirds of its board. British citizens own the remaining 51%.

Since a majority of the voting equity is owned by British citizens and the definition of "an investor of a party" does not recognize board control, the company is an "American" but not an "investor of a party".

The Rationale: Whey did the free trade negotiators use two slightly different definitions for "American" and "investor of a party"? Simple majority ownership, they obviously thought, not a board test, should determine whether a widely held company like IBM can benefit from the FTA.

Also, they were stuck with the concept of "control in fact" (already in the *IC Act*). Consequently, this concept had to be used in defining an "American". However, the negotiators apparently thought that disagreement might arise over what factors should be looked at, in addition to the share register, when assessing where "control in fact" lies. Accordingly, when drafting the definition of an "investor of a party", which was to govern the main portion of the investment chapter of the FTA, they chose to word the definition in a slightly different fashion.

The Investor of a Party Test: How does a solicitor determine if a corporation is an "investor of a party"? He or she begins by asking two questions:

1. What does the phrase "ultimately controlled directly or indirectly through the ownership of voting interests" mean? (What facts do you look at?)

2. Is the corporation ultimately controlled by its shareholders or by its board of directors?

With respect to the first question, there exists a mountain of decisions on the meaning of "control" in other statutes. In most of these cases, the courts stress that the search is for *de jure* control (the person or group who has a majority of votes that can be used for the election of directors). The expression "ultimate control" in the FTA suggests that the search may be broader when that agreement is being interpreted. If, for instance, one class of shares has the right to elect the directors and another class has the power to do everything else, including the dismissal of the directors, ultimate control may lie with the holders of the second class of shares. In other words, "ultimate control" may refer to the power to control all events of significance at general meetings, rather than just the election of directors.

The phrase "ultimate control" is further modified by the words "direct or indirect". This is simply another way of stating that direct share ownership is not the only basis of control. Control can be indirect if a party owns shares in a corporation which in turn owns shares in another corporation.[64]

---

[64] In *Rochester Telephone Corp. v. U.S.*, 23 F. Supp. 634, a judge stated that "broadly used, 'control' may embrace every form of control, actual or legal, direct or indirect, negative or affirmative". In that case, no vote of shareholders could be effective unless concurred in by 80% of the common stock. This gave negative control to a shareholder with one third of the voting stock. This decision was upheld by the U.S. Supreme Court:

Are there any exceptions to the ownership test? Might the location of *de jure* control be affected by shareholders' agreements (or trust agreements) that restrict the freedom of shareholders to vote as they please, or impose special quorum or voting requirements? This is a grey area. Some cases dealing with other statutes suggest that shareholders (and trust) agreements are immaterial.[65]

Shareholder-Controlled Companies: If the corporation is shareholder-controlled, the next question is:

3. Are the controllers

    (a) U.S. nationals;

    (b) a U.S. federal, state or local government or its agencies; or

    (c) a board-controlled company (or other entity not controlled through its voting interests) that is majority-owned by U.S. nationals. (See the discussion below.)

EXAMPLE (Shareholder Control): The shares of Eagle Company are owned by many Americans, who collectively hold 60%. However, Japan's Mitsubishi Corp. controls the company with 40%. Is Eagle Company an "investor of a party"?

Although it may be politically difficult for Americans to swallow, Eagle Company is not an investor of a party, despite 60% American ownership, because it is controlled in Japan. (The country of incorporation is not a factor when there is shareholder control.)

Board-Controlled Companies: If a corporation is controlled by its board of directors (because its shares are widely-held), a straight majority ownership test applies.[66] To ascertain if the company is an "investor of a party", a solicitor must ask another question:

Are the majority of the shares of the board-controlled company owned by:

    (a) U.S. nationals;

    (b) a U.S. (federal/state/local) government or its agencies; or

    (c) a company (or other entity) *incorporated* (or constituted) *in the U.S.*:

---

307 U.S. 125.

[65] Two articles discussing the concept of control for income tax purposes are: David Matheson, "Corporate Control Concepts and Tax Reform" (1972), 20 *Can. Tax J.*, 1, at 45; Richard Miner, *Associated Corporations*, (Toronto: Carswell, 1983).

[66] A straight majority test only applies if a company (partnership, trust or joint venture) is *not* controlled through its "voting shares" (or "voting interests"). A company that is controlled by its Korean shareholders is not an "American" even if individual American shareholders own 51% or more.

(i) that *carries on business in the U.S.* (this requirement does not apply to holding companies that do not carry on business anywhere),

(ii) that is not controlled by nationals of a third country,

(iii) in which nationals of third countries do not own a majority of the voting interests.

Should the corporation be publicly traded, the nationality of individual shareholders owning less than a 1% interest may be determined from their street addresses.

EXAMPLE (Board of Director Control):

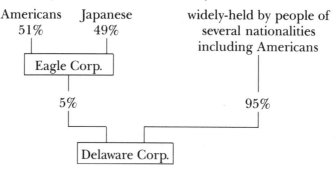

Americans   Japanese   widely-held by people of
51%   49%   several nationalities
                               including Americans

Eagle Corp.

5%   95%

Delaware Corp.

Consider the facts presented in the above diagram. Imagine that you are a lawyer who must determine if Delaware Corp., which is board-controlled, is majority-owned by Americans. Should Eagle Corp.'s 5% interest be added to the total American interest?

This depends on whether Eagle Corp. is U.S.-controlled. If Eagle Corp. is a holding company and incorporated in the U.S., it will be presumed to be a U.S.-controlled shareholder. If instead, Eagle Corp. is an operating company, it must also carry on business in the U.S. ("U.S. situs") for this presumption to apply.

The presumption that Eagle Corp. is a U.S. shareholder of Delaware Corp. arises as soon as the Americans have established U.S. incorporation and U.S. situs. If Canada disagrees with this outcome, Canada would have to rebut the presumption by demonstrating:

(1) that Eagle Corp. is controlled by the Japanese, or

(2) that the Japanese have a majority interest in Eagle Corp.

If Canada cannot rebut the presumption, is Eagle Corp.'s 5% interest partitioned (to take into account the 49% Japanese interest)? No. Eagle Corp.'s entire 5% interest is added to the shares held by other Americans to determine if Americans have a majority interest in Delaware Corp.

Appendix B

American Status Rules for Corporations and Other Entities[67]

1. If one American or two or more American members of a voting group own a majority of the voting interests of an entity, it is American-controlled.

2. If one non-Canadian, other than an American, or two or more members of a voting group who are non-Canadians other than Americans, own a majority of the voting interests of an entity, it is *not* American-controlled.

3. If Americans own a majority of the voting interests of an entity, it is an American-controlled entity if it can be established that the entity is not controlled in fact through the ownership of voting interests by one non-Canadian, other than an American, or by a voting group in which non-Canadians, other than Americans, own one half or more of the voting interests owned by the voting group.

4. If less than a majority of the voting interests of an entity are owned by Americans, it is presumed *not* to be an American-controlled entity unless it can be established that:

   • the entity is controlled in fact through the ownership of voting interests by one American or by a voting group in which Americans hold a majority of the voting interests owned by the voting group, or

   • in the case of a corporation or limited partnership, the entity is not controlled in fact through the ownership of voting interests and Americans comprise two thirds of:

     • its board of directors, in the case of a corporation,

     • its general partners, in the case of a limited partnership.

5. If it can be established that a trust is not controlled in fact through the ownership of its voting interests, the trust is an American-controlled entity if two thirds of its trustees are Americans.

6. If two persons, one being a Canadian and the other being an American, own equally all voting shares of a corporation, the corporation is deemed to be American-controlled.

Note: There is a special rule for board-controlled companies, in which American shareholders have a minority interest, if two thirds of

---

[67] Subss. 14.1(10), 26(1) and (2).

the company directors are a combination of Americans and Canadians. See paragraph 14.1(9)(d) of the Act. A similar special rule exists for widely-held limited partnerships and certain trusts.

CHAPTER 18

THE BANK ACT AND THE INVESTMENT CANADA ACT

The precise relationship between the *Bank Act* and the *Investment Canada Act* is a puzzle for many foreign investors. Most of the time, it is a puzzle they need not solve. However, investors (and their advisers) must still understand some basic concepts.

This understanding is essential, in order to ascertain which branch of government has jurisdiction over a transaction. If a mistake is made, and information is filed with the wrong arm of the bureaucracy, government officials may not always detect the error. This is most likely to happen if a notification form is submitted to Investment Canada concerning a transaction which falls under the *Bank Act*. There is simply not enough information on the notification form to permit the discovery of all jurisdictional errors.[1]

1. General Rule

The general rule is: if the *Bank Act*[2] applies, the *IC Act* does not. This rule is expressed in paragraph 10(1)(h) of the *IC Act*.[3] It exempts transactions to which section 522 of the *Bank Act* applies.

Occasionally, a transaction is composed of several parts, one of which comes within the ambit of the *Bank Act*, the other within the jurisdiction of Investment Canada. When this happens, each statute governs its respective portion of the transaction.

---

[1] A completed notification form contains the name of the investor and the Canadian business but not much else.

[2] *Bank Act*. All citations refer to Bill C-19, given first reading in Parliament on May 31, 1991. As of November 1991 the bill was still being discussed.

[3] The same rule can be found in s. 522 of the *Bank Act*. (Bill C-19 amends para. 10(1)(h) of the *IC Act* by substituting a reference to s. 522 for a reference to s. 307.)

To determine if section 522 of the *Bank Act* applies, solicitors should examine the nature of the transaction. The identity of the investor (and, in particular, the links between the investor and its affiliates) will usually be relevant as well.

The following four classes of transactions are listed in section 522 as falling within the *Bank Act*. (Note that section 522 is paraphrased.)

1. The acquisition of control (within the meaning of the *IC Act*) of a bank or a foreign bank subsidiary.[4]

2. The establishment of a new Canadian business (within the meaning of the *IC Act*) that is a bank or foreign bank subsidiary.[5]

COMMENT: These types of transactions should cause no problems. Even if the investor is a non-Canadian, it is unlikely that a solicitor will mistakenly file an application with Investment Canada.[6] (Observe that "control", "acquisition of control" and "new Canadian business" have the same meaning in section 522 of the *Bank Act* as they do in the *IC Act*.)

3. The acquisition of control[7] of an entity by a foreign bank or the establishment, directly or indirectly, of a new Canadian business by a foreign bank, whose principal activity in Canada consists of:

   (i) providing banking services;

   (ii) providing fiduciary services;

   (iii) performing the functions of an investment dealer, stock broker, investment counsellor, or portfolio manager;

   (iv) the business of insurance, including the function of an insurance agent or broker;

   (v) any combination of the above.[8]

COMMENT: If an investor wishes to acquire or establish a business that provides (or will provide) banking, fiduciary, insurance or stock brokerage services, it is essential to ascertain if the investor is a "foreign

---

[4] Ibid., subs. 522(a) and subpara. 518(3)(a)(i).

[5] Ibid., subs. 522(b) and subpara. 518(3)(a)(ii).

[6] The *Bank Act* gives the Superintendent of Financial Institutions exclusive jurisdiction over the establishment or acquisition of a bank irrespective of whether the investor is a Canadian or a foreigner.

[7] Section 522 of the *Bank Act* uses the words/phrases "acquisition of control", "entity", "establishment" and "new Canadian business", then refers readers to the *IC Act* for their meaning.

[8] *Bank Act*, para. 518(3)(a). The intention is that, whenever a foreign bank or an affiliated company seeks to establish or acquire a new financial business in Canada, the review is to be made pursuant to the *Bank Act* and not the *IC Act*.

bank". This broadly defined term includes[9] a foreign-incorporated company that:

(a) is a bank according to the laws of any foreign country where it carries on business,

(b) carries on a business in any foreign country that, if carried on in Canada, would be wholly or to a significant extent, the business of banking,

(c) engages, directly or indirectly, in the business of providing financial services and employs, to identify or describe its business, a name that includes the word "bank", "banque", "banking" or "bancaire", either alone or in combination with other words, or any word or words in any language other than English or French corresponding generally thereto,

(d) engages in the business of lending money and accepting deposit liabilities transferable by cheque or other instrument,

(e) engages, directly or indirectly, in the business of providing financial services and is affiliated with another foreign bank,

(f) controls another foreign bank, or

(g) is a foreign institution, other than a foreign bank within the meaning of any of paragraphs (a) to (f), that controls a bank named in Schedule II,

but does not include a subsidiary of a bank named in Schedule I.

As a first step to ascertaining whether a corporate investor is a foreign bank, counsel should examine its financial statements. These statements may indicate that the investor either:

(1) controls a foreign bank (by owning more than 50% of its voting shares), or

(2) (directly or indirectly) provides a financial service and is controlled either by a foreign bank or by a company which controls a foreign bank. (See the definition of "affiliated".)[10]

However, if the financial statements are silent, counsel should make further inquiries. This is because the definition of a "foreign bank" casts a wide net. If one member of a group of companies is a foreign bank, all group members which engage in financial activities and are controlled by the same company which controls the foreign bank, in turn become foreign banks.

---

[9] *Bank Act*, s. 2. For the meaning of control in (f) and (g) of the definition of a "foreign bank", see s. 3. Note that the concept of "control in fact", which caused controversy when it was in the *FIR Act*, is now in the *Bank Act*.

[10] "Affiliated" is defined in ss. 2 and 6 of the *Bank Act*.

Any foreign company which carries on banking activity, no matter how insignificant that activity may be in relation to its main business,[11] is a foreign bank. Such a foreign company will need the approval of Canada's Minister of Finance before it can get involved in financial activities in Canada.

Presented below is an example designed to explain the concept of a foreign bank. Examine the diagram and decide which companies are foreign banks.

1. EXAMPLE (Foreign Banks and Associates):

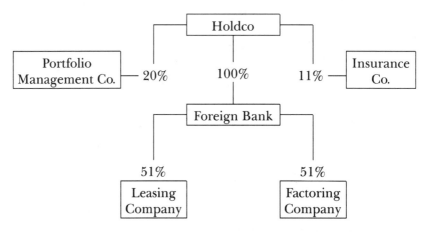

Leasing Company and Factoring Company are "foreign banks" since they are controlled by a foreign bank. (A foreign bank owns more than 50% of their voting shares). Portfolio Management Co. and Insurance Co. are "associated with a foreign bank" since a "foreign bank" (Holdco) owns more than 10% of their voting shares.[12] Holdco is classified as a foreign bank since Holdco controls a foreign bank.

The next two examples further explain the concept of a foreign bank.

2. EXAMPLE (Manufacturing Company): Not all companies that are affiliated with a foreign bank qualify for "foreign bank" status. Although there are exceptions, generally a manufacturing company that provides no financial services cannot be a foreign bank, even if all of its shares are owned by a foreign bank.[13]

---

[11] The activity must be wholly, or to a significant extent, the business of banking. See paragraph (b) of the definition of a "foreign bank".

[12] See subss. 507(2) and 10(1).

[13] See paragraph (e) of the definition of a "foreign bank". "Financial services" is not

By way of illustration, consider automobile manufacturer Daimler-Benz A.G. Because Deutsche Bank owns 28.5% of Daimler-Benz's voting shares, Daimler-Benz is an "associate" of a foreign bank. If Deutsche Bank were to increase its interest to 51% (or 100%), Daimler-Benz would be "affiliated" with a foreign bank. However, Daimler-Benz would not (on these facts alone) be a foreign bank.

One common exception to this general rule is a manufacturing company incorporated outside Canada that buys and sells conditional sales contracts, or makes loans to finance the sale of its products. Because the manufacturing company is providing a financial service, it is a foreign bank. In addition, a manufacturing company which controls a foreign bank is itself a foreign bank.

3. EXAMPLE (Controller of a Foreign Bank): The Royal Bank of Scotland Group P.L.C. is a holding company which is the sole owner of the Royal Bank of Scotland. Consequently, the "parent" holding company is a foreign bank.

If a solicitor has decided that a client, which wants to expand to Canada, is a foreign bank, the solicitor should ask this question: will the "bank" be engaging in financial activities? The answer will determine which of the two Acts (the *Investment Canada Act* or the *Bank Act*) governs the transaction. The following three examples illustrate this:

4. EXAMPLE (Foreign Bank Sets Up New Manufacturing Business): A foreign manufacturing company wants to assemble luxury sports cars in Canada. Because the company grants loans to help finance the sale of its products, it is characterized under Canada's *Bank Act* as a "foreign bank". Although Canada no doubt will welcome this new automobile assembly plant, what arm of government must give its approval?

Since the assembly of automobiles is not within the scope of the activities referred to in subsection 522(c) of the *Bank Act*, Investment Canada has jurisdiction. The approval of the minister responsible for Investment Canada is not needed for a new business. However, the "foreign bank" must advise Investment Canada of its plans.

5. EXAMPLE (Foreign Bank Buys Denison Mines): The foreign manufacturing company in the previous example is a foreign bank because it grants loans (to help finance the company's sales). The company has just announced public takeover bids for Denison Mines and Stelco. What are some of the regulatory hurdles it faces?

---

defined. Such a manufacturing company may be an associate or a non-bank affiliate of a foreign bank.

Section 522 of the *Bank Act* ousts the *IC Act* when a foreign bank is acquiring a Canadian-incorporated company that provides banking, fiduciary, insurance or stock brokerage services. However, section 522 does not apply when a "foreign bank" wants to buy a Canadian company that engages in non-financial activities. The foreign bank must, therefore, convince Investment Canada and its minister that the takeover of Denison Mines and Stelco will benefit Canada.[14] (If a foreign bank such as U.S.-owned Citibank owns shares in a foreign bank subsidiary such as Citibank Canada,[15] the foreign bank will be restricted by subsection 508(1) of the *Bank Act* from owning more than 10% of the shares of another Canadian-incorporated company.)

6. EXAMPLE (Banking Services): Manufacturers Hanover Trust Company, based in New York City, is a foreign bank. If it wants to buy a bond rating company, is the transaction reviewable under the *IC Act*?

No. Since bond rating is a service that a bank is permitted to provide,[16] the transaction falls within the *Bank Act*.

If an investor is a company incorporated in Canada, that company can never be a foreign bank. That means, for instance, if an investor is a Canadian-incorporated life insurance company, which is controlled by a foreign bank, the insurance company is not itself a foreign bank.[17]

Until 1985, this was a potential loophole. Foreign banks could circumvent the *Bank Act* by incorporating a company in Canada, which then would not be subject to the *Bank Act*. To close this loophole (and oust the jurisdiction of Investment Canada when a corporation that is ultimately controlled by a foreign bank makes an acquisition or establishes a new business in the financial sector), the word "indirectly" was placed in what are now subsections 521(1) and 522(c) of the *Bank Act*. The intention is to subject to the *Bank Act*:

(i) the direct or *indirect* acquisition by a foreign bank of a business engaged in financial activities in Canada; and

(ii) the direct or *indirect* establishment by a foreign bank of a business engaged in financial activities in Canada. [Emphasis added.]

---

[14] This analysis is based on the assumption that Denison Mines and Stelco do not have divisions that finance the sale of uranium and steel.

[15] A "foreign bank subsidiary" is a bank named in Schedule II of the *Bank Act* that is a subsidiary of a foreign bank. Among the banks named in Schedule II are: the Bank of Singapore (Canada) and Barclays Bank of Canada.

[16] *Bank Act*, subs. 522(c) and subpara. 518(3)(a)(i).

[17] To be a "foreign bank", a company must be incorporated outside Canada. However, a Canadian-incorporated insurance company controlled by a "foreign bank" would be "a non-bank affiliate of a foreign bank" and, therefore, prohibited from lending money if it accepts deposits. See the *Bank Act*, ss. 507 and 514.

Unfortunately, there is no definition of what "indirectly" means.

> EXAMPLE: A Canadian subsidiary of a foreign bank wants to establish a financial business in Canada. Since the company making the investment is incorporated in Canada, it is not a foreign bank. However, because a foreign bank is establishing a financial business indirectly, section 522 of the *Bank Act* applies.
>
> Consequently, a notice should not be sent to Investment Canada. Instead, the Office of the Superintendent of Financial Institutions should be contacted in order to obtain the prior approval of the minister of Finance and the Governor in Council.[18]

Here is another example. Portfolio Management Company (see the diagram below) plans to expand to Canada. Should it seek *Bank Act* approval?

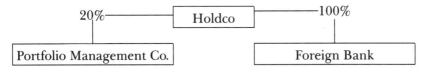

If Holdco had a 50.1% interest in Portfolio Management Co., the answer would be clear: approval under the *Bank Act* would be needed. Because Holdco has only a 20% interest, approval will only be needed if a foreign bank is indirectly establishing a portfolio management business in Canada. The meaning of "indirectly" is therefore a key issue.

2. Confusion over Jurisdiction

Because of the complexities of the interlocking definitions in the *Bank Act*, solicitors who are not *Bank Act* experts may find it difficult to ascertain if their client is a foreign bank. If an application for review is submitted to Investment Canada accompanied by a letter expressing some doubt about which government body has jurisdiction, Investment Canada will discuss the issue with the Superintendent of Financial Institutions. The next example illustrates how confusion over jurisdiction can arise.

> EXAMPLE: A foreign bank wants to buy 30% of the shares of a stock brokerage company. Which Act (the *IC Act* or the *Bank Act*) governs the purchase?

---

[18] There may be some question whether the acquisition by a Canadian subsidiary of a foreign bank of, for instance, a trust company would be "indirect".

According to paragraph 28(3)(d) of the *IC Act*, the acquisition of less than one third of the shares of a corporation is deemed not to be an acquisition of control. Consequently, the *IC Act* does not apply.

Subsection 522(c) of the *Bank Act* does not apply either. That subsection would remove such a transaction from the jurisdiction of Investment Canada—if there was a proposed acquisition of control. However, subsection 522(c) refers to acquisitions of control within the meaning of the *IC Act*.

That does not mean the foreign bank can proceed with its purchase. Another section of the *Bank Act*—paragraph 519(1)(b)—bars it from doing so without the consent of the Governor in Council.

4. The acquisition or holding of all or substantially all of the assets of a Canadian entity whose principal activity in Canada consists of:

    (i)   providing banking services;

    (ii) providing fiduciary services;

    (iii) performing the functions of an investment dealer, stock broker, investment counsellor or portfolio manager;

    (iv) the business of insurance, including the function of an insurance agent or broker;

    (v)   any combination of the above.[19]

3. Corporations Associated with a Foreign Bank

Some European banks own shares in industrial and commercial corporations. The best-known example is Deutsche Bank, which has a 28.5% interest in Daimler-Benz A.G. When a foreign bank has a substantial investment (more than 10% of the voting rights) in a company, that company becomes a "corporation associated with a foreign bank".[20]

Large investments made by such "associated corporations" are reviewable on a case-by-case basis under the *IC Act*. However, if the European bank also owns a bank in Canada, section 518 of the *Bank Act* imposes further restrictions on investments by these associated corporations. Apart from special exemptions, such foreign banks and their associated corporations cannot own more than 10% of the voting shares of a Canadian corporation.[21]

---

[19] *Bank Act*, subs. 522(d).

[20] Subs. 507(2) sets out other circumstances, when a corporation is associated with a foreign bank.

[21] *Bank Act*, subs. 518(1) and para. 518(3)(b)(ii). A foreign bank with foreign bank subsidiary in Canada cannot (without ministerial approval) acquire a substantial investment in an entity except through the foreign bank subsidiary.

EXAMPLE: Compagnie des Machines Bull ("Machines Bull") is quoted on the Paris, Zurich, Geneva and Frankfurt stock exchanges. Approximately 90% of its shares are owned by the French government, which, in turn, owns four banks (e.g., Banque Nationale de Paris). Each of these four banks owns a Schedule II bank in Canada (which bears the same name as the parent bank).[22] What can Machines Bull buy in Canada?

Machines Bull is a "corporation associated with a foreign bank", namely, Banque Nationale de Paris. This bank, in turn, has a foreign bank subsidiary in Canada. Consequently, Machines Bull cannot buy more than 10% of the shares of a Canadian company without the approval of the Minister of Finance. Investments made by Machines Bull will also be notifiable or reviewable under the *IC Act*.

4. Exemptions from Foreign Bank Status

The *Bank Act* permits the Minister of Finance to exempt a company from being classified as a "foreign bank".[23] If the minister grants such an exemption, the *IC Act* will then govern the company's activities. This may be to the company's advantage since the regulatory requirements imposed by the *IC Act* are, in most instances, easier to meet than those of the *Bank Act*.

---

[22] E.g., Banque Nationale de Paris (Canada).

[23] The minister's power to grant exemptions is found in s. 12 of the *Bank Act*.

CHAPTER 19

THE ACCESS TO INFORMATION ACT AND THE INVESTMENT CANADA ACT

The *Access to Information Act*[1] ("*AIA*") came into force on July 1, 1983. Its purpose is to provide all individuals and corporations in Canada with a right of access to information contained in government records.[2]

However, foreign investors need not worry that the documents they provide to the agency will appear in the newspapers. As a vehicle for allowing the general public to discover what has been submitted to Investment Canada, the *AIA* is of little assistance.

1. The Procedure

The first step in obtaining any information is to consult the Access Register. This register, which is found in post offices, public libraries, and government offices across Canada, contains descriptions of government records and their probable locations. The next step is to complete the access request form, taking care to specify as many details as possible concerning the desired records. This form, and the appropriate fee, can then be forwarded to Investment Canada. (Alternatively, just send a letter and the fee.)

Investment Canada must reply within 30 days of receiving the request, unless the president of the agency elects to extend the time limit.[3] This can be done for a "reasonable period of time" if there are many files to examine or if third parties must be notified.[4]

---

[1] *Access to Information Act*, ("*AIA*"), R.S.C. 1985, c. A-1.

[2] *AIA*, subs. 4(1). Access to Information Act Extension Order, No. 1. (published in the *Canada Gazette*, Part II, Vol. 123, No.9, p. 2287).

[3] *AIA*, s. 7 and s. 9. The minister has delegated his duties under the *AIA* to the president of Investment Canada. The statutory authority for this delegation is in s. 73.

[4] Ibid., subs. 9(1). Applicants have the right to lodge a complaint with the Access to Information Commissioner about any extension of the 30-day time period.

If Investment Canada refuses to disclose the information, the agency's letter to the applicant must state the provision of the Act on which the refusal is based.[5] The applicant then has the option of making a complaint to the Information Commissioner who will investigate the matter. During this investigation, the Information Commissioner will contact Investment Canada and make recommendations about what information should or should not be released. The Information Commissioner will then prepare a report. If disclosure is still denied after the Information Commissioner has sent a copy of the report to the applicant, the applicant (or the Information Commissioner, with the applicant's consent) may ask the Federal Court to review Investment Canada's decision to withhold the information.

The *AIA* states that an application for judicial review must be made within 45 days after this report has been received.[6] Sometimes, on such an application, it may be necessary to show the court that the Information Commissioner has conducted an investigation and has submitted a report to the applicant. If so, the Information Commissioner will provide a certificate to that effect for use in court.

2. Privileged Information

Section 24 is the reason why the *AIA* is of little assistance to people who want to inspect Investment Canada's files. This section contains a mandatory exemption from disclosure for any "record" that is restricted by the confidentiality provisions of several Acts of Parliament, including section 36 of the *Investment Canada Act*.

Under section 36, "all information obtained with respect to a Canadian, a non-Canadian or a business" by the minister or a government employee in the course of administering the Act is privileged and cannot be knowingly disclosed to anyone.[7] These words are open to interpretation, but they would appear to render privileged:

    (i) the fact that an application for review has been filed, and its contents;

    (ii) undertakings given by a foreign investor (provided that the minister does not want to disclose such undertakings);[8]

---

[5] Ibid., subs. 10(1).

[6] Ibid., s. 41.

[7] There are a few exceptions. For instance, for the purpose of administering the Act, information may be disclosed to provincial government officials.

[8] See para. 36(4)(b) and subs. 36(5) of the *IC Act*. But *quaere*: is para. 36(4)(b), which allows the minister to disclose undertakings, really a statutory restriction? If not, s. 24 of the *AIA* does not apply. (Disclosure may still be barred by s. 20 of the *AIA*.)

(iii) representations submitted by a province, an investor, the general public, and government departments in connection with a proposed takeover or new business;

(iv) the memoranda prepared by Investment Canada for the minister (which outline the details of proposed transactions and contain the agency's recommendations);

(v) details of the performance record of investors;

(vi) letters and memoranda that agency staff prepare when investors request written opinions.

Despite the restrictions in section 36, it may still be possible to get privileged documents. However, these documents must first be sanitized by the removal of personal information and confidential business information.

The *AIA* renders this procedure mandatory. Section 25 of the Act is a severability provision which overrides all other sections. This section states:

> 25. Notwithstanding any other provision of this Act, where a request is made to a government institution for access to a record that the head of the institution is authorized to refuse to disclose under this Act by reason of information or other material contained in the record, the head of the institution shall disclose any part of the record that does not contain, and can reasonably be severed from any part that contains any such information or material.

In other words, Investment Canada cannot claim an exemption for an entire document if privileged information can be removed, and if the remaining information is reasonably comprehensible.

(a) Other Exemptions

There are several mandatory exemptions in the *AIA* that either overlap or extend beyond the confidentiality restrictions in the *IC Act*. These mandatory exemptions prevent a number of "records" from being released, including:

(i) information obtained in confidence from foreign, provincial and municipal governments (section 13);

(ii) financial, commercial, scientific or technical information supplied by third parties on a confidential basis;

(iii) information, the disclosure of which could prejudice the financial, competitive or negotiating positions of third parties; and

(iv) trade secrets (section 20).

In addition, the *AIA* contains some discretionary exemptions. For example, government departments and agencies such as Investment Canada may refuse to disclose information "which could reasonably be expected to be injurious to the conduct by the Government of Canada of federal-provincial affairs" (section 14). Details about discussions between Ottawa and the provinces on how to promote investment in Canada could be refused on this basis.

A second discretionary exemption is directed at legal advice given by government lawyers. Investment Canada may refuse to disclose any "record" which contains information that is subject to solicitor-client privilege (section 23).

This exemption would cover legal opinions prepared for Investment Canada by the Department of Justice. An example of such an opinion would be a memorandum concerning possible interpretations of the *IC Act*. However, this exemption does not encompass non-legal advice, such as policy advice, given by government lawyers.[9]

Applicants under the *AIA* may wish to contend that the exemption for information subject to solicitor-client privilege should be narrowly construed. In particular, they may argue that the exemption should only apply to documents prepared in anticipation of litigation.

The third important discretionary exemption covers policy advice (section 21). The president of Investment Canada may refuse to disclose: "advice or recommendations" developed for a government department or a minister; an account of deliberations involving government officials; and negotiating plans or positions.

This "policy advice exemption" encompasses a lot of terrain. In particular, it may bar from disclosure: the views of the agency concerning the programs of other government departments that may interfere with Ottawa's objective of increasing investment in Canada; what other government departments think about any proposed amendments to the *IC Act*; briefing notes provided by External Affairs Canada to Investment Canada on how the U.S. and other countries are trying to attract foreign investment; policy initiatives respecting investment; and details of any discussions between Investment Canada and other

---

[9]The exemption for information subject to solicitor-client privilege does not apply unless three elements exist: a communication with someone qualified to practice law; the seeking or giving of legal advice; and an intention by the parties that the advice be kept confidential. Consequently, the privilege does not cover advice given by a government employee who has a law degree but is not a member of a provincial bar, or advice given by lawyers working for Investment Canada who are not employed as legal advisers. *Solosky v. The Queen*, [1980] 1 S.C.R 821; *Alfred Crompton Amusement Machines Ltd. v. Customs and Excise Commissioners* (No. 2), [1972] 2 Q.B. 102, *per* Lord Denning.

government departments on how to co-ordinate their activities. If one government employee writes to another, giving an opinion on Canada's obligation under the Free Trade Agreement, that "advice" can be exempted as well.

Applicants seeking information may want to assert that the reference to "advice or recommendations" in section 21 (the policy advice exemption) covers only predecisional documents. Their assertion should be that once a decision has been rendered, the exemption for policy advice does not warrant the withholding of background information or statistical data that explains the decision.

3. Information Available to the Public

With so many restrictions and exemptions surrounding the *AIA*, business people may wonder if *any* information is available. Certainly, Investment Canada cannot be used as an alternative to Dun and Bradstreet,[10] and with good reason.

However, lists of investors, whose proposals have been approved or whose notifications have been filed under the *IC Act*, are published. The agency's Annual Report to Parliament, industrial analyses and market profiles that the agency has prepared, and speeches given by senior agency officials are also available, as are details about the manner in which the agency is co-operating with international organizations and universities, and details of any consultations with business, industry and law associations.

Lawyers may be interested to note that they can obtain internal memoranda on the interpretation of the *IC Act*, provided the memoranda do not contain privileged information. And students who want to know what laws of other countries affect foreign investment or what foreign countries think about Canada's approach to regulating foreign investment, can see this information if the agency has it.[11] Government policies on various industrial sectors, and internal guidelines and discussion papers that do not contain privileged information under section 36 of the *IC Act*, can also be provided.

Investors and their counsel who resort to the *AIA* should keep in mind that, within a narrow range, the confidentiality provision (section 36) of the *IC Act* is subject to different interpretations. Thus, the amount of information that can be divulged is, to some degree, a policy decision.

---

[10] Dun and Bradstreet provides business reports on companies.

[11] Students should contact the appropriate embassy.

For instance, section 36 could be used as the basis for a blanket refusal to provide most types of information. Alternatively, an agency file can be sanitized as required by section 25 of the *AIA*, and a more liberal interpretation given to the confidentiality provision. This may allow the release of at least some information.

Counsel seeking information may want to quote the purpose clause found in section 2 of the *AIA*, and insist that the severability principle in section 25 be rigorously followed. In the event of ambiguity or disagreement, counsel might also refer to the *Maislin* case, in which Mr. Justice Jerome stated that "public access ought not to be frustrated by the courts, except upon the clearest grounds, so that doubt ought to be resolved in favour of disclosure".[12]

4. Examples of Requests

The following are some documents that foreigners and Canadians may want to see, and the legal parameters within which a response may be given.

(a) Written Undertakings

Section 24 of the *AIA* prohibits disclosure of any information that is privileged under section 36 of the *IC Act*. However, there is one important exception. After an investment has been approved by the minister, information in any written undertakings relating to the investment loses its privileged status and may be released by the minister. Such undertakings also become accessible under the *AIA* (after consultation with the party that provided the undertakings) unless these undertakings fall within one of the exemptions contained in the latter Act.

Written undertakings may retain or regain their privileged status, but only if the minister opines that the disclosure of such information is not necessary for the administration or enforcement of the *IC Act* and would prejudicially affect the business affairs of the person who gave the undertakings. If the minister gives this opinion, he cannot be forced, through legal proceedings under the *AIA* or any other law,[13] to release the contents of the undertaking. But if the minister does not so

---

[12] *Re Maislin Industries Ltd. and Min. for Industry, Trade and Commerce, Regional Economic Expansion* (1984), 10 D.L.R. (4th) 417, at 420. Also, s. 11 of the *Interpretation Act*, R.S.C. 1985, c. I-23, contains a mandate for liberal construction.

[13] *IC Act*, para. 36(4)(6).

opine, and someone makes a request under the *AIA* for written undertakings, they must be released, unless an exemption in the *AIA* can be
brought into play. Two exemptions that often apply are in paragraphs
20(1)(b) and (c). These paragraphs state that:

   (i) confidential financial, commercial, scientific and technical in-
       formation that is supplied to a government institution, and is
       treated in a confidential manner by the third party, and

   (ii) information that could reasonably be expected to cause finan-
        cial loss or gain, or harm the competitive position of a third
        party,

is not subject to disclosure without the consent of the third party (that
is, the foreign investor) who supplied the information.

Procedures are set out in the *AIA* preventing the disclosure of such
information until the third party (namely, the foreign investor) has
been notified and given the opportunity to show that the information
is exempt from disclosure. If, despite the representations of the foreign investor, the president of Investment Canada still intends to
release the information, the foreign investor has the right to request
that a court reviews the president's decision.[14]

Here is a hypothetical scenario which illustrates how the process
works:

   A foreign investor, who last month bought a Canadian corporation, shuts
   down one of its plants. An angry labour leader denounces the takeover
   and demands to see all the commitments the investor gave to government
   officials. Two business competitors make the same request.

The first question government officials will ask is whether any
undertakings were given. Most investors only provide plans, which are
not undertakings, and cannot be released.

If there are undertakings in the file, the next issue is whether they
should be withheld. The minister has the discretion to withhold them
(under subsection 36(5) of the *IC Act*) and the agency could seek his
authority for doing so. However, the minister has a heavy workload, so,
instead, the *AIA* is relied upon if a legal basis is needed for keeping the
undertakings secret.

If there are undertakings, the foreign investor is contacted and
told: "There has been a request under the *AIA* for the undertakings
you provided. Under that Act, information is disclosed unless it falls
within one of the exemptions. Do you consider your undertakings to
be confidential, or will you permit their disclosure?"

---

[14] *AIA*, ss. 28 and 44.

If the investor is adamant that the undertakings are confidential and government officials think that that stance is without foundation, the government could then legally release the undertakings, subject to the investor's right to block that action in court.

Most undertakings will be covered by the exemptions in the *AIA*. That means foreign investors will be able to contest any requests for disclosure made by competitors or the general public. However, if—and this may one day be the case—no exemption applies, and if the minister has not opined that disclosure of the undertakings will prejudicially affect the business affairs of the foreign investor, then the undertakings must be released.

On the other hand, suppose the minister believes that the disclosure of an undertaking will indeed prejudice the foreign investor. Since the undertaking then remains privileged, does an outsider have any legal basis for demanding information?

Section 25 (the "severability section") of the *AIA* can still be relied upon. If an undertaking contains any information unrelated to the investment (and does not fit within an exemption), that portion of the undertaking must be disclosed.[15]

(b) Discussion Papers

The *AIA* does not apply to most Cabinet documents. Some critics have labelled this the "Mack truck exclusion". Cabinet documents are excluded from the ambit of the Act for 20 years. They include: memoranda presenting proposals to Cabinet; "discussion papers", the purpose of which was to present background explanations, analyses of problems or policy options for consideration by Cabinet in making decisions; records reflecting discussions between ministers on policy matters; ministerial briefing papers; draft legislation; and most important, any document containing a record of the above-mentioned matters.[16]

Certain Cabinet documents may be open for release to the public. These are:

(i) Cabinet documents that are more than 20 years old;

(ii) "discussion papers" containing explanations, analysis or policy options for consideration by the Cabinet, if:

---

[15] Admittedly, it would be hard to conceive of an undertaking that would contain information unconnected with the investment.

[16] *AIA*, s. 69. These Cabinet documents are referred to in s. 69 as "confidences of the Queen's Privy Council of Canada". Not even the Information Commissioner can see excluded Cabinet documents.

(a) the decisions to which the papers relate have been made public, such as through a news release or an announcement in the House of Commons, or

(b) the decisions to which the papers relate have *not* been made public, but four years have passed since the decisions were made (not four years since the date of the "discussion papers").

Should these conditions be met, the "discussion paper" is subject to the *AIA* (after any references to the "Confidences of Queen's Privy Council" have been removed or "severed"). But that does not mean the document will be released. Other exemptions in the statute may still bar the door.

To understand how these provisions work, imagine that a discussion paper on Investment Canada's operations is presented to a committee of Cabinet in 1991. This paper contains both background material and policy opinions and thus qualifies as a discussion paper of the type described in paragraph 69(1)(b) of the *AIA*. Cabinet quickly reaches a decision, but it is not made public.

In 1995, this discussion paper would become accessible to the general public. Should this paper contain any information coming within the exclusion for Cabinet confidences set out in section 69 of the *AIA*, or exempt material, or privileged information protected by section 36 of the *IC Act*, such information would first have to be deleted before the paper was released.

Consider another illustration. A document containing proposals for amendments to the *IC Act* is drafted by government officials. Can the public see it? Probably not. The document would (likely) be classified as a memorandum, the purpose of which is to present proposals or recommendations to Cabinet (paragraph 69(1)(a)).

Fortunately, government departments have many documents which no one ever intends to send to Cabinet. These documents can be made public if all information that is excluded or exempted by the *AIA* is removed.

What kind of information must be removed? Here are some examples:

(i) "Cabinet agreed to . . ."

Because this paragraph would reveal the contents of a record recording a decision by Cabinet, it would have to be deleted (paragraph 69(1)(c)).

(ii) "The Memorandum to Cabinet concluded . . ."

This section would have to be eliminated, because it would reveal the contents of a memorandum by virtue of which proposals to Cabinet had been presented (paragraph 69(1)(a)).

Proposed legislative changes to which Cabinet has agreed would also have to be taken out before the document could be made accessible.[17]

If an applicant is met with an outright refusal to release a document on the grounds that it is a Cabinet confidence, a complaint can be filed with the Information Commissioner. However, before doing so, the applicant might want to urge the government official he is dealing with to adopt a restrictive view of what constitutes a Cabinet document. Perhaps a paper that was prepared for ministers, but was never seen by them or never made it into the Cabinet paper system, should not be classified as a Cabinet confidence.

Even if a policy or background paper is not a Cabinet confidence or if the offending paragraphs can be removed, it might not be released for other reasons. Sections 21 and 23 of the *AIA* contain discretionary exemptions for "advice or recommendations" developed for a government institution, and for "records" that are subject to solicitor-client privileges. These sections could still be invoked.

(c) Correspondence from Company Officers

It will be difficult to obtain copies of most letters that Investment Canada receives. Many of these letters come from company officers or their lawyers and deal with cases that are before the agency. They are, therefore, shielded by the exemption in section 36 of the *IC Act*.

Even letters of a general nature may be inaccessible, particularly if they contain personal or commercial information. Subsection 19(1) of the *AIA* protects personal information, such as personal views or opinions that have been expressed. Section 20 would be claimed if any letter contained financial or commercial information of a confidential nature.

Company management can therefore relax. Any letters they have written, criticizing competitors or government policies, requesting

---

[17] The names of the government officials who wrote a background paper often appear on its front cover. Can probing researchers obtain these names? Yes, since these names are legally accessible. Under s. 19 of the *AIA*, personal information as defined in the *Privacy Act* cannot be released. However, the definition of personal information (in s. 3 of the *Privacy Act*) excludes "the name of an individual on a document prepared by the individual in the course of employment" and "the personal opinions or views of the individual given in the course of employment" (*Privacy Act*, subs. 3(j)).

favourable treatment, or advising Ottawa that a competitor has not complied with the *IC Act*, are safe from prying eyes.[18]

(d) Status/Non-Status Opinions and Background Memoranda

The *IC Act* authorizes the minister to issue opinions on whether an individual or an entity is a Canadian or an American. These are known as status opinions. Non-status opinions deal with any other matters. Prior to such opinions being issued, agency staff prepare a draft letter and an explanatory memorandum.

Most or all of this supporting documentation will not be accessible. The explanatory memoranda cannot be seen since they contain information with respect to a non-Canadian or a business that has been obtained by a government employee in the course of administering the Act.[19] Although it might be possible to release a "sanitized" opinion letter after removing the name and the description of the transaction, what would remain would be of no use to anyone.

The list of status opinions that had been issued during the previous year used to be published in the agency's Annual Report. That is no longer done since publication is not specifically authorized by the *IC Act*.

(e) Representations from the Provinces

When Investment Canada is reviewing an investment, it seeks the views of any province that will be significantly affected by the decision. When a major Canadian company is about to be purchased by a foreign investor, newspaper reporters may be anxious to ascertain what the views of the provinces are.

Unfortunately, from the perspective of the press, the basic obligation in the *AIA* to make government information available to the public, is overridden by the confidentiality provision of the *IC Act*. The opinions of the provinces on whether a takeover should be approved are therefore barred from disclosure.

Sometimes letters from the provinces deal with topics other than transactions that are before the agency. Such letters are not protected

---

[18] S. 19 of the *AIA* covers personal expressions of opinion but may not encompass the views of a corporation or its board. (However, other exemptions in the *AIA* may apply.)

[19] Such memoranda are rendered privileged by subs. 36(1) of the *IC Act*. Consequently, subs. 24(1) of the *AIA* prohibits their release.

by the *IC Act*.[20] Members of the general public may, therefore, attempt to see copies of such letters. However, before doing so, they should take a look at sections 13 and 14 of the *AIA*.

Section 13 contains a mandatory exemption for information obtained "in confidence" from a provincial government. Section 14 provides the president of Investment Canada with a discretionary right to withhold information that could be injurious to the conduct of federal-provincial affairs.

It is not always easy to determine if information has been obtained "in confidence" from a provincial government.[21] For instance, does innocuous material that a provincial government clerk has routinely stamped "in confidence" fall within the mandatory exemption in section 13? If it does, the consent of the province will be needed before even innocuous material can be released.

5. Provincial Access to Information Acts

Investment Canada's practice of seeking the views of the provinces (when investments are subject to review) raises another interesting question. Can members of the public use provincial access to information legislation to obtain information that is privileged under the *IC Act*? If so, they need look no further because Investment Canada provides all provinces that will be significantly affected by a foreign investment with a photocopy of the complete application.[22]

Provincial officials who receive these applications are governed by the confidentiality provision[23] in the *IC Act*. Consequently, they cannot disclose the information. But what would happen if provincial access to information legislation took a different stance and granted a right of access to information received from other governments[24] and if

---

[20] S. 36 of the *IC Act* protects only those letters which contain information about a Canadian, a non-Canadian or a business obtained during the administration of the *IC Act*.

[21] Some provinces and companies try to seek protection under ss. 13 and 20 by claiming that everything is confidential. The extent of their success will depend on whether the courts apply a subjective or objective test as to what confidential information consists of.

[22] Para. 36(3)(b) of the *IC Act* permits this.

[23] S. 36.

[24] For instance, subs. 15(b) of Ontario's *Freedom of Information and Protection of Privacy Act*, S.O. 1987, c. 25, gives a deputy minister the discretion to disclose information received in confidence from another government. S. 18 of Quebec's *Loi sur l'acces aux*

provincial officials did not exercise any discretionary rights they might have in their legislation to refuse to release the information?

The federal government or the foreign investor would then have to make an immediate court application. The courts would probably rely on the doctrine of paramountcy and rule that the confidentiality provision in the *IC Act* takes precedence over any right of access created by provincial law.[25]

---

documents des organismes publics et sur la protection des renseignments personnels uses similar wording.

[25] Para. 36(4)(f) says that nothing in s. 36 prohibits the "disclosure of. . .information to which a person is otherwise legally entitled". One question that may disturb investors is whether a person who has a right of access under provincial law is a person "otherwise legally entitled".

CHAPTER 20

THE NATIONAL TRANSPORTATION ACT, 1987 AND THE INVESTMENT CANADA ACT

Non-Canadians who wish to invest in one of Canada's large transportation companies (airline, bus or trucking) may confront a triple-tiered review process under the *National Transportation Act, 1987*, (the "*NTA, 1987*"),[1] the *Competition Act* and the *Investment Canada Act*.

Under the *NTA, 1987*, anyone[2] (irrespective of nationality) who proposes to acquire:[3]

(1) substantially all of the assets to be held or controlled directly or indirectly, or

(2) 10% of the issued and outstanding voting shares

of a federally regulated transportation company (or other "undertaking") that has assets or annual sales in Canada of $10 million or more must file a notice with the National Transportation Agency.

The agency then sends the person making the application a receipt stating that the notice is complete, informs the Minister of Transport of the proposed acquisition, and publishes a notice of the proposed acquisition in the *Canada Gazette* and any other publication it considers appropriate (such as a local newspaper).

If objections are received within the prescribed time, claiming that the proposed acquisition is against the public interest, the agency must inform the Minister of Transport and the person who made the application of the objections and it must review the proposed acquisition. The agency may hold hearings on the matter at its discretion.

Otherwise, if no objections are submitted within the prescribed time, the agency informs the person (who made the application) that the proposed application is not subject to review by the agency.

---

[1] R.S.C., 1985, c. 28 (3rd Supp.).

[2] And associates. See subs. 251(3) for definition.

[3] The Act applies to direct or indirect acquisitions by any means, including an amalgamation. *NTA, 1987*, subs. 252(1).

Should the government want a proposed acquisition reviewed, it must also file an objection (since the government falls under the definition of "person").[4] This is why the procedure under the *NTA, 1987* is referred to as a selective review scheme.

When a proposed acquisition is subject to review, the agency has 120 days after the sending of the receipt to decide whether the proposed acquisition is against or not against the public interest. To be in the public interest, an acquisition must be consistent with the national transportation policy as set out in subsection 3(1) of the Act and any policy directives issued by the Governor in Council.[5]

If the National Transportation Agency has not reached a decision at the end of the 120 days, the proposed acquisition is deemed not to be against the public interest. However, any decision or deemed decision may be rescinded by the Governor in Council within 30 days of the decision or deemed decision. This is called "the Governor in Council override".

If a proposed acquisition is subject to review, an investor cannot close the deal until the National Transportation Agency has allowed or disallowed it. In addition, the investor must wait until the 30-day period has expired during which time the Governor in Council can rescind the proposed acquisition. Otherwise, the investor may face some stringent penalties.

1. Non-Canadian Purchasers

Foreign investors who want to purchase a major "transportation undertaking" may face a particularly long delay. According to subsection 253(4) of the *NTA, 1987*, a notice must *not* be filed under that Act until the proposed acquisition has been approved under the *IC Act*. This is to ensure that two review proceedings do not take place at the same time.

Delay will not be such a problem, however, if the foreign investor is proposing to acquire less than 33% of the voting shares[6] of a transportation company (or is buying a larger percentage interest but is not

---

[4] *NTA, 1987*, subs. 251(1); ss. 255(1) 255, and 256. A "person" can file an objection. The government is included in the definition of a "person".

[5] See the definition of "public interest" in s. 4.

[6] Note that the definition of "voting shares" in the *NTA, 1987* and the *IC Act* are different. A voting share in the *NTA, 1987* means "a share. . .that carries, under all circumstances, or by reason of an event that has occurred and is continuing, a right to vote" (subs. 251(1)).

acquiring control). In that event, Investment Canada will have no jurisdiction. A notice can, therefore, be filed (if required) with the National Transportation Agency immediately.

2. Control Test

The notice requirement under the *NTA, 1987* is not premised upon a change of control of a "transportation undertaking". The purchase of a 10% interest is unlikely to constitute even a *de facto* change of control, unless the buyer already owns a sizeable interest.

This is a different approach from that found in the *IC Act*. Instead of a semi-rigid control test which misses some *de facto* changes of control (like the *IC Act*), or a more discretionary test which catches *de facto* changes, but causes uncertainty for investors, those who drafted the *NTA, 1987* settled on a flat 10% threshold. This test catches any transaction which results in effective control passing into different hands, as well as many transactions that do not have any effect on the locus of control.

Such a low threshold, and the definition of "associate" in subsection 251(3) of the *NTA, 1987* may make it difficult for investors who want to make an end run around the regulators. In the case of other statutes, these end runs can sometimes be achieved by setting up a network of companies (or using existing corporate groups) whose share ownership structure conceals the fact that the corporate throttles are in the hands of one investor.

The use of such corporate structures where *de jure* control, (that is, majority ownership) is in one set of hands, and real control is held by someone else, will face a few hurdles under the *NTA, 1987*. That Act states that a corporation is controlled by a person if that person has "any direct or indirect influence which, if exercised, would result in control in fact of the corporation".[7] This test, which is in addition to a *de jure* control test, gives the administrators at the National Transportation Agency considerable discretion in determining where real control lies.

---

[7] *NTA, 1987*, para. 251(4)(c).

CHAPTER 21

CANADA AND THE INTERNATIONAL COMPETITION FOR FOREIGN INVESTMENT

Some foreign investors make their first contact with the Canadian government when they buy or set up a business. For others, this initial encounter occurs much earlier—at a seminar, conference or trade show in the investor's home country. These are not chance meetings. Instead, they are part of an organized effort known as Canada's "Investment Development Program", designed to market the country abroad and attract foreign investors.

Investment development is a term which puzzles most Canadians. However, it is not a new government activity. To some extent, the federal and provincial governments, plus a few municipalities, have been involved in investment development ("efforts by governments to encourage domestic and foreign investment") for decades.

1. History

As long ago as the late nineteenth century, Canadian municipalities were pitting themselves against each other in fierce competition for manufacturing businesses. To entice industrialists, these local governments offered a variety of incentives or bonuses, such as cheap land, tax and utility concessions, as well as cash. Citizens of the time soon labelled this phenomenon as "bonusing".[1]

In this century, central governments in Canada and other countries have used monetary, fiscal and regulatory policies to attract selected forms of investment. Tax incentives and subsidies have been

---

[1] Michael Bliss, *The Evolution of Industrial Policies in Canada: An Historical Survey*, Discussion Paper No. 218, (Ottawa: Economic Council of Canada, 1982), p. 11.

the most popular and, arguably, the most wasteful means of doing this.[2]

Investment development (often labelled "economic development" or "investment promotion" in the past), therefore, has a lengthy tradition. But in the last decade there have been some remarkable changes, quite apart from the relatively new double-barrelled name.

2. The Change in Scope and Strategy

Most noticeable has been the expansion in the scope of investment development. Government departments of industry, in years past, might court a U.S. or British automobile parts manufacturer. Today, these same governments pursue foreign investors of all kinds in more than a dozen countries.

Accompanying this expansion has been a rapid growth in the human and financial resources devoted to investment development, and the adoption of more sophisticated techniques. In part, this is because investment development, which used to be principally the responsibility of local governments, is now a central government activity in many countries.

The qualities demanded of the personnel have changed as well. In the 1950s and 1960s, the local investment development commissioner was a retired businessman with a gift of the gab and a desire to travel. Although these characteristics are not absent in today's investment developers, the latter are more often career civil servants with a university degree in economics, marketing or communications.

Frequently, these civil servants work hand-in-hand with senior politicians. Investment development, always the subject of covert lobbying and shrewd tactics at the local level, has become, since the early 1980s, one of the most highly politicized activities of national and state governments. Even the most eminent government ministers (Mulroney, Bourassa, Major) have been used like loudspeakers, to convey the message that investment within their jurisdiction is both welcome and profitable.

In 1989, for instance, Saskatchewan's deputy premier led a provincial investment mission to China (trips by government and business leaders are called "missions"). Quebec's Ministre des Communautés

---

[2] What are the incentives used to attract high-tech companies? Read: Jack Lyre, "States, Provinces Accelerate High-Tech Chase", in *Industrial Development & Site Selection Handbook*, June 1988, p. 630.

culturelle et d'Immigration shook hands in Korea, Malaysia, Singapore and Hong Kong.[3] Canada's Minister of International Trade (John Crosbie) visited Europe, and the chairman of China's National People's Congress travelled across Canada. Hundreds of similar trips took place during that year, by "top hats" of many nations in search of foreign investment. (Some of these "top hats" visit the same locations every year.)

Another break with the past lies in the strategy underlying investment development. Governments used to think that if they created a favourable business climate, market forces would attract foreign companies. Then the private sector would help these companies set up their businesses. When market forces did not operate as expected, governments used grants, subsidies, low interest loans and tax concessions to entice foreign investors.

Governments still use these traditional tools. Indeed, tax concessions are being employed more than ever. (France, for instance, has three "Free Enterprise Zones". Companies which locate in these zones get a ten-year tax holiday.) However, over the last two decades, many western and Third World governments have taken on a new "activist" role—as investment counsellors and salesmen.

3. The New Role of "Salesman"

In these nations, government employees woo and counsel foreign investors. They also aid foreign investors with site selection, give investors advice on regulatory procedures, locate potential suppliers and partners, and provide other forms of assistance that, until recently, everyone considered to be within the exclusive preserve of the private sector.

In most countries, this new role began quietly, with the establishment of a "reactive" program. Upon receiving an unsolicited inquiry, civil servants would respond with information and assist the investor in arranging meetings with government officials. Sometimes, branch offices would be set up in foreign consulates and embassies. As the size of the program grew, a central body like Ireland's Industrial Development Authority might be created to handle all government regulatory requirements affecting foreign investors.

More recently, a number of governments have established "proactive programs". Under these programs, government-employed

---

[3] Paul Cauchon, "Robic cherche des Investisseurs en Asie. Elle en profit pour prendre ses vacances à Bali", *Le Devoir*, Feb. 3, 1989, p. 1.

"salesmen" seek out, then contact, foreign business people who have never expressed any interest in investing abroad.

Like Canadian municipalities in the nineteenth century, these governments are directly competing against each other.[4] In the hope of emerging as winners in this competition, they are adapting the glossy brochures and sophisticated marketing techniques of the large corporations they hope to attract. However, these governments are not marketing consumer products. Instead, they are marketing their country, its infrastructure, their nation's lifestyle and its economic opportunities. Like the sales divisions of many corporations, they are also appealing to the panoply of human emotions, especially envy and greed.[5]

(a) Thailand and Singapore Lead the Way

One of the first nations to organize such a national marketing strategy was Thailand. In 1960, Thailand established its "Board of Investment"—chaired by the prime minister—to promote investment and administer the country's investment incentive programs. The Thai Board of Investment now has promotion centres in four cities overseas: New York, Frankfurt, Sydney and Tokyo. These centres provide "one-stop service" to potential investors, and seek out joint venture partners for Thai companies.[6]

Has the Board of Investment been successful? Sony, Nestle and Dow Chemical carry on business in Thailand. MMC Sittipol Group (the Thai affiliate of Japan's Mitsubishi Motor Corp.) exports Thai-assembled Dodge and Plymouth Colts to Canada.[7] Partly on account of foreign investment, Thailand (with a population of 56 million) is forecast to become another "Asian economic tiger" within the next decade.

Singapore followed suit in 1961. At that time, unemployment was over 10%. Because of its small domestic market, Singapore could not

---

[4] "National Economies Are Engaged in a Silent War in the Marketplaces of the World", Canadian Manufacturers Association, *The Aggressive Economy: Daring to Compete*, June 1989, p. ES-1.

[5] A 1987 seminar presented by the Canadian Consulate General in New York was entitled "Making Money in Canada". Canada's competitors are equally explicit.

[6] Like Investment Canada, Thailand's Board of Investment promotes foreign and domestic investment. Unlike Investment Canada, the board can grant tax incentives when it approves a project.

[7] Jonathon Sikes, "Thais Out to Spur Chrysler Colt Exports", *Financial Post*, April 15, 1989, p. 11.

pursue a policy of import substitution. So, it established an "Economic Development Board" to seek out foreign investment and implement a plan for export-led growth.[8] Singapore's Economic Development Board subsequently set up offices in eight countries. An official with Becton Dickinson, a U.S. company with operations in Singapore, has spoken highly of the assistance his company received from the board:

> When you arrive in the country somebody from the ministry of trade and industry will escort you to industrial sites and take you to established companies. If you want certain kinds of engineers, they will find out where they are, and take you to visit them so you can see the quality of tooling work done locally.[9]

(b) Investment Development in Europe

Compared to the countries of the Far East, western nations were laggards in organizing national marketing strategies. This is easily explained; they were relatively rich and home to most of the world's industry.

Ireland (often called the poor man of Europe) was one of the first to perceive how useful national marketing could be. Ireland set up its program in the early 1960s, after the government had abandoned its protectionist policies toward native industry. That is when the Industrial Development Association ("I.D.A.")—an autonomous state body—began promoting Ireland and pursuing foreign investors.

During the 1960s, the I.D.A. tried to attract mature labour-intensive industries. In the 1970s, it pursued growth industries (electronics, pharmaceuticals, healthcare, engineering and consumer products). In 1981, the I.D.A. was restructured and given a mandate to attract high technology and value-added industry and to promote technology transfer agreements. Presently, the I.D.A. has 600 employees and 19 offices on four continents.

This effort has paid dividends. Over 350 U.S. manufacturing and service companies operate in Ireland. Ireland has also succeeded in attracting investment from Japan (Fujitsu, NEC), Taiwan (Tatung, consumer electronics) and South Korea (Sachan Media, video tapes).

---

[8] In the 1960s, Singapore's Economic Development Board tried to attract export-oriented companies; in the 1970s, skill-intensive industries; in the 1980s, high-technology and service industries. Singapore Economic Development Board, *Economic Development Board Yearbook 1987/1988*, (Singapore: Saik Wah Press Pte. Ltd., 1988).

[9] Andrew Kupfer, "How To Be A Global Manager", *Fortune*, Mar. 14, 1988, p. 52 at 58.

Such success is not surprising. Attracting foreign manufacturers is not difficult when they are offered cash grants and a maximum tax rate of 10% until the year 2010.[10]

Britain's "Invest in Britain Bureau", on the other hand, was not established until 1977. London-based civil servants thought Britain could do better if a central body marketed the country to foreigners, instead of a mob of competing salesmen from district, county and regional councils.

This reasoning was not appreciated by the Scots.[11] At the time, the Scottish Development Agency had its own marketing effort overseas (carried out, since 1981, through a joint venture called "Locate in Scotland"), which the Scots did not want placed under London's wing. Partly because of such regionally-based resistance, it was not until 1985 (the same year Investment Canada was created) that the Invest in Britain Bureau spearheaded its first integrated U.K. effort abroad.

Since the early 1980s such national marketing strategies have been copied by many nations. Portugal has its Foreign Investment Institute; Indonesia, its Investment Co-ordinating Board.[12] Both bodies welcome foreign investors, help them find projects in which to invest, and issue authorizations on behalf of other state organizations ("one-stop service"). The Netherlands' Foreign Investment Agency[13] (offices in the Hague, Tokyo, Taipei, Seoul and New York City), has aided more than 260 North American companies. Brazil, Mexico,[14] Australia,

---

[10] Ireland is a tax haven for Canadian business people. Accrued earnings of an Irish subsidiary are not subject to Canadian tax and accumulated capital can be remitted to Canada free from Canadian tax. Moreover, companies building new facilities in Ireland usually pay no tax.

Foreign investors have often enjoyed an average return on their investment of 30%. However, a 1984 government white paper questioned how much this investment benefits Ireland. Foreign investors, the paper noted, import five sixths of their raw materials and repatriate about 60% of their profits. "Industrial Development: Irish Answer", *The Economist*, July 14, 1984, p. 70.

[11] "Inward Investment: Let a Thousand Flowers Bloom", *The Economist*, Nov. 24, 1984, p. 645. Wales set up its own single-door agency in April 1983.

[12] Like Investment Canada, Portugal's Foreign Investment Institute and Indonesia's Investment Coordinating Board can block investments.

[13] Holland's prime minister once boasted: "the Netherlands . . . provided a return on U.S. investment that . . . exceeded 34% in 1986". *The Netherlands Foreign Investment Review*, (The Hague: Ministry of Economic Affairs (undated)). The N.F.I.A.'s sale message stresses Holland's stability, geographic position, universities and infrastructure.

[14] In Mexico, a division within the Ministry of Commerce and Industrial Development (Secretaria de Commercio y Fomento Industrial) promotes investment. The National Commission on Foreign Investment in the same ministry screens certain

Japan,[15] Taiwan and several European countries have similar, though less formal groups within government departments.[16]

Even New Zealand has an Investment Unit (within that nation's Department of Trade and Industry) which seeks foreign companies wishing to establish an Asia/Pacific headquarters. This indicates a change of attitude in New Zealand. In 1977, New Zealand refused to allow a Belgian millionaire and his French girlfriend to live there because millionaires were "not needed in New Zealand".[17]

(c) The U.S. Peacock Parade

The United States is also a vigorous competitor in this peacock parade, but with a difference. In that country, the movement towards central government management of economic development, so visible in other nations, is not present.[18] Instead, because of Ronald Reagan's "New Federalism" and the consequent reduction or elimination of many federal economic development programs, the responsibility for implementing an industrial strategy was undertaken by the governments of the individual states.

They have readily shouldered that burden. Georgia and North Carolina (just two examples) produce glossy promotional brochures (emphasizing their "pro-business attitude", the low wages, low unionization rates, and "less government regulation"). Sales missions to foreign countries by mayors or state governors, accompanied by local business people occur many times a year.[19] Tax breaks, employee

---

investment proposals.

[15] Jetro (Japan External Trade Organization) is a Japanese government body with offices overseas. It hosts seminars and introduces foreign investors to potential Japanese partners.

[16] Malaysia's M.I.G.A. and France's D.A.T.A.R. have offices in twelve and eight countries respectively. (Sometimes, central and regional governments compete in promoting investment; an example is the rivalry between the Spanish government and Catalonia.)

[17] Reuters, "New Zealand Rejects Millionaire", *The Globe and Mail*, Oct. 29, 1977, p. 2; New Zealand's Overseas Investment Commission still screens investment proposals (over 25% foreign ownership). See n. 95.

[18] The Americans and West Germans leave investment development activities to local and state governments. Great Britain and France, which are more concerned about helping disadvantaged regions, run more centralized investment promotion campaigns. In Canada, both options have been adopted.

[19] For techniques of the U.S. states, see "States Are Going Down Industrial Policy

training assistance, site identification assistance and videotapes in foreign languages are other ways U.S. states compete for foreign investment.

Some of these state-run promotional campaigns have been remarkably intense. Kentucky has an office and a Japanese-speaking representative in Tokyo. Nonetheless, when Kentucky Governor Martha Collins was courting Toyota, she did not respond to Toyota's requests for additional information with telexes. Instead, she sent her development people to Tokyo to make personal presentations. When she went to Tokyo herself, she found "11 [U.S. state] governors in Japan, practically at the same time", all offering tax and financing packages.[20]

Thirty-one states actually joined in the competition. Kentucky won; Toyota chose Georgetown, Kentucky, as the site for its automobile assembly plant. But at a price! Before Toyota's decision was announced, Kentucky had offered Toyota (one of the world's wealthiest corporations) $125 million in subsidies, bought the land Toyota was interested in, hosted a lavish dinner, complete with fireworks for a visiting Toyota delegation, and taken Toyota officials on an inspection tour by helicopter, (the cost per job: $108,333).[21]

Presently, U.S. state governments have 38 offices in Tokyo.[22] A number of U.S. states have offices elsewhere: in West Germany (10), the United Kingdom (7), Korea (12), Canada (5) and twenty other countries. What are the staff in these offices doing? A California state government official explains:

Lane", *Fortune*, Mar. 5, 1984, p. 112.

In 1986, 48 states sent trade or investment missions to Europe and Asia. Marianne Clarke, *Revitalizing State Economies: A Review of State Economic Development Policies and Programs*, (Washington, D.C.: National Governors' Association Centre for Policy Research and Analysis, 1987), p. 82. In addition, in several states, the utilities (e.g., Georgia Power Commission, Niagara Mohawk Power Corporation) promote investment by providing economic data, and information on site selection and community profiles.

[20] Harold Seneker, "Faces Behind The Figures", *Forbes*, June 16, 1986, p. 163.

[21] The actual cost to Kentucky taxpayers of the incentives given to Toyota over 20 years is $354 million. On the other hand, the Toyota plant and additional enterprises may generate $488 million in taxes, assuming there are no recessions or layoffs. John Miller and Alecia Swasy, "The Wooing of Toyota: Kentucky Adds up the Bill." *Lexington Herald-Leader*, Sept. 28, 1986, p. 1; Norman Glickman and Douglas Woodward, *The New Competitors*, (New York: Basic Books, 1989), p. 232.

[22] Figures obtained from the Japan Desk, International Trade Administration, U.S. Department of Commerce. U.S. state offices in Tokyo promote Japanese investment in the U.S. and U.S. exports.

We now have a man in our Tokyo office who can meet with Japanese representatives at their offices to discuss site locations, permits, and all other elements that go into locating an investment in California.[23]

Similar offices have been set up in Canada by New York State (Toronto, Montreal), New Jersey (Montreal), Vermont (Montreal), Georgia, Illinois and the Association of Great Lakes States (all in Toronto). They want to entice Canadian investment dollars to the south.[24]

(d) Canada's Pursuit of Foreign Investment

Canada did not establish its Investment Development Program until 1985 (several years after the Invest in Britain Bureau had been set up). However, that date did not mark the commencement of government-sponsored investment promotion campaigns overseas.

During the previous decade, while Ottawa looked askance at increases in foreign investment, Canada's provinces had, ironically, been developing programs (ministerial visits, participation in industrial exhibitions) to encourage it.[25] By 1985, Quebec, Ontario, Alberta and British Columbia had established a number of offices overseas and were busy making presentations to prospective investors.[26] Even some

---

[23] Jim Rinehart of the State Office of Business Development. Quoted in: Niels Erch, *Striking Gold: A Pacific Rim Guide to Investing and Trading in California* (Northridge, California: Windsor Publications, Inc., 1987), p. 60.

[24] The Canada Desk, International Trade Administration, U.S. Department of Commerce. The U.S. Commerce Department also conducts "Investment in U.S.A" seminars in Canada. See "26 U.S. States Court Investment from Quebec", *The Gazette*, Nov. 7, 1986, p. B-6, and Giles Gherson, ". . .But Some States Still Put Out the Welcome Mat", *Financial Post*, July 20, 1987, p. 5.

[25] For example, during a 1979 mission to Japan, Ontario Industry minister Larry Grossman "was busy convincing Japanese government and business leaders that Ontario is a good place in which to invest". "Immediate Sales Result from Mission to Japan", *Ontario Business News*, May/June 1979, p. 1. As a result of a 1978 mission to New York City, an Ontario government official said he expected 12 to 14 joint ventures or U.S. branch plants to be established in Ontario. *Ontario Business News* June/July 1978, p. 3. In the fall of 1977, 350 Japanese business people attended two investment seminars in Tokyo and Osaka organized by the Ontario government. *Ontario Business News*, Dec. 1977, p. 6.

[26] By 1979, Ontario had trade and investment offices in ten cities (London, Paris, Frankfurt, Tokyo, New York, Chicago, Atlanta, Dallas, Los Angeles and Hong Kong). See Don Butler, "Ontario Starting Program to Lure U.S. Firms Here", *Ottawa Citizen*, Jan. 23, 1980, p. 74; *The Profit Centre: Why You Must Consider North America's Strategic Market*, (Toronto: Ministry of Industry and Tourism, 1979). Manitoba's first overseas office, established in 1985, pursues wealthy Hong Kong business people, although those

cities were sending their mayors (Ralph Klein, Calgary) on tax-funded sales missions to Europe and Asia.[27]

At the federal level, a limited effort had also been undertaken for several years. The Department of Regional Industrial Expansion (now called Industry, Science and Technology) was furnishing sectoral and regional information, as well as advice on incentive programs, to foreign investors who contacted it. In certain industry sectors, this department also engaged in investment prospecting. First, Canadian firms in need of capital or technology were identified, then departmental officials would promote these firms as "opportunities" to domestic and foreign business people.

Offshore, Canada's trade commissioners were doing some promotional work from their embassy offices (providing information, assisting the provinces in organizing investment missions), in addition to their trade-related responsibilities. As part of External Affairs Corporate Liaison Program, these trade commissioners were also pursuing a dialogue with senior executives of foreign multinationals that had subsidiaries in Canada. The object was to uncover problems these executives might have experienced in Canada, and to encourage them to consider expansion plans for their Canadian operations.

However, this multi-centred structure for promoting investment presented several difficulties. Most troublesome was the duplication, the lack of co-ordination, and a support system that was often weak or non-existent.

For instance, Canadian embassies and consulates regularly received questions about wage rates, transportation costs, and incentive programs. Yet there was no centralized infrastructure within the federal government that compiled packages of information for investors. Neither was there any federal organization willing to hold the hand of

---

who have settled in Manitoba have a dismal record for job creation. Michael Bociurkiw, "Investing for the Future", *The Free Press*, Feb. 11, 1989, p. 17.

[27] By 1988, former Calgary Mayor Ralph Klein had been on 16 missions. Total cost per mission: $10,000. Calgary's Economic Development Authority even has a director of international relations. Montreal has an office in Hong Kong. Part of the $2.2 million budget of Toronto's Economic Development Department is used to pursue Asian investors. (The budget of Investment Canada is $10 million.) Claudia Cattaneo, "Klein Set to Woo Investors During Trip to Europe", *The Calgary Herald*, Aug. 22, 1981, p. B1. Sheldon Alberts, "Cheap Real Estate Gives Calgary Added Appeal", *The Calgary Herald*, June 18, 1989, p. F4. Bruce Gates, "Putting Their Cards on the Table. The Stakes Are High when Cities Court Business, Industry", *The Financial Post*, Aug. 29, 1988, p. 44. Miville Tremblay, "Vendre Montreal aux investisseurs, ca prend du charme et des chiffres", *La Presse*, Feb. 19, 1989 p. E1. In 1977, the city of Niagara Falls sent its industrial commissioner on a five-week trip to Europe to attract foreign investment. *Ontario Business News*, Dec. 1977, p. 9.

individual investors and lead them through the red tape surrounding the establishment or acquisition of a business.

Furthermore, there was little co-ordination. Representatives from the federal government, the provinces, and Canadian cities would visit companies overseas or attend conferences and trade fairs without first contacting each other. And often no one would contact Canada's embassies abroad for information, leads, and prearranged meetings.

As for Canada's trade commissioners, they had many brochures on the Foreign Investment Review Agency. But with that exception, they had few publications to send to potential investors. Even brochures on the most mundane of topics—such as Canada's strengths in comparison with other countries—were not available.

Not surprisingly, these trade commissioners often wondered just how hard they should be promoting Canada to foreign investors. Investment development activities at Canada's posts abroad were pushed behind the posts' other duties.

4. 1985: Canada's "Investment Development Program" Begins

This state of affairs began to change in June 1985. FIRA was within a few weeks of dying, and a new two-headed creature, called Investment Canada, was about to be born. Its mandate was both to screen and to encourage foreign investment.

This twin mandate set off a tiny thunderclap. Some investors were surprised that FIRA's replacement had been assigned both roles. As for Ottawa's jostling bureaucrats, they realized, with a new player about to step on stage, they had no choice. Some harmony had to be brought to the promotional efforts of federal government departments.

So, in June 1985, Ottawa set up an interdepartmental program. Designed to attract foreign investment, it brought together the resources of three government departments: Investment Canada, External Affairs and the department now called Industry, Science, and Technology Canada. Ottawa christened this program the "Investment Development Program".

(a) The Program's Focus

But what, exactly, was the program to focus on? That was not clear. Parliament had given Investment Canada, or rather, the minister responsible for Investment Canada, a mandate to:

(1) encourage investment by Canadians and non-Canadians;

(2) assist Canadian businesses to exploit opportunities for investment and technological advancement,

(3) do research on domestic and foreign investment issues;

(4) provide investment services; and

(5) assist in the development of industrial and economic policies that have an impact on investment.

But Parliament had issued no further instructions. Instead Parliament left it up to the minister and government officials to determine the scope of the mandate and devise ways to encourage investment.

It was not long before government officials defined this mandate in the broadest terms. Canada, they decided, needed capital, technology and market know-how to become more competitive internationally. As a result, they expanded the concept of encouraging "investment" to encompass far more than a search for foreign capital. Perhaps Parliament should have instructed the minister to promote Canadian enterprise because any initiative which economists suggested might make Canada more competitive—joint ventures, technology transfer agreements, licensing agreements, more R&D, the training of employees—was called an "investment" and became something to be encouraged.

(b) Co-ordinating Ottawa's Octopus

However, before much could be done, there had to be a means of synchronizing the performances of the several actors on stage. These actors included Investment Canada (general promotion), External Affairs Canada (embassies overseas), and Industry, Science and Technology Canada (industry sector experts), all of which occupied lead roles. The National Research Council (technology transfer), Employment and Immigration Canada (business immigration program), and the Federal Business Development Bank were also important members of the federal cast. Then there were the provinces, the municipalities, and private sector bodies, such as the boards of trade, banks, and investment dealers.

Some type of structural linkage was needed. Accordingly, in the summer of 1985, senior Ottawa bureaucrats created an "investment development steering committee" to pull together a few arms of the federal octopus.

This steering committee consisted of deputy ministers from Investment Canada, External Affairs, Industry, Science and Technology, and Employment and Immigration, plus a senior representative from Finance Canada. Its task was to map out strategy and the broad outline of projects, and to advise the minister on goals. A working level committee of departmental officials was also formed to prepare recommendations for the steering committee to consider. As for Investment Canada, it saw itself as co-ordinating the country's promotional effort by becoming "the focal point for the investment development activities of a number of federal government departments".[28]

At the same time that Investment Canada and the other major players were trying to define their roles, two meetings took place between federal and provincial ministers responsible for economic development. At a meeting held July 28-29, 1985, these ministers discussed how to co-ordinate federal and provincial programs to encourage investment. One outcome was a press release in which they agreed "to work with the support of the private sector towards a National Investment Development Plan".

In October 1985, federal and provincial ministers concurred on which countries Canada should focus its efforts to obtain more foreign investment. The United States was a clear choice. The United Kingdom, France, West Germany, Japan, Hong Kong and the Netherlands were also selected. The ministers concluded that a few other nations, such as Switzerland and South Korea, should receive a lesser degree of attention.

However, little additional progress was made towards co-ordinating their respective programs. Although federal, provincial and municipal officials work closely together at the officer level to help foreign investors seeking a Canadian location for their businesses, this is not done within the framework of one overall plan.

Meetings also took place in 1985 between Investment Canada officials and Canadian municipalities (through the Industrial Developers Association of Canada). Since many Canadian cities actively encourage greater domestic and foreign investment within their respective boundaries, various ways in which the federal government and Canadian municipalities could work together were canvassed. These meetings yielded promises of co-operation but again, no impetus towards a single national plan.

As a result, there are several independent programs in Canada designed to promote greater investment. The Investment Development Program and the business immigration program are the best known. Then there are the programs of the provinces and the municipalities, and the "industry sector campaigns" of Industry, Science and Technology Canada ("I.S.T.C.").[29]

---

[28] Investment Canada, *Annual Report*.

[29] I.S.T.C. promotes investment in various industry sectors. Many of these "sector campaigns" are not connected with Canada's Investment Development Program.

5. The Meaning of Investment Development

While the organizational structure of Canada's Investment Development Program was evolving, the federal government was trying to increase foreign investment in Canada. The techniques used will be recounted shortly. But first, the meaning of "investment development" must be explained.

"Investment development" is an obscure term. One aspect is investment promotion, that is, the pursuit of foot-loose industry by waving carrots such as low tax rates, cheap transportation, and government grants. However, there is more to investment development than casting lures.

Investment development, as defined by many government officials, has two components. The most visible is "targeted" marketing and promotion. The other is policy development.

Investment developers decide: which industries offer the most promise for the future. Then they identify investment opportunities in those industries which they communicate to potential investors.

These activities are sometimes backed by a four-part plan:

1. *Targets:* identifies promising industries (e.g., Canada's biotechnology industry) to be promoted, and potential investors with technology, capital or market access. Those who design this aspect of the plan should know what domestic (e.g., Canadian) industry needs to become more competitive, and what foreign companies can offer.[30]

2. *Communication Strategies:* designed to make investors aware of investment opportunities (e.g., in Canadian biotechnology firms).

3. *Promotional Activities:* range from participation in trade shows to direct mail campaigns. Promotional activities are distinguished from communication strategies because the former involve person-to-person interaction.

4. *Services:* answers inquiries. Collects information on incentive programs, comparative wage rates, energy costs and other subjects that companies need in order to make investment decisions. Helps business people find partners.

The other component of investment development—and its distinguishing feature—is policy formation. "Economic development" (programs to expand/attract industries) touches upon policy

---

[30] Some of this information can be obtained from the annual I.S.T.C. *International Plan* which identifies sectors in each country that I.S.T.C. believes are important to Canada from the perspective of increased trade and investment. Some of the staff at Canadian embassies overseas have also done research on local industry.

considerations. But investment development goes further; it seeks to alter the nature of society by changing both attitudes and policies that inhibit investment.

The objective is two-fold: first, to improve the competitiveness of key industries; second, to produce an economic environment that welcomes/rewards investment, and a society that is more entrepreneurial in nature.

(a) Strategies

There are two basic strategies for achieving this objective (see the diagram below):

investment environment

*CANADA

investment promotion

One strategy focuses on the investment environment: taxes, interest rates, the exchange rate, labour costs, the educational system. The theory is—provide the right environment ("till the soil") and domestic industry will prosper. The sight of this prosperity will result in more foreign investment. For this strategy to be most effective, a government body (like Investment Canada) would have to monitor the investment climate of competing nations and be prepared to tactfully challenge other branches of the government (and, in Canada's case, the provinces) when their policies adversely affect investment.

The opposite strategy—"targeted" promotion—is directed at selected companies ("company specific"). It requires a staff of investment counsellors in the home country (to answer questions) and sales people abroad. "Strategic analysts" are also needed to prepare presentations for foreign companies on how a particular (e.g., Canadian) location can improve their (the foreign company's) competitive position. Investment promotion strategies provide an advantage to the nations that first set them up, until all nations have established their own.

The Canadian government was pursuing the first strategy when it introduced its framework policies:

- reduction in corporate and personal taxes (underlying theory: people will save/invest more);

- the sale ("privatization") of Crown corporations;

- a reduction in the number of regulations affecting the transportation, financial services and energy sectors (goal: to strengthen market forces);

- a goods and services tax;

- an easing of the paper burden on small business;

- free trade.

The marketing component of Canada's investment development program is an example of the second strategy.

The United Kingdom under Margaret Thatcher was following the same course when it changed its tax system and regulatory policies, privatized several industries and promoted the country through the Invest in Britain Bureau. Nevertheless, investment development is not tied to any political ideology.

The People's Republic of China has set up a legal structure within which foreign companies can operate.[31] In the summer of 1988, the Chinese opened an office in Edmonton to encourage joint ventures between Canadian and Chinese companies. Obviously, Communist leaders, if they decide their countries must copy some elements of capitalism to succeed economically, can become investment developers too.

(b) The Example of Midland

One way to learn more about investment development is to examine a program in operation. Let's visit the Republic of Midland as it launches its first promotional campaign. (Try to remember the tools and tactics that Midland uses. Many countries, e.g., Australia, Canada, use similar ones.)

Midland, like Canada, suffers from high unemployment. Much of its industry is uncompetitive (high cost) in comparison with that of other countries. The leaders of Midland want to improve their nation's economic performance. So they establish an investment development program. Their goal is to encourage foreign business people to invest

---

[31] Foreigners establishing a joint venture in China used to need approval from 48 government departments. Now all the work is done in one centre. Scott Anderson, "Queen's Professors to Probe Mysteries of Chinese Law", *The Kingston Whig-Standard*, July 29, 1988, p. 1.

in Midland, and to enter into joint ventures and licensing agreements with Midland's entrepreneurs.

The program begins with a visit by a Midland government minister to a European country, which we shall call "Sumoto". The object is to promote investment in Midland's aerospace and electronic sector. During this visit, Midland's many attractions are emphasized: a skilled labour force, cheap energy, a world-class transportation system and good access to international markets.

About the same time, consultants are hired to identify firms in Sumoto that could benefit from investing in Midland ("investment prospecting"). Some firms are chosen as prospects because they have proprietary technology, are dependent on exports, are growing rapidly, or are well-capitalized. These companies might be interested in investing in one of Midland's businesses or establishing a subsidiary. Other companies are selected because they have expressed an interest in exploring opportunities for joint ventures and licensing arrangements. The same consultants also identify prospective Midland counterparts and prepare brochures, highlighting Midland's comparative advantages.

Then, a direct mail campaign is undertaken. Aimed at Sumoto's leading business people, its object is to make them aware that entrepreneurs in Midland can make a lot of money. Throughout this direct mail campaign, special attention is paid to the investment advisory industry (lawyers, the banks, stock brokerage firms, management consultants, and other intermediaries), because investors rely on such advisers for information and advice. Finally, literature promoting Midland is sent to firms, such as high-tech firms, on specialized mailing lists.

These tools constitute the first phase of Midland's investment development program. During this phase, the administrators of the program are learning about Sumoto's industries and what they can offer Midland. At the same time, these administrators are networking ("chatting with Sumoto business people") and finding out what they perceive as obstacles to investment.

The next phase of Midland's program opens with an exhibition in the nation's capital. The aim, according to government officials, is to encourage technology transfers, especially in "industries of the future", such as telecommunications and the computer industry. Foreign firms are invited to attend this exhibition and display their wares. To increase attendance, Midland's Department of External Affairs picks up most of the tab.

The following Monday, venture capital firms from Sumoto are invited to a venture capital conference in Midland. Two days later, portfolio managers from Sumoto are flown to Midland for briefings from high level officials. After the briefings, these portfolio managers are given the opportunity to explore investment possibilities.

At the same time, mid-level bureaucrats from the government of Midland are travelling in the other direction. They are on their way to attend trade fairs in Sumoto, in Germany and in other foreign countries. After arriving there, they mingle, hand out literature and sit in a large booth, answering questions from business people.

While these visits are taking place, several Midland officials are organizing an advertising campaign. Full-page advertisements appear in business publications in Sumoto. The themes in these advertisements are woven around what consultants say are the ambitions and concerns of Sumoto business people.

Midland does not ignore the press either. Press tours of Midland are arranged that bring together leading Sumoto journalists, in the hope of generating news coverage. Seminars about doing business in Midland are organized as well, to which business people and opinion leaders from Sumoto are invited.

Some of these seminars are for large audiences. Others, such as seminars to demonstrate the capabilities of Midland's machinery companies and the opportunities for joint ventures, are intended for only a few people. Five or six people (including a lawyer hoping the trip will bring him more clients) comprise the seminar team. Among the topics they address:

(1) the legal aspects of doing business in Midland,

(2) taxation and financial incentives for investors,

(3) the economic climate.

Sometimes, a representative from Midland's National Research Council will speak about technology transfer agreements between foreign and domestic firms. Next, a short film about Midland is shown. Finally, a testimonial speech by a foreign businessman, relating the story of his company's successful investment in Midland, concludes the seminar.

In addition to these seminars, Midland uses the direct approach to "dig out" potential investors: "Have You Ever Thought of Midland as a Source of Joint Venture Partners and Place for Investment?" ask advertisements which appear in local newspapers in Sumoto cities. If not, the ads say, why not make an appointment with a Midland Embassy official who will be visiting the city shortly.

Midland is especially keen on attracting more foreign entrepreneurs as immigrants, particularly if they have lots of cash. Sometimes

Midland has to be discreet about this because Sumoto's leaders do not like it. Privately, they accuse Midland of stealing their entrepreneurs. Consequently, officials attached to the Embassy of Midland only deliver low-key presentations and then counsel foreign business people who show an interest.

This is one vision of investment development. It has two unusual features: Midland does not offer financial incentives to investors. Also, the government has not undertaken structural and legal reforms (e.g., changes to tax, competition and environment laws) to encourage investment because it is still weighing them against social policy goals. An idea presented by a researcher with Midland's C.D. Howe Institute—that the government set up a program of adjustment assistance to compensate "those who personally lose, so that society might gain"[32]—is under discussion as well.

6. Canada's Tools and Techniques

Canada's investment development program and the programs of Canada's provinces are not the same as Midland's. But there are similarities in the tools and tactics used.

Both Canada and Midland, for instance, have a program to attract foreign entrepreneurs as immigrants. Under Canada's program, a person who promises to buy or start a business that will employ one or more Canadians can gain entry to Canada. In addition, Canada has a program aimed just at the wealthy. By making an investment of just $350,000 ($250,000 in some provinces), a foreign citizen can get landed immigrant status.[33] (Critics usually describe this program as a "passport for sale" scheme.)

Another similarity is in the overseas missions that each nation organizes. Both countries believe that if ministers and government officials are sent on speaking tours, foreign investment dollars will eventually follow them home.[34] Seminars, participation in trade shows,

---

[32] Byrne Purchase, *The Innovative Society: Competitiveness in the 1990s*, (Toronto: C.D. Howe Institute, 1991), p. 11.

[33] The Ontario government's director of business immigration told the Canadian Bar Association that Chinese nationals from Hong Kong often use the federal-provincial business immigration programs to buy Canadian passports without much benefit for Canada. Jean Pierre Bonhomme, "Les avocats doutent de l'efficacité de l'aide aux immigrants investisseurs", *La Presse*, Aug. 23, 1988, p. B1. Michael Bociurkiw, "Entrepreneurs Hard to Track after Landing", *The Free Press*, July 15, 1988, p. 30.

[34] A number of delegations from other countries, such as Japan, have come to

and direct-mail campaigns are other promotional techniques that both governments favour.

Canada and Midland also engage in investment prospecting. At Investment Canada, one-page outlines or profiles of Canadian companies with interesting technology (e.g., opto-electronics) are developed. These companies are then presented as potential partners to European firms seeking access to the North American market. The object, according to Investment Canada officials, is to get companies talking to each other. If a European firm wants to establish a business in Canada, Investment Canada may receive the news by telex from one of Canada's investment counsellors overseas. Meetings are then arranged between company officers, provincial government officials (e.g., the "plant location" division of provincial ministries of industry) and municipal economic development commissioners.

Sometimes, groups of business people from Japan and other countries (incoming missions) visit Canada. Federal and provincial government officials, including Investment Canada officials, meet and speak with them, and accompany them during part of their tour.

One tool common to the programs of many countries, including Canada's, is a heavy reliance on media advertising. Indeed, in the first few months after Canada's investment development program was set up, advertising was the predominant tool.

That was in the summer of 1985. Surveys had shown that some foreign business people viewed Canada as a relatively unattractive location for investment for various reasons: its labour force was inefficient, its climate severe, and its market potential small.

Government officials were concerned. Such opinions, they thought, were misperceptions of reality that could harm the country's investment plans. What was the best way to dispel such images? That was their main concern. Also, how to communicate a new message that Canada was receptive to foreign investment ("open for business").

The tools government officials chose were the traditional ones employed in any awareness program. Government ministers gave speeches overseas, printed promotional brochures, organized seminars and, of course, there was advertising.

These advertisements highlighted Canada's comparative advantages. Designed to appeal to high income people, chief executive officers and politicians, they appeared in prestigious international

---

Canada. "Japanese Business Leaders Tour Canada", *Montreal Gazette*, Oct. 18, 1989, p. E1.

business publications such as *Der Spiegel* and the *Far Eastern Economic Review*. Among the themes chosen were:

- "If you want to know how great Canada is, look beneath the surface" (Canada's wealth of natural resources);
- "271,000 kilometres of highway" (the extensive transportation system);
- "From vacant lot to making a lot" (profitable opportunities);
- "We are proud to say that Alexander Graham Bell was the start of it all" (the communications system).

Did this media blitz accomplish its goal? Cause and effect are hard to determine. Nonetheless, in 1987, the Conference Board concluded, after a survey of foreign companies, that the government's "open for business" message had gotten "through to the investment community".

Even if advertising is effective, it is not sufficient for any government to merely shout welcome. Image, after all, is only one determinant of investment flows. Economists who study site location theory have identified many more: comparative wage rates, transportation costs, taxation, access to markets, energy costs, and regulatory practices. In addition, there is the quality of life, such as the number of cultural, educational and recreational facilities which a particular location offers. This is increasingly important to companies wanting to attract the best employees.

These site selection factors—examining them, ranking Canada and other nations in relation to them, and talking to foreign business people about them—are at the heart of Canada's Investment Development Program. In almost every speech that a government official gives to foreign business people, Canada's advantages as a site for investment will be discussed.

Those who give these speeches—ministers of industry, international trade and their deputies, and the president of Investment Canada—are well-known. They are Canada's boosters or "salesmen". However, there are many other promoters who are not public figures. They are found at different levels within Investment Canada, Industry, Science and Technology Canada, External Affairs, and Canada's embassies abroad. These lower level officials—which include seven investment counsellors in the U.S., U.K., France, Germany, Hong Kong and Japan—make direct contact with individual company executives, answer questions, entice and persuade.

Some of these officials are part of the "investor services" component of the program. In Ottawa, this aspect of the program is performed by the Business Services Division of I.S.T.C., the Investment

Development Division of External Affairs, and Investment Canada. If one of these centres cannot answer an investor's question, the investor is referred to another part of government. If he is seeking technology, the investor is put in contact with the National Research Council.

What do these officials do when they are not answering questions? Some—especially the investment counsellors and trade commissioners at Canada's embassies—organize seminars, advertising campaigns and direct mailings to successful business people.

This is called the shotgun approach to investment prospecting. Its aim is to promote inquiries. One-on-one meetings, on the other hand, are termed the rifle approach. Sometimes, both approaches are combined, such as at the conference hosted annually by the World Economic Forum ("W.E.F.") in Davos, Switzerland.

The W.E.F.'s Annual Symposium at Davos is actually a series of forums that last for a week. Over 800 company executives and government leaders meet there every year, attracted by the opportunity to exchange ideas, visit the national exhibits and, of course, ski after hours.

One Canadian government minister and his delegation always attend. They give speeches in the forum rooms, deliver audio-visual presentations on Canada's economic performance, talk to corporate executives, and distribute literature such as "Canada the Trading Nation". Making foreign business people aware of Canada's potential in the hope they will invest, is the object of this effort.

The federal government has a different goal when it encourages private sector participation in European trade fairs. If Canadian companies are placed in contact with their European counterparts, Ottawa reasons, they may enter into mutually beneficial technology transfer, co-production and co-marketing agreements.

Every year there are hundreds of trade fairs in Europe, such as the Milan fair, and the Hannover fair (the world's largest industrial fair) which attracts 600,000 visitors annually. Government officials seek out Canadian firms interested in acquiring technology from, and forming partnerships with overseas companies. Then they organize corporate missions to attend these fairs.

Most investment development programs in other countries have a research and policy division. Canada's program is no exception. Canadian researchers gather data on wage rates and other locational factors, and identify foreign sources of technology. They also provide the intellectual justification for many of the program's initiatives.

For example, they study the sources and destinations of foreign investment funds. This topic interests Canada's investment promoters—the officials who give the uplifting speeches and prepare the brochures—because it tells them where to direct their efforts.

Researchers serve as an adjunct to Canada's program in another way—by identifying potential corporate investors. How might this be done? One way is "old hat" to many entrepreneurs who have searched for a market niche to fill. First, make a list of those subsectors of the Canadian economy where imports are highest in terms of quantity and value. Next, find out from which countries those imports are coming. Finally, identify the foreign firms which are supplying the imported goods. These firms are potential investors, if not now, then in the future when their Canadian customer base is of sufficient size to support a branch business.

The flow of goods going the other way may also be a beacon to locating potential foreign investors. For instance, foreign businesses that import industrial raw materials produced in Canada are candidates for setting up processing plants in this country.

But probably the most important role of the researchers has been to devise the themes around which Canada's Investment Development Program have been built. It was their task to examine current economic literature, come to a conclusion on the forces shaping Canadian and world economies, and ascertain the elements successful companies have in common.

7. Themes and Messages

The ideas they chose for improving Canada's competitiveness are popular these days. One is the need for companies to adopt a global orientation.

(a) The Global Marketplace[35]

Globalization (the integration of markets on a global scale) has many causes: declining tariffs, lower transportation costs, the high standard of living in many parts of the world.

An important cause is improved communications. New products become known more quickly. Consumers in Sweden, China and

---

[35] Milton Friedman claims that the revolution in communications technology has warped our vision, and that the world is less internationalized than in 1929. Milton Friedman, "Evidence Shows the Internationalized Economy is Nonsense", *The Globe and Mail*, May 6, 1989, p. B2.

everywhere else want jeans and hand-held calculators. Another factor is rapid technological change. This shortens product life and spurs companies to market their products in several countries as quickly as possible.

The accelerated cost of R&D is another impetus to globalization. Some companies sell globally to recover their R&D costs faster. In the case of a few products, such as certain drugs, R&D costs can be justified only on the basis of world-wide sales.

Because of these forces, global markets are developing for a number of products. Ford, Toyota and Fiat, for instance, compete in several countries, so do Kodak, Fuji and Agfa (photographic film). Another example is Tata Consulting Services of Bombay, India, which supplies computer software to American Express.

Canada's investment development program has two messages related to globalization. For Canadian companies, the message is to think globally. A presence in Europe, Asia and the U.S. may be necessary for competitiveness.

For foreign companies, the message is a little different. Multinational companies want to locate their businesses in countries with an infrastructure that allows them to operate world-wide. These companies are told that Canada's relatively small market is no handicap, since Canada can offer them the opportunity to service North American and world markets.

(b) The Competitive Advantages of Partnerships

A second theme is that new forms of industrial co-operation are needed to keep Canada competitive. Canadian firms should consider entering into "strategic alliances", a term that embraces national and international partnerships, joint ventures, licensing and technology transfer agreements and sales/distribution arrangements. Joint ventures, government officials tell business people, are an effective way for Canadian firms to penetrate distant markets.

To foreign audiences, such as those in Japan, the message is slightly changed. They are told that tremendous business opportunities are being missed which might involve the exchange of technology, co-marketing and co-production arrangements, and joint ventures in third countries.[36] Canada, they are reminded, is an attractive international partner.[37]

---

[36] Notes for a Presentation by Paul Labbé, President, Investment Canada, to the Keidanren, Tokyo, July 7, 1988.

[37] "Canada: A Powerful Partner", remarks by Paul Labbé, President of Investment Canada, to the Swedish Delegation, Ottawa, Mar. 14, 1988.

International partnerships or joint ventures are not a new idea. Prior to World War II, a number of international joint ventures existed involving trade, mining and plantation agriculture. By the 1970s, the joint international business venture had "become the predominant form of foreign investment in developing countries".[38] However, it was not until the 1980s—about the time that Kenichi Ohmae wrote *Triad Power*[39]—that the idea of international business arrangements acquired popular appeal.

Because of rapid technological change, plus the associated risks and costs, Ohmae sees global partnerships as the wave of the 1990s. He also believes that firms, in order to remain competitive, must establish themselves in Japan, Europe, and the U.S., and then serve the rest of the world from these bases. Strategic alliances—since they offer companies a way of spreading risks, piercing foreign markets, and acquiring a "technology window"—form part of his prescription.

Australia,[40] France[41] and China[42] must agree. As part of their development efforts, they are seeking Canadian companies interested in partnerships and joint ventures. Canadian companies which have followed this road include Bombardier (partnership with Hitachi of Japan to produce and market locomotives) and Vencap Equities of Alberta (working with U.S.-based Biotechnica International to develop herbicide-tolerant canola seeds). Northern Telecom is another example.

Many Canadian companies are too small to enter into international partnerships. For such companies, the message is to consider licensing and cross-distribution arrangements.

(c) The Need to Acquire Technology

A third theme stresses that technology is the basis of competition among industrialized countries. In the words of one government publication:

> The world's nations are moving from the traditional industrial economy towards a new economy based on technology and innovation . . . advances

---

[38] Wolfgang Friedman and Jean-Pierre Beguin, *Joint International Business Ventures in Developing Countries*, (New York: Columbia University Press 1971), p. VI.

[39] (New York: The Free Press, 1985).

[40] Erik Floren, "Aussies Woo Alberta", *Edmonton Sun*, July 21, 1988, p. 44.

[41] Patricia Lush, "France Promotes Alliance with Canadian Companies", *The Globe and Mail*, Nov. 16, 1988, p. B17.

[42] Nick Lees, "Chinese Open Edmonton Office to Spur Joint Ventures", *Edmonton Journal*, Aug. 17, 1986, p. H1.

in areas like microelectronics, robotics, biotechnology and advanced industrial materials are transforming the way business operates and the way
nations compete in world markets.[43]

During the 1970s, several economists made similar forecasts. They
argued that as Third World countries become major manufacturers of
automobiles and other standardized products, competition among
industrial countries would be increasingly based on technology and
know-how.

Such views have brought about a new direction in government
thinking. In the past, the Canadian government restricted its concern
to ways of increasing Canada's low rate of spending on R&D (1.3% of
annual output on R&D compared to 3% for Japan). The Canadian
government is now trying to assist Canadian industry to acquire technology from abroad (e.g., through External Affairs' Technology Inflow
Program).

In their speeches, government officials are also suggesting that
Canadian companies shift towards more knowledge-intensive forms of
production, and acquire foreign technology through licensing agreements. A related message is that Canadian companies should consider
entering into R&D partnerships. In the words of a senior Investment
Canada official addressing foreign journalists:

> . . . foreign investment is deemed vital to strengthen our research and
> development activities. Joint ventures, research consortias, resource ex-
> changes and technological pooling are of great interest to us.[44]

(d) Canada as an Attractive Place to Invest

The fourth theme is the best known: Canada is a profitable place
in which to invest. Foreign companies which locate in Canada can gain
a comparative advantage.

To create this awareness, Canadian government officials visiting
Korea and other countries remind business people that:

- "corporate profits in Canada tend to be higher than in the
  United States, while labour, energy and real estate costs tend to
  be lower";[45]

---

[43] Science and Technology Canada, *Innovation: The Canadian Strategy for Science and
Technology*, p. 9. The high cost to develop advanced technology has driven European
companies to share research by entering into consortia like Esprit and Eureka.

[44] "The Climate for Foreign Investment In Canada", notes for an address by Alan
Nymark, Executive Vice-President, Investment Canada to a group of foreign economic/
business journalists, Ottawa, Oct. 2, 1989, p. 10.

[45] Notes for an address by John Church, Vice-President, Investment Canada, at the
Canada Product Show, Seoul, Korea, Mar. 28, 1990, p. 14.

- Canada has a "highly-skilled, well-educated labour force";[46]
- "as of 1988, average wage and benefit costs in Canadian manufacturing were below those of the United States, France, Japan and West Germany".[47]

In addition, foreign business executives are told that Canada has an enviable quality of life and is a leader in the scientific and technological revolution (e.g., Spar-Aerospace with its remote manipulator arm on the American space shuttle). Finally, because of free trade and an integrated system of highways, railways and telecommunication links, a company that establishes in Canada can get easy access to the U.S. market. (The Canada-U.S. market has 270 million people.)

Industry, Science and Technology Canada contributes to this communications effort by preparing industry profiles. External Affairs Canada helps by distributing information[48] on Canada through its posts abroad and by placing advertisements in foreign publications.

8. The Planning Process

The preceding themes form the backdrop to the planning of Canada's investment development program. This planning begins in August of every year. That is when officials at Industry, Science and Technology Canada prepare their development strategies for each industrial sector. In November, these strategies are communicated to Canada's embassies and consulates. These embassies and consulates then put together a set of projects as part of each post's annual plan.[49]

In these plans, there will be a list of economic sectors and the reasons they were chosen. For instance, if Canadian embassy officials in Britain should decide to direct their efforts at the aerospace sector, they might justify their choice by pointing out that Canadian aerospace firms could enter into mutually beneficial joint venture and technology transfer agreements with their British counterparts. This rationale will then appear in the plan.

In the next section of the plan, the embassy's (or consulate's) promotional projects and the anticipated results will appear. In the

---

[46] Ibid., p. 15.

[47] Ibid.

[48] An example of a publication is "Canada - an Investment Perspective". This 18-page document describes Canada's business environment.

[49] *Investment Program: Investment Promotion Operational Plans of Missions in Selected World Markets*, (Ottawa: External Affairs Canada - various years).

case of the British Embassy, one project may be to give technical briefings on Canada's aerospace industry to British executives. A possible rationale is that this is one way of locating British companies interested in joint ventures with Canadian companies.

After the plans of Canada's posts overseas are complete, they are forwarded to Ottawa. The plans are then collated and reviewed by External Affairs Canada, Investment Canada, and I.S.T.C. Is there an overlap? Will a seminar be effective? Is the right type of investment— such as investment that will bring technology to Canada—being sought? These are some questions that are asked.

9. A National Investment Development Plan

Officials involved in investment development sometimes talk wistfully about the idea of a National Investment Development Plan. Such a plan would reflect a national consensus among federal and provincial governments and the private sector, on the priorities for economic development within Canada and its regions. It would also set out a program to attract selected industries from abroad and increase the amount of investment in Canada by foreigners and Canadians.[50] Needless to say, no such plan presently exists. The major obstacle is Canada's regional rivalries. Each province views the other nine as competitors.

There are other problems too. Which level of government should carry out such a plan? Should Ottawa concentrate on Canada-wide promotions and market research and let the provinces handle specific projects? Or should the federal government be the pre-eminent player and directly court investors?

Then there is the question of bias. If a National Investment Development Plan focused on sectors such as electronics and transportation equipment, it might be biased in favour of central Canada. That could worry the Maritimers.

Since 1867, Canada has had an array of industrial policies. They have ranged from regional development and worker retraining to R&D incentives, energy self-sufficiency, and reduction in foreign investment. None of Canada's industrial policies, however, has been as

---

[50] On July 29, 1985, provincial and federal government ministers responsible for economic development met in St. John's, Newfoundland. Afterwards, they announced that they had agreed "to work with the support of the private sector towards a national investment development plan which would reflect the overall priorities of Canada and all its regions" (press release).

explicit as those of France and Japan, which clearly designate the industries to be encouraged or restructured based on their prospects for international competitiveness.

Canada's "Investment Development Program", to the extent that it picks industry sectors to be promoted, is another in this country's series of industrial policies. The adoption of a National Investment Development Plan would be a major step along the same road.

10. Measuring the Success of "Investment Development"

Bringing Canada's potential to the attention of foreign business people and ensuring that the country's environment is attractive in comparison with that of other countries is at the heart of Canada's investment development program. But ultimately, it will be the real or perceived rate of return that will determine whether investments are made in Canada or elsewhere.

Many factors outside the control of governments will influence this rate of return and, therefore, the impact of the investment development program. For example, Canada's attempts to attract and encourage the growth of firms with a global horizon will only work if other countries do not introduce protectionist measures and if Third World debt problems or a new oil crisis do not throttle world trade. Notwithstanding this, is there any means of evaluating Canada's Investment Development Program? Several methods of measurement can be proposed. None of them is satisfactory.

The first method is to presume that all foreign investment benefits Canada and to calculate how many dollars and yen came in. Another approach is to inquire whether Canada's competitive position has improved. A more exacting criteria would be whether the standard of living of the average Canadian has been increased.

Unfortunately, even starting with the simplest measure and looking at inflows of foreign capital, there are problems linking cause and effect. The investment decision-making process involves a complex interplay of variables which cannot be isolated.

On an elementary level, an indication of the program's impact can be gauged from the number of inquiries generated by advertisements and seminars. One aspect of investment development, the Business Immigration Program, might be assessed in terms of the value of the investments it yields. But such figures overestimate the impact, since they include inquiries and transactions that would have occurred in any event. As for achievements in actually attracting investment—and increasing technological diffusion from abroad—there are obvious difficulties in arriving at any conclusion.

In addition to investment inflows, other "macroeconomic indicators" might be looked at. Success in creating employment is relatively easy to size up, although linking such success with the investment development program will pose a challenge. In the event there are increases in Canada's productivity and exports, substantial replacement of imported goods by those manufactured locally, and a decline in the average age of Canada's manufacturing equipment and plants, then one might conclude that efforts to improve the international competitiveness of Canadian industry have left their mark.

But not much more can be said about the effect of the program on Canada's international competitive position without some consensus on what international competitiveness is all about. Alas, there is none.

To the average person, the measure of competitiveness between nations is a favourable balance of trade. Economists, on the other hand, use a variety of indicators, such as productivity measurements (unit labour costs or gross domestic product per employed person) and debt *per capita*. The World Economic Forum goes the furthest of all. In its 1989 annual report on the competitiveness of nations, the W.E.F. relies on 292 criteria.[51]

The most satisfying method of evaluating Canada's Investment Development Program would be in terms of its impact on the average standard of living of Canadian citizens. But that is not something that can be done scientifically. Even if it were possible to isolate individual factors affecting real income, the gap in time between a promotional activity and its effect, if any, on real income, is too great.

Nevertheless, there is one certainty. As the federal and provincial governments assume a more visible role in selecting industry sectors in which foreign investment and the development of international alliances will be encouraged, economists will have much to discuss.

11. Ottawa Versus the Provinces

The first topic they might examine is: which level of government can best promote foreign investment? The provinces (as always) want

---

[51] I.M.E.D.E. and the World Economic Forum, *The World Competiveness Report 1989*. The W.E.F. used statistical indicators and impressionistic (subjective) accounts from 2,000 business people.

the limelight. And to buttress their position, they can point to the U.S., where the individual states devise their own strategies for attracting investment. However, this has led to bidding wars between American states. Other disadvantages include: the inability of the poorer states/ provinces to compete successfully, their limited authority over trade and tax matters, and the difficulty that regional governments have in dealing with companies whose business transcends borders.

In Canada, this issue is currently academic. Ottawa and the provinces are all pursuing foreign investors and marketing their economies.[52] A leading example is Ontario and its Ministry of Industry, Trade and Technology ("M.I.T.T."). Five of M.I.T.T.'s branches are entitled: Business Immigration, Investment Marketing, Strategic Alliances, Industry Development, and Industry Promotion.

The scope of their promotional efforts "demonstrate[s] that, like the federal government, the provincial governments are 'open for business'".[53]

12. The Effectiveness of the Tools

Another topic for economists to discuss might be the effectiveness of the tools being used. These days there are so many national, regional and municipal governments seeking foreign capital that the international arena resembles a circus midway. All have the same message: their country has low taxes, skilled labour and an excellent infrastructure.

What are the best tools to operate in such an environment? For instance, are overseas missions by government ministers productive when every country is arranging them? These missions bring Canada considerable publicity in foreign news media. Nevertheless, the president of the Winnipeg Chamber of Commerce called missions by Manitoba government officials "holidays for ministers". They do not accomplish much, she said, because building a rapport with Asian businessmen takes a long time.[54]

---

[52] For instance, Ottawa and five provinces (B.C., Alberta, Saskatchewan, Ontario, Quebec) have offices in London; Ottawa and four provinces (B.C., Alberta, Quebec, Ontario) have offices in Tokyo; Newfoundland and P.E.I. have no offices abroad.

[53] "Globalization: Lessons for Canadian Investment Policy and the Federation", notes for an address by Alan Nymark, Executive Vice-President, Investment Canada, I.R.P.P. Conference on Canadian Federalism: Global Economic Challenges, Mont Gabriel, Mar. 30, 1990.

[54] "Failure Predicted for Group Hunting Asian Investment", *The Free Press*, Nov. 4, 1987, p. 11.

Speeches by ministers may pique the curiosity of foreign business-men. That is an important first step. But as for what really motivates investors, Michael Howard, who spent three years at the Canadian embassy in Tokyo as an investment counsellor, has some thoughts. Japanese investors come to Canada, Howard says, for three strategic reasons:

(1) to secure access to markets (e.g., automobile assembly plants);

(2) to secure products they need (e.g., coal, fuel);

(3) to secure or acquire technology.

Howard bluntly asserts: "If you can't convince the Japanese that it is in their strategic interest—not financial but strategic—to make the in-vestment, you are wasting your time".[55]

13. The Competition

Next there are the international implications of Canada's Invest-ment Development Program (and similar programs at the provincial level). All the world's advanced countries are trying to shift into the high-technology and knowledge-intensive sectors, and to become ex-porters of products embodying sophisticated technology.

Japan's strategy for the twenty-first century, for instance, focuses on biotechnology, optics, microelectronics, and advanced industrial materials. The Canadian government is emphasizing the same sectors. So is Australia,[56] Singapore, and the Netherlands. Will such policies clash? Will there be duplication of capacity? And if so, will this lead (as "free market" critics of industrial policies claim) to more protectionism as nations champion their newly acquired industrial structures?

Questions can be asked about joint ventures as well. They are politically popular; almost every nation seeking foreign investment encourages them. They are also a growing phenomenon: some U.S. companies have entered into dozens of domestic and international joint ventures. However, they have their dangers. One partner may extract the skills of the other and then compete with it directly. South

---

[55] Lillian Rukas, "Interview: Michael Howard", *Investing in Canada*, Fall 1989, p. 4.

[56] Australia wants foreign investment in the "brain-driven industries": bio-technologies, advanced material, information, scientific and medical equipment, com-munications and processing technologies. The Investment Commissioner, *Investment Australia: Business News Update*, (New York, Australian Trade Commission, 1989).

Korean and Japanese companies have used such alliances as stepping-stones to become internationally competitive.[57]

14. Strategies and Scope

The most important issue, however, is which strategy[58] should be used to promote investment. There are two:

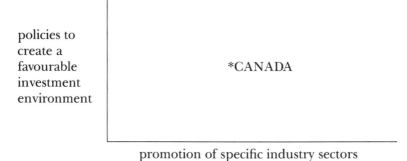

policies to
create a
favourable   *CANADA
investment
environment

promotion of specific industry sectors

Germany and the U.S. federal government favour the first strategy. Singapore and Ireland emphasize the second. Most countries, including Canada, have chosen mixtures of both strategies.

After countries choose an appropriate strategy, they must select the industries in which foreign investments and partnerships are to be encouraged. The issue is the criteria to be used. Investment Canada, Quebec, Ontario and Alberta are focusing on firms in the biotechnology, optoelectronics and software sectors. These are "companies of the future". Canadian embassy employees in the Netherlands are targeting industries involved in food processing, health care, transportation, electronic composites and machinery equipment. On the other hand,

---

[57] Christopher Lorenz. "Japanese Use Partnerships with West as Damaging New Form of Competition", *The Globe and Mail*, Oct. 28, 1986, p. B26. An M.I.T. study describes how start-up firms in the U.S. semi-conductor industry were forced by lack of funds to issue licences or sell technology to the "heavyweights of Japanese industry", which then became their competitors. Michael Dertouzos, *Made in America: Regaining the Productive Edge*, (Cambridge: M.I.T. Press, 1989). Japanese companies enter partnerships to learn. The goal of Western companies, on the other hand, is often just to avoid making an investment. Gary Hamil, Yves Doz and C.K Prahalad, "Collaborate with Your Competitors—-and Win" *Harvard Business Review*, January-February 1989, Vol. 67, No. 1, p. 133

[58] Investment Canada Vice-President Alan Nymark says: "Canada has no choice but to meet international standards in a wide range of areas. . .industrial R&D. . .education and training; competition policy; the cost of capital; transportation and communications services; industrial/regional development policies; and interprovincial barriers to trade", *Globalization: Lessons for Canadian Investment Policy and the Federation*, op. cit.

if industry sectors were ranked in terms of present employment levels, export earnings and R&D, the automotive, pulp and paper, and metals sectors would receive the highest priority.

15. Who Benefits: A Gamut of Views

Finally, there are the more philosophical questions. Who benefits the most from efforts to attract foreign investment? Does anyone lose?

One might seek an indication by asking the converse: who benefits from nationalism? Opponents of nationalism have an answer: the upper middle class and business people in protected industries (who make higher profits).[59] Nationalist policies, free market supporters claim, open up opportunities for aspiring managers at the expense of workers and consumers, who must contend with reduced employment and product choice because of restrictions on foreign investment.[60] The real beneficiaries of a foreign investment screening process, these critics suggest, constitute 2% to 3% of a country's population (500,000 to 800,000 people in the case of Canada).

To many people, this is a simplistic view. Over the last few years, several companies whose transactions were in the process of being reviewed by Investment Canada have announced that they would grant their Canadian subsidiaries world product mandates. The spin-offs[61] from a world market mandate can benefit an entire community. The value of these two differing views is that they serve to emphasize two points. Those who investigate the welfare consequences of restricting or encouraging the inflow of foreign capital often abandon empiricism for speculation. Secondly, there are interest groups behind most economic prescriptions.[62] One reason they arise is because the costs and benefits of economic programs are seldom spread equally.

---

[59] According to one political scientist, salaried professionals (e.g., private sector managers) were the greatest supporters of Canadian nationalism after 1965, and its greatest beneficiaries. Philip Resnick, *The Land of Cain*, (Vancouver: New Star Books, 1977), p. 210. For another writer's views, read Steven Globerman, "Canadian Science Policy and Technological Sovereignty", *Canadian Public Policy*, Winter 1978, pp. 34-45.

[60] However, in Canada, the trade union elite wants to reduce the level of foreign investment while the corporate elite favours it. William Johnston, "Class and Economic Nationalism: Attitudes Toward Foreign Investment" (1985), 10 *Canadian Journal of Sociology* 23.

[61] These include: R&D, increased employment and additional spending in local stores, as well as opportunities for suppliers to specialize. Mark Witten, "Branch Plants Bear New Fruit", *Canadian Business*, Nov. 1980, p. 54.

[62] For example, Chrysler's nationalistic President Lee Iaccoca (1986 earnings: $20 million in salary and stock options) and the Big Three automakers want Washington to

Despite the conceptional difficulties, it is important to ponder how these costs and benefits are distributed. Most economic goals—such as making Canadian industry more competitive—can be reached by several routes. Society cannot choose the best route without knowing who bears the burden.

Foreign direct investment can bring many benefits. It may provide new channels to foreign markets (for instance, through the marketing and distribution network of the foreign company), or strengthen a country's industrial structure, especially when accompanied by technology and proven management skills. There are a number of examples of foreign companies which have purchased a Canadian business, or entered into a joint venture with a Canadian company, and then transferred production or other technology to Canada. Foreign capital can also save a financially troubled company. Amoco's takeover of Dome was an example of that.

Foreign direct investment, if it is in the form of a new business, also enlarges the potential market for domestic suppliers. This pleases those corporations able to obtain another customer, and senior company managers whose bonuses are linked to their company's income statements.[63] In part, this explains why the Canadian Manufacturers' Association has praised Ontario's efforts to attract foreign investment, despite the risk of new competition for C.M.A. members.

Finally, foreign direct investment often creates jobs. These are just two of many examples: the Hyundai plant in Bromont, Quebec, and the Cami Automotive plant (a General Motors-Suzuki joint venture) in Ingersoll, Ontario, employ 1,200 and 2,000 people respectively. The spending of these employees has a multiplier effect throughout the local economies, creating additional jobs. Foreign multinationals are able to increase employment in Canada, because they have access to export markets and possess valuable technological, marketing and organizational skills.

On the other hand, foreign investment can also eliminate jobs, A new foreign-controlled company may displace an existing Canadian business. As for takeovers, they may save jobs if the target company is bankrupt. However, they seldom create new employment. On occasion, takeovers cause cutbacks. The merger of Molson and Carling O'Keefe led to a reduction of 1,400 jobs.

---

impose a 25% tariff on imported mini-vans.

[63] Bruce Constantineau, "Business Leaders Welcome Cash Influx", *The Vancouver Sun*, Feb. 18, 1989, p. A8.

The net effect is hard to determine. American economists Glickman and Woodward[64] looked at U.S. data but could not determine the effect of acquisitions, sales and liquidations on employment. As for jobs created by *new* foreign-controlled businesses established in the U.S., the numbers varied widely: from 4,139 jobs in 1984 to 33,871 jobs in 1988. For their calculations, Glickman and Woodward chose the period 1982-86 (which included the 1982 recession). They added the jobs created by new businesses and the expansion of existing foreign-controlled firms, then deducted cutbacks by other foreign-controlled firms. The resulting figure was negative, indicating net job loss.

The number of new jobs created by foreign investors increased after 1986. Glickman and Woodward believe that, during the latter part of the 1980s, there was a net annual job gain of between 15,000 and 25,000 jobs. The two economists concluded that "foreigners have added only a few drops to the large American job pool". On the other hand, "foreign manufacturers have the potential to offset some domestic factory closings in U.S. communities".[65]

Are the figures different in other countries? The U.S. has a mature economy. Foreign investment in, say, Ireland or Singapore has clearly increased the level of employment. As for Canada, no comprehensive analysis is available. However, some statistics on Canada have been published. On the notification forms submitted to Investment Canada, investors who are establishing new businesses must indicate the number of employees they plan to hire over two years. In 1988-89, this figure was 5,202. In 1989-90, it was 7,068.[66]

One of the ways Canada encourages more investment is through its business immigration program (administered by Employment and Immigration Canada). The entrepreneurial category, designed to attract experienced people, allows a person to immigrate to Canada if he promises to start or continue a business which he will manage. The business must employ at least one Canadian or permanent resident (in addition to the entrepreneur and his dependants).

According to External Affairs Canada, 2,843 entrepreneurs were accepted at Canadian immigration offices abroad in 1989. Prior to

---

[64] Norman Glickman and Douglas Woodward, *The New Competitors: How Foreign Investors Are Changing the U.S. Economy*, (New York: Basic Books, 1990). Some U.S. state governors and mayors seem to believe that all foreign investment creates jobs. This is not so. Jobs are sometimes redistributed or lost.

[65] Ibid., pp. 135 and XVIII.

[66] Investment Canada, *Annual Report* for the appropriate year.

acceptance, each entrepreneur had to submit a business proposal, which are the sources of the statistics shown below:[67]

Year	No. of Entrepreneurs Accepted	Jobs to Create	Jobs to Retain	Funds to be Transferred to Canada
1989	2,843	11,837	1,449	$3.6 billion

The number of jobs created appears to be substantial. However, "the economic benefits attributed to the Entrepreneur Program are based solely upon the declared intentions of the successful applicants".[68] Because there has been little monitoring, no reliable data exists on the actual number of jobs created (or the actual amount of funds transferred or what happened to the funds).

One study, covering the period 1979-84, discovered that the "jobs created were predominantly situated in the retail and services sector" and were "primarily in the unskilled manual labour category".[69] The authors concluded that "the entrepreneurial program (was) contributing most to employment in the youth category". (A glance at the data reports from External Affairs Canada, which records what entrepreneurs intend to do, shows that the service sector continues to be the site of most new jobs.)[70]

A second category in the business immigration program is for "investor immigrants". Wealthy foreign citizens, who want Canadian immigration visas and who otherwise qualify, write a cheque for $350,000 ($250,000 in some provinces) payable to a privately administered investment fund. This fund then invests in eligible businesses. The money is locked in for five years.

Fund managers like First Generation Resources Ltd. (an investment company which manages Canadian Maple Leaf Fund Ltd.)

---

[67] Source: Masent and Invest Reports produced by External Affairs Canada. These reports contained data based on accepted applications. However, not all immigrants who are accepted come to Canada. In addition, these reports were based on investors' declared net worth. In 1990, External Affairs Canada discontinued these reports.

[68] John DeMont and Thomas Fennell, *Hong Kong Money*, (Toronto: Key Porter Books, 1989), p. 100.

[69] C.G. Wong, C.A. Schutz and G.A. Crone, "Evaluation of the Entrepreneurial Immigration Program", prepared for Employment and Immigration, Immigration Directorate, Program Evaluation Branch, Ottawa, September 1985, p. 118 and para. 8 of the Introduction. This study is referred to in Alan Nash, *The Economic Impact of the Entrepreneurial Immigration Program*, (Ottawa: The Studies in Social Policy Program of the Institute for Research on Public Policy, 1987), p. 30 and Table 19.

[70] Employment and Immigration Canada keeps statistical data (available under the *Access to Information Act*) showing business immigrants admitted by sector of the economy. To ascertain how goods-producing industries are distinguished from service-producing industries, see Nash, op. cit., Table 21.

receive a fee based on a percentage of the fund's assets. (Annual management fees are 2% to 4%. In addition, many funds charge as much as one third of annual profits after the initial outlay is returned to the investor.)

Eligible Canadian businesses profit as well. They get low-cost capital (e.g., term loans below the prime interest rate). More commonly, the funds buy preferred or common shares. The businesses, which often have no earnings history, can then qualify for bank loans.

Some Canadian companies even market their own investor immigrant funds. Lakeview Development of Canada is an example. It uses the money from its fund to finance its budget hotels. Another fund, marketed by the Beacon Group, finances the distribution of its feature films. (Many fund managers, like the Beacon Group, have people on staff who counsel potential investor immigrants.)

The purpose of the investor immigrant category is to create a source of risk capital for small and medium-sized Canadian business. However, that source may be smaller than it could be. After the investor has received a return (e.g., 3%) on the loaned money, and management fees (e.g., 4%) have been paid, any remaining profits go to the investment fund. This creates an incentive for the money to go into low-risk projects.

The investor immigration program has brought the banks and investment dealers substantial fees and new clients. Perhaps they foresaw this when they lobbied for the program.

Although its precise impact on employment and national welfare will always remain the subject of debate, many corporations, employees and communities are major beneficiaries from the pursuit of foreign investment. In the U.S., some of these beneficiaries have formed an organization, called the Association for Foreign Investment in America, to fight restrictions on foreign investment that are being advocated by some members of Congress.[71]

Opposing this association is the Citizens Against Foreign Control of the United States. Founded by the president of an automobile parts manufacturer, it unites those who fear that their jobs and their country's sovereignty are in jeopardy. In Canada, the Business Council on National Issues, consisting of 150 chief executive officers, confronts the Council of Concerned Canadians.

People of means with assets to sell also benefit from the influx of foreign capital. They often get a higher price for their companies and

---

[71] The *New York Times* Service, "Foreign Investment in U.S. Making Waves: Yeutter", *The Globe and Mail*, Feb. 23, 1988, p. B2.

real estate. One reason is that Canadian (and American) prices are comparatively cheap in terms of Asian currencies (such as the Japanese yen). Also, many Asian buyers are not well-informed about North American market conditions. Middle-class professionals in Tokyo or Hong Kong listen to the presentation of a Canadian or American promoter then buy a condominium sight unseen. This has caused the Japanese government to worry about its lax disclosure laws.[72]

Another factor (boosting demand and price) is foreign investors' political fears. These investors see American and Canadian assets as offering long-term security. Some Pacific Rim investors have apparently concluded that they should invest their wealth elsewhere in case the poor in southeast Asia gain political power.

Unfortunately, not every Canadian is a winner from this inflow of funds. Some have seen their living standards decline as housing prices have risen.

Incoming foreign capital is not the only cause. The baby boom, internal migration, and purchases by Canadian speculators have played a role. However, investment and immigration from the Far East have helped to drive up the costs of housing in Toronto and Vancouver.[73] Other cities have experienced a spill-over effect. Retailers and those who rent office space have suffered also as commercial rents are pulled upward by the spiralling price of office buildings.[74]

The same phenomenon has occurred internationally in several cities such as Sydney, Australia; Bangkok, Thailand; and Honolulu,

---

[72] Elisabeth Rubinfein, "The Price Is Right: In Reverse Land Rush, Americans Now Pitch Property to the Japanese", *Wall Street Journal*, June 15, 1988, p. 1.

[73] Susan Gitten, "Yacht People Find B.C Property a Good Place to Drop Anchor", *Financial Post*, Aug. 29, 1988, p. 52. Calgary home builders have sent sales people to Hong Kong. "Calgary Builders Court Asians", *The Leader-Post* (Regina), Oct. 7, 1989, p. C-1.

It is impossible to know the impact of foreign investment on real estate prices because there are no comprehensive reporting requirements. The *IC Act* catches purchases of apartment buildings and commercial real estate (hotels, shopping centres, office buildings) but not farms, homes or raw land. Moreover, some investors forget to file a notification. Land titles documents such as affidavits of residency are of little assistance. Foreigners often buy real estate through nominees (lawyers and relatives), trusts or numbered companies. For comments on a study done for the Laurier Institute, read Donald Gutstein, *The New Landlords: Asian Investment in Canadian Real Estate* (Victoria, B.C.: Press Porcépic Limited, 1990), pp. 198-99. Some real estate agents and lawyers play down the impact of offshore capital because of their financial interest in a continuing flow of foreign money into real estate.

[74] Author Donald Gutstein tries to identify winners and losers. He says that those being hurt by globalization "are having enormous difficulty impressing their concerns on the politicians". *The New Landlords*, op. cit., p. 229.

U.S.A. Among the buyers are Japanese, South Korea, Taiwanese, Malaysian and Hong Kong investors. One result is that Australia and Thailand have passed laws to curb land speculation by foreign purchasers.[75] After a 32% jump in residential prices in one year, Honolulu's mayor called for a similar law.

Government officials in most countries do not welcome offshore property investment. Those involved in Canada's Investment Development Program, for instance, try to promote "technology bearing investments". That includes "green field joint ventures" (new businesses established by joint ventures) and corporate alliances, but excludes most mergers. Real estate investment is not promoted.

Attitudes are different at the provincial and municipal levels. Promoters working for the B.C. and Quebec governments seem prepared to use real estate—and almost any other lure—to attract Taiwan's and Hong Kong's wealthiest citizens.

Municipal governments also seek foreign real estate investments. Hamilton, Brantford, Saskatoon, Calgary, Ottawa (through the Ottawa Carleton Economic Development Corporation), and Vancouver are just a few of the cities that send missions to Asia for this purpose.[76] City governments do this, they say, to increase employment and tax revenues. Their critics, on the other hand, claim that the purpose of these missions is to please local real estate development companies. *Globe and Mail* reporter Jock Ferguson has revealed that these companies are the main source of funds for many municipal election campaigns.[77]

The major promoters of foreign investment in Canadian real estate, however, are in the private sector. While the federal and provincial governments tout Canada's "profit potential" in order to attract foreign technology and job creating investment, real estate firms use the same slogan to boost their own profit and the sale of real estate.

---

[75] Foreigners cannot buy residential real estate in Australia unless they have permission to immigrate. They can buy homes under construction provided not more than 50% is bought by foreign interests. They can also buy non-residential commercial real estate. However, all purchases of houses and other urban real estate by foreign persons must first be approved by the Foreign Investment Review Board. Australia. *Foreign Investment Review Board: Report 1987-88*, (Canberra: Australian Government Publishing Service, 1989). Paul Handly, "No Rights to Land: Thailand Moves to Curb Land Speculation", *Far Eastern Economic Review*, May 12, 1988, p. 76. In South Korea, foreigners cannot own land. Mark Clifford, "South Korea: Foreigners Need Not Apply", *Far Eastern Economic Review*, March 29, 1990, p. 54.

[76] A mission to Hong Kong by the mayor of Vancouver cost $500,000. Suzanne McGee, "Wooing the Orient: Attracting Investment to Ottawa", *Ottawa Business Life*, April 1988, p. 23.

[77] Jock Ferguson, "Toronto Land Developers Found to Be Main Backers of Municipal Campaigns", *The Globe and Mail*, Aug. 8, 1989, p. 1. He published related articles in 1987 and 1988.

Canada's Royal Le Page, for instance, has added Hong Kong and Taipei to its international computer network. As a result, Vancouver homes appear on Hong Kong computer screens the instant they are listed. Another company, Canada Trust, has formed a joint venture with Hambros PLC (an international merchant banking group) to attract southeast Asian investment into Canadian real estate.[78] These companies and their many competitors court foreign capital because they want to share in the $80 billion (U.S.) in the Pacific Rim that Royal Trust estimates is available for real estate investments.

The merriest group of beneficiaries from the inflow of foreign investment, however, may be Canada's members of Parliament. Without it, both they and the country would face difficult policy choices.

Interest rates might be higher (since the pool of available capital would be smaller). Socially desirable public (or private) investments might have to be cut back. And to improve competitiveness, the politicians might be forced to make controversial concessions to the business community, such as further reductions in corporate tax rates.

This observation caused U.S. newspaper columnist Jack Anderson to write, with reference to American politicians:

> Foreign investment has become a narcotic and the politicians have become addicted. They have come to rely on foreign money to stimulate the economy, create new jobs and expand the tax base.[79]

16. The Pyramid of Wealth

Another philosophical question touches upon disparities of wealth that exist in Asia. The Philippines, for instance, is a land of contrasts. Thirty million Filipinos live in absolute poverty.[80] Hordes of people hunt for food every day in Manila's garbage dumps, yet, in the same country, millionaires seek overseas investment opportunities.

Life is better in Hong Kong. However, there is no statutory minimum wage or government-run social security nets (e.g., unemployment insurance). Across the border, an immense pool of cheap labour lies waiting in China's Guangdong province.

---

[78] "Canada Trust, Hambros Launch Real Estate Venture to Attract Asian Investors", *Toronto Star*, Mar. 2, 1989, p. D8.

[79] Jack Anderson, "Who Owns America?", *Parade Magazine* (Supplement to the *Washington Post*), Apr. 16, 1989, p. 6.

[80] According to a World Bank report. James Clad, "Philippines: Poor Get Poorer", *Far Eastern Economic Rev.*, Aug. 18, 1989, p. 34.

These conditions have allowed some Hong Kong residents to hire workers for very low wages[81] and amass millions. Others traded land, becoming spectacularly wealthy as population pressures caused Hong Kong property prices to skyrocket.

The result is a number of nouveau riche in Hong Kong, as well as Indonesia, Taiwan and the Philippines, hoping to safeguard their money from their less fortunate countrymen. (One out of three people in southeast Asia is wretchedly poor.)

One way is to export the money to Australia, the U.S. and other countries. Many Canadians hope they choose Canada. But is there a cost? In particular, will the peoples of the Third World become less friendly when they realize that money which could have provided them with hospitals and roads is sitting in foreign (including Canadian) bonds and real estate?[82]

During 1989-90, more than twenty nations contributed $3.5 billion to help the Philippines. Canada's economic aid program to that country costs over $150 million per year. However, the Council of Maritime Premiers recently invited potential investor immigrants from the Philippines (as well as Hong Kong and Taiwan) to visit the Maritime provinces.[83] Canada's First Generation Resources Limited (which manages an investor/immigrant fund) even has a representative in Manila.[84]

In 1989, Canada accepted 35 entrepreneurs and investors from the Philippines, who indicated they would bring $45.9 million to Canada. Compared to the amount of investment capital flowing from the Philippines to the U.S., this is a small sum. On the other hand, perhaps Canada's interest might be better served if the money was invested in the Philippines.

A related matter involves perceptions that entrepreneurial and investor immigration programs sometimes create. In a few foreign

---

[81] A 300-page report by SRI International states: "Many Hong Kong factories are no more than sweatshops. They produce to order for large foreign companies and have little expertise of their own in product design, marketing or manufacturing technology". "Hong Kong Urged to Play New Role in Economic Future", *The Globe and Mail*, Oct. 6, 1989, p. B2.

[82] Conservative M.P. Robert Brisco expressed concern about the sources of incoming capital and mentioned the Marcos family. They allegedly invested in U.S. property some of the economic aid given to the Philippines. House of Commons, *Minutes of the Standing Committee on Regional Industrial Expansion*, May 12, 1987, Issue No. 14, p. 14:27.

[83] "Investors from Far East to Visit Province October 5", *The Guardian* (Charlottetown), Sept. 28, 1989, p. 11. Filipino billionaire Eduardo Cojuangco Jr. has a $30 million cattle ranch and horse farm in Australia.

[84] Also Hong Kong and Taipei.

capitals (e.g., Singapore, Hong Kong), concerns have been expressed about the loss of wealth and skilled labour to countries like Canada, Australia, and New Zealand.[85]

Observers refer to statistics published in Canadian newspapers to underline the extent of the transfer:

Year	Category	Number of Individuals	Total Fund To Be Transferred
1988	Entrepreneurs	3,097	$7.5 billion
	Investors	322	$5.8 billion
1989	Entrepreneurs	2,843	$3.6 billion
	Investors	586	$1.05 billion

After allowing for the exaggeration of aspiring immigrants, the movement of wealth still appears awesome. In 1989, net immigrant transfers were $6.3 billion. This amounted to 4.1% of Canada's current account receipts.[86]

To people in other countries, this inflow of wealth must appear like a windfall for Canada. However, a report from the Economic Council of Canada states that "the gains are far from obvious. All immigrants retain title to their investments and its yield. The host gets no direct benefits".[87] Indirect benefits can arise if world capital markets do not function in a perfect fashion. That will leave investment opportunities unexploited by domestic or foreign capital. In such circumstances, the money raised by Canada's investor immigration program may finance projects that could not otherwise have gone ahead.

Where do the funds brought to Canada by investor and entrepreneurial immigrants really come from? Hong Kong, and nations like Taiwan, South Korea, Lebanon and Germany are the major source countries.

---

[85] The Hong Kong government says that the rising emigration among skilled and professional workers is hurting the economy of the colony.

[86] These figures come from Royal Bank economist Allan Yarish. See Brian Milner, "Hong Kong Cash Boom for Canada" *The Globe and Mail*, Dec. 29, 1989, p. B1. Statistics Canada has since changed the way it accounts for migrants' funds in Canada's Current Account. Statistics Canada now records only funds in possession of migrants at the time of arrival, not the migrant's declared net worth. One problem was that some migrants exaggerated their net worth. Statistics Canada, *Canada's Balance of International Payments*, 1st quarter 1991, pp. 14–17.

[87] Economic Council of Canada, *New Faces in the Crowd: Economic and Social Impacts of Immigration*, (Ottawa: Supply and Services Canada, 1991), p. 9. An editorialist in the *Financial Post* commented that "although functioning capital markets should theoretically ensure there are no unexploited investment opportunities, in practice, it is difficult to believe that where investors live does not affect their investment decisions". *Financial Post*, Aug. 9, 1990, p. 5.

17. Growth and Its Consequences

The final issue is the most difficult. Is the value system underlying the international competition for foreign investment, with its emphasis on making money and accumulating wealth, in tune with the "conserver" society that the world may be entering—or forced to enter—because of the "greenhouse effect", ozone holes and other environmental problems. Or is this competition, in part, a manifestation of the growth paradox, that is, the assumption that rapid growth will solve a country's major problems when, in fact, growth does not solve some critical problems and sometimes cause new ones, such as urban overcrowding, the displacement of the poor as housing prices soar, and environmental disruption.

From another perspective, to what extent should Canadians admire the "irresistible dynamism of Hong Kong"? A greater dynamism (or a "restless drive") would make Canada more competitive and help achieve the "aggressive economy" that the president of the Canadian Manufacturers' Association advocates for Canada.[88] However, dynamism sometimes has another side. According to one businessman, in Hong Kong "money is worshipped", "tycoons are the gods" and "ethics often do not survive the pursuit of money".[89]

Perhaps Canadians would be richer if there was less emphasis on growth and development. That alternative would leave Canada less wealthy in terms of *per capita* G.N.P. than other nations. On the other hand, there could be compensating benefits, including the preservation of valuable agricultural land and the environment. By the year 2000, the income of the average North American will be two thirds that of the average person in Japan. But will the quality of life in Japan be one third higher?

Twenty-five years ago, there were still some open fields in Metropolitan Toronto. People went cycling along country lanes on the outskirts of the city. Newly married couples looked forward to owning a home. Now, after more than two decades of development (funded mostly by Canadian money), similar amenities are not readily available.

What is needed is a new way of measuring international competitiveness and economic performance, in which the destruction of the ecosystem will be accounted for as a minus. Then competitiveness

---

[88] David Vice, "The Aggressive Economy - Daring to Compete", *Area Development* (Special Edition - 1989), p. 9.

[89] Richard Gossen, "The Great Property Wave", *Canada-Hong Kong Business*, p. 6 at 7. Mr. Gossen is the managing director of a Hong Kong-based company, Kolex Property Development.

would no longer be "about continuously raising the real income of Canadians".[90] Instead, the goal of competitiveness would be to ensure all Canadians are employed, enjoying an adequate (but not necessarily increasing) standard of living, at a minimal cost in terms of damage to the environment. This new concept would bring about major changes. Japan would suddenly be listed among the less competitive of nations. The development of farm land would be called destruction. Advocates of economic expansion and a steady state economy would start debating in a common language (cost-efficiency). Finally, Canada and its competitors would spend more time pursuing foreign companies which possess environmentally benign technologies (e.g., technologies that use recyclable material and renewable resources). That would benefit everyone, at least in the long-run.

18. Looking Ahead

Canadian industry needs access to international markets and the latest technology. The targeted promotion of foreign investment—based upon prior study and careful selection of foreign firms—can bring considerable benefits to the country. Programs like External Affairs' Technology Inflow Program, where staff at missions abroad search for new technologies on behalf of Canadian companies, may do the same.

Canadian companies should be encouraged to develop links with Japan. That country has emerged as the world leader in the export of technology and capital. Canadians can tap some of this technology (microelectronics, robotics, lasers, artificial intelligence) through joint venture agreements and direct Japanese investment in Canadian manufacturing plants.[91] In this way, Canada's structural problems (low level of R&D, low level of resource processing, high propensity to import manufactured and high-tech products) may be ameliorated.

Joint ventures with companies in the Far East may also open markets for Canadian products. The opportunities there are vast, as wide-eyed business people point out. By the year 2000, there will be 4 billion people in Asia. Asia will produce 50% of the world's goods and services. (The same business people do not ask how the planet can support an industrialized population twice its present size.)

---

[90] Thomas Kierans in the foreword to a book by: Bryne Purchase, *The Innovative Society: Competitiveness in the 1990s*, (Toronto: C.D. Howe Institute, 1991).

[91] The Japanese have traditionally invested in Canadian resources (to secure a supply of raw materials) or merchandising (to distribute Japanese made goods). Richard Wright, "Investment from Japan: Small but Growing Rapidly", *CA Magazine*, May 1987, p. 40.

Canada's Investment Development Program, therefore, has potential. It is also needed, if only because Canada's competitors are spending more than Canada (especially in the area of financial incentives) to attract foreign investment. Small firms overseas may think only of the U.S., unless they realize what Canada has to offer (e.g., inexpensive energy, an educated labour force, safer cities).[92]

However, the pursuit of foreign investment has another dimension. Infatuated by the wealth in southeast Asia, not caring how the money was made, an international chorus (bankers, real estate sales people, government officials from many countries) is serenading the super-rich.[93] Unlike traditional foreign investment, however, the greater portion of the capital of these wealthy individuals is not being invested in industry.

Do the recipient nations really benefit? Like so much else in economics, there are several perspectives. One issue is whether simply increasing a nation's aggregate level of foreign investment improves its productivity (more output for the same/less input). If money is invested in real estate, does it indirectly find its way into companies seeking to produce higher value-added products, or achieve economies of scale?

The international competition for foreign investment raises other issues worthy of reflection. The main ones for many economists are: In what industry sectors should the government concentrate its promotional efforts? Will foreign investment make Canada a vigorous international competitor?

Social scientists ask:

1. To the extent that a conflict exists, to what degree are Canadians willing to trade off their political and social goals (e.g. sovereignty and more comprehensive social programs than competing nations) to obtain the economic benefits of foreign investment?

---

[92] One of Canada's competitors is Georgia, which has no minimum wage laws. Employees can be dismissed without notice or just cause. Georgia, according to the critics, is an attractive location for a ruthless employer. John Valorzi, "Riding High in the Deep South", *Ottawa Citizen*, Oct. 24, 1989, p. D10.

[93] A number of nations, such as Australia, Canada and its provinces, the U.S.A. and South Africa, are welcoming all suitors, as long as they have lots of cash. However, a larger investment is required to gain entry to Australia and the U.S. in comparison with Canada. Under Australia's business migration program, the price to gain entry is U.S. $260,000 (migrants under 40 years old); U.S. $375,000 (ages 40 to 57); U.S. $640,000 (age 58 and over). The U.S. has an investor immigrant program that allows an applicant who invests $1 million (U.S.) and employs at least 10 Americans to get a green card (the permanent resident category). Jamaica, on the other hand, grants permanent residence status in exchange for a $100,000 investment. Belize charges U.S. $24,000.

2. Is "nationality of ownership" still important in an era when a "Canadian" company (e.g., Northern Telecom) may have many of its operations located abroad, and a foreign-owned company may be a major employer of Canadians?[94]

3. Should Canada, like Australia, control foreign purchases of urban real estate? (By ensuring that the burden of changes in the global economy does not fall unfairly on one sector of the population there may be less opposition to other changes.)

Finally, a few people are beginning to wonder how long nations on a planet, whose ecosystem has already suffered extensive damage, can continue to pursue a value system in which rapid growth and development is the paramount goal.[95]

---

[94] For a discussion of this issue in a U.S. context, see Robert Reich, "Who Is Us", 1990 *Harvard Business Rev.* 53.

[95] Did the New Zealand government lose its senses when it barred a millionaire in 1977, or was the government trying to create a less materialistic society? If so, was New Zealand pursuing a value system that other nations on a polluted planet may soon have to adopt? See n. 17.

CHAPTER 22

A PLETHORA OF EXAMPLES

In the pages that follow, a number of hypothetical examples are presented, with analyses. These analyses illustrate how Investment Canada or the courts might interpret the *Investment Canada Act*. Nevertheless, readers should keep in mind that some sections of the Act can be interpreted in two or more ways. Until the legislation has been considered by the courts, any analysis of it must remain an academic exercise. Foreign investors who want to be confident about their legal position should request a written opinion from Investment Canada.

Table of Illustrations

1. Several Non-Canadians Purchase Small Interests in a Canadian Business—Joint Venture

FACTS: Richard Street is a Canadian engineer. He has invented an automobile engine that runs on water. The company he set up constructed a prototype, but he needed money. Over the last few months, he has sold shares in his company to five American engineers. The Americans bought interests ranging from 5% to 30%. There exist no written agreements between the Americans, but they have invested together in one other enterprise.

The American engineers now own 80% of an exciting Canadian company. Has anyone acquired control for the purposes of the *IC Act*?

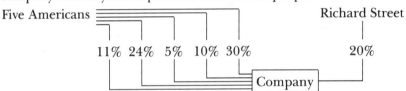

RESPONSE: Probably not! None of the Americans has purchased more than 33% of the company's shares. Therefore, no individual has acquired control.

Might the Americans constitute a joint venture (which has acquired 80% of the company's shares)? Three questions should be asked:

1. Does a joint venture exist? (Unclear)

2. If so, who controls it? (Americans)

3. Has the joint venture acquired "control" by buying more than 50.1% of the shares of a Canadian company?[1] (Yes)

For a joint venture to exist, the participants must be associated with each other. A common purpose (e.g., to invest together) will suffice. In this example, the Americans know each other. They have invested together before. They bought shares near the same point in time. These facts create a suspicion that a joint venture exists.[2] If so, a notification will have to be filed with Investment Canada (not an application for review—the company is too small). On the other hand, if the purchases by the five Americans were unconnected events,[3] Investment Canada does not have to be notified.

---

[1] Over 50% is a deemed acquisition of control (para. 28(3)(a)).

[2] This reasoning illustrates how the joint venture concept was intended to work. A potential technical difficulty is mentioned elsewhere in this book.

[3] If the purchases were unconnected events, no joint venture exists.

2. Lender's Exemption—Pledge of Shares as Security

FACTS: A Canadian businesswoman owns a Canadian company. She wants to buy a luxury condominium in Florida.

To obtain the funds, the businesswoman arranges for a loan from a U.S. bank and pledges 51% of the shares of her company as security. She then buys the condominium. Unfortunately, she later defaults on the loan. As a result, the U.S. bank acquires control of the Canadian company.

There is an exemption in the *IC Act* for takeovers that occur because a lender is forced to realize upon its security. (See paragraph 10(1)(c).) Can the U.S. bank rely on this exemption?

RESPONSE: Maybe. The lender's exemption does not state that the loan must be given to help the borrower carry on a business, although this might be implied. Therefore, it could be argued that the acquisition by the U.S. bank of a 51% interest in the Canadian company is an "exempt" acquisition of control.[4]

Foreign lenders who provide loans to Canadian business people for personal expenditures and take shares as security should, however, tread warily.

3. Loan by Foreigner to Canadian Company—Option to Acquire Shares

FACTS: A Swedish industrialist makes a loan to a Canadian company. As additional consideration, the shareholders of the company give him an option to buy all of their shares. The option can be exercised on ten days' notice, at a price calculated according to a formula. Is the exercise of that option exempt from Investment Canada's jurisdiction?

RESPONSE: Control of a Canadian business cannot be acquired by contract. The loan agreement is, therefore, not subject to the Act. If a borrower defaults, a lender is also free to realize upon any security granted in connection with the loan. (See the lender's exemption in paragraph 10(1)(c).)

Unfortunately for the Swedish industrialist, he cannot rely upon the lender's exemption if he wishes to exercise his option, because his

---

[4] If the acquisition is "exempt", it is because the lender's exemption applies.

option to acquire shares is not tied to a default under the loan agreement. Neither can he use the financial assistance exemption (paragraph 10(1)(d)) unless he is willing to divest himself of control within a two-year period![5]

This means that the exercise of the option will be subject to the *IC Act*. However, the Swedish industrialist should read subsection 30(1). This subsection states:

> . . . a non-Canadian who has an absolute right under a written contract to acquire voting interests of an entity . . . may, at the option of that non-Canadian, treat that right as if it had been exercised and as if that non-Canadian owned the voting interests or assets that are the subject of that right.

Because no conditions precedent exist before the Swedish industrialist can exercise his option, it qualifies as an absolute right within the meaning of this subsection. He therefore has a choice: he can file a notification/application for review now, or when he exercises the option. (If the company is growing and will soon be over the threshold for review, he should file a notification now.)

4. Rollovers—Acquisitions of 50% Interest— Jointly Owned Corporations and Partnerships—Attempting to Avoid Review

FACTS: Bill Johnson owns Simcoe Corp. He wants to transfer the assets of the business to a new company or partnership which will be jointly owned by himself and a non-Canadian. He is considering three ways of doing this:

(1) incorporate a *new company* ("Canco") which will buy the assets of Simcoe Corp.; the non-Canadian will then purchase 50% of Canco's shares;

(2) establish a *partnership* made up of himself and the non-Canadian which will then acquire the assets of Simcoe Corp.; the two partners will have equal interests in the partnership;

(3) establish a *partnership* composed of himself and his sister, Monica; after the partnership has acquired the Canadian business, Monica will sell her 50% partnership interest to the non-Canadian.

Which of these schemes is least likely to be subject to the *Investment Canada Act*?

---

[5] Also, the financial assistance exemption can only be used if the takeover is for the purpose of facilitating the financing of the business.

RESPONSE: If the implications of each scheme are carefully evaluated (see below), it will be apparent that the third one is least likely to be subject to the legislation.

1. *Acquisition by Canco of Business; then Acquisition by Non-Canadian:*

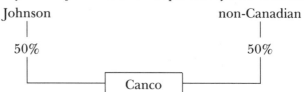

When the non-Canadian acquires his 50% interest in Canco, he is presumed to have acquired control of a Canadian business. (This presumption may be rebutted.)[6]

2. *Acquisition by Non-Canadian of Partnership Interest; Acquisition by Partnership of the Canadian Business:*

A partnership owned by Johnson and the non-Canadian is presumed to be controlled by the non-Canadian. (This presumption may be rebutted.)[7] Any acquisition by such a partnership is subject to the Act.

3. *Acquisition by Partnership of Business; Acquisition by Non-Canadian of Partnership Interest:*

If a partnership composed of Bill Johnson and his sister, Monica first acquires the Canadian business, then Monica sells her 50% interest to the non-Canadian, the non-Canadian will be deemed not to have acquired control.[8] However, a word of caution: this scheme may be considered to have been implemented for a purpose related to the Act, and thus be open to attack under sections 29 or 39.

5. Business Arrangements with Agents in Canada—Establishing a New Canadian Business?

FACTS: A U.S. book publishing company signs an agency agreement with a new Canadian company ("Canco"). Under the terms of the agreement, Canco will seek orders for the books of the U.S. company, then forward these orders to the U.S. company which in turn will send

---

[6] Para. 28(3)(c).

[7] Para. 26(1)(d).

[8] Para. 28(3)(b).

the books to the purchasers. Canco will be paid a commission. The U.S. company is one of the founding shareholders of Canco and has a 20% interest.

Is the U.S. company establishing a book distribution business in Canada? Can the Canadian government stop the Americans from doing so?

RESPONSE: For a Canadian business to legally exist, there must be a place of business in Canada, assets in Canada and a person employed in connection with the business.[9]

The U.S. company will have neither a place of business nor assets in Canada. Therefore, it is *not* establishing a Canadian business.[10]

If, instead of 20%, the U.S. company owns 51% of Canco, either Canco or the U.S. company will have to file a notification with Investment Canada.[11] The Canadian government can then order a review and (if it wishes) prevent the business from being established.

6. Status—Company Whose Shareholders Are Partnerships, Trusts and Joint Ventures

FACTS: Beaver Ltd. ("Beaver"), which operates a Canadian business, is owned by a limited partnership and a pension fund trust in the proportions set out below.

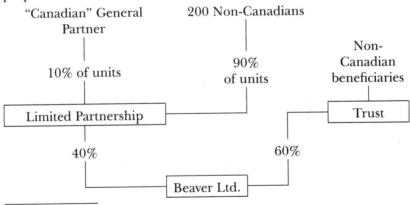

---

[9] S. 3.

[10] Control cannot arise through a contract. If the agency agreement gives the U.S. company effective control over the business of Canco, that will not change the legal result (i.e., there will, in law, be no establishment of a business by the U.S. company). Similarly, if a U.S. business person enters into an agency agreement with a close relative in Canada on the same basis as outlined above, their non-arm's length relationship will not be relevant. The relative's business will be regarded as his or her own.

[11] See the status rules.

Ninety per cent of the units in the limited partnership are owned by 200 non-Canadian limited partners. A Canadian general partner owns the balance. You, in your capacity as a solicitor, have decided that the limited partnership is not controlled by the unit holders. Since the general partner is a Canadian, the limited partnership is, therefore, Canadian-controlled.[12]

The pension fund trust is also Canadian-controlled.[13] The trustees are Canadians and you have determined that the beneficiaries are not in control.

Both shareholders of Beaver Ltd. are, therefore, Canadians. Does that mean the company is also Canadian-controlled?

RESPONSE: Remember the look-through principle? When trying to determine the status of a company whose shareholders are trusts, joint ventures or partnerships, the Canadian or non-Canadian status of these shareholders must be ignored. Instead, the ownership of the shares held by the trust, joint venture or limited partnership is traced back to the beneficiaries, joint ventures or partners.[14]

Because of this look-through principle, the non-Canadian limited partners are deemed to own 90% of the voting shares held by the limited partnership. This means they "own" 36% (90% x 40%) of Beaver's shares.

The look-through principle does not apply to a trust controlled by its trustees, such as the pension fund trust in the example above. Since the trustees of this pension fund trust are Canadians, it is Canadian-controlled. Consequently, 64% (60% + 4%) of Beaver's shares are "owned" by Canadians, which means Beaver is Canadian-controlled.[15]

Would the results have been different if the trust had been controlled by its foreign beneficiaries? Definitely. In that case, foreigners would have been deemed to own 64% (60% + 4%) of Beaver's shares (which would have turned Beaver into a foreign-controlled company).

7. Board-Controlled Company—Distribution of Shares of Wholly Owned Subsidiary to Shareholders of Parent Company

FACTS: A widely held U.S. corporation that is controlled by its board of directors has a subsidiary that carries on a Canadian business. The

---

[12] Subpara. 26(1)(d)(ii).

[13] Subs. 26(2).

[14] Subs. 27(a).

[15] Para. 26(1)(a).

parent corporation (U.S. Corp.) proposes to distribute the shares of the subsidiary to its (the parent's) shareholders. At the time the distribution takes place, it is possible that the board of directors of the parent corporation and the subsidiary might be composed of different individuals. Does this proposed transaction come within the purview of the *Investment Canada Act*?

Shareholders

RESPONSE: No. For an acquisition of control to occur, a "non-Canadian" must purchase at least one third of the shares of a Canadian company. (A "non-Canadian" can be a person, partnership, trust, joint venture or a company.)

The shareholders of the parent company cannot be considered as "associating" themselves for the purpose of acquiring the subsidiary's shares. Therefore, these shareholders cannot be classified as a joint venture. Neither are they a partnership or trust. Accordingly, no "non-Canadian" is acquiring more than one third of the shares.

Another way to view the problem is to examine the method of acquisition. According to section 28, "control" can be acquired in only two ways: through the purchase of shares or assets. After the share distribution takes place, the aforesaid subsidiary will be a widely held company controlled by its board. If the directors of this subsidiary are completely different from the directors of the parent, the ultimate controllers of the Canadian business will certainly have changed. However, no board member will have acquired shares or assets.

8. Purchase of Customer Lists—Substantially All the Assets? Separate Business?

FACTS: 1. A U.S. oil company purchases the customer list of Reliable Fuel Delivery Inc. together with the exclusive right to use the name "Reliable Fuel".

2. Collection Ltd., which carries on a waste disposal system in the U.S., purchases the customer lists and contracts of a Canadian company, which is in the same business. However, pursuant to an agreement between the two companies, the Canadian company, which still owns a fleet of trucks, will continue to service the Canadian customers.

Has a Canadian business been purchased?

RESPONSE: Here are the issues:

1. Is a customer list an asset? (Yes, assets are defined to include intangible property.)

2. To acquire control of a business through an asset purchase, a non-Canadian must buy all, or substantially all of the business' assets.[16] Can a customer list by itself constitute substantially all of the assets of a business? (This is a debatable point.)

3. Do the assets being acquired (e.g., customer list and trade name) constitute "part of a business that is capable of being carried on as a separate business"?[17] Is substantially all of that "separate business" being purchased?

For aid in answering these questions, counsel should read Interpretation Notes 2 and 3. According to Interpretation Note 3, the phrase "substantially all of the assets" may have either a qualitative or quantitative meaning.[18] If a qualitative meaning is adopted, the issue is whether the most important part (the essence) of the business is being acquired.

The better view is that the first example involves the purchase of a business and the second does not.

9. Purchase of Non-Voting Convertible Preferred Shares—Conversion Would Give Control of Canadian Business to Non-Canadian

FACTS: A lawyer in New Guinea purchases all of the non-voting convertible preferred shares of a Canadian company. These shares can be converted into common shares at the option of the holder. If these shares are converted, the lawyer will own 60% of the Canadian company's voting shares. Does Investment Canada have jurisdiction?

RESPONSE: No (at least not at the present time). Under the *IC Act*, control of a corporation can only be obtained through the acquisition of voting shares.

However, a non-Canadian who has an absolute right to acquire voting shares may elect to treat that right as having been exercised and pretend she owns the voting shares (subsection 30(1)). This would

---

[16] Para. 28(1)(c).

[17] Subs. 31(2).

[18] Interpretation Note 3 begins: "The test is not purely a quantitative one. . . ."

allow the lawyer in New Guinea to pretend she has converted her preferred shares and make the appropriate filing under the Act. However, she need not do this.

What will influence her choice? If the Canadian company is growing rapidly and will soon be so large that any takeover will have to be reviewed, she may decide to make a "deemed takeover" right away (and thus avoid Canadian government review at a future date).

10. Leases and Leasehold Interests

FACTS: A Canadian company, which owns five hotels, leases the hotels to an American hotel management company for ten years. Is Canadian government approval needed?

RESPONSE: No. Under the *IC Act*, control of a business cannot be acquired through a lease of assets. (On the other hand, if a non-Canadian were to buy all of the leases owned by a Canadian business, this might constitute an acquisition of control. The issue would be whether the leasehold interests constituted all or substantially all of the assets used in carrying on the Canadian business.)[19]

11. Rollover of Assets

FACTS: A foreign-owned Canadian company has several divisions, each of which manufactures a different product. The company wishes to incorporate a subsidiary and transfer the assets of one division to the subsidiary. Does the *IC Act* apply?

RESPONSE: The Act does not apply to a mere sale of assets, only to the sale of a business. Therefore, the first question to ask is: can the division be considered a separate Canadian business?[20]

Most divisions meet that test. However, the transaction described above does not fall within Investment Canada's jurisdiction because ultimate control of the business will not change.[21]

---

[19] This example illustrates one way in which the *IC Act* differs from its predecessor. Under the *FIR Act*, which contained a provision that "the acquisition of a leasehold interest in any property used in carrying on a business shall be deemed to constitute the acquisition of that property", a transaction such as the one outlined above would have been subject to review.

[20] Subs. 31(2).

[21] Para. 10(1)(e).

12. Real Estate—Purchase of Commercial Complex—Substantially All

FACTS: A non-Canadian wants to purchase an office and commercial complex in Calgary from its sole owner. The book asset value of the complex is above the threshold for review.

Initially, the non-Canadian will only purchase a 50% interest. However, the purchaser will also obtain a contractual "no strings" right to acquire the remaining 50%, which can be exercised at any time. (Management of the complex will remain with a Canadian property management company.) Is the approval of the Investment Canada minister needed?

RESPONSE: No. An office and commercial complex constitutes a Canadian business. To acquire control of this business, a non-Canadian must purchase all or substantially all of the assets.

The non-Canadian will only be acquiring a 50% interest, which is not substantially all of the business from either a qualitative or quantitative perspective. Therefore, government approval is not necessary even if the non-Canadian will be managing the property. (Under the *IC Act*, control cannot be acquired through a contract.)

The non-Canadian will also obtain an unrestricted right to purchase the remaining 50% interest. This is an absolute right within the meaning of subsection 30(1). The non-Canadian can elect to have this right treated as if it had been exercised. If this election is made, the non-Canadian will be deemed to own 100% of the complex and can file an immediate application for review. In this way, he can find out in advance whether the Investment Canada minister will allow the purchase of the entire complex.

13. Non-Canadian Owns 51%—Acquires Remaining 49%

FACTS: Is a non-Canadian, who owns 51% of the shares of a company that carries on business in Canada, free to acquire the remaining 49%?

RESPONSE: Yes. Although there is a rebuttable presumption in the Act that the acquisition of between one third and one half of the shares of a corporation constitutes an acquisition of control,[22] that presumption does not apply if the non-Canadian already has control. (This principle is stated nowhere in the Act but must be implied in light of the purpose of the Act.)

14. New Business—Relatedness Issue—50:50 Joint Venture

FACTS: Williams Restaurant ("Williams") is an American-controlled company that already operates a number of restaurants across Canada. Williams wants to enter into a 50:50 joint venture with a Canadian to establish a new restaurant in Toronto.

Does a notification have to be filed with Investment Canada?

RESPONSE: The Act (section 11) states that the establishment of a new Canadian business by a non-Canadian is subject to notification. A "new Canadian business" is defined as a business that is not already being carried on in Canada by the non-Canadian and that is unrelated to any other business being carried on in Canada by the non-Canadian.

Two questions, therefore, arise:

(1) is the joint venture a non-Canadian?

(2) since Williams already operates restaurants across Canada, is the new business related to Williams' existing business?

A joint venture that is owned on a 50:50 basis by a Canadian and a non-Canadian is presumed to be controlled by the "non-Canadian".[23] As for the nation-wide restaurant operations, the "relatedness rights"[24] that a non-Canadian acquires by carrying on business alone cannot be transferred to a joint venture, because it is a new entity. Conclusion: the joint venture must file a notification.

---

[22] Para. 28(3)(c).

[23] Para. 26(1)(d).

[24] What is a "relatedness right"? That is the right of a foreign investor who already has a business in Canada to establish a new, related business without having to file a notification with Investment Canada (exception: a new cultural business).

15. Business—Mining Claim

FACTS: Eagle Corporation is a foreign mining company. It wishes to acquire 46 mining claims. The property in question has no proven reserves. Do these mining claims constitute a Canadian business which, if acquired, is subject to the *IC Act*?

RESPONSE: Interpretation Note 4 sets out how the minister interprets the term "business". It states: " . . . mineral properties which are only at the exploration stage are not considered to be businesses".

Consequently, the 46 mining claims are not a business.

16. A Company to Be Incorporated

FACTS: A Canadian and an American intend to incorporate a company to establish a business in Canada, but have not yet done so. Who should they identify as the investor when they file a notification form with Investment Canada?

RESPONSE: A company that is to be incorporated is not an "entity".[25] Therefore, it cannot be identified as the investor. The parties who intend to incorporate the company constitute a joint venture. If this joint venture is "non-Canadian-controlled", it must file the notification. Both joint venturers should sign the form unless one party has the authority to sign on behalf of the other.

17. Two-Step Acquisition—Creation of a Branch Business Followed by the Acquisition of the Shares of the Foreign Parent

FACTS: Mid-Atlantic Corp. is a foreign company that has a subsidiary in Canada (Can Sub.).

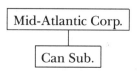

An Australian wishes to purchase the Canadian business, but for tax reasons, wants to do it in a two-step transaction:

---

[25] The "investor" whose name appears on the notification form must be a "non-Canadian". A non-Canadian means an individual, a government or an entity.

Step 1: Mid-Atlantic will acquire the *assets* of its Canadian subsidiary. This will create a branch business (since Mid-Atlantic now owns all the assets in its own name).

Step 2: The Australian will purchase the shares of Mid-Atlantic.

Does Investment Canada have jurisdiction?

RESPONSE: The *Investment Canada Act* contains an exemption for corporate reorganizations when there is no change in the ultimate controller of the business. Step 1 (the creation of a branch business) falls within this exemption.[26] When the Australian buys the shares of Mid-Atlantic (step 2), he will be indirectly acquiring control of a branch business in Canada. Normally, the indirect acquisition of a branch business is not caught by the Act. (For the reason, see Chapter 6 of this book.) In this example, however, because the two transactions occur within a short period of time, the step transaction provision (section 29) can be used to combine them into one transaction. This allows Investment Canada to assert jurisdiction.

18. Indirect Acquisitions—Branch/Joint Venture Distinction—Oil and Gas

FACTS: A U.S. Company owns several oil and gas properties in Canada. It also has a number of undivided interests (ranging from 10% to 90%) in other oil and gas properties in Canada. A non-Canadian is proposing to acquire the U.S. company. Is this acquisition subject to the *Investment Canada Act*?

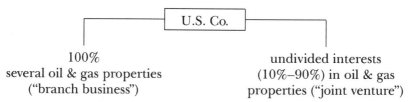

100%	undivided interests
several oil & gas properties	(10%–90%) in oil & gas
("branch business")	properties ("joint venture")

RESPONSE: The indirect acquisition of a 100% interest in the branch businesses is not caught by the statute. As for those properties in which the U.S. company has an interest varying between 10% and 90%, they constitute "joint ventures". The indirect acquisition of a *majority* interest in a joint venture does come within the jurisdiction of Investment Canada. (The U.S. company is deemed to control any joint venture in which it has a greater than 50% interest).[27]

---

[26] Para. 10(1)(e).

[27] Subpara. 28(2)(b)(i).

If the U.S. company has a majority interest in five joint ventures, which have a total book asset value in excess of $5 million (and constitute more than 50%[28] of the book value of all entities acquired),[29] an application for review must be filed.[30]

19. Trusts—Change in the Number of Trustees—Change in Beneficiaries—The Devolution of Estates Exemption—Joint Venture

FACTS: In 1990, Roger Portfolio established a trust to which he transferred all his shares in Beaver Corp. The trustees were Roger Portfolio and Aladdin Trust Company. The beneficiaries were Roger Portfolio himself, and his children (who are U.S. citizens). Under the terms of the trust, Roger Portfolio was entitled to receive all of the income earned by the trust during his lifetime. If he died during the term of the trust, his children were entitled to receive the income earned by the trust for the balance of the term, and then the principal. Subsequently, the following events happen:

(1) the Aladdin Trust Company is replaced by the Northwest Trust Company,

(2) Roger Portfolio dies.

Does Investment Canada have jurisdiction over the change in the trustees and the acquisition by Roger Portfolio's two children of the right to the income from the trust and, at a later date, ownership of the shares of Beaver Corp.?

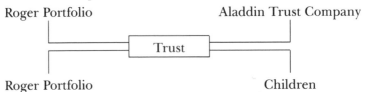

RESPONSE: A change in the identity of trustees can never constitute the acquisition of control of a business owned by the trust. This is

---

[28]The 50% plus proportionate test. See Chapter 6.

[29]The U.S. company and the joint ventures it controls (by having a majority interest) are the entities acquired.

[30]What happens if the U.S. company has many other assets in addition to those Canadian joint ventures that it controls? If the result is that the Canadian joint ventures constitute 50% or less of the book asset value of all entities acquired, Canada's review threshold for indirect oil and gas acquisitions rockets up to $50 million.

because section 28 of the Act states that an acquisition of control can only occur through an acquisition of assets or voting interests. At worst, a change of trustees may affect the status of a subsection 26(2) trust, that is, a trust controlled by the trustees, by turning it into a non-Canadian.

The other issue is whether the children of Roger Portfolio— each of whom, upon his death, acquired a 50% voting interest in the trust— have acquired control.[31] If they have, the exemption in paragraph 10(1)(i) of the Act (which deals with the involuntary acquisition of control of a Canadian business on the devolution of an estate or by operation of law) will not assist them, since this exemption does not cover acquisitions that occur pursuant to an *inter vivos* trust.

Happily for the children, the acquisition of a 50% interest in a trust is deemed not to be an acquisition of control.[32] The only remaining question is: do the children constitute a joint venture which has acquired a 100% voting interest in the trust?

There is probably an element of voluntariness or intention needed before a joint venture can exist. If this is correct, the two children are not a "joint venture".[33]

20. Acquisition of Three Separate Businesses from One Vendor—Different Treatment Depending on Whether Operations Are Incorporated

FACTS: A Canadian company carries on three businesses—bottling soft drinks, canning fruit and brewing beer. These businesses constitute "separate businesses" within the meaning of subsection 31(2) of the Act. The book value of each separate business is $3 million. Should

---

[31] A voting interest in a trust is an ownership interest that entitles the owner to receive a share of the profits and to share in the assets on dissolution. The children of Roger Portfolio did not acquire voting interests in the trust until his death because, up to that point, Roger Portfolio was entitled to all of the income generated by the trust.

[32] See para. 28(3)(b) and subpara. 28(1)(d)(i). A non-Canadian does not acquire control of a trust until he or she acquires a majority interest.

[33] The death of a life tenant or life beneficiary under a trust may result in the "remaindermen" acquiring a voting interest in the trust and therefore acquiring control of the trust and, indirectly, a Canadian business. In the example above, that would have happened had there been only one U.S. beneficiary instead of two since a single beneficiary would have acquired a "greater than majority" interest (i.e., a 100% interest) in the trust.

a non-Canadian who wishes to buy these businesses file a notification or an application for review?

bottling   canning   brewing

RESPONSE: This example shows how a decision to structure a transaction as an asset or a share purchase and the form of business organization employed by the vendor can dramatically change the legal consequences.

1. Asset Purchase—Divisions

If the corporate vendor operates the three businesses as divisions, the non-Canadian should file an application for review. This is because the book asset value of the three divisions amounts to $9 million. (If the non-Canadian buys each of the divisions in separate transactions, then argues that he has bought three separate businesses, he may be checkmated by the anti-avoidance provision in section 29.)

2. Asset Purchase—Subsidiaries

If the corporate vendor carries on its business through three subsidiaries, and causes the three subsidiaries to sell their assets to the non-Canadian, three separate notifications will have to be submitted. Why? The asset value of each business ($3 million) will be below the threshold for review. There is no provision in paragraph 14(3)(a) for the assets of the three businesses to be added together.[34]

3. Share Purchase

If (i) the three businesses are carried on as three divisions and the shares of the Canadian company are purchased, or (ii) the three businesses are operated as subsidiaries, and their shares are purchased, the transaction is reviewable. (In accordance with paragraph 14(3)(b), the book asset values of each subsidiary are totalled.)[35]

---

[34] If the three operations can be conceptualized as being *one* Canadian business carried on by a joint venture, the legal result will be different. This illustrates how the *IC Act*—-and most legislation—-can be interpreted in more than one way in order to obtain the desired result.

[35] That total is $9 million.

21. Purchase of Assets Including Shares—Need for Separate Filings—Calculating the Thresholds

FACTS: A non-Canadian purchases all the assets of a Canadian company, including the shares that the Canadian company holds in a wholly owned subsidiary. The shares are shown on the balance sheet of the Canadian company as being worth $2 million. The remaining assets have a balance sheet value of $4 million.

Is the value of the shares "counted in" when determining if the transaction is reviewable?

RESPONSE: Paragraph 14(3)(a) states that an investment is reviewable if the value of the assets acquired exceeds $5 million. There is no stipulation that the assets must be operating assets.[36]

Accordingly, if an asset purchase includes shares, the book value of the shares is added to the book value of the other assets for the purpose of determining if the value of the transaction exceeds the threshold for review. In the example above, the value of the assets is $6 million, and the acquisition is reviewable. A curious result is that two forms must be filed: an application for review form with respect to those $4 million of assets used in carrying on the Canadian business, and a notification form covering the share transaction. This double filing is necessary because section 28 distinguishes between asset acquisitions and share acquisitions. There is no provision in the Act permitting shares and other assets to be "put in one pot" so that only one form need be filed.

22. Acquisition of Shares of Canadian Company with Foreign Subsidiary—Calculation of Thresholds

FACTS: A Canadian company that carries on a business in Canada owns a French subsidiary. The Canadian company has a consolidated

---

[36] Whenever lawyers meet, there are always differences of opinions. A counter-argument can be constructed by reading paras. 14(3)(a) and 28(1)(c) together.

book value of $6 million which includes a value of $3 million attributed to the French subsidiary. A non-Canadian wants to purchase the shares of the Canadian company. What is the book value of the Canadian company (for the purpose of determining if the transaction is reviewable)?

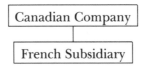

RESPONSE: $6 million. That is the most sensible interpretation of subsection 14(3). Thus, if a foreign investor buys all of the shares of Alcan Aluminum, its subsidiaries would be included in the computation of Alcan's asset value.

23. Acquisition of Canadian Company with Subsidiaries—Acquisition of Company with a 50% Interest in Another Company

FACTS: A non-Canadian wishes to buy Canada Corp. Canada Corp. owns shares in two other companies (see the diagram below). Must an application for review be filed?

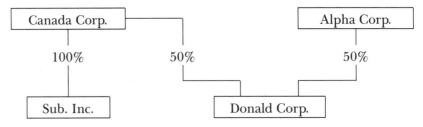

RESPONSE: When a company has an interest in a second company, it is necessary to examine the "chain of control presumptions" to determine if the target company controls the second company.

One of these presumptions (paragraph 28(2)(b)) states:

an entity controls another entity directly

(i) where the controlling entity owns a majority of the voting interests of the other entity, or

(ii) where the other entity is a corporation, the controlling entity owns less than a majority of the voting shares of the corporation but controls the corporation in fact through the ownership of one third or more of its voting shares.

Canadian Corp. obviously controls Sub. Inc. But does it control Donald Corp.? If the answer is no, Canada Corp.'s interest in Donald Corp. can be deducted when determining whether the book asset value of Canada Corp. exceeds the threshold for review.[37]

24. Asset Acquisition—Determining Asset Value when the Number of Assets of a Class Has Decreased Since the Fiscal Year-End

FACTS: In November, a non-Canadian buys 40 trucks from a moving and storage company. These trucks constitute substantially all the assets of the company. Nine months previously (January 31), at the end of its fiscal year, the company owned 200 trucks. At that time, the book value of the 40 trucks was $1 million, and $5 million for all 200 trucks. However, since then, 160 trucks have been sold. (The company has been winding down the business.)

For Investment Canada purposes, what is the value of the business?

RESPONSE: Subsection 3(1) of the regulations can be interpreted in two ways. The book value of the 40 trucks is either:

(1) the total book value of the 40 individual trucks ($1 million), or

(2) the total book value of the entire category of trucks ($5 million) at the end of the company's fiscal year.

Investment Canada has chosen the second interpretation in order that share and asset acquisitions can be treated in a similar fashion. (In the case of a share purchase, the book value of all assets of the business as of the last completed fiscal year represent the business' worth for reviewability purposes, even though many of those assets may have been dissipated between the end of the fiscal year and the date of the share purchase.)[38]

---

[37] When the certificate of receipt is issued, it must name each company acquired. If the target company controls 100 companies in Canada, the certificate of receipt will contain 101 names. (This was not the case under the *FIR Act*. That Act stated that a parent company was deemed to carry on the business of its subsidiaries. Consequently, it was proper in the certificate of receipt only to refer to the target company.)

[38] If part of a business that constitutes a separate business (e.g., a division) is being purchased, only the values of the assets of that part should be ascertained, not the value of the whole business.

APPENDIX

**Distribution of FDI in Canada By Area of Ownership
1983 & 1987**

United States 75.5%

Others 5.1%
PACRIM 0.7%*
Switz. 1.7%
Japan 2.1%
Netherlands 2.3%
W. Germany 2.5%

United Kingdom 10.1%

United States 71.1%

Others 5.1%
PACRIM 3.0%*
Switz. 1.8%
Netherlands 1.8%
Japan 2.5%
W. Germany 2.6%

United Kingdom 12.1%

1983 Total = $ 77.4 Billion

1987 Total = $ 101.5 Billion

* The Pacific Rim excludes Japan

Source: Statistics Canada, Canada's International Investment Position.

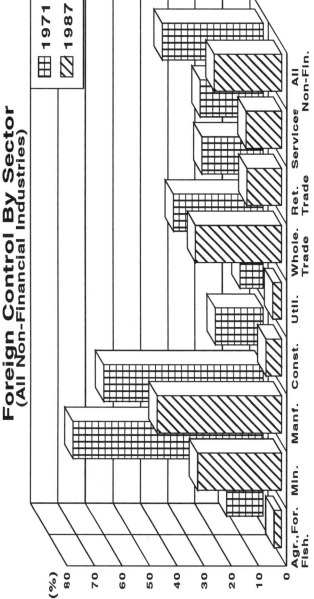

Foreign Control By Sector
(All Non-Financial Industries)

1971
1987

(%)
80
70
60
50
40
30
20
10
0

Agr.,For. Min. Manf. Const. Util. Whole. Ret. Services All
Fish. Trade Trade Non-Fin.

Source: Statistics Canada, Canada's International Investment Position.

Sources Contributing to Changes in Book Value of FDI in Canada: 1983 to 1989

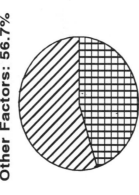

Reinvested Earnings and Other Factors: 56.7%

Net Capital Flows: 43.7%

1986 - 1989

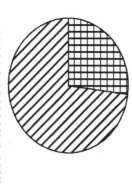

Reinvested Earnings and Other Factors: 73.8%

Net Capital Flows: 25.2%

1983 - 1989

Source: Statistics Canada, Canada's International Investment Position.

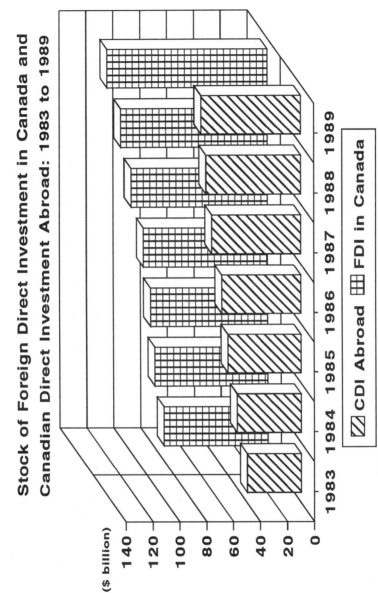

Stock of Foreign Direct Investment in Canada and Canadian Direct Investment Abroad: 1983 to 1989

($ billion)

140 120 100 80 60 40 20 0

1983 1984 1985 1986 1987 1988 1989

CDI Abroad FDI in Canada

Source: Statistics Canada, Canada's International Investment Position.

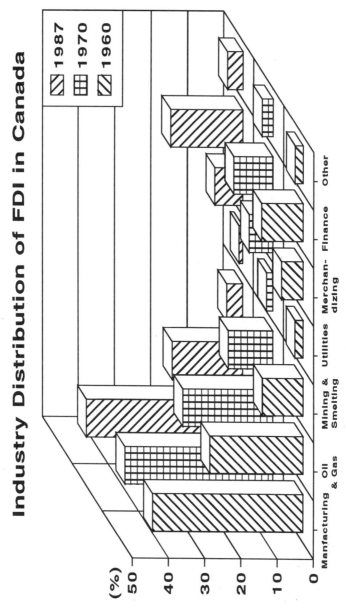

Industry Distribution of FDI in Canada

Source: Statistics Canada, Canada's International Investment Position.

FOREIGN CONTROL OF CORPORATE ASSETS
BY MAJOR INDUSTRY

INDUSTRY	1971	1987	CHANGE 1971-87
	%	%	%
Agriculture, Forestry & Fishing	13	3	-10
Total Mining	62	31	-31
Total Manufacturing	53	46	-7
Food	46	37	-9
Paper & Allied Industries	46	22	-24
Primary Metals	41	19	-22
Metal Fabricating	42	25	-17
Transport Equipment	82	75	-7
Electrical Products	67	46	-21
Chemicals & Chemical Products	79	72	-7
Construction	18	6	-12
Trans., Sto., Comm., & Pub. Util.	10	3	-7
Wholesale Trade	33	31	-2
Retail Trade	22	13	-9
Services	23	13	-10
Total Non-Financial Industries	37	25	-12

Source: Statistics Canada, Corporations & Labour Unions Returns
Act, Annual Reports 1972 and 1987, Cat. #61-210.

CALURA data cannot be compared to other Statistics Canada figures on FDI stock. For example, if a foreign firm controls a Canadian firm through the ownership of 70% of its shares, Statistics Canada stock data would show 70% of that firm's assets as foreign-controlled. In other words, in Statistics Canada stock data, figures on foreign-owned assets are proportional to foreign-owned equity. In the same circumstances, CALURA would designate 100% of the Canadian firm's assets as foreign-controlled. CALURA data are about three years behind the current date.

INDEX

453